# A History of Long Island

## From Its Earliest Settlement to the Present Time

## Volume 2

PETER ROSS
JUERGEN BECK

*A History of Long Island 2, Ross/Beck*
*Jazzybee Verlag Jürgen Beck*
*86450 Altenmünster, Loschberg 9*
*Deutschland*

*ISBN: 9783849679255*

*www.jazzybee-verlag.de*
*admin@jazzybee-verlag.de*

*Printed by Createspace, North Charleston, SC, USA*

# CONTENTS:

# KINGS COUNTY

## CHAPTER XXV. KINGS COUNTY

Kings County in its beginning was essentially a Dutch community. Gravesend, of course, was English, but its existence does not change the fact of Dutch pre-eminence, for it was permitted to be established by the authority of a Dutch Governor, and was at first as completely under Dutch laws and Dutch protection as was any other settlement on the island. When Col. Nicolls made his memorable descent upon New Netherland and forced the surrender of New Amsterdam and the abdication of the lion-hearted Peter, and wiped out the authority of "Their High Mightinesses," he formed the towns in what is now Kings county, with Newtown, Staten Island and part of Westchester into one of the Ridings — the West Riding — of his then newly created Yorkshire. That was in 1664. The reconquest by the Dutch under Governor Colve was too brief an interlude to permit much of a change in geographical nomenclature, or such frivolous things as territorial divisions, and so the West Riding of Yorkshire may be said to hold good for the west end of the island until 1683, when the present county of Kings was formed along with those of Queens and Suffolk. It had an area of some 70,000 square miles, and was divided into six towns, — Brooklyn, Bushwick, Flatbush, Flatlands, New Utrecht and Gravesend. These towns, with the exception of Gravesend, "just grew," — that is, they were not definitely settled at first with the idea of becoming towns and rose into that pre-eminence simply because local conditions attracted settlers to given points, and also because it was necessary that the settlers should have rallying places for defense. Gravesend on the other hand was settled at first as a town colony. Over the territory included in these townships, and indeed over all the territory west of Oyster Bay, the authority of the Dutch rulers of the New Netherland was nominally supreme until Capt. Nicolls' upheaval sent Stuyvesant into retirement to his "Bouwerie," and not even the claims of Connecticut acting under its charter of 1662, which awarded it territorial jurisdiction over the whole of Long Island, could change the allegiance of the sturdy Dutch farmers, there was nothing to gain by the change, and they understood their rules, although the paternal rule of such men as Kieft and Stuyvesant was sometimes felt irksome. Of Long Island outside of the towns in Kings County it can hardly be said that the rule of the West India Company was ever secure with the exception of Hempstead, Jamaica and Newtown; but these towns, like Gravesend, were permitted to choose their own officers and to manage their own affairs subject to review and approval by the Governor, a right that was rarely exercised. Oyster Bay, too, the boundary town, was another English settlement over which the Dutch claimed sway, but it finally was' yielded up to Connecticut. In the Dutch towns of Kings county (to use the best-known name for the territory) the rule of the

Governor in New Amsterdam was supreme. It used to be the boast of the old chroniclers that the Dutch honestly bought from the aborigines — and honestly paid the stipulated price — all the land in what afterward became Kings and Queens counties. In this claim they are perfectly justified by the record, although it seems to us that they drove a pretty hard bargain on their part, while, so far as the Indians went, it was a question of either sell or fight, for the white man had come to stay and the time had come for the native to go west in search of new lands, or remain and accept the virtues or the vices of the new order of things. Most of them remained; most of them, nay all of them, it might be said, the exceptions were so few, accepted the vices of the white man; and gradually, but surely, disappeared from the face of the earth. The Dutch Governors, as we have seen, were autocrats; but autocracy is inseparable from a system of paternal government. They were loyal, except perhaps Minuit, to their task of building up the province over which they ruled, or making the people happy and contented and as comfortable in surroundings and wealth as possible, — always, however, remembering the paramount claims of their High Mightinesses and the success of the West India Company's venture. Every effort was made to build up Long Island — or what they could see of it from the New Amsterdam shore of the East River or could discover of it in a day's journey. By order of the company a settler could easily get a patent for a piece of meadowland, more indeed than he could cultivate, on a scale of payment little more than nominal and which would have made the modern phrase of "easy terms" to seem extortionate. To some farmers, indeed, free passages from Holland were given, and there is no doubt that the company did its best to people the territory. Large estates were even given to enterprising capitalists who promised to induce settlers, and patents for land were freely given at times to all who had interest with the Governor and Council or could show a probability of their turning them to some use. A few of these people held the land simply for speculative purposes, much as property is similarly held in our day. But the bulk of those who crossed the East River with a patent went there to stay. In this way was the territory of Kings County first built up, but the process was naturally a slow one, and its early difficulties and dangers were many and serious.

The leading event in the history of Kings county is the Battle of Brooklyn (or Battle of Long Island, as it is generally and incorrectly called); but as that is fully narrated in one chapter, and the story of the British occupation told in another, there is no need of recurring to it here beyond this scanty mention. The part which Long Island played in the war of 1812 is also told — and these practically exhaust its story — with the momentous change which took place on Jan. 1, 1897, when, as the result of the vote of a majority of its inhabitants, it became part and parcel of the Greater New York, although still retaining its standing as a district county. A forecast of this great amalgamation was seen in 1857, when an act of the Legislature turned the counties of New York, Kings, Westchester and Richmond into a single police district, under the designation of the Metropolitan district, under the direct control of the State. This innovation did not last long, nor can it be said to have been in any way a success, although it seems to have proved beneficial to the police administration in Brooklyn.

Kings County and the Borough of Brooklyn are coterminous in their boundaries; but for administrative purposes the county administration is maintained, — that is, there is a distinct set of county officials in Kings, — sheriff, county clerk, public administrator, district attorney, etc., — the county administrations of the component parts of Greater New York not having been altered in that respect by consolidation. The County Courts are also maintained, and the general Government appears in its arrangements to have ignored the great fact of consolidation altogether. Kings County may be described as occupying the entire southwestern end of Long Island and to be bounded on the north and west by the county of New York: on the west by New York Bay; on the south by Gravesend Bay, the Atlantic Ocean and by Jamaica Bay, and on the east and north by the county of Queens, including all wharves, piers, docks and basins lying southerly and easterly of the center line of the East River.

The history of Kings County is simply a history of its townships and that history we will now proceed to relate.

# CHAPTER XXVI. FLATLANDS.

By a narrow margin of a few months the old town of Flatlands could claim, in fact did claim, when the claim was worth anything, priority over Breuckelen and the other towns of Kings county. The first recorded purchase of land in the old' town was dated June 16, 1637, when Andres Hudden and Wolfert Gerretse Van Couwenhoven bought from the Canarsie Indians "the westernmost of the three flats (prairies), called by the sellers Kaskutenu." On July 16th in the same year Gov. Van Twiller secured by patent another of the flats; and Jacobus Van Curler (or Corlear), who in 1638 was a teacher in New Amsterdam, secured a patent for the third flat. The two latter transactions seem to have been in the nature of land speculations, but Hudden and Van Couwenhoven bought a place on which they might settle and earn their living. Their holding they called Achtervelt. In 1639 Hudden gave up, or sold, his interest in the plantation to Van Couwenhoven, although they appear to have continued for some time in partnership as regards other lands which they held in the neighborhood, and removed to New Amsterdam. Hudden seems to have been a politician, an almost continuous office-holder. Such was the beginning of Flatlands. In an inventory taken in 1638 it seems the owners of Achtervelt "had a house set around with long, round palisades, the house being twenty-six feet long, twenty-two feet wide, forty feet deep, with the roof covered above and around with plank; two lofts, one above another, and a small chamber at their side; one barn forty feet long, eighteen feet wide, and twenty-four feet deep; and one bergh with five posts, forty feet long. The plantation was stocked with six cows, old and young, three oxen and five horses."

It was not long before the plantation became the center of a settlement. Peter Stuyvesant had a Bouwerie there which was farmed for him by Peter Wyckoff, who worked it, apparently in connection with sixty acres he had bought from Van Couwenhoven. Hans Hansen or Jansen, the ancestor of the Van Nostrands, also bought a tract of land, as did Elbert Elbertse, the ancestor of the Stoothoffs. Elbert appears to have had the land fever quite strong, for he not only kept steadily adding to his purchases on shore but became the possessor of Bergen's Island and Barren Island. In 1673 Governor Colve appointed him Captain of a company of militia, with Roelof Martense as his lieutenant and Derrick Janse as his ensign. He became the possessor of Achtervelt by marriage with the widow of the pioneer Couwenhoven's son and assumed the care of her young family. This Elbert faithfully performed, for he appears to have been a most honorable and upright man. By the time he thus came into prominence, Flatlands had become quite a settlement, and the Strykers, Van Sigelens, Romeyns, Ammermans and a dozen other families were located around the palisadoed mansion of the original settler, a mansion that was so arranged as to be a stronghold to which the people might readily fly for refuge should Indian or other dangers arise.

But while first as regards settlement — if it was first, for the old records are a little confusing — Flatlands was much slower than some of its neighbors in acquiring municipal rights. Gravesend and Flatbush secured such privileges ahead of it. The people were to a great extent more isolated than those in the other settlements and probably attracted little attention in New Amsterdam. It really needed little attention from the ruling powers. It was essentially a religious community, and in its earlier days the dictum of the Dominie and Elders at Flatbush was sufficient to settle all the little disputes which might arise. To a certain extent, too, when it required some decision at law, it had to arrange with the Magistrates at Flatbush to hold the scales of exact justice, and that was too troublesome a procedure to be invoked except on very grave occasions. In 1661 it assumed the dignity of possessing a local government, for it then was empowered to elect three Magistrates of its own, and the people chose Elbert Elbertsen, Pieter Cornelissen and Simon Jansen as the holders of this dignity — the old dignity of Schepen; and their successors were to be elected annually. It was not until the arrival of Col. Nicolls and the overturn of the Stuyvesant regime that the town was called into being with the full dignity of a charter; and in that document, which was dated Oct. 4, 1667, it is called "Amersfoort, alias Flatlands." The boundaries of the town were laid down so indefinitely in this charter that an amended one was issued February 3, 1668, by Gov. Lovelace, and yet another by Gov. Dongan March 11, 1685, but none of these proved clear enough to prevent litigations more or less bitter and acrimonious and tedious between Flatlands and Flatbush. In fact a local historian tells us that Flatlands in June, 1679, got a judgment against Flatbush for £10, and that the amount with interest is still due! In 1788 Flatlands was officially recognized as a town by the State Government of New York, and it continued its independent existence until Jan. 1, 1896, when the town was wiped out and its territory became the Thirty-second ward of the then Greater Brooklyn.

A list taken in 1687 gives the following as the names of those who took the oath of allegiance to the British authorities in accordance with the orders of Gov. Nicolls, and as the list is a valuable one for genealogical purposes we here give it in full:

Pieter Claes Wyckoff, 1636; Gerret Pieterse Wyckoff, Claes Pieterse Wyckoff, Hendrick Pieterse Wyckoff, Jan Pieterse Wyckoff, natives; Elbert Elbertse (Stoothoff), 1637; Gerret Elbertse (Stoothoff), Hans Janse (Van Nostrandt), 1640; Roelof Martense Schenck, 1650; Jan Martense Schenck, 1650; Jan Roelof Schenck, Martin Roelof Schenck, Derick Janse Ammerman, 1650; Jacob Stryker, 1651; Fferdinandes Van Sickelin, 1652; Christoffle Janse Romeyne, 1653; Ruth (or Rut) Bruynsen, 1653; William Davies, 1653; Jan theunis Van duyckhuys, 1653; Simon Janse Van Arts Daelen, 1653; Cornelius

Simonen Vanarsdalen, Pieter Cornelius Luyster, 1656; Thys Pieter Luyster, 1656; Pieter Pieterse Tull, 1657; Jan Brouwer, 1657; Dirck Brouwer, hendrick Brouwer, Dirk Stofflese, 1657; Stoffle Dirckse (Langstraet), Adriaen Kume, 1660; Court Stephense Van Voorhees, 1660; Albert Courten Van Voorhees, Luycas Stephense (Van Voorhees), 1660; Jan Stephense (Van Voorhees), 1660; Abram Williamse, 1662; Johannis Williamse, 1662; Evert Janse Van Wickelen, 1664; theunis Janse Van Amach, 1673; Gerret Hansen (Van Nostrandt), Gerret Hendrickse Bresse, Wellim Gerretse Van Couwenhoven, Gerret Williamse Van Couwenhoven, Anthony Warnshaer, William Williamse Borcklo, Jan Albertse Terhune, Pieter Nevins, Pieter Manfoort.

The date appended to some of these names indicate those in which were of foreign birth and show when they settled in the country. Of course such a list is not a complete census. The Rev. Dr. Du Bois prepared the following list from church and other records of those who resided in the town in 1687 and previously:

Gerret Seerjersy, Hendrick Freemensen (here in 1670); Gerret Gerretsen, Abram Joeresy (Brinkerhoff), Jan Cornelis, Jan Barrentsen (Van Driest), Albeirt Albertse (Terhune), died 1672, and Vaereyck Flieksen, all here in 1672; William lobbertse, Wm. Williamise (Wyckoff), Gerrrt Remers, Barent Jureyaensy, Thunis Helebrantsy, here in 1673; Klaes Kornelesen, Barent the Tailor, Sawaern Jans, Hans Janse (Van Nostrandt), Hendrick Hermanze, Widow of Frederick Ebbcott, here in 1674; Widow of Gerraen Keest, Willem Gansen Van Barkelo, Klaes Smit, Widow of Geromus Boeck. Willem Kuyken, Jan Snedeghyer, here in 1675; Abraham Jorissen (Brinkerhoff), Fookie Hansen, 1679; Cornelius Barentsen, Simon Jansen (Romeyne), Simon Jdrisen, 1680; Albert Terhune, Jr., Lawrence Koeck, Hendrick Aswerus, 1682; Jan Hansen (Van Nostrandt), Johannis Machgilssen, Jan Manfordt, Vis Homes, Jammes Wilier, William the Shoemaker, De Fris the tanner, Jacob Fardon, Jan Albert Terhune, 1685; Rut Joosten (Van Brunt), Cornelis Simonsen Van Arsdalen, Joost Rutjen (Van Brunt), Johannis Holsa, Jan Kilement a mason. Master Toon, the Doctor, here in 1687; also 1677-1685; Bruno Hendrickse, Rutgert Brunoos, Tjelletje Reimers (Wizzelpfinnig), Pieter Tull, Jan Poppe, William Stryker, Gerret Remmerts, Jan Kiersen, Dirckye Roelffsen, Pieter Hendricksen, Albert Steven (Voorhees), Steven Coerten (Voorhees), Martin Pieterse (Wyckoff), Luykas (Voorhees), Teunis Jansen, Swaen Jansen, Adam Michilse, Dierckie Williamse, Lourens Cornelise, William Hulett.

A census taken in 1698 showed a total of 40 men, 39 women, 130 children and 40 negro slaves. The name of the heads of families are given as follows, the first figure after the name (when two are given) being the number in the family and the second the number of slaves:

Gerret Elbert Stoothoff, 7, 4; Jan Teunis Dykhuys, 5, 5; Roelif Martense (Schenck), 6, 4; Coert Stevense, 5, 2; Gerret WyckofiE, 5, 2; Hendk Wykof,

2, 2; Dirk Jans Amerman, 9; Adriaen Kenne, 8; Dirck Langstraet, 5; Jans Kiersen, 2, 1; Alexander Simson, 10; Jan Hansen, 5; Pieter Nevins, 9, 1; Jacob Tysse Lane, 6; Helena Aertsen, 5; Simon Jantz Van Aersdaelen, 5, 1; Cornelis Simontz Aersdaelen, 8, 1; Willem Gerrittz Van Couwenhoven, 8; Aernont Viele, 2, 2; Jan Albertz ter hennen, 8, 2; Jan Brouwer, 8, 1; Thunis Jantz Amack, 7; fferdinando Van Sigelen, 7, 4; Claes Wykof, 8; Jan Wykof, 4, 1; Willem Bruynen, 7, 4; Adriaen Langstraet, 1; Lucan Stevense, 12, 4; Pieter Pieterse Wyckoff, 1; Hendrick Brouwer, 1; Albert Amerman, 1; Pieter Van Couwenhoven, 4; Martin Schenck, 5, 2; Jan Stevense (Voorhees), 12, 1; Pieter Monfoor, 8, 1; Steven Caerten (Voorhees), 5; Rutgers Bruyn, 9.

According to a census taken in 1738 the population consisted of 195 whites and 42 negroes, so that there was evidently no land boom or other excitement to disturb the even tenor of the place during these pre-Revolutionary years. In fact, outside of a scrap or two with Flatbush the annals of Flatlands were of the quietest description possible and centered round the story of the local church. The good people claimed that their religious history began with 1654, as they had an equal interest with Flatbush in the church then built, there, and whose history had been already told in an earlier chapter. Certainly the structure at Flatbush was legally their religious home. The Governor said so. They contributed $48 toward the cost of its erection; and Dominie Polhemus, they held was their pastor as much as he was the spiritual director of their neighbors in Flatbush and Brooklyn. Indeed he was pretty regularly in Flatlands, preaching in barns and private houses until 1663, when they finished the construction of a church building in their midst.

It was a quaint little structure, according to our ideas, but doubtless Dominie and the people were equally proud of it, standing as it did on quite a commanding site on a piece of already sacred ground, — ground which had been consecrated by the Indians as a burial spot from remote ages. In appearance the building was similar to the other temples of worship in the Dutch towns. Like them, it was octagonal in form, with a high-pitched roof, surmounted with an open cupola, over which a weather-cock showed the citizens the direction of the wind and assisted the local weather prophets in their prognostications. The cupola, of course, was to contain a bell, but by the time the building was finished the resources of the brethren for church decoration were exhausted and so the people were called to public worship by the beating of a drum until 1686, when a subscription netted 556 guilders and a bell was imported from Holland. The building was fitted up in the interior in quite elaborate style. The pulpit was a lofty structure, but rather a slender arrangement, surmounted with a sounding board that looked heavier than the pulpit it covered. The worshippers were seated on wooden benches except that a chair was reserved for the minister's wife and another for the magistrate. The accommodation was for 130 and the Dominie could see every corner of the building when he was conducting the sermon: perhaps even when sitting on the hard bench provided for him in the pulpit he could mentally note the absentees and prepare to admonish the late-comers. The little edifice stood in its original form until 1762. At that time the members were Cornelius Voorhees, 5 sittings; Steve Schenck, 4; Johannes Lett, 7; Hermann Hooglandt, 5; William Kouwenhoven, 5; Roelof Voorhees, 4; Fammetie Ditmars, 3; Roelof Van Voorhees, 4; John Van Der Bilt, 5; Jeremiah Van Derbilt, 1; Abraham Voorhees, 5; Folkert Sprong, 2; Abraham Dorye, 4; Coustyn Golneck, 1: Peter Wykof, 3; Johannes Lott, Jr., 3; William Van Gelder, 3; Derrick Remsen, 4; Henrick Lott, 4; Jan Schenck, 5; Wilhelmus Stoot.hoof, 7; Jan Ouke. 1; Marte Ouke, 1; Samuel Garreson, 1; Bernardus Ryder, 3; Albert Terhune, 4; James Holbert, 2; Fernandus Van Segelen, 1; Barent Vanderventer, 1; Abraham Schenck, 1; Callyntje Janse, 1; Garrett Wykoff, 3; Getore Heyn, 2; Jan Amerman, 6; Annatie Wykof, 5; Petrus Amerman, 3; Jacob Ouke, 1; Helena Ouke, 1; Eisack Selover, 1.

The church at that date was enlarged by having the three front octagons of the walls built out in a straight line so as to make a square side and in that way twenty-eight new sittings were added. The sittings in the church were allotted to the farms— not to individuals — and were part and parcel of the property of each holding and subject to transference with it, and the dues to the church seemed to have been regarded down even to the year 1876 as a lien on certain pieces of property in exchange for the right to sittings. In 1794 the old weather-beaten building began so plainly to show the effects of time that an entire new structure was demanded. So the octagon building was torn down and a new church was erected which was opened for public worship December 26, that year, with a sermon by the Rev. Peter Lowe, one of the ministers of the home church in Flatbush. This structure lasted until 1848, when the present church building was erected. This has since been improved several times, and its usefulness was increased in 1853 by the erection beside it of a building for school and lecture purposes. The connection between the churches in Flatbush and Flatlands terminated in 1820, and in 1824 Flatlands and New Lots were united ecclesiastically and the Rev. William Cruikshank accepted the joint pastorate. During his term the church at Flatlands underwent one great change, inasmuch as it was, for the first time in its history, heated in winter by the introduction of a wood-burning stove. In 1827 a new pulpit was introduced and the ladies of the congregation subscribed a sufficient sum to have it appropriately dressed.

Mr. Cruikshank resigned in 1834, and was followed in 1836 by the Rev. J. Abeel Baldwin, who served until 1852, when the association with New Lots came to an end, and the Rev. T. M. Davie became minister of Flatlands. Since then the church has prospered under a succession of pastors, on the work of one of whom, the Rev. Dr. Anson Du Bois, much of this sketch has been founded. Before leaving the church history of Flatlands we may here state that the Methodist Church at Canarsie was organized in 1840, with twelve members, and that the Methodist Episcopal Church at Flatlands had its beginning in 1851. The other churches are of recent date.

In every old Dutch community school and church generally went hand in hand and formed part of the same organization. We have already seen this exemplified in the chapter wherein the story of the church at Flatbush is told. Such was undoubtedly the case at Flatlands, although the earliest records have been lost. The Rev. Dr. Du Bois in his historical sketch tells the early story of education in this town so completely that we quote it:

We have found no records touching it (the school) earlier than 1675, when it was evidently in a mature and vigorous career under the care of the church elders. It was called "The School of the Town." The first notice we have of it is in regard to a supply of books by the deacons; and entries and bills, of elementary and religious books paid for, appear in their accounts from 1675 for a long period of years, along with every variety and order of expenses.

According to the tradition in our town, and the well-known usages of other Dutch settlements, the schoolmaster was, by virtue of his office. Reader in church. Chorister, and commonly Sexton also. If this be true, we are able to name some of the honored leaders of mental progress in Flatlands from very early times.

The first who claims this honor is Willim Gerretse (Van Couwenhoven), 1675; the next Jan Brouwer, 1688; the third Pieter Tull, 1691, though the fact that he afterward became a pauper does not argue liberality of salary. Various items were paid "to the schoolmaster," for salary and other services, until 1704, when the incumbent was Martin Schenck, who was also a deacon of the church. Isaac Sllover was teacher in 1712; Yan Sudani in 1715 and apparently to 1729; when Yohannes Van Siggelon succeeded him. In 1733 Abraham de Lanoy occupied the place. His name would indicate that he was French, while has receipts for his salary of £6 a year are written in a bold and elegant English hand. He was doubtless able to teach in English. Isaac Voorheesi held the place in 1742; Johannes Nevius in 1743; Abram Voorhees, 1744-47; Luykas Voorhees, from 1748 to 1752, when Derick Remsen served part of a year, and Luykas Voorhees again, 1755-1757. As no new name occurs, it is fair to infer that Voorhees continued to receive the annual salary of £4 from the deacons as chorister, and probably an additional sum from the elders as schoolmaster, until 1768, when he was succeeded by Abraham Voorhees, the same probably who had served in 1744-47, and who now held the position until 1792. This teacher first introduced a stove into the school-house in June, 1789, costing £12 15s. 6d. We judge the previous winter must have been uncommonly cold and they would no longer trust to an open fire even though they had to bring in the stove in the first month of summer.

We have assumed that the chorister was also the school teacher as was the universal custom of the Dutch. But the practice was now falling into disuse. It seems that Thomas Whitlock was employed during the latter years accredited to Abram Voorhees and that John Baxter, whose journal of daily events continued by his son Garret extends from 1790 to 1840, taught the school about 1790. We have also the following as teachers: Peter Labagh, 1792; Geo. Parker, 1795; Jas. Smith, 1798; Elijah Elwell, 1801; Patrick Noon and Hugh McGarron, 1802; John Burns and Alex. Johnson, 1804; Cuthbert, 1805: Cassidy, 1810; Hugh McGarron again, 1811-16; Tibbetts and Blundel taught a short time; James Bolton some years; Esterbrook, Bledsoe, Kingsley, Topping, and Leach; Slauson to 1827, when Chas. Leach resumed and taught to 1830: Ed. Berry, 1830, when David Baldwin (whose conversion is recorded by his pastor in a tract of the American Tract Society) assumed charge, but retired from ill health; Albert Smith, 1831; Willis, and the same year H. D. Woodworth, now principal of a public school in Brooklyn: W. S. Webb, 1833; and after him E. S. Johnson and Stephen Voorhees; since whom Messrs. Sutton, Wade, Blake and Sowles have taught.

Principal Voorhees Overbaugh took charge of this school in 1845. He was then expected to teach from 8 o'clock A. M. to 4 o'clock P. M., with a noon recess, five days each week, without a vacation of any kind during the whole year. He did not receive a stipulated salary, but a fee per capita on the scholars, and collected his own bills.

The original school-house of District No. 1 probably stood on Hubbard's Lane, opposite John L. Williamson's. On February 3rd, 16967, the heirs of Elbert Elbertse, viz., Garrett Stoothoof, Thos. Willes and Jan Van Duyckhuisen, deeded to Coert Stevense, Derick Amertman and Claes Peterse, for themselves' and others, freeholders, etc., premises described as follows: "All that house and garden spot, as it is now in fence, lying * * * in the town of fflatlands, adjoining to the house and land of fferdinanno vasycklyn, and now used and occupied for a school-house for said town." Van Sickelin lived at the southeast corner of the church-lot, where his son Johannes lived in 1747.

Confirmatory of this view is the fact that on the next day, viz., February 4th, 1697, the Stoothoff heirs, who seem to have been engaged in settling up the estate conveyed to the same parties, "Elders of the Dutch Church of fflatlands," the church-lot and burying ground, and describe the latter as "Bounded north by Tunis Janse's fence, south by the pound, west by the highway," with the church-lot at the east. Thus the whole of the present school-lot and burial-ground is included, without any mention of the school-house being then upon it, and excluding the Van Syckelen lands from contiguity. The evidence seems conclusive that the original school-house stood east from the residence of John B. Hendrickson. A new school-house seems to have been built about this time. Between September, 1694, and

August, 1697, the Deacons paid "for the school-house" in various items of material and work no less a sum than $654.40, which could not have been for repairs. Probably, at this time, the new school-house was placed on an unused part of the burial-ground. The lot described in 1696 as the school-house lot must, soon after this, have fallen into private hands, for, in 1729, it is deeded by Abram Westervelt, and Margaret, his wife, to the Town, together with an acre where the house of B. Stafford now stands. We know that the school-house was near its present location in 1733, for in that year Pieter Wyckoff conveys "a certain piece of land adjoining the school-lot, being in breadth two rods and in length as far as the school-lot runs, bounded southerly by said school-lot, northerly by ground of said Pieter Wyckof, westerly by the highway, and easterly by the land belonging to the church." The school-house first placed within the original lines of the grave-yard, in 1699, was extensively repaired about 1765, the work having been begun in 1762, simultaneously with the extensive improvements and enlargement of the church. At this time the sum of £356 was paid for materials and work "for the school-house." In 1771 "a well for the schoolhouse" cost £1, I11S. 3d.

In April, 1816, the town ordered a new school building. It was completed and occupied two years later, and the old house sold to Nicholas Schenck for $20. This new building continued to be used by the school until 1861, when it was sold to John L. Ryder for a carriage-house. The school-lot was fenced in by the trustees, as such, in 1861, by advice of counsel. The building of 1861 was enlarged to more than twice its former capacity in 1876.

A school was early established in Flatlands Neck, the section of the town that lies between Jamaica Bay, New Lots and Flatbush. A new school-house was built there in 1835 and another at Carnarsie in 1844. The modern story of education in Flatlands, however, is associated with that of Brooklyn.

It has been said that the annals of Flatlands are uneventful and uninteresting, yet at the same time the story of the battle of Brooklyn might be woven into its history. There was, of course, rare excitement in the township when the British troops landed, and the excitement deepened during the strategical operations that followed. But after the battle was over things resumed their usual quiet sway. One regiment, Colonel Kniphausen's horse, was quartered for some time on a farm in Flatlands, but this is only a tradition and it does not seem likely that they were there beyond a few days. A few guards were placed on duty in residences at Canarsie Point and Flatlands Neck, but they seemed not to have been very offensive and made themselves humbly comfortable in the kitchens of the houses to which they were assigned. The British, of course, took possession of the grain, the produce and much of the livestock, — that was part of the incidents of any war, and nothing else could be expected. But the best evidence that Flatlands was not seriously molested lies in the fact that services in the church were regularly conducted all through the British occupation, although there was a strong patriotic sentiment in the town, and the Dominie expressed himself very freely on all occasions against the invaders, and nowhere on Long Island was the triumphant close of the war celebrated with more enthusiasm than in this old stronghold of the Dutch sentiment. With the return of peace Flatlands retained her quiet mode of living, advanced slowly but surely, and the years passed on so uninterestingly that the historian finds little to narrate in the routine of its calm, domestic, home-living current. It was the last of the suburbs of Brooklyn to feel the quickening influence of that city, but when the influence was felt the dwellers in the community met it with avidity. The old farms were placed on the market, the land-boomers got in their work, and "lots" instead of acres began to dominate in the real-estate transactions. With the introduction of the trolley the old seclusion of Flatlands began to vanish, and since it has itself disappeared and become simply a city ward it has been wholly cut up into streets and avenues, and everywhere the march of improvement represented by the modern builders is apparent. It has many new features, but Barren Island is still devoted to the manufacture of fertilizers and its smells are as fragrant as ever; Canarsie is still a haven for fishermen and those who enjoy rowing or yachting, and Jamaica Bay yet yields a harvest of pleasure or profit; but Bergen's Island has become, under the name of Bergen Beach, a resort of the nature of Coney Island, and on each Sunday in the season more people pass through Flatlands in trolley cars than has been seen in it since that eventful day in August, 1776, when an old lady said that "the red coats were so thick in Flatlands you could walk on their heads."

## CHAPTER XXVII. FLATBUSH.

One local writer has given 1630 as the date of the first settlement at 't Vlavke Bros., Middle-Wout, or Midwout, the earliest names by which Flatbush was designated. There is, however, no definite proof as to this. It would seem that the patents given for lands in Flatlands to Hudden and Van Couwenhoven and Van Twiller included ground which overlapped into what was afterward across the border of that township and into the township of Midwout, but even that would hardly give us the right to claim the date of these patents as the beginning of the story of this, in many ways the most interesting of the five Dutch towns. From Flatlands an Indian trail led to Brooklyn, and while using this trail the rich and fertile fields, now the streets of Flatbush, lay invitingly open and the overflow of population, so to speak, from Flatlands took them up. These early Dutch farmers were mighty particular as to places of settlement. They were strong believers in meadow land, and those who can recall Flatbush before the rush of the trolley and the march of modern improvements changed things all around could easily imagine it, in its still more primitive stage, as lying ready and prepared for adaptation into farm, garden and grazing ground with but little labor. By 1651 the place had a sufficient population to warrant the issuance to it of a town patent, and Governor Stuyvesant incorporated in the document the names of Jan Snedecor, who had prospered as a tavernkeeper in New Amsterdam; Arent Van Hatten, burgomaster of the same city; and one of its ministers, Johannes Megapolensis. The lands of Midwout also began very early to have a speculative value, for in 1653 we find that Edward Griffin bought fifty acres of land "on the west side of the road near the Flatbush" in February, and he sold the same in July to Bartel Loot and Peter Loot (Lott). When the patent was issued. Dr. Strong says, "farms were laid out into forty-eight lots, or tracts of land, extending 600 Dutch rods east and west on each side of the Indian path and having generally an average width of twenty-seven rods." Before the farms were drawn for, 102 lots were laid aside for the use of the church, which it was even then determined should be built, while the unappropriated lands, mainly stretches of woodland on the outskirts of the town, were left for the common use and so continued for many years.

It seems that there was not enough meadow land to satisfy the wants or ambitions of the Dutch farmers in Flatbush, and they squatted on some of the rich meadows of Canarsie, which the Flatlands people claimed as their own. This led to trouble between them; and to end it, and also with the view of substituting an English charter for the Dutch one. Governor Nicolls caused a fresh survey to be made, and then issued a new patent which bore the date of October 11, 1667. It was then that Flatbush, the English rendering of 't Vlacke Bosche, came into legal use. But the good farmers no sooner had this trouble adjudicated than a new and even more serious one arose. The land comprising their town had originally been bought from the Canarsie

Indians, but in 1670 another tribe, the Rockaways, claimed the soil, denying the right of the Canarsies to ownership, and demanding payment. The probability is that the Canarsies were honest in their intentions, but they sold more than they ought to have done, and unwittingly disposed of some territory to which the Rockaways had some claim. Lands were not very closely surveyed in those days. Of course the Flatbush title was clear, so far as the settlers were concerned. They had complied with all the forms of the law, Dutch as well as English, and could have defended their holdings in any court of law successfully. But the Indians had ways of enforcing their demands which were much more unpleasant than those of the courts, and an angry dispute with them meant much loss of life and destruction of property — all the horrors, in fact, of Indian warfare. So the settlers made the best of the situation and secured a fresh deed from the wily claimants. It reads as follows:

To all Christian people to whom this present writing shall come: Eskemoppas, Sachem of Rockaway, upon Long Island, Kinnarimas and Ahawaham his brothers, send greeting: Whereas they, the said Sachem Eskemoppas, and his two brothers aforementioned, do lay claim to the land now in the tenure and occupation of the inhabitants of Midwout, alias Flatbush, as well as other lands adjacent thereto as the right born Indian owners and proprietors thereof: Know ye that in consideration of certain sums of seewant, a certain sum of wampum and divers other goods (hereinafter specified) unto the said Sachem and his brothers in hand paid, and received, from Adrian Hegeman, Jacob Stryker, Hendrick Jorise and Jan Hansen, for and on behalf of themselves and the rest of the inhabitants of Midwout alias Flatbush, the receipt whereof they do hereby acknowledge, and themselves to be fully satisfied and paid: Have given granted contracted and sold * * * All that said parcel of land where the said town of Midwout stands, together with all the lands lying therein, stretching on the east side to the limits of Newtown and Jamaica, on the south side to the meadow ground, and limits of Amersfort; on the west side to the bounds of Gravesend and New Utrecht, and on the north side along the Hills; that is to say, all those lands within the limits above mentioned &c. * * * in witness whereof, the parties to these presents have hereunto set their hands and seals this 20th day of April, in the 22nd year of his Majesty's reign, in the year of our Lord 1670.

Eskemoppas £ Mark, (seal.)

Kinnarimas & Mark, (seal.)

Ahawaham *f* Mark (seal.)

Signed and delivered in the presence of Thomas Lovelace. Cornelius Van Ruyven.

Recorded the day and year within written, per Mathias Nichols, Secretary.

The consideration agreed upon in the purchase herein mentioned was as follows viz.: 10 Fathoms of black seewant; 10 Fathoms of white seewant; 5

Match coats of Duffells; 4 Blankets; 2 Gunners sight Guns; 2 Pistols; 5 Double handfulls of Powder [Gispen bunches of Powder]; 5 Bars of Lead; 10 Knives; 2 Secret Aprons of Duffell (Cuppas of Duffell]; I Half vat or half barrell of Strong Beer; 3 Cans of Brandy; 6 Shirts. All the above particulars were received by the Sachem and his two brothers, in the presence of the persons under written, as witnesses hereof.

John Manning, Jacob Van Cortlandt.

Sylester Salisbury, Teunis Jacob Hay.

John Hough, Edward Carlisle.

Acknowledged before me, the Sachem and his two brothers, and the goods delivered in my oresence, the day and year within written. Francis Lovelace.

In drawing up this deed the Flatbush people took good care to have their old boundaries clearly fixed, and it would seem that the territory known as Oostwoud was thrown in by the Rockaways in their joy at the prospects of the possession of the powder and beer and brandy and Other commodities stipulated by their head men. This territory, afterward known as New Lots, claims 1670 as the beginning of its history, although it was not until 1677 that Adrian Lambertsen and thirty-four others secured a patent for ownership in it. For many years, in fact until 1721, the most notable feature of the history of Flatbush was its constant defense of its territory against claims made by Flatlands, Newtown and even by private individuals; but as the course of events has long since rendered the story of such disputes of no practical value, of no responsible bearing on the real history of the town, there is little use of recounting them here. There seems no doubt that the Flatbush settlers were in some of these disputes the real aggressors, — the courts so more than once decided; but the probability is that in most cases the trouble arose from want of exact knowledge as to boundaries, or, as is equally likely, indifference on the part of the settlers to political divisions. It was probably with the view of settling all this on an enduring basis that the inhabitants in 1685 applied to Governor Dongan for a new patent which should confirm to them all that had been granted at various times and for which various patents had been issued. That application was granted, and the document, one of the most important in the early local history, reads as follows:

Thomas Dongan, Lieutenant-Governor and Vice-Admiral of New York, &c., under his Majesty James the Second, by the Grace of God, King of England, Scotland, France and Ireland Defender of the Faith, &c., Supreme Lord and Proprietor of the Colony and Prince of New York and its dependencies in America. To all to whom these presents shall come, sendeth Greeting: Whereas, there is a certain town in Kings County, upon Long Island, called and known by the name of Midwout, alias Flatbush, the bounds whereof begin at the mouth of the Fresh-Kill, and so along by a certain ditch which lies betwixt Amersfoot and Flatbush Meadows, and so running along the ditch and fence to a certain white-oak marked tree, and from thence upon a straight line to the westernmost point of a small island of woodland lying before John Stryker's bridge; and from thence with a straight line to the northwest hook or corner of the ditch of John Oakie's meadow, and from thence along the said ditch and fence to the swamp of the Fresh-Kill, and so along the swamp and hollow of the aforesaid Kill to the land of Keuter's Hook: thence along the same to a white-oak tree; from thence with a straight line to a black-oak marked tree standing upon the northeast side of Twiller's Flats, having a small snip of flats upon the southeast side of the line; and so from thence to a white-oak tree standing on the west side of Moschito Hole to a small island, leaving a snip of flats in the Flatlands bounds; and from thence to a certain marked tree or stump standing upon the highway which goes to Flatlands, upon the Little Flats, about twenty rods from Flatbush Lots, and so along the fence six hundred Dutch rods to the corner of Flatbush fence, and so along the rear of the lots to a sassafras-stump standing on Cornelius Jansen Berrian's lot of land; and from thence with a straight line to a certain marked tree, or stump, standing by the Rush Pond under the hills, and so along the south side of the hill till it comes to the west end of Long Hill, and so along the south side of the said hill till it comes to the east end of the Long Hill; and then with a straight line from the east end of said Long Hill to a marked white-oak tree standing to the west side of the road, near the place called the gate or port of the hills, and so from the east side of the port or gate aforesaid, upon the south side of the main hills, as far as Brooklyn Patent doth extend, and so along the said hills to the bounds of the Jamaica Patent; and from thence with a southerly line to the kill or creek by the east of Plunder's Neck, and so along the said kill to the sea, as according to the several deeds or purchases from the Indian owners, the patent from Governor Nicolls, and the award between Brooklyn and the town of Flatbush, relation thereunto being had, doth more fully and at large appear: And, whereas, an application to me hath been made for a confirmation of the aforesaid tracts and parcels of land and premises: Now, Know ye, that by virtue of the commission and authority unto me given by his Majesty, James the Second, by the Grace of God of England, Scotland, France and Ireland, King, Defender of the Faith, Supreme Lord and Proprietor of the Province of New York, in consideration of the premises and the quitrent hereinafter reserved, I have given, granted, ratified and confirmed, and by these presents do give, grant, ratify and confirm unto Cornelius Vanderwyck, John Okie, Joseph Hegeman, Aries Jansen Vanderbilt, Lafford Pieterson, William Guilliamsen, Hendrick Williamse, Arien Ryers, Peter Stryker, John Stryker, John Remsen, Jacob Hendricks, Derick Vandervleet, Hendrick Ryck, Okie Johnson, Daniel Polhamus, Peter Lott, Cornelius Vanderveer, Derick Johnson Hooglandt, Denise Tennis, John Johnson, Ditimus Lewis Jansen, William Jacobs, Hendrick Hegeman and Garret Lubbertse, for and on behalf of themselves and their associates, all the freeholders of the said town of Flatbush, and to their heirs and assigns forever, all the before recited tract and tracts, parcel and parcels, of land and islands within the said bounds and limits, together with all and singular, the woods, underwoods, plains, hills, meadows, pastures, quarries, marshes, waters, lakes, causeways, rivers, beaches, houses, buildings, fishing, hawking, hunting and fowling, with all liberties, privileges, hereditaments and appurtenances to the said tract of land and premises belonging, or in any wise appertaining; To have and to hold, &c. * * * To be holden of his Majesty in free and common soccage according to the tenure of East Greenwich, in the county of Kent, in his Majesty's Kingdom of England. Yielding, rendering and paying therefor, yearly, and every year, at the City of New York, to his Majesty, his heirs or successors, or to his or their officer or officers, as by him or them shall be appointed to receive the same, eighteen bushels of good merchantable wheat, on or before the five and twentieth day of March, yearly, and every year. In Testimony whereof, I have caused these presents to be entered upon record, in the Secretary's office in the said Province, and the seal thereof, have hereunto affixed, and signed with my hand the twelfth day of November, in the first year of his Majesty's reign. Anno Domini, 1685.

Thomas Dongan.

Governor Dongan willingly granted such charters not only because their issuance added to the income of his office and settled many vexed questions as to boundaries, but they provided an income from the townships in the shape of a tax which was termed "quit rent" and which in the case of Flatbush was placed at "eighteen bushels of good, merchantable wheat." No objection seems to have been raised anywhere to this certainly very moderate impost. It was some years later changed to a regular cash payment, and continued in force until 1786, when future payment was commuted on payment of a lump sum, according to an act passed by the Legislature April 1 of that year. It seems that Flatbush fell in' arrears from 1765 until 1786 and was required to pay up the amount which then accrued with a rebate of eight years' payments, covering the period of the Revolutionary struggle.

The early story of Flatbush centers around the story of the church, and it, with the school-house and later the court-house, made up the dorp or town, — the rallying point of the life of the village. As in most of the Dutch settlements, the homes of the farmers were located as close to the dorp as possible and spread into what used to be called Rustenberg, a trace of rich sandy loam to the south of it, which was within easy reach. In the dorp the Schout posted his notices and the Schepens held their meetings. These functionaries were the representatives of the Governor, of law and order. Jan Teunissen, Schout in 1646 of Brooklyn, held that office for Middlewout and Amersfoot, and seems to have been succeeded in 1654 by David Provoost, although there is some dubiety about the latter's appointment, so far as his jurisdiction over the territory outside of Brooklyn is concerned. The first local man appointed to this office was Adriaen Hegeman, who was thus honored in 1661, his authority extending over Brooklyn and Flatlands. Adriaen was the ancestor of the family bearing his name and appears to have been a prominent and popular citizen. He came here from Holland in 1650 and was one of the Schepens of Flatbush from 1654 until his appointment as Schout. Afterward he became again a Schepen and secretary of the five Dutch towns, and rounded off his appointments by acting as auctioneer. He owned two valuable lots of land in Flatbush and prospered generally. His death took place previous to 1688. The Schout was the direct representative of the Governor and Council, and was appointed by them, but the Schepens, or local magistrates, were appointed on the nomination of the people. Midwout enjoyed three of these dignitaries.

At first the nominations for these representatives of the people seem to have been practically dictated by the Governor. But the Midwout flocks were not remiss in asserting what they considered their just rights even at this early period in their history, and we find them represented at the conventions held in 1652, which demanded that the laws by which they were governed should resemble those of the old land from which they had emigrated. The story of this primitive constitutional struggle has already been fully told, and may be dismissed here by saying that Governor Stuyvesant fully asserted his authority, and the towns lost some of their privileges. They did not long remain under the Governor's displeasure, however. The shores of Long Island, and even of Manhattan Island, were at that time infested with river thieves and desperadoes, who often made a successful descent upon a village or farm-house and easily escaped with their plunder. It was held that most of these thieves were English, or that at all events they made Gravesend their headquarters and had the sympathy of the people there, whose property it seems was unmolested. To protect themselves the three Dutch towns of Breuckelen, Flatlands and Midwout in 1854 organized a company of militia, with a sergeant for each town and a regularly organized patrol.

This movement, undertaken by the people themselves without apparently any urging on the part of the authorities, appealed to Stuyvesant's military sympathies, and he granted to the Dutch towns, of his own volition, all the privileges they had formerly asked and which he had so stubbornly refused. Midwout became entitled to send a list of six names to the Governor as the choice of the people for their Schepens, and from this list the ruler selected three to whom the usual commissions were issued. It is believed that the first three so appointed were Adriaen Hegeman, Willem Jacobse Van Boerum and Jan Sueberingh. A district court was also instituted, composed of delegates from each town along with the Schout, and this court had charge of all local matters, such as the laying out and maintenance of roads, establishment of schools and the like. This condition of things continued until 1661, when

New Utrecht and Bushwick were added to the combination and the whole formed into a district called the Five Dutch Towns. Over these a Schout Fiscal was placed as the head of the legal and municipal authorities, while a secretary or clerk was appointed to perform much of the duties of the modern town clerk and notary, — acknowledge deeds, wills and other legal papers, and probably to act as the legal adviser of the Schout Fiscal. The first to hold the latter office (1661) was Adriaen Hegeman, of Midwout, quite a standing officeholder, his successor being Nicasius de Sille, of New Utrecht. Michil Hainelle, of Brooklyn, was the town clerk from 1674 to 1680. The fact of his holding this office so long after the Dutch regime had passed away shows that the changes introduced by Governor Nicolls as to the Five Dutch Towns did not affect them greatly. The changes, in fact, were more in name than anything else; and although the New Netherland passed under a "proprietor," the changes which were effected were in reality in the direction of a broadening of the liberties of the people.

Under Nicolls, as we have seen. Long Island became the main portion of the new county of Yorkshire, the Dutch towns became part of the West Riding, Midwout became Flatbush, the Schouts and Schepens became memories, and law was administered by a deputy sheriff and a selected array of justices. The local government in the towns was under the care of overseers, — "men of good fame and life chosen by plurality of voices of the freeholders," — and a constable was to be chosen from among the ex-overseers, and seems to have been the executive officer of the latter. The overseers assessed the local tax rate, kept the church and roads in repair, looked after the poor, saw to it that the minister's salary was forthcoming, regulated bounds and fences and held court in all cases in which less than £5 was involved. When an overseer or constable was elected and refused to serve, a fine was imposed — £10 for an everseer and £5 for a constable. The overseers continued to administer affairs under that name until 1684, when the first Colonial Legislature, under Gov. Dongan, changed their title to supervisors, and so they remained until the end of the history of Flatbush. That same Legislature did away with the nonsensical arrangement of Yorkshire and the West Riding became Kings county. One particularly beneficial result of Governor Dongan's legislation to Flatbush was the settlement of the courts within its bounds. In 1668, by the desire of the Hempstead Convention, the courts were transferred from Flatbush to Gravesend. By an act passed November 7, 1685, Flatbush was again made the center of the legal world of what was then Kings county, and, as if to perpetuate this distinction, a court-house was at once erected. In 1758 this building was superseded by another, which served until 1793, when a larger edifice was constructed. In 1832 that building was burned and with the flames passed the legal glory of Flatbush, for Brooklyn then became the county town. In 1695, beside the first court-house, a whipping-post and a pair of stocks were erected as terrors to evil-doers as well as for use, while the village pound was not far away.

The progress of the years passed slowly and uneventfully in Flatbush until the outbreak of the Revolutionary War, and that memorable struggle found the inhabitants sadly divided in their allegiance; but it would seem as if the majority was in favor of taking no part in the contest. Possibly the older residents, not from any love for King George and British rule, but from a dislike to radical changes, desired matters to remain as they were. They admitted that wrongs existed, but hoped for their abatement by peaceful agitation. The younger element, however, seemed to throw their hearts into the cause of the Patriots, and were anxious to demand their rights and a removal of all obstacles to the liberty of the people; but their ardor appears to have been restrained by the counsels of their elders. Still Flatbush was desirous in bringing about reforms in the government relations, it hated the stamp duties as much as did New York or Boston, and it was represented in the convention that met in New York City April 10, 1775, to choose delegates to the First Continental Congress, by David Clarkson, Adrian Voorhees, Jacobs Vandeventer and John Vanderbilt. These were elected at a meeting held in Flatbush five days previously, and the convention elected three citizens of Flatbush to the congress, — Johannes Lott, John Lefferts and John Vanderbilt.

These three men deserve more than a passing notice, for they were foremost among the upbuilders of Flatbush. Johannes Lott was the great-grandson of Peter Lott (or Lodt), who emigrated from Holland in 1652. In 1662 he secured a patent for twenty-four morgens of land in Flatbush, which he sold in 1674 to Jan (Cornelise) Boomgaert. He held other tracts of land in the town, and his name appears in Governor Dongan's patent to Flatbush in 1656, and he took the oath of allegiance there in 1687. For a time he was one of the local magistrates. His son, Engelbert, also took the oath of allegiance to Britain, in 1687, and in 1698 was High Sheriff of Kings county. John Lott, the eldest son of this latter dignitary, was born in Brooklyn July 21, 1701, and died prior to 1733, leaving among other children a son, Johannes, born September 2, 1730, who was the Patriot already named as being returned to the Continental Congress. Mention has already been made of John Vanderbilt in connection with the history of Flatbush Church. "The Senator," as he was familiarly called, afterward rendered considerable aid in the Provincial Legislature. John Lefferts was a prominent member of a family whose story is elsewhere told in these volumes.

But while the good folks of Flatbush were as loud, if not as strenuous, in their complaints as others against the wrongs inflicted on the colonies by the British Parliament prior to the outbreak of hostilities, they were, as a whole, of a rather halting turn of mind when the time came to choose at the parting of the ways. At a meeting of delegates held in Flatbush on May 22, 1775, at which all the towns in Kings county except Flatlands were represented, the Flatbush representatives, Nicholas Cowenhoven and Johannes E. Lott, reported that their constituents desired to remain neutral in any conflict which might arise. "Prudence," as one writer said, "had taken the place of valor." The fact is that the proximity of Flatbush to New York and Brooklyn, both of which were Tory in their sympathies, had overawed the local patriotic sentiment, and, besides, the Tories who resided in the township itself were active, powerful and influential. Flatbush answered to the call of the Provincial Congress for troops so far as to provide a company for the Long Island regiment of militia, but there is no evidence that it ever furnished its full quota. Cornelius Van der Veer was captain; and Peter Lefferts and John Van Duyn lieutenants, and John Bennem, ensign, were the other officers, but it is doubtful whether the company ever fired a shot for independence, although it is vaguely hinted that they actually did outpost duty prior to the landing of the British. Mayor Mathews, of New York, had his county seat at Flatbush, and, as has already been chronicled, kept up an active intercourse from there with Governor Tryon, while the latter maintained his gubernatorial chair and dignity on the quarter-deck of the Asia or one of the other British ships in the harbor while the city of New York was in the hands of the Patriots. His neighbor. Colonel William Axtell, was equally pronounced in his devotion to Toryism, and there seems no .doubt that it was in Axtell's mansion, Melrose Hall, that the plot for the abduction of Washington was hatched. Until the British landed, August 22, 1776, Flatbush, indeed, appears to have been the center of Tory plots and projects and schemes of all sorts. That landing and the story of the seven or eight days which followed until Washington had carried his troops from Long Island to New York is Flatbush's real contribution to the history of the nation. The story of that brief and interesting campaign has already been told in this work, and we need only refer here to a few local incidents related in Field's elaborate monograph on the history of the battle, by which it would seem that most of the few honors gained by the American troops in the short campaign were won in Flatbush on its western boundary. The vanguard of the British forces under Colonel Donop got to Flatbush late on the evening of August 22. Says Field:

Three hundred American riflemen, who had occupied the village, abandoned it as soon as the Hessian battery of six guns had taken position and opened fire. The possession of this slumberous little Dutch village by the Hessians was not, however, destined to be maintained without a struggle. The awe inspired by the imposing array of the German troops had worn away in the cool night, and early on the morning of the 23rd the slumbers of the heavy-eyed Hessians were broken by a dash upon their right wing, resting near the west end of the village. On the thickly wooded hills near Flatbush, Colonel Hand was in command of the whole Pennsylvania battalion of riflemen, consisting of 553 officers and privates. Believing that the familiarity acquired by combat with the formidable strangers would dissipate the increasing dread with which they were regarded. Colonel Hand ordered an assault upon their lines. The attack was spirited, though feebly maintained, as the Americans retired to the woods as soon as a field-piece was brought to bear upon them.

On the afternoon of the same day the Continentals again tried to drive Donop out of Flatbush. So impetuous and fierce was the assault that that portion of the Hessian corps was driven back upon the main body, then lying south of the Dutch church, and the whole detachment was held at bay for more than one hour. The fire of the American riflemen was so galling that the Hessians were compelled to improvise redoubts, from the houses of Adrian Hegeman and Lefferts Martense, for the purpose of repelling their attack. In these buildings they cut holes, wherever these afforded them position for firing upon the American sharp-shooters. At length the cannon, from which the Hessian gunners had doubtless been driven by our riflemen, were brought into position, and opened their fire upon the assaulting party. At this time the houses of Jeremiah Vanderbilt. Leffert Lefferts and Evert Hegeman were in flames, and added, by their conflagration, to the horrors which war had brought upon this quiet village. Although it has been a popular habit to charge this incendiarism upon the Hessian invaders, it is yet certain that these dwellings were fired by the Americans to prevent their occupation as defensive positions by the enemy.

On the 25th the Americans determined to meet the Hessian artillery with the same arms; and, accordingly, a strong body of riflemen, accompanied by several guns, pushed forward beyond the edge of the woods, and opened fire with round and grapeshot upon the devoted village, behind whose walls the enemy sought shelter from the rebel sharpshooters. The attack was well maintained for a time, but was at length repulsed by the greater weight and steadiness of the Hessian artillery.

We read of several other annoying attacks upon the Hessians by the daring American militia, the latter even arousing their enemies to fight at two o'clock one morning, an hour which was against all well regulated notions of warfare, but the defeat on the 27th practically ended the fighting on Long Island and the crisis was settled elsewhere. During the British occupation Flatbush seems to have been prosperous enough except that signal vengeance was wreaked, immediately after the battle of Brooklyn, on those whose sympathies were known to have been with the Patriots. Most of the farmers lost their cattle and horses and growing crops were destroyed. Many houses were burned and the vast number of unburied dead infected the air and fever became epidemic. Those who could left the town, and business for a time was at a standstill. Soldiers were quartered in dwellings without regard to the wishes of the owners and without any compensation, while on the least sign of grumbling or discontent all sorts of rude pranks were played and property was wantonly destroyed. We read of feather beds being emptied into wells, of woodwork and furniture being slashed and destroyed, of fences and tables and chairs being torn up for firewood; and not only property but life was in constant danger. Thugs and thieves crowded the streets and even took possession of the court-house and held their orgies in it, as well as made it the receptacle of much of their plunder. After a while matters quieted down considerably and law and order resumed sway, — as much as was possible under martial law. The township began to prosper even under British rule, but the Long Island campaign, brief as it was, had left a trail of havoc and disaster behind and the people learned a grim lesson of the uselessness of being neutral when the dogs of war have been unchained and are sniffing at their gates.

With the passing away of the British occupation Flatbush fell into line as an American township, and as the angry passions between Patriot and Tory died out it resumed its quiet, dreamy existence with hardly a ripple, except in connection with church affairs or around election time, to disturb the sweetness of its repose. As the legal center of Kings county it attracted many visitors at intervals from the outside world, was the scene of some general business and loomed up considerably in the affairs of the county. It had even progressed a little on modern lines, its sidewalks were kept in good order and well graded, and in 1830 a daily line of stages was introduced by Smith Birdsall to run between Flatbush and Brooklyn, replacing the farm wagons which had previously been in use. But the progress of Flatbush was ruthlessly arrested by the fire which in 1832 destroyed the court-house and so led to the transference of the courts to Brooklyn, which became the county seat. Flatbush then quietly sank into the status of a mere country village; its glory had apparently departed: even its kerche only shed its light within its own territory and was no longer a lamp that sent its spiritual rays over almost an entire county. But the citizens made the best of the situation, and with wealth and energy on their side seemed determined that Flatbush should not be altogether forgotten. Its beauties as a residential neighborhood were soon exploited and every effort was made to induce new settlers. For a time these efforts seemed to bring very slow results, for the town was removed from any center of population; it had no manufactures and transit was slow, uncertain, and in winter time decidedly unpleasant. However, a beginning was made in 1834 when Gerrit L. Martense (a descendant of "Martin the Boor," who settled in Flatbush prior to 1687), laid out a tract of land into lots and opened two streets, —Johnson and Erasmus. Some six or eight cheap houses were built on this property, but the scheme was not a financial success.

In the following year Dr. Adrian Vanderveer had his farm surveyed and mapped out in city lots, opened Vernon avenue, and laid out Bedford avenue and Lott, Prospect, Lawrence, Franklin and Clinton streets. This enterprise likewise failed for the time, and the survey lay practically dormant for some thirty years, when its provisions began to be put in operation. In fact it was not until 1866 that Flatbush began to grow in the modern sense, and since then there has gone on within it a steady stream of street-opening and homebuilding. Land booms of all sorts have flourished and faded within its boundaries, but, in spite of the misfortunes which always attended such schemes, its beautiful situation, superior surroundings and healthful climate have carried it safely through many a forced march and enabled it to grow prosperous, while other boomed localities have disappeared from the map and returned to wildwood. Two notable results of judicious booming were the establishment, in 1852, of two villages in the township, — Greenfield (afterward Parkville) and Windsor Terrace. They flourished for a while and brought to their sites quite r. number of particularly desirable settlers, most of whom erected beautiful homes and spent money in embellishing their neighborhood; but neither village ever commanded a large population and both are now simply sections in Brooklyn's Twenty-ninth Ward.

There is no doubt that the upward movement in 1866 was brought about by the introduction of street cars in 1860, following the opening up of Flatbush avenue from Fulton avenue, Brooklyn. At first there were grave doubts as to the success of the venture, but when these were removed and the village could be reached by a reliable, and, what was then considered an expeditious, mode of transit, its upward progress was assured. In 1864 gas was introduced and in the same year the fire department (which had existed since 1821, when it was called the "Flatbush Engine Company") was equipped with a modern engine and equipment, at a cost of over $6,000; and in 1872 the town reached the dignity of having a newspaper, when the "Kings County Rural Gazette" was issued. The old Dutch Reformed church long ere 1866 had several neighbors, — the Methodist Episcopal church, organized in 1844, and St. Paul's Protestant Episcopal church, organized in 1836, being among the earliest, while, as might be expected in such a community, schools were abundant and all the resources of social and religious life and culture found ample scope. The town had had a board of health since 1832, and could point to its usefulness with justifiable pride. Saloons increased naturally with the population; but the establishment in 1874 of an excise commission served to curtail the number of these places, while a Law and Order Association, organized in 1880 under the presidency of the Rev. Dr. C. L. Wells, closed many objectionable resorts which had crept into the town — overflowed into it from its big neighbor, in spite of the organization in 1878 of a small police force and Police Board. The establishment of a Board of Improvement in 1871, just when the upward movement was beginning to gain headway, did much not only to preserve the amenity of the place but proceeded to open up streets and avenues only when the public welfare so demanded, and with the most scrupulous care that the interests of the property-owners and the public should be equally safe-guarded. To this body of seven residents, serving without compensation, modern Flatbush owes much. Not the least of their good works was the building of the much-desired Town Hall. On this subject the Rev. R. G. Strong wrote:

"The subject of a town hall was repeatedly agitated in the local village paper. After the destruction of the county court-house at Flatbush, great difficulty was experienced in finding a suitable place to hold the village courts, the town elections and other public meetings. For many years the elections were held at the hotels of the village; and the justices held their courts either at their own houses, or in the parlor of one of the numerous hotels of the village. There being no place in which to confine prisoners, or persons awaiting trial, constables were compelled to take such persons to the jail in Brooklyn, and then return them for trial to the village. After the erection of the public school-house, in 1842, the elections and justice courts were held, for nearly twenty years, in its upper story. About the year 1861 it became necessary to use this room for school purposes. During this year Schoonmaker's Hall, on Flatbush avenue, was completed, and was used for ten years as a place for all public gatherings, church fairs, sessions of court and for election purposes. The discussion of this subject in the local paper brought the matter prominently before the public.

"A call for a public meeting to consider the subject of a town hall appeared in the Rural Gazette of February 14, 1874. Pursuant to this call a large and enthusiastic meeting of prominent citizens was held at Schoonmaker's Hall on Thursday, February 19, 1874, Supervisor J. V. B. Martense being Chairman, and Abraham Lott, Secretary; at which, after various motions and considerable discussion, the matter was referred to the Board of Improvement, with power, the expense for land and building being limited by resolution to $40,000. At this meeting the town authorities were directed to issue thirty-year bonds, and provision was made for payment of interest and principal by taxation. The Board of Improvement immediately entered upon the accomplishment of the task assigned to them. A building committee, consisting of John Lefferts, John J. Vanderbilt and John L. Zabriskie, M. D., was appointed. Architect John Y. Cuyler was engaged to draft plans for the building. On May 18, 1874, the Board procured the enactment of a law authorizing them to proceed legally in their work (Chap. 456 of the Laws of 1874 of the State of New York). A section of land (100 feet front and 200 feet deep) was purchased on Grant street (then Union Place) 200 feet east of Flatbush avenue, at a cost of $5,800. The contract was let to William Vanse for $29,000, the building to be completed September 1, 1875. Though not completed, the building was nevertheless used on November 2, 1875, for the annual fall election. On February 7, 1876, the new town hall was formerly transferred by the Board of Improvement to the town authorities. On this occasion a large and enthusiastic meeting was held. The formal transfer was made by Hon. J. A. Lott in an able address, a portion of which, in these days of robbery in high places, is worthy of historical record, and is as follows: ' It was found, on adjustment and settling of the interest realized on the money deposited in the bank, and in making up the final account, that the said expenditure exceeded the sum of forty thousand dollars borrowed, and the interest realized thereon, by the amount of ninety-eight dollars. That excess was paid by the seven members of the Board out of their own pockets, in equal sums, to the treasurer, who was thus enabled to defray and pay the entire expenditure incurred without leaving any outstanding indebtedness therefor, beyond the amount authorized by law under which the Board acted.' "

While Flatbush had been enlarging her population and increasing the extent of her streets and the number of her homes, Brooklyn had been advancing with mighty strides. In 1855 the latter had gathered in to itself one of the five Dutch towns, — Bushwick (including Williamsburg and Greenpoint); and it had no sooner got settled down with that increase than it began to cry out for more, to bring into its bounds the three remaining Dutch towns — Flatbush, Flatlands and New Utrecht — and the old English town of Gravesend. The question naturally created a great deal of earnest discussion, but it reached the stage of action on June 28, 1873, — seven days after the first telegraphic message was sent from Flatbush to the outside world, — when a bill was passed in the Legislature directing the local Supervisors to meet and appoint five commissioners who, with six to be appointed by the Mayor of Brooklyn, were to draft a plan for consolidation. The commissioners were duly named as follows: Brooklyn — J. N. Wyckoff, Jr., E. J. Lowber, A. G. Bayliss, Edmund Briggs, George C. Bennett and George L. Fox; Flatbush, Hon. John A. Lott; New Lots, C. Warren Hamilton; Flatlands, Peter Lott; Gravesend, William Bennett; and New Utrecht, Teunis G. Bergen.

There were many difficulties in the way of the proposed consolidation, not only in the matter of local taxation, but from the fact that the city would occupy all of Kings county, and unless some arrangement was made there would be two sets of officials to be paid with any amount of future trouble in the way of conflicts over jurisdiction. The credit for grappling with the numerous intricate questions which arose has been awarded to John A. Lott, president of the commission, and the plan outlined by him was adopted by the entire body. The scheme was submitted to the electors at the election of November, 1873, and repudiated. Brooklyn was in favor of the annexation by a majority of some 20,000, but the other towns decided against it by a majority of 21,568. Even in face of that the question of annexation was not permitted to rest and the agitation in its favor was kept up until in January, 1894, separate bills for the annexation of each town were introduced in the Legislature and all were passed. That for the annexation of Flatbush came before Governor Morton for his signature April 28. 1894, and as he laid down his pen the separate history of old Midwout came to an end _ and it became simply Brooklyn's Twenty-ninth Ward.

Since consolidation, the progress of Flatbush has been little short of wonderful. Almost every month has seen improvements, — streets and avenues opened up and homes of all sorts, from the princely villa to the mechanic's cottage, erected. Even the tenement house is finding sites in some of its streets. Much of the old has disappeared, few of the ancient landmarks remain. Melrose Hall has been torn from its site, lost its glory, and what remains of it re-erected at Winthrop and Robinson streets, and is but, as it were, the shadow of the old structure. The Dutch church still stands in its hallowed God's-acre. The Bergen house, erected in 1735, is still extant in all its old-time usefulness, and so are the Lefferts' homestead, the Vanderbilt homestead, the old home of the Vanderveers, and that of the Birdsalls, the Martenses and several others. But time is against them and it seems only a question of a few years when Flatbush will have little in the way of antiquity to show the stranger within its gates. Flardly a building season passes without at least one of these survivors being torn down to make room for a modern structure or permit a street to be laid out. Even during the past year (1901) the old home of Dominie Freeman was torn down. It was erected in 1707, was badly shattered during the battle of Brooklyn and roughly used afterward by the British troops; but it survived until the demand of modern progress finally secured its demolition. It is a pity that we could not make certain the retention of some at least of such local historical landmarks.

# CHAPTER XXVIII. NEW UTRECHT.

One of the prettiest and the most popular of the old stownships in Kings county, New Utrecht, has less of a really interesting history than any of them. It somehow had, until the arrival of the ubiquitous trolley, always lived practically within itself. It covered an area of eight square miles — rather more — and boasted of its villages of New Utrecht, Bath, Fort Hamilton and Bay Ridge. The New Utrecht water front as a place for summer residence has been popular since early in the past century. For many years the Hamilton House, kept by Hawley D. Clapp, was a favorite resort for summer boarders. Curiously enough, a point on the New Utrecht shore was selected by Drs. Bailey, Bard, Rogers, Tillary and others as the site for the first bathing establishment erected on Long Island. This institution flourished, and when burned, in 1802, was rebuilt and long continued to be a favorite resort of New Yorkers. As time went on hotels and boarding houses increased in number and popularity. Of late years, however, many attractive all-the-year-round settlements have been added to it, of which Bensonhurst may be regarded as the chief. The land boomer has been particularly busy in New Utrecht and to his efforts we owe such communities as West Brooklyn, Van Pelt Manor, Homewood, Blythebourne and, as the auctioneers say, "a host of others." It is now all surveyed, a mass really of streets, driven with mathematical-like regularity in straight lines and at equal distances in spite of all natural obstacles, historical association or family sentiment, and while only a few of these streets, comparatively, have been thoroughly opened and built up, still every year is adding to the number and the time is not far distant when New Utrecht will be but a memory and it will recognize as gracefully as possible its new position as Brooklyn's Thirtieth Ward. It was the last of the five Dutch towns to come into existence, and it was the last which really threw off the old condition of things and accepted emphatically the new, — those which now prevail.

The first patent issued for lands in what afterward became the township was granted in 1643 by Governor Kieft to Anthony Jansen, who came here from Holland at an early age. He did not seem to succeed on his 200 acres and sold them in 1660. In the meanwhile Cornelius Van Werckhoven essayed to start a colony in the territory, but the unfortunate result for that colonizer has already been told in these pages. Jacques Cortelyou, who succeeded to his interests, established a settlement in 1657 and named it in honor of the ancient city of Utrecht. Twenty-one grants, each of fifty acres, and a house lot were that year issued by Governor Stuyvesant. Nineteen of these were given to the settlers and the remaining two were reserved for the poor. Those to whom the patents were issued were: Jacques Cortelyou, Nicasius de Sille, Peter Buys, Johann Zeelen, Albert Albertson (Terhune), William Willemse (Van Engen), Jacob Hillickers (alias Swart), Pieter Jansen, Huybert Hoock, Jan Jacobson, Yunker (or Squire) Jacob Corlear, Johann Tomasse (Van

Dycke), Jacobs Backer, Rutgert Joosten (Van Brunt), Jacob Pietersen, Peter Roeloffse, Claes Claessen (Smith), Cornelis Beeckman and Tennis Joosten.

The most noted of these pioneers was Do Sille. He emigrated from Gelderland in 1653 and settled at New Amsterdam, where he became a close friend of Governor Stuyvesant, who at once appointed him to the high office of First Councilor. De Sille was a widower when he came here, and in 1655 he married a Dutch lass; but the marriage proved an unhappy one and the couple separated on account of incompatibility of temper; but which of the two was to blame in the matter the records fail to state. The lady survived him, however, and the law records show that she had something to say in the disposal of his property; so that very likely it was the husband's temper that was out of joint. Stuyvesant, however, did not lose faith in De Sille on account of his matrimonial misfortune, and in 1656 he appointed him Schout Fiscal of New Amsterdam. On receiving his patent in New Utrecht De Sille appears to have at once removed there and built a house, where he resided until his death, some time prior to 1674. "This house (which was demolished in 1850) was," says Van Bergen, "a fine relic of colonial life. Substantially built after the manner of the Dutch architects of the time, with its thick stone walls, its capacious fireplaces, its prominent chimney, its long, rambling sort of roof of red tiles brought from Holland, its heavy beams and long rafters, and its odd windows with their little panes of glass, — this ancient colonial house was for nearly 200 years an evidence of the care, stability and comfort of the early settlers of New Utrecht. Into this house General Nathaniel Woodhull, the Long Island hero in the Revolution, was taken to die, and before the old fireplace which had warmed the colonists for more than a century the brave patriot enjoyed some comfort before his death.

"De Sille was a man of many accomplishments, well versed in the law, not unacquainted with military affairs, of fine character, a poet and a historian." For the last named quality we still have evidence in his "History of the First Beginning of the Town of New Utrecht," which was translated by the late Tennis G. Bergen. De Sille's only son returned to Holland in 1662 and died there. Of his two daughters, Gerdientje married Gerretse Van Couvenhoven, of Brooklyn Ferry, and Anna married Hendrick Kip, Jr. It is curious to note as an instance of how things were done in those days that when Anna's son, Nicasius, was fourteen years of age "she bound him to Jan Montange (Flatbush) to learn the cooper's trade. Montange was to board the apprentice, find his washing and mending, give him eight stivers every Sunday for spending money, send him to evening school and at the end of his term give him a Sunday and every-day suit of clothes."

Bergen tells us — and no man was a better authority — that of the pioneer settlers of New Utrecht named above Joosten Van Brunt is alone represented by male descendants in the town to this day, although Cortelyou, De Sille, Van Dyck and Terhune are represented through female descendants, while

Jansen Van Salee, the first patentee, is represented by the Sicklen and Emmanis families. Joosten Van Brunt was quite a prominent man in his day and a useful and prosperous citizen. He came here from the Netherlands in 1653, and was a Magistrate of New Utrecht for several years, extending his landed property considerably beyond the limits of his original patent by judicious purchases as well as by securing additional patents. In 1674 he bought De Sille's house, when it was put up at auction by the latter's administrators and it continued in the possession of his descendants until its demolition, in 1850. Some of his descendants still reside on property which he purchased or secured. He had three sons, — Nicholas, Cornelius and Joost. Nicholas, who was a farmer on some one of the parental holdings, married Helena, daughter of Jacques Cortelyou, and died in 1684, leaving a son, also named Nicholas, who was born in the same year. The latter, on the death of his grandfather prior to 1713, became heir to most of his property, but did not long survive, for his own will was probated in 1714. He was married, but his children appear to have died in infancy and the bulk of the original owner's estate reverted to his second son, Cornelis, who had long before that time won wealth as well as prominence in the affairs of the colony. He was assessed in 1706 on 144 acres of land in New Utrecht. From 1698 to 1717 he was a member of the Colonial Assembly. 1718 he bought the Pennoyer patent in Gravesend for £365, rather a large transaction for those days. Cornelis died in 1748, leaving a family of four sons and five daughters. His younger brother, Joost, was of a military turn, and was in succession Ensign, Captain, Lieutenant Colonel and Colonel of militia. For over forty years he held the office of Supervisor. He died in 1746, leaving a son, Rutgert, who in 1744 succeeded him in his office of Supervisor and was a Captain in the local militia. Rutgert acquired considerable wealth, — so much that be was known as "Ryke Bood" or rich brother, and he became the owner of considerable real estate. In 1752, six years before his death, he transferred, for £2,200, a tract of 246 acres in New Utrecht to his son-in-law, Joris Lott, husband of his daughter Maria. Such were the pioneers of a family which has continued to be connected with New Utrecht to the present day.

Governor Stuyvesant gave New Utrecht a patent in 1662, when Jan (Tomassen) Van Dyke, Rutger (Joosten) Van Brunt and Jacob Hellakers were chosen as Magistrates and the dominion of Adriaen Hegeman as Schout was extended over the new township. Soon after the patent was issued Stuyvesant made a visit to New Utrecht in solemn state, hoisted the flag of the Netherlands, and wound up by partaking at a feast in the home of the pioneer. Van Brunt. This may be said to be the first excitement in the history of New Utrecht. The second occurred in 1663, when the adventurer John Scott rode into the village with his gang of braggadocios, took possession of the unguarded blockhouse, fired one of its guns, and proclaimed Charles H the sovereign ruler of New Netherland. Scott tried to make Jacob Hellakers and others swear allegiance to the English sovereign, threatened several women with the sword and then clattered away to win fresh victories. Little over a year later there was a still more serious excitement, for on December 8, 1664, a fleet of English vessels appeared in Nyack Bay and it was not long before Colonel Nicolls' coup changed New Netherland into an English colony, sent Peter Stuyvesant, indignant and bellicose to the last, into retirement and brought New Utrecht as well as the other Dutch and English towns on Long Island under the British flag. New Utrecht seems to have submitted to the change with placid submission and was represented by two delegates at the convention which Governor Nicolls called in 1665 after he had secured a firm grip of the reins of government. In the following year it accepted a new patent from his hands, found itself one of the towns of the West Riding of Yorkshire, and the "Duke's Laws" became the supreme legal code of the town. The English rule lasted for nine years and then disappeared as suddenly as it came, for on July 29, 1673, a fleet of vessels with the flag of Holland at each of their mastheads was seen in Nyack Bay and were heartily welcomed and soon New Netherland was Dutch once more. Governor Colve's rule was especially welcomed in the Dutch towns on Long Island, and on August 29 every male inhabitant of New Utrecht of suitable age took the oath of allegiance to the Fatherland and swore to it undying fidelity. They also accepted a new charter or patent for the town from the astute Colve, for that enterprising potentate had found out, like Nicolls and Stuyvesant and all the rest, that there was money in such things.

Matters were just beginning to settle down into their accustomed dreary routine when a fresh change occurred. On August 27, 1674, another fleet was discovered lying in Nyack Bay, and before the burghers fully realized the nationality or purpose of the strange craft the sailors were in possession of New Utrecht, helped themselves to beef and other good things and took possession of all the cattle, grain and vegetables in the place. That night New Utrecht was once more annexed to the British crown and it was not long afterward that the Dutch rule in New Netherland became forever a thing of the past. English laws and government were planted again, to stay this time until revoked by the people themselves. In 1686 Governor Dongan issued another patent to the town, and in it the quit rent was fixed at six bushels of winter wheat, payable in the city of New York March 25, in each year.

Beyond what has been related above, the story of New Utrecht is practically destitute of interest until the time of the Revolution. It made progress but slowly. In 1647 it had a population of some 35, in 1698 it had 259, of which 48 were slaves. Perhaps the only matter which aroused general interest was the local congregation, and even that had but little incident to record excepting the same quiet progress which characterized the civil history of the town. Ecclesiastically New Utrecht was the ward of Flatbush. Church services were at first held in the schoolhouse when the weather was unpropitious, but those who were able were expected to walk to the sanctuary at Flatbush. Provision was made in the schoolhouse, however, for the spiritual edification of those who were unable for one reason or another in any weather to undertake such a journey. In 1677 the people formed themselves into a congregation and the dedicatory services were conducted by the Rev. Casparus Van Zuren. Bergen tells us that "the names of the first elders were: Jan Guysbertz and Myndert Korten; the first deacons were Arian Willemsen (Bennett) and Jan Hansen (Van Nostrand). More than 26 families formed the congregation, and 27 persons were communicants at the beginning of the church organization. The following is the list of the original members: Jan Hansen (Van Nostrand) and wife; Myndert Korten and wife; Daniel Vorveelen and wife; Jau Gysbertz; Willemtje; Neeltje; Adrian Willemsen Bennett and wife; Jan Pietersen Van Deventer and wife; Nyntie Van Dyck; Gysbert Tysz Van Pelt and wife; Adriaantje; Joost Du Wien and wife; Pieter Veritie; Jean du Pre; Nicholas du Pre; Lourens Jansen and wife; the mother of Joost du Wien; Annetje Bocquet; Magdalena Van Pelt."

It was not until 1700 that the first church building was erected, an octagonal stone structure something like that of Flatlands with a large rooster perched on the top of an iron cross over the belfry.

Like so many other Long Island towns, the control of New Utrecht's civil government was vested for many years in the same hands by which the affairs of the church were managed. On this point a recent writer says:

The first church officers chosen performed the duties of overseers of the poor. The control of town and church affairs by the same individuals thus early begun was continued throughout the eighteenth and into the present century. Here as elsewhere in the county the past died hard and the town records were kept in the Dutch language until 1763. Oddly enough church officers were elected at town meetings, the same as other functionaries, and were ex officio poor overseers. It was also common to confer the offices of constable, collector and poundmaster on the same individual, for the plausible reason that neither alone was of much value and might be considered a burden rather than a favor to the incumbent. So unwelcome was the post of constable that it was necessary to assign it to the married men of the community in rotation, and in case the receiver of the honor was unable to serve he had the right to name a substitute, whose fidelity he was willing to vouch for. At first five and afterward ten pounds was the compensation allowed to the collector. In 1799 the elders of the church were chosen commissioners and the deacons trustees of common schools, which regulation continued till 1812, when the present state common-school system was adopted. Political distinctions were not recognized in town affairs.

Apropos to the long-continued church government it is interesting to recall a case of a dominie who performed his own marriage ceremony in 1663, while another wife was still living. The defendant alleged that the first wife had eloped and he therefore presumed that he might perform the ceremony for himself as well as for anyone else. This plea was set aside, the marriage annulled and the defendant fined in two hundred guilders and forty beaver skins, besides forty guilders more for his insolence and impertinence to the court.

At first the ministers were those of Flatbush, but when the collegiate compact, as it was called, was dissolved, the Rev. Dr. John Beattie became sole minister of New Utrecht. His pastorate lasted from 1809 to 1834, and he was succeeded by the Rev. Robert Ormiston Currie, who continued until 1866, when the Rev. David S. Sutphen became pastor. He held the pulpit until 1880, when he was succeeded by the Rev. Alfred H. Brush. The old graveyard of New Utrecht, which still is preserved amid all the modern changes at what is now Sixteenth avenue and King's Highway, may be said to mark also the site of the first church. In his sketch of New Utrecht, of which much use has been made in preparing this sketch. Tennis G. Bergen wrote:

The old graveyard of the village, near where the first church edifice stood, still preserves the old lines and shows the grassy mounds over the graves of the early dead of pioneer times, as well as over the remains of those who died but a short time ago. The graceful monument erected to the memory of Drs. DuBois and Crane commemorates deeds of noble sacrifice. In the year 1856 some shipping in the quarantine, then opposite Staten Island, communicated the fatal seeds of yellow fever to the inhabitants of Bay Ridge and Fort Hamilton. Family after family was broken up or sadly ruined by the terrible scourge. In the endeavor to stay the ravages of the disease and help the afflicted, these two physicians bravely did their utmost until they, too, fell victims to the pest and were interred in the ancient church-yard. Since then the quarantine hospitals have been established lower down in the bay, near Sandy Hook: and nothing has occurred to detract from the salubrity of the air of New Utrecht throughout its whole area.

Of late years, however, this old burying ground has been sadly neglected, and a recent visitor described it as "uncouth and unkempt," the weeds luxuriant, the stones decaying, broken or fallen, the inscriptions fast becoming unreadable, and the whole place, with the exception of a few plots, left "to hang as it will grow." This reproach to New Utrecht, this slur upon the memories of the village fathers who there rest, should not be permitted to continue. The people should strive to preserve as long as possible the amenity and sacredness of the little enclosure. It is a part of the history of the old town.

For a month or two prior to the landing of the British forces on August 22, 1776, New Utrecht was the scene of constant excitement. In 1740 or thereabout a ferry was established between Bay Ridge and Staten Island and the landing on the Long Island end was beside the bluff now occupied by

Fort Hamilton and was locally known as Denyse's ferry. A small battery was placed there early in August, 1776, by the Americans with the view of stopping the traffic between the shore and the British ships then in the harbor. The good folks of New Utrecht were not above turning an honest penny by supplying the enemy with fresh meats and farm and garden produce, and the ferry to Staten Island not only carried over to the enemy an abundance in the way of provender but was the means of much information being conveyed concerning the doings of the patriot forces which should have been zealously withheld from the British troops then on Staten Island or from the British sailors in the bay. From its very nature the water front of New Utrecht presented many convenient places for sending to the enemy on the waters or on the land across the bay the persons or the communications of spies and informers of all sorts, and it also gave the British a stretch of coast line which from its extent and unguardedness almost invited a descent. The little battery of two or three twelve-pounders gave a good account of itself while it had the opportunity. It put a stop, to a great extent, to the illicit and unpatriotic traffic in its vicinity and it opened fire on the frigate Asia when that famous ship came within its range. The Asia responded, and while the battery escaped harm the houses in the neighborhood suffered severely. Bergen says that this battery opposed the landing of the British on August 22, but there seems no clear warrant for this. The invaders in the disposition of their fleet on that eventful morning certainly placed a vessel — the Rainbow — to cover the place where the little fort was supposed to be. All the historical evidence shows that the British landing was practically unopposed, and indeed General Parsons in his minute report of the matter to John Adams mentions nothing of such a defense. Probably, therefore, the armament had been moved to some of the forts in the established line of defenses where it might be enabled to do more effective service than in an outpost to which was opposed an entire fleet and a veteran army.

It is generally held that the landing from the British army was effected at Denyse's ferry, but probably the coast from there to what is now Bensonhurst was soon alive with the red-coated troops and the European mercenaries. For two or three days New Utrecht swarmed with the invaders, and roar of cannon and -the din of musketry deadened all other sounds, while fields of grain were ruthlessly trampled down and farm houses and cottages despoiled of their provender, battered by shot, or doomed to flame by the exigencies of the short campaign or the brutal malice of the soldiery. It was a terrible episode in the story of the quiet township, a whole epoch as it were crowded into a few days; but after it passed matters resumed their wonted quiet and the people were given a chance to repair the damage and prepare their fields for fresh crops. During the British occupation the town felt the iron hand of the invader more heavily than those of any other of the old Dutch towns, for they had lived even more among themselves than had the others, and their

Dutch doggedness, and determination and loyalty, were more marked; but when the occupation, with all its bitterness, became a thing of the past New Utrecht gradually resumed its old ways and contentedly sowed and reaped, laughed and dozed, as the seasons came and went and the years slipped on.

It got another awakening when the war of 1812 broke out, for then a rock lying off the then famous Denyse's ferry and locally known as Hendrick's Reef was selected as the site of one of the forts forming the defenses of the harbor. This fort was originally called Fort Diamond, on account of the shape of its little island site, but the name was afterward changed to that which it now bears, — Fort Lafayette. In the other defenses of Long Island, when the war of 1812 seemed to threaten them with another British invasion, the people of New Utrecht took an equal interest with their neighbors. On August 22, they worked on the Brooklyn fortifications and the New Utrecht company in the Long Island (Sixty-fourth) Regiment was maintained easily at its full strength. It was officered by Captain William Denyse, Lieutenants Barcalo and Van Hise, and Ensign Suydam. There was also another military company formed under Captain J. T. Bergen, while in New Utrecht was an armed camp for drill and instruction which bore the name of General Morgan Lewis.

In 1824 Fort Hamilton (the locality known to the Indians as Nyack) was commenced and was pronounced as completed in 1832. But military evolution is a constant evolution and even to the present day it is still undergoing enlargement and improvement. It now occupies a reservation of 155 acres and ranks as one of the most complete fortifications on the North Atlantic coast. At the time of this writing an army board is considering several very extensive improvements, to cost in the neighborhood of $1,000,000. The barracks are to be rebuilt, and the parade ground will be graded and enlarged and also beautified by extensive tree planting. The government reservation is to be transformed into a fine park through which will pass a driveway connecting Bay Ridge with Bath Beach, Bensonhurst and Coney Island. Fine macadamized streets are to take the place of the old dirt roads. The redoubt at the southeastern corner of the grounds will be leveled, as it is in the way. The stables, store-room, hospital and the quarters of the non-commissioned officers are to be left standing. The improvements include a new sewer system. In fact little of the old barracks will be left when the improvements now under consideration are completed. Most of the officers' quarters, however, will remain, and it is hoped that the old Cortelyou mansion at the southeastern corner of the grounds will be spared. It is a historic landmark, having been General Howe's headquarters when he effected his landing on Long Island in August, 1776.

The modern history of New Utrecht is one simply of peaceful progress. Its villages — Bay Ridge, Fort Hamilton, Bath, Lefferts Park, Dycker Meadow, Bensonhurst — are, as we see them, mainly new developments, whose existence in these later days are due to the general desire for suburban homes and the wiles and ways of the land boomer. None of them has any history in the strict sense of the word, — any interest beyond their own borders, — although Bay Ridge came into unkind prominence in 1873, when one of the supposed abductors of Charley Ross, of Philadelphia, was shot while engaged in an attempt to rob the old Van Brunt mansion which then stood on the site now occupied by the Crescent Athletic Club.

In 1831 the Methodists first organized a church in Bay Ridge, and in 1834 St. John's Episcopal church was organized at Fort Hamilton. It was founded mainly by people connected with the military reservation, and the late Robert E. Lee, the Confederate General, was one of its vestrymen in 1842, at which time he was a Captain in the United States army. In 1852 another Episcopalian body was founded, — Christ Church, Bay Ridge, — mainly through the efforts of the late J. A. Perry, the first Comptroller of Greenwood Cemetery, who died August 26, 1881. The advent of the street car, the laying of a line of railroad right through its farms to the seaside, and, more potent than all, the introduction of the trolley, have opened its every nook and corner to the outside world. Streets now cross each other on the map with mathematical nicety, all over its old-time territory, farms have been cut up into city lots and every season new communities are being brought together. The time of the change from urban to suburban conditions was marked by many curious cantrips, none more curious than those of Cornelius Furgueson, who among other things, had the township nightly lighted up with 3.900 gas lamps at a time when there was neither house nor barn to benefit, — one gas lamp it was said for every three persons in the township, or ten for each house! The company which supplied the gas received $28 for each one every year and paid a handsome commission on the contract. There were stories afloat of other jobs and it was just such stories, backed up by strong evidence, that hastened the end of New Utrecht's separate existence. Governor Morton signed the bill for its annexation to Brooklyn May 3, 1894, and the measure went into effect on July I following. Since then New Utrecht has been reduced to the official position of a city ward, but its progress as such has been much more rapid than it ever experienced as a township, while its future is of the brightest possible description.

# CHAPTER XXIX. BUSHWICK.

Williamsburg, Greenpoint — The Adventurous Life of Neziah Bliss.

Unlike the other Dutch towns on Long Island, Bushwick does not seem to have sprung into existence as a town duly backed up by a patent, and must rather be considered as a place which simply grew until it had township honors conferred upon it by the progress which its own people made in numbers and importance. Lying in a fertile belt of land, some 5,000 acres of extent, it seemed from the beginning an agricultural paradise, while it was so adapted by nature that almost any portion of it was easily accessible. Extending, roughly speaking, from the Wallabout to Newtown Creek, it had a splendid stretch of water front on the river facing New Amsterdam, while in its rear Newtown Creek and its tributaries formed another highway by which a farmer might send his produce to market. It seemed a stretch of land designed by nature for farming operations, and so far as we may judge its advantages were very early perceived by the pioneer prospectors of the West India Company. In 1638 most of the territory afterward incorporated into it was bought from the Indian proprietors, and some of it even then is said to have been occupied by enterprising pioneers who saw that the land was good and had pre-empted as much as they could and then waited the advent of "law and order to award them titles and make peace with the red man. By 1650 it boasted a mixed population of Swedes, Dutch and Norwegians. As early as 1641 we learn of one of these settlers, Cornelius (Jacobse) Stille, having sold his farm in Bushwick, so that the territory by that time had so far advanced from its primeval condition that its land had become the object of barter and sale. We do not propose to follow here the story of the early patents to such settlers as Jean_Meserole, or Lambert Moll, or Claes Carstensen, or George Baxter, or Jan the Swede, or David Andriese, or Jan Forbus, or Pieter Jans the Norman, and merely present their names to show that Bushwick was primarily settled by as cosmopolitan a population as was New Amsterdam itself.

It was not until 1660 that the settlers began to draw together and the object then was simply that of self-protection. The Indians were at that time ugly and troublesome, and a blockhouse was erected on a bluff beside the river near the foot of the present South Fourth street, which was given the name of the Keike, or Keikout (look-out), which became the popular designation of a stretch of contiguous territory. That fortification protected the settlers, or at least inspired confidence in their hearts, especially of those near the Wallabout; but the farms seem to have rapidly — rapidly, for the time — spread over a wide stretch of territory. On Feb. 16, 1660, fourteen Frenchmen, recently arrived, along with a Dutch interpreter, waited on Gov. Stuyvesant and asked him to lay aside a section of the territory as a town plot and a few days later the redoubtable Peter, with his officials, crossed over to Long Island and designated, or more likely approved, a site between Mespat

Kill (Newtown Creek) and Norman's Kill (Bushwick Creek), on which he ordered twenty-two house lots to be laid out and building was at once begun, the first house being that of Evert Hedeman. A year later Stuyvesant revisited the place, saw that everything was really prospering, and, in answer to the request of the inhabitants that he should give the village a name, dubbed it Boswijck, the "town in the woods." But he was greeted with another request, a petition signed by twenty-three male inhabitants — all there was undoubtedly, — asking for the usual town privileges, such as being ruled by local magistrates; and Peter the Impetuous, being in a better humor than usual, seems to have at once assented. They submitted six names and from the list he selected three, — Peter (Janse) de Witt, Jan (Cornelise) Zeeaw, and Jan Tilje, — who thereupon became the first magistrates. The Schout, however, was Adriaen Hegeman, who held that office over the other Dutch towns, for Bushwick took its place at once among these in spite of the cosmopolitan complexion of its population. Stuyvesant also advised the surrounding settlers to build their houses so as to be in, or within easy reach of, the new settlement, and so they might help each other in case of danger. This suggestion was so evidently useful and practical that it was carried into effect with such zeal that within a few months the magistrates had to apply to the Governor and Council for an increase in the number of town lots, a request that was at once granted. It does not appear that Stuyvesant, in spite of his evident partiality for the "town in the woods," ever conferred on it a town patent; at least none has been discovered.

The early history of Bushwick is one of steady prosperity. On Dec. 26, 1662, say the Dutch records: "The magistrates of the village of Bosswyck, appeared before the council, representing that they in their village were in great need of a person who would act as clerk and schoolmaster to instruct the youth; and that as one had been proposed to them, viz, Boudewyn Manout, from Crimpen op de Lecq (a village in Holland), they had agreed with him that he should officiate as voorleeser or clerk, and keep school for the instruction of the youth. For his [services] as clerk he was to receive 400 guilders in [wampum] annually; and, as schoolmaster, free house rent and firewood. They therefore solicited that their action in the matter might meet the approval of the Director General and Council in Nieuw Netherland, and that the Council would also contribute something annually to facilitate the payment of said salary." From this beginning we can trace the progress of primary education in Bushwick, the story of which has already been outlined.

Except a record of slow progress after the first exciting start, there is little to relate of the early Dutch history of Bushwick, but with the advent of Gov. Nicolls in 1664 there came quite a ripple of excitement. The town accepted the change of government quietly enough, though perhaps not loyally, and was represented in the Hempstead Convention of March 1, 1665, by Jan Stelman and Guisbert Teunissen. It was in the latter's house that the excitement commenced, for there a minister, a preacher from New Amsterdam, delivered a sermon by order of the Governor. The name of this clergyman is unknown, and only a few of the inhabitants went to listen to him. In the first place he was a minister of the Church of England, a body of which few, if indeed any, of the people knew anything except from hearsay; in the second place, like most Protestants, they did not care to have a minister thrust upon them; and in the third place they had learned that they were to be taxed for the support of the new religious teacher. The amount was first fixed at 175 guilders, but when the extent of the opposition to the move became apparent. Gov. Nicolls reduced the impost 100 guilders. This there was no evading, grumble as they might, and the amount was paid yearly until Gov. Colve took the reins of government, in 1673. But the people, while forced to pay, could not be compelled to listen, and most of them preferred to stay away from the services thus thrust upon them and adhered in their allegiance to the Dutch Reformed Church, traveling generally to the little tabernacle in Brooklyn. Gov. Nicolls, however, in spite of all this, willingly acceded to the request of the people for a municipal charter, and issued one on Oct. 25, 1667, in which the boundaries of the town are set forth, but in language which would be unintelligible to the general reader. Of course such a charter meant a fee and that was probably the main reason for the prompt response which the request met with. Another patent was issued in 1687 by Gov. Dongan. When the brief rule of Colve came to an end and British supremacy was re-established, no attempt seems to have been made to thrust a minister once more on the people, and it was not until the time of the British occupation, after the Battle of Brooklyn, that the Episcopal Church again asserted itself. Considering themselves under the spiritual guidance of the Collegiate Church, the people, except possibly the French who did not understand the language and very likely degenerated in religious observances, contributed to the support of that body; and there is still in existence a receipt given by Dominie Freeman for the Bushwick contribution to his salary, dated 1709. It was probably a year before, 1708, that the first church was built, the usual octagonal structure with steep roof and open belfry, surmounted by an eagle or a dove, or some other emblematic design in gilt. A part of the first communion service, still extant, bears the date 1708, and there is also a receipt for a church bell dated 1711, so that the former year may be accepted as the date of erection; and as the queer-looking little box, with trifling alterations and improvements, lasted until 1829, when it was demolished, it must have been a good honest piece of construction.

Notwithstanding its magnificent situation, Bushwick did not prosper or increase in population in the same proportion as the other Dutch towns. It remained' a farming community mainly, and seemed to live in a measure within itself, attending to its own business, its people settling their troubles by arbitration among themselves, steadily keeping alive their ancestral traditions, jealous of any interference with their local affairs, supporting their own poor without the necessity of any legal edict, paying their quit-rent tax with the usual mild grumbling and finally becoming outspoken in their denunciation of the imposts and the laws of their English rulers. But they could do little more than grumble, for they were a mere handful. Probably in 1776 the whole population did not number over 250.

Bushwick, despite the disparity of its numbers, was more pronouncedly patriotic and outspoken than any of the other King's County towns in the crisis which preceded the outbreak of the Revolutionary War. It was represented in the Provincial Congress at New York in 1775 and 1776 by Theodorus Polhemus. The town seems to have fully complied with the calls of the Congress for militia and Capt. Titus's company is claimed to have done its full share of duty in the Battle of Brooklyn. The result of that battle, however, effectually silenced the Revolutionary spirit in Bushwick, and many of its most ardent Patriots moved away, while not a few entered the military service of the struggling republic. The town seems to have suffered many hardships all during the years of the British occupation, the trees and fences were made to furnish firewood for the camps or taken for use in such defenses as were thrown up, while farm and garden produce was transferred from raiser to consumer by the easy methods of martial law; and to that rude code in fact the civilization and property of the entire township had to give way. The most obnoxious feature of the occupation was perhaps the billeting of the soldiers on the people. A Hessian regiment, for instance, was quartered in Bushwick in the winter of 1776-7. Many of them were sheltered in barracks which they constructed on the farm of Abraham Luqueer, using whatever wood, growing or otherwise, came handiest. A great number, however, were quartered in private residences and defiled and destroyed the property which they occupied with reckless wantonness. So filthy were they in their habits that they received the name of "the Dirty Blues," and one of the results of their stay in Bushwick was a malignant fever which made a vacant chair in many a household. Gangs of toughs and thieves — human scum — later on in the occupation crossed over from New York or marched from Brooklyn and infested the whole territory, while from 1778 until 1783 McPherson's Guides, although nominally under British discipline, proved little better than a squad of thugs and freebooters. No wonder that Bushwick rejoiced when the victory was won and the occupation became a thing of the past. Its citizens joined in an address to Gen. Washington, to which he sent a most dignified reply. On Dec. 2, 1783, they had a grand festival at which they joined in thirteen regular toasts, beginning with "The United States of America" and "His Most Christian Majesty (of France)," and "the States of Holland." Then they pledged New York, Clinton, Washington, the Council and Assembly, and closed with sentiments, the last of which was, "As the roaring of a lion is to animals, so may the frowns of America be to Princes."

The chronicles tell us that "the day was spent in greatest good humor, decency and decorum. Every countenance displayed in the most lively manner the joy and gratitude of their hearts upon this most happy and important event."

"Among the patriots of Bushwick," says Stiles, "we may here record the names of John Provost (grandfather of Hon. A. J. Provost), who escaped the pursuit of a detachment of British soldiers on Greenpoint and was obliged to secrete himself for three days in Cripplegate swamp, during which time he sustained life by milking the cows which pastured there; of John A. Meserole, who was taken and confined in the Provost jail at New York; of John I. Meserole, who was mistaken for John A., while out gunning in a skiff, and arrested as a spy, but subsequently released; and of Abraham Meserole, another member of the same family who was in the American army. Jacob Van Cott and David Miller were also in the service, and taken prisoners. William Conselyea was taken during the war, and hung over a well and threatened in order to make him confess where his money was; Nicholas Wyckoff was engaged in vidette duty with a troop of horse; and Alexander Whaley was one of those decided characters of whom we should be glad to learn more than we have been able to ascertain, in spite of much inquiry and research. He was a blacksmith, residing at the Bushwick Cross Roads, on land forming a part of Abraham Rapalye's forfeited estates, and which he purchased at the commissioners' sale, March 21, 1785. (Liber VI, Convey., Kings Co., 345). The building which Mr. Whaley occupied was erected by himself, on the south side of the present Flushing avenue, his liberty-sign pole rising from a little knoll some twenty feet west of the house. His blacksmith shop was on the site of the present house, east of the old Whaley house. He died at Bushwick, in February, 1833, in the eighty-eighth year of his age. Bold, faithful, and patriotic, and odd withal, he made his mark upon the day and generation in which he lived. His obituary notice (all too brief) says that "he was one of the pioneers of American liberty; being one of those who assisted in throwing the tea overboard in Boston harbor. He was the confidential friend of Washington, and in all the relations of life he always did his duty."

"Several estates were confiscated, among which were those of William Rapalje and others; the owners finding it convenient to go to Nova Scotia.

"Although opposite political opinions were frequently entertained by different members of the same families, it is worthy of remark that they always acted honestly towards one another. Though a great number of the inhabitants of Bushwick were Whigs, the Royalists even were men of peaceable character and integrity. This fact, as recorded by a venerable eye witness of the Revolution, speaks volumes in favor of the ancestry of Bushwick."

With the close of the Revolutionary struggle Bushwick resumed the quiet tenor of its ways and did not manifest to any extent the progress made by the other Dutch towns. Probable its people were averse to change, — to receiving and fraternizing with new-comers. They tilled the soil season after season, ate the produce of their, fields, sold what they could, or what they did not want, and were happy. The center of their little world was Het Dorp, where was located their church, their town house, their school-house and the little God's acre where after life's little battle they were gathered to their fathers. This was the spot on which Stuyvesant stood when he named the place Boswijck and probably the visitor who nowadays passes along Humboldt avenue, between North Second and Skillman streets, may tread in the footsteps of the valorous Peter when he viewed the landscape and graciously assented, in the passing fullness of his heart, to all the people asked of him. Now its glory has departed and rows of houses stand on once fruitful fields. Even the old burying-ground has disappeared. It became practically unused and an eyesore, and in 1879 the graves were opened, the remains reverently gathered together in boxes and deposited under the modern Bushwick church. There was quite a settlement around Het Dorp, for it was the rallying place of the inhabitants, and the courthouse and church and school caused it to be frequented by strangers at intervals; but even in spite of these things it was a sleepy village, even in its busiest days. There was also a little settlement at the junction of what is now Flushing avenue and Bushwick avenue, which rejoiced in the name of Het Kivis Padt, or The Cross Roads, and another, Het Strand, stood on the shore of the East River. But they were inconsiderable hamlets and looked to Het Dorp as the center of their social sphere, their business world.

There was still another section which, although its distinct existence was not recognized until long after, really existed in Bushwick. This was Cherry Point, afterward known as Greenpoint, lying in a neck with Newtown Creek as one boundary, and the East River and Bushwick Creek as others. It was divided at the time of the Revolution between a few Dutch families, the Praas, the Meseroles, the Colyers, the Bennets, and it is known that a troop of Hessians held sway here during part of the occupation and played sad havoc with John A. Meserole's house, in which they were quartered. The family managed to save one cow out of the wreck of their livestock by hiding it away in an out-of-the-way clump of trees. From its peculiar location and the absence of roads the people at Cherry Point were so cut off from the rest of the township as to be hardly considered a part of it. Their main communication with the outer world was by boat, and a boat was as necessary a part of the farm's outfit as was a wagon at Flatbush. The people rowed over to Manhattan with their produce, and even journeys to Brooklyn were made by boat. In 1796 a bridge was built across Newtown Creek, but its facilities were for a long time of little practical use to the dwellers in Cherry Point.

But while Bushwick after the Revolution relapsed into its primitive state of what might be termed in words of a modern statesman "innocuous desuetude," part of the territory was suddenly given over to modern ways, and its population and resources and importance began to expand. But the pressure to expand came from without in the chain of circumstances which led to the foundation of Williamsburg. The story of that erstwhile city is that of a succession of land booms and reads more like a romance than a piece of veritable history. As the early history is so involved as to be clearly stated only by one who has given the subject close study combined with a personal acquaintance with many of the undercurrents of events, I venture to quote at considerable length from a sketch written by Mr. John M. Stearns, probably the best authority on the history of Brooklyn's once famous "Eastern District."

After the close of the Revolutionary War, the farmers of Bushwick pursued in peace their occupations of raising grain and cultivating garden vegetables for the New York market. But, ere long, upon the shores of the river which formed their western border appeared the nucleus of a village, and even while they rubbed their astonished eyes, it expanded to the fair proportions of a city. Instead of slowly amassing money by plodding labor and close-fisted huckstering, they found fortunes fairly thrust upon them by the enhanced value of their farms, due to the enterprise of others, whom they considered as Yankee intruders. They hesitated at first, dazzled by the prospect and suspicious of the motives of those who offered it. But finesse prevailed and, the first purchase made, the rest was simply a matter of time.

Richard M. Woodhull, a New York merchant, of intelligent and comprehensive views, albeit somewhat speculative in his conclusions, was the pioneer in this movement. He had already established a horse ferry, from Corlaer's Hook (near the foot of the present Grand street, New York) to the foot of the present North Second street, in Brooklyn; and the concentration of trade from Long Island at this apology for a ferry naturally suggested to him its probable occupation, to a limited extent, near the eastern terminus of the ferry, for a village. Had he reasoned from experience as to the growth of cities, he might have been deterred from this venture. New York City, which at the period of the Revolution had but 24,000 inhabitants, possessed at this time (1800) less than 61,000. There was, indeed, a highway from the settled parts of the city to Corlaer's Hook; but Chatham street was then the margin of the built-up city, and the scattered farmsteads, shops and hotels along the Bowery were mere suburbs of the town. Had he stopped to consider that from thirty to forty years would be required to crowd three square miles of vacant lands with houses, and to occupy the De Lancey and Willet farms with population, before his projected city on the opposite Long Island shore could become a practical success, he might have saved himself from infinite trouble and ultimate bankruptcy. True, he had a ferry established. But this could not accommodate the people whose employment was in New York. A horse ferry, with two miles of travel on the New York side, before the business portion of the city could be reached, was to most persons a most formidable objection to locating so far from their employment. But Woodhull was infatuated with his scheme; and, as he could not easily, in the then temper of the old Dutch residents, purchase the much coveted land in his own name, he employed one Samuel Titus, of Newtown, to secure the title from Charles (old "Charlum") Titus of some thirteen acres of his farm, which he afterward repurchased from the said Samuel Titus, at cost. This land, situated in the vicinity of North Second street (then called Bushwick street), was soon laid out by Mr. Woodhull in city lots, and named Williamsburgh, in compliment to his friend. Col. Williams, U. S. engineer, by whom it was surveyed. A shanty ferry house and a tavern nearby were erected; one Lewis bought some lots and put up a hay-press and scales near the present North Third and First streets, where it was intended to bale the hay crop of Long Island for shipment and the New York market; and an auction was held, at which a few building lots were disposed of. But the amount realized came far short of restoring to Woodhull the money he had thus prematurely invested. His project was fully a quarter of a century too soon. It required half a million of people in the city of New York before settlers could be induced to remove across the East River, away from the attractions of a commercial city. Woodhull found that notes matured long before he could realize from his property, and barely six years had passed before he was a bankrupt, and the site of his new city became subject to sale by the sheriff. By divers shifts the calamity was deferred until September 11, 1811, when the right, title and interest of Richard M. Woodhull in the original purchase, and in five acres of the Francis J. Titus estate, purchased by him, in 1805, near Fifth street, was sold by the sheriff, on a judgment in favor of one Roosevelt. James H. Maxwell, the son-in-law of Woodhull, became the purchaser of Williamsburgh; but not having means to continue his title thereto, it again passed under the sheriff's hammer, although a sufficient number of lots had by this time been sold to prevent its reappropriation to farm or garden purposes. Woodhull and Maxwell's experience was that which is common to men who think in advance of their times; but they will ever be mentioned with respect as the "fathers of the town."

Meanwhile another rival was in the field, Thomas Morrell, of Newtown, who had purchased from Folkert Titus the ancient Titus homestead farm of twenty-eight acres; and who, with James Hazard, to whom he sold a moiety, had laid it out in city lots, and had a map made of the same, whereon Grand street was laid down as a dividing line. Morrell then, in 1812, obtained from the city of New York a grant for a ferry from Grand street, Bushwick, to Grand street, New York, — the same point to which Woodhull's ferry also ran. Yorkton was the somewhat pompous name given to the territory along the river between South First and North Second streets, and Loss' map of Yorkton was dignified to the position of a public record. The Morrell ferry gradually superseded Woodhull's in the public estimation, so that both owners became rivals; and disputes ran so high between them that they would not permit each other's teams to pass over their respective lands; all this tended to retard the progress of the village. Grand street became the permanent site of the ferry; and the old Titus homestead (on the northeast side of South First street), long known as "Old Charlum's" Fountain Inn, became the headquarters of village politics, where the destinies of town and county were often discussed, on winter nights, over hot flip and brandy slings.

But while Morrell succeeded as to the ferry Woodhull managed to preserve the name Williamsburgh, which applied at first to the thirteen acres originally purchased, and had extended itself to adjoining lands, so as to embrace about thirty acres, as seen in Poppleton's map, in 1814, and another in 1815, of property of J. Homer Maxwell. But the first ferry had landed at Williamsburgh, and the turnpike went through Williamsburgh out into the island. Hence, both the country people and the people coming from the city, when coming to the ferry, spoke of coming to Williamsburgh. Thus Yorkton was soon unknown save on Loss' map and in the transactions of certain land jobbers. Similarly, the designations of old farm locations, being obsolete to the idea of a city or a village, grew into disuse; and the whole territory between the Wallabout Bay and Bushwick Creek became known as Williamsburgh.

At the time the ferries were established there was no open road to the water side except that of the Newtown & Bushwick Bridge Co., which came to the shore at Woodhull's ferry. There was no open shore road connecting the two ferries, nor any from the Wallabout to Williamsburgh; for, blind to their own interests, the owners of the shore land refused to have any road opened over their property along the shore. Consequently the ferries could not prosper, their cost exceeded their income, and both owners died in embarrassed circumstances and with blighted hopes. Subsequently the ferries were consolidated.

While Woodhull (and his successor) and Morrell were at variance about towns and ferries. Gen. Jeremiah Johnson had purchased the farm of Charles Titus second; and, in his goings to and fro between his farm and Williamsburgh, became much annoyed at having to open and shut no less than seventeen barred-gates, within a distance of half a mile along the shore. His proposition to the owners of these lands to unite with him in securing a legislative act for the opening of a two-rod road, along the front of their property from the Wallabout Bridge to the Newtown and Bushwick Bridge road at Woodhull's ferry, was not only declined but strenuously opposed. Whereupon, taking the matter in his own hands, he himself surveyed the proposed road, gave due notice of application, got up a petition, and by personal interest at Albany secured the required authority, and within a month the road was opened by commissioners of the two towns. The effect was magical, for before this there had been no means of vehicular travel with Brooklyn, except by the Newtown road from the Bushwick Cross Roads. Now the business largely increased at the ferry, and public attention began to be drawn more than ever to the many advantages of residence afforded by Williamsburgh. For, situated as it was, — opposite the very heart of New York City, with a bold water-front upon the East River of a mile and a half extent (entirely under the control of its own local authorities), with a sufficient depth for all ordinary commercial purposes, and with the ground rising gradually from the river to the height of about forty-five feet above water level, — it seems as if, on the whole. Nature had designed the territory for the site of a city.

The village grew apace. The M. E. Church (organized 1807) erected, in 1808, the first place of worship; the North American Hotel was built about the same time; and by 1814 the town numbered 759 persons.

About 1819 a distillery was established at the foot of South Second street, by Noah Waterbury, whose enterprise has earned for him the appellation of the "Father of Williamsburgh." A native of Groton, Ct., he came, in 1789, at the age of fifteen, to Brooklyn, where he learned to be a shoemaker. At the age of twenty-one years, together with Henry Stanton, he took Catharine Street ferry, and after carrying it on awhile entered into the lumber trade, and subsequently established a rope walk. He removed to Williamsburgh, in May, 1819, where he purchased from Gen. Jeremiah Johnson the half acre of land on which, with Jordan Coles, he built the distillery above referred to. Subsequently purchasing eight adjoining acres, he laid it out in city lots: gradually got into the real-estate business; frequently loaned money to the village in its financial embarrassments; originated the City Bank, of which he became the first president; as also of the Board of Trustees of 1827; and in many ways promoted the welfare of the village. His life was one of enterprise, public spirit and high integrity.

It was early found that the laws relating to common highways were entirely inadequate to the opening of streets and other improvements needed by a village or city. If the plan had been adopted of opening all streets by common taxation, improvements might have been effected, and in the end their expense would have been equitably apportioned, that is, when the whole village plot was improved alike and paid for; but in this new community every person wished his particular property improved, and had rather pay the expense than have such improvements deferred till the general public were willing to assume the special burden of such improvements. Mr. David Dunham, a merchant and citizen of New York, became interested in Williamsburgh, by purchase at the Sheriff's sale, when the right, title and interest of James H. Maxwell (Woodhull's son-in-law) were sold out on execution in favor of James J. Roosevelt, who continued to follow the property with his financial accommodations until 1818 brought the final extinction of the original pioneer interest of these two founders of the village. Dunham shared his purchase with Moses Judah and Samuel Osborn, established the first steam ferry from New York to Williamsburgh, and had his name applied to Grand street, as laid down on "'Loss' Yorkton Map." But, though the street was soon widened ten feet on the north side, the new name would not stick. Grand street it was, and is to this day. In 1820 David Dunham, above named, donated land near North First street, on which a school-house was erected, known as District School No. 3 of the Town of Bushwick; and the population of the town, including the village, was at this time 934, of which 182 were colored.

In July of this year an advertisement in the Long Island Star announces a bear-shooting, at the Fountain Inn, which "the rifle companies of Major Vinton and Captain Burns are particularly invited to attend with their music. Green-turtle soup to be ready on the same day, from 11 A. M. to 10 P. M." In October, following, three persons were indicted at the Kings County General Sessions for bull-baiting at Williamsburgh! which argues well for the moral sentiment of the new community. In 1823 the village sustained a severe loss in the death, by drowning, of Mr. David Dunham, "merchant and citizen of New York," whose efforts had "materially changed the appearance of Williamsburgh and were adding constantly to its improvements. The Williamsburgh Ferry and Turnpike, maintained by him, are real and lasting benefits to the city and to Long Island." "Never disheartened by disappointment, nor diverted from his object by indolence or opposition," he was justly considered "the friend and founder of the village." His ferry continued to run; manufacturers (especially of whisky or rum and ship cordage) acquired something of a foothold in the place; and there appeared one or more corner groceries and a village tavern, besides "old Charlum" Titus's Fountain Inn. In 1825 Garret and Grover C. Furman, New York merchants, purchased twenty-five acres on South First street, about 150 feet from what is now Grand, near corner of Second street, at $300 per acre, and had it mapped into city lots. They then offered the Dutch Reformed congregation their choice of a lot 100 feet square upon which to erect a church, which was accepted; then building lots began to be enquired about in that neighborhood. The first two lots were sold to Dr. Cox for $150, after which they sold so fast that the price was advanced to $200, and in less than six months to $250, etc.

It was not long before the necessity of a village organization, with officers possessing the power to compel the opening and improving of streets, the digging of wells and the erection of pumps, and other public conveniences, and to restrain and limit the unneighborly selfishness of particular citizens, was made fully apparent. Moreover, no general survey of a village plot had been made; and the people, in public and private, began to discuss, and gradually to agree upon, the need of a village charter. Finally John Luther and Lemuel Richardson (or rather George W. Pittman), having purchased sites for two rope walks between North Third and North Fourth streets, procured a survey of the adjacent lands into street and lots, and made application to the legislature for an act which should confer upon the place the usual village powers. The desired act of incorporation was passed April 14, 1827, defining the village boundaries as "beginning at the bay, or river, opposite to the Town of Brooklyn, and running thence easterly along the division line between the towns of Bushwick and Brooklyn, to the lands of Abraham A. Remsen; thence northerly by the same to a road or highway at a place called Sweed's Fly, thence by the said highway to the dwelling-house late of John Vandervoort, deceased; thence in a straight line northerly, to a small ditch, or creek, against the meadow of John Skillman; thence by said creek to Norman's kill: thence by the middle or center of Norman's kill to the East River; thence by the same to the place of beginning." The charter named five Trustees to serve till the time of the village election, viz.: Noah Waterbury, Abraham Meserole; Lewis Sanford, and Thomas T. Morrell; also, John Miller, who declined serving; which Board were duly sworn in April 26th, and organized April 30th, by choosing Noah Waterbury, President; Abraham Meserole, Secretary; and Lewis Sanford, Treasurer. Their only noteworthy acts were the granting of several tavern licenses (the proceeds, $10 each, accruing to the poor of Bushwick), and procuring a survey of the village to be made by Daniel Ewen, for which $300 was raised by special tax. The first village election was held Nov. 5, 1827, and the old trustees were reelected, by a nearly unanimous vote, except that Peter C. Cornell was elected in place of John Miller. The votes being one to six of the population gives 114 as the population of the village proper.

While the new city fathers speedily evinced a commendable degree of enterprise in their efforts towards the improvement of the place, their wisdom was not altogether commensurate with their zeal. The charter itself lacked precision, in some respects, and its vagueness seems to have been often improved by the early trustees as a warrant for the exercise of extraordinary powers. This embroiled them in legal and political contentions with private owners of property, who, for the first time, became subject to municipal regulations. Thus, the attempt to open First street along the East River front between South First and South Second streets, gave rise to a long and bitter lawsuit between Jordan Coles, as plaintiff, and the village, in which Coles was partly successful; but the open street remained in the hands of the public. Again, the Board, unwittingly, became the cats-paw of certain domestic speculators who rendezvoused at the old Fountain Inn, during; the days of its decline, and these hatched schemes to possess themselves, under color of the law, of the parcels of land owned by non-residents and outsiders.

By instigating taxation and assessment sales of these lands, with and without law, they were enabled to purchase them "for a song," much to the detriment of the village, as it gave rise to much uncertainty as to land titles. Yet the practice continued until probably 10,000 lots were sold for non-payment of taxes or assessments, while there was not law enough in these assessments or tax titles under which to acquire or hold the lands. But thus were matters too often managed by those who "had the ear" of the little handful of trustees, who held their sessions in a small, wooden house, with its gable to First street, about seventy-five feet north of Grand; wherein, also, was a tin and stove store, and the office of a Justice of the Peace.

In January, 1829, the village had reached a milestone in its career: it had a debt! In February it had a post office, Lewis Sanford, postmaster; in June, a hook and ladder company was formed; and, during the year. North Third and South Second streets were built, and First street between Grand street and the Brooklyn line was opened. In 1829 a school census revealed these facts, — that Williamsburgh had a population of 1,007, including 72 blacks; 148 dwelling houses, including 10 stores and taverns; 5 other stores; 5 rope walks; 1 distillery; 1 turpentine distillery; I slaughter-house, and 2 butchers; 3 lumber-yards; 1 M. E. church; 1 Dutch Reformed church; 1 district and 3 private schools, etc., etc. In 1832 a Methodist Protestant church was formed by secession from the M. E. church. In 1835 a census of the town of Bushwick (inclusive of Williamsburgh) gave a population of 3,314; and 2 distilleries, 4 rope walks, and one gristmill, with a total of $398,950 of raw material' consumed, and $481,272 produced — all of which (except the gristmill) were within the village limits, as were also 3,000 of the population. This was exclusive of many smaller establishments, wood-yards, storehouses, etc., together with 72 village streets, of which 13 were opened, and about 300 houses. This year, also, the Williamsburg Gazette was started.

These facts illustrate the progress the village had made, despite the errors of its trustees, the machinations of land-jobbers, and the depressing failures of its first founders; and, encouraged by these facts, its inhabitants bestirred themselves to procure an enlargement of their charter and a strengthening of their corporate authority. On their application, a legislative act was passed, April 18, 1835 extending the village limits by adding all the present Sixteenth Ward, of Brooklyn, from the Sweed's Fly road to Bushwick avenue, and the present Eighteenth Ward, as well as a portion of the Eighteenth Ward, between Humboldt street and the old Wood Point road. The new charter created a Board of nine Trustees, to be annually elected, of which Edmund Frost was chosen President, and the energy and enterprise of the new board soon inaugurated a new era in the history of the place. Several large and substantial wharves and docks were built, new avenues of trade opened by the construction of turnpikes, more streets laid out, and (against the strenuous opposition of New York) a new ferry established to Peck Slip, a movement which, more than anything else, perhaps, contributed to the increase of Williamsburgh's population and prosperity, — adding, as it did, an inducement to many New Yorkers to locate their residences on some of the beautiful and eligible sites covering the eastern shore of the East River.

Speculation had now grown to enormous proportions. In 1828, in addition to the "Williamsburgh" and "Yorkton" settlements, the Jacob Berry farm, of twenty-five acres, next to the East River and Brooklyn line, and the Frederick Devoe farm, of ten or twelve acres, extending from the river to Seventh street and along South Fifth and Sixth streets, had been laid out in village lots and mapped. In 1833 one Holmes Van Mater, of New Jersey, having purchased the David Van Cott property, of twenty-four acres, extending from Sixth street to the old Keikout road, near Tenth street, and from South Third to Grand street, and for the space of a block to North First and beyond, between Ninth and Tenth streets, including the "common" near Ninth and North First streets, had it mapped out into lots. John Miller had a map made of eleven acres, the northerly half of the land, inherited from David Miller, his father, being part of the old Keikout farm and of a piece of land extending from Seventh to Tenth streets, bought by David Miller of one Roosevelt. Maria Miller Meserole had the south half of the same land, mapped by the village and then in partition in 1849.

Nearly all of the present Thirteenth and Fourteenth wards of Brooklyn — the original chartered limits of Williamsburgh — was laid out into lots before 1834, when a general map of the village was made by D. Ewen, setting out the entire chartered village into prospective city lots. Prior to this Edmund Frost, Silas Butler, Charles O'Handy and William Sinclair had laid out twenty-five acres, extending from near North Second street to North Tenth, and from Sixth street to Ninth street.

Sharp and Sutphen had also seventeen acres laid out from North Second to North Seventh, and from Third to Sixth street. These parcels were of irregular shape and matched to contiguous lands by irregular lines.

A company purchased several farms and combined them in a map of 939 lots of land in Williamsburgh, the title being vested for convenience of sale and the execution of deeds in one William P. Powers, a handsome, amiable and honest young man, who was a law clerk in the office of John L. Graham, in New York. Powers also held title to one hundred and ninety-seven lots located between Ninth street and Lorimer street, and South Third street and North Second street, and lying on both sides of Union avenue; also, he held title to the Abraham Meserole farm, west of Graham avenue.

The greatest rivals of Powers' associates were one John S. McKibben and Thomas Nicholls, and, associated with them as banker and friend, one George D. Strong. Nearly all the land south of the Meserole farm, held by Powers as above, to the Brooklyn line and the cross-roads, was purchased by McKibben, Nicholls and Strong, and mapped into city lots, both upland and swamp. The only portion of what was made the third district of Williamsburgh, remaining to the original owners, was the part of the Meserole farm lying between Graham avenue and Bushwick avenue, the John Skillman farm, near North Second street, to the northerly village line and to the meadows, and from Union avenue to near Leonard street, — the land formerly of John Conselyea, deceased, afterward owned by Andrew J. Conselyea, as to part, and Mrs. D. W. Townsend and Mrs. Schenck as to other portions, and John Devoe as to land on the southerly side of North Second street, from Lorim.er street to Bushwick avenue. But all these several farms and lands were mapped as city property by their old farm-owners and put on the market in competition with the landjobbers' stock in trade. The village had already assumed jurisdiction, under an act extending its limits, passed in 1835, and laid out the streets as they are now recognized.

Such are the mater-of-fact details of the growth of the paper suburbs of our growing town. Its springs of life were hid away in the speculating haunts of New York City in dingy upper rooms of No. 142 Fulton street and No. 5 Nassau street, where often at midday and at early nightfall gathered those who thought there was something more than Kidd's money hid away in the meadows and uplands of the old town of Bushwick.

At public and private sale large numbers of lots were disposed of, moneys were paid for margins, and mortgages were taken back for part of the purchase money to twice the intrinsic value of the property. All went merrily, the land-jobbers were reputed to have become wealthy, and their customers saw fortunes in their investments; and the pasture lands and fields which then made up nine tenths of the territory of Williamsburgh were clothed in the hopeful imaginings of the holders of lots with all the incidents of a busy, bustling town.

During the year 1836, a company purchased the Conselyea (formerly Daniel Bordet's) farm, together with an adjoining estate, traversed by the present Grand street, laid it out (part of map of 939 lots), and erected thereon fourteen elegant first-class dwellings, designed to be the pattern houses of a new and model city. The advance in real estate and population was unprecedented — lithographed property-maps set forth in glowing colors the unrivalled opportunities and advantages for profitable investments, which were eagerly caught up by the uninitiated, until by this time (1836) real estate in Williamsburgh actually exceeded its present value.

Finally the bubble burst, and in the crash which followed — known as the "General Commercial Crisis of 1837," Williamsburgh suffered deeply. A perfect business paralysis ensued, which seriously shattered the foundations of real and substantial property. Between cause and effect, intervening circumstances delayed the ultimate catastrophe to collateral investments: so that not until 1839 or '40 did Williamsburgh fully realize that the prestige of her second founders was lost. The fourteen model dwellings were followed by no similar erections; here and there a half-finished building, abandoned by its owner, suggested the vanity of all human hopes; the noise of the axe and hammer was stilled throughout the village. From 1840 to 1844 the Court of Chancery was fully busied in clearing away the rubbish of private bankruptcies from investments made in these lots, that they might stand discharged from judgments and liens in the hands of responsible capitalists, and in a condition for improvement. But healthful legislation and increasing facilities of access gradually restored business to its wonted channels. So rapid was the progress of the village that in less than ten years its population had doubled, and its ultimate position as a city became a fixed fact in the public mind. For, during the period (1835-1844) when political and financial history had been so unhappy, social, religious and educational advantages had rapidly increased and helped to lighten the general gloom. In 1837 the Episcopal Church was organized in the city; in 1838 the Williamsburgh Lyceum was established; in 1839 the Baptist denomination gained a foothold; in 1840 the opening of the Houston Street ferry opened a convenient transit to residents employed in the great manufactories along the eastern water front of New York City; the village press was augmented by the advent of The Williamsburg Democrat; and the first omnibus line was established. The village census gave a population of 5,094. In 1841 the Roman Catholic denomination established itself in the Dutch village neighborhood; and the Odd Fellows organized a branch. In 1842 the First Presbyterian, and in 1843 the First Congregational Church, was commenced; while during 1843-'4 the place became a favorite resort of the "Millerite," or Second Advent craze. In 1844 an amended village charter was adopted, under which three trustees and one collector were chosen for each district. From this point up to 1850 the social, educational and literary interests of the village assumed more definite proportions and vigor, while the number of church organizations was rapidly increased in each of the denominations, and the Williamsburgh Bible Society was formed. In 1848-'9 appeared the first village directory, published (as also the year following) by Henry Payson, and continued by Messrs. Samuel and T. V. Reynolds, the increase of population from 1845 to 1850 being 19,448. The year 1851 saw the establishment of the Williamsburgh Savings Bank, the Williamsburgh Dispensary, the Division Avenue Ferry and three new churches.

Williamsburgh now aspired to be a city. Several motives conspired to this result. The village government had often exercised doubtful powers in matters of public improvement. Its several charters, subjected, as they were by the courts, to the strictest construction, were found to allow of too little discretionary power to be always available in emergencies which were constantly arising. Again, the Village Trustees being mostly men of limited business experience, could not readily work up to a technical and strictly constructed law. It is due, however, to the old Village Trustees, to say that their carelessness, as to the provisions of the charter, oftener arose from an over-ambition to serve the public in its needed improvements of the village than from any corrupt motives of personal profit. And, not infrequently, they found themselves, as a board, involved in litigations initiated by the very persons who had petitioned for improvements, and whose property was benefited thereby, perhaps to even double the assessments charged to it for the expenses. An unwise fostering of the fire department, for the sake of its political influence, also gave undue influence to the Towdy element of the population, which soon showed itself in an increased turbulence of the town meetings, at which alone legal taxes could be ordered. This, with the impossibility of getting, in the town meeting, a fair expression of the real public voice — since the meetings could be so "packed" as to leave nine-tenths of the village voters out on the sidewalk — led to legislation for the establishment of a Board of Finance, which should determine the amounts to be raised for specific objects and provide for their insertion in the tax levy.

Such a Board was created March 1, 1849, by act of Legislature, and consisted of the President and Trustees of the village, with the Town Supervisor and nine other men especially elected for the purpose. But this did not suffice; and finally the required city charter, drawn by Mr. S. M. Meeker, village Counsellor, received the sanction of the Legislature April 7. 1851; the election for city officers was held in November following, and the charter went into effect January 1, 1852.

The names of public streets frequently express fragments of local history. Some are only to be interpreted by traditions. Men who lay the foundations of a city. or map the locations so to be occupied, are apt to respect a Scripture example in calling their cities "by their own names," or by the names of favorites and friends. Bushwick had no very conspicuous men; so, when it became the site of a future town, no local denizen had sufficient sympathy with the matter to wish to couple his name with what seemed so absurd a project.

Thus, in old Williamsburgh no streets preserve the memory of the Titus, the Miller, the Meserole, the Devoe, the Berry families, nor even that of its founders, Morrell or Woodhull. Mr. Dunham sought, indeed, to apply his name to the present Grand street; or, at least, to sixty feet wide of the southern portion of it. But the widened street, as a center line of departure in the designation of all the streets, took the more significant name of Grand street. And Woodhull street, in designating the streets by numbers, was succeeded by "North Second" street. All the regular streets of the village were designated by numbers, except Grand street and the lane known as Water street, a portion of the old road along the East River shore; and a street laid out on the Commissioners' map as "River street," whose site was over the waters of the East River, has been closed.

In the designation of the streets First street ran along the East River, Second street was parallel or nearly parallel to it, and so the streets were numbered as we went east from the East River up to Twelfth street; and north from Grand street the first street having the same general directions was North First street. The old Jamaica turnpike, from the old Ferry out, was North Second, and so on to North Thirteenth street, at or along Bushwick creek; then, south of Grand street and running in the same general direction, though not exactly parallel. South First street to South Eleventh street, at the old Brooklyn line. In the use of numerals there was a certain degree of convenience; but strangers were often confused by confounding First street with North First, or South First, etc.

But it is in the present Fifteenth and Sixteenth Wards that we find the streets designated by historical names. Lorimer commemorates the middle name of John and James Lorimer Graham, two famous land-jobbers there in 1836. Ewen street was named after Daniel Ewen, City Surveyor, residing in New York, who surveyed both the old and new village. Graham avenue still flatters the above-named Grahams. Smith street commemorated Morgan L. Smith, and Bushwick avenue was the boundary, between Williamsburgh and Bushwick. North Second street was extended on the map of the new village to Bushwick. Powers street, in the present Fifteenth Ward, was named after William P. Powers, a clerk in the office of John L. Graham, who was made nominal proprietor of 939 lots for the convenience of their sale and conveyance to purchasers; also of several other parcels of land. He appears on the record as the greatest landjobber of the period. While, however, the profits belonged to others, the responsibilities and losses were sometimes fathered on him. But he has always borne the character of an upright, honest and cultured gentleman. Ainslee street was named after Mr. James Ainslee, who for many years administered local justice in Williamsburgh. Devoe street represented the Devoes, who owned a block or two of land adjoining North Second street on the South side, and whose home was in Bushwick, and not Frederick Devoe, whose farm was on the East River shore. Going north of North Second street, or the old Jamaica turnpike, the first street parallel to it is Conselyea street, whose eastern portion runs through the farm late of Andrew J. Conselyea, and about an acre of land of William J. Conselyea, his brother; hence the name. Skillman street, now Skillman avenue to distinguish it from Skillman street in old Brooklyn, derived its name from John Skillman, Sr., who lived and died on the same farm, at or near the present residence of Charles M. Church, son-in-law to John Skillman. Jackson street was probably named from Daniel Jackson, who, in connection with Graham and Reuben Withers, had some landed interests in Williamsburgh. Withers street was named after Reuben Withers, late proprietor of the Houston Street Ferry. Frost street was named from Edmund Frost, who was associated with Handy, Sinclair and Butler in a tract of land in the Fourteenth Ward.

Richardson street was named for Lemuel Richardson, whose worthy name is elsewhere mentioned as one of the pioneers in building up Williamsburgh. Sanford street (changed to Bayard) was in honor of Edward Sanford, a distinguished lawyer associated with John L. Graham in many real-estate transactions. His name had been applied to a street in the Seventh Ward, Brooklyn; hence the change. The substituted name was probably taken from the name of a street in the city of New York.

Going south from Grand street, Remsen street was named after Abraham A. Remsen, who owned land at its junction with Union avenue. There is another Remsen street near the City Hall, old Brooklyn, and the name of the E. D. street was changed to Maujer street in respect to Air. Daniel Maujer, who, about the time, represented the Fifteenth Ward as Alderman.

Nicholas Wyckoff, the late worthy President of the First National Bank, has his name perpetuated in Wyckoff street. Stagg street, with its homely name, has doubtless outlived its patron, who is probably known to but few, if any, of the existing citizens. Scholes street represents the family of James Scholes, deceased, late of what is now the Nineteenth Ward. Meserole avenue was named from the Abraham Meserole through whose farm it ran, and not from Abraham Meserole, husband of Maria Miller, of the present Thirteenth Ward. Johnson street, or avenue, commemorates the memory of the late General Jeremiah Johnson. Boerum street was named from old Jacob Boerum, who had a farm of fifty-eight acres within the limits of the present Sixteenth Ward, Brooklyn. This farm was the subject of the great Cleveland lawsuit. McKibben street was named after John S. McKibben, who caused a map of a part of the Jacob Boerum farm, as the land of McKibben and Nicholls, to be made and filed. Sigel street, which (on changing the name of duplicate streets in Williamsburgh by the Common Council of Brooklyn) superseded Marshall street, was in honor of General Sigel, of the Civil war. Moore street was named for the late Thomas C. Moore, a manufacturer of wire sieves and netting, who owned lands in that neighborhood. Varette street was named from Lewis F. Varette, a land speculator, who operated on the sale of village lots there and elsewhere. Cook street was probably named from an old resident near the Cross Roads. Debevoise street (covering a part of the old Brooklyn and Newtown turnpike, by the Cross Roads) was named from Charles Debevoise, who lived on Flushing avenue, near the western terminus of this street.

The custom of perpetuating the names of the oldest inhabitants by those of streets is more marked in the old city of Brooklyn than in Williamsburgh. In the latter place many whose names are thus perpetuated were really residents of the city of New York, and interested in Williamsburgh only as speculators.

From 1817 until 1852 the local government of Williamsburgh was carried on by a President and Board of Trustees. By a law which passed the

Legislature in April, 1851, it was raised, on January 1, 1852, to the dignity of a city, and Dr. Abraham J. Berry was elected the first Mayor, the population being at that time about 45,000. The possession of a city charter at once added influence and strength to the community, and it began to expand with bewildering rapidity. In 1852 the Farmers and Citizens' Bank was incorporated, with a capital of $200,000, and the Williamsburgh City Bank with a capital of $320,000. In the following year the Mechanics' (Manufacturers' National) Bank was formed, with a capital of $250,000, and these financial institutions, with several local fire insurance corn companies, gave force to the idea of the citizens that Williamsburgh was destined to become the business center of Long Island. New churches were organized in almost all denominations, and twenty-five Sabbath-schools, with 4,600 registered pupils, showed that the active element in the city's growth was not unmindful of the higher interests of the community. Everything was hopeful, and a roseate hue colored every move by the municipality. Expenses were increasing rapidly, much more so than the local revenues warranted, but then the future was bright with promises. Thirty miles of streets had been opened up, paved and flagged, and that itself was boasted about as being a grand item, even though the treasury was empty.

The curse of the new city, as it was in a lesser degree that of the village, was its politics. A class of men forged to the front who lived of the spoils, and these were urging the city fathers to rush into all sorts of rash expenditures, — expenditures far beyond the financial ability of the local treasury to meet, and the municipal indebtedness began to pile up in a way that caused thinking people to desire a halt. But the politicians in office could not halt even if they had desired, which is doubtful, for those not in office had to be provided for, while their dependents, — those who by their votes gave them the power they enjoyed, — had to be "looked after." The fire department, for instance, being an excellent vote-getter, was carefully nourished by the local authorities until the city had a system far beyond its needs; but, then, each fire company was a powerful factor in local politics. In 1852 the Williamsburgh Water Company was organized, and proved the beginning of the end, for it was its extravagance and grasping methods that, more than aught else, turned the eyes of the Brooklyn people to the city that was rising into prominence on their border and to the dangers which its exigencies suggested and presented. The water company, soon after it was incorporated, proceeded promptly to buy up some sources of supply on the south side of the island, for which Brooklyn had been cautiously negotiating, and its scope of action promised still further to interfere with the future development of the water department of the City of Churches. The condition of things that presented itself to Brooklyn was not a pleasant one, for it was seen that all the local schemes of improvement were apt to be hindered by the new city, which was rapidly increasing in population, in ambition, in a knowledge of the wiles of local statesmanship, and in debt. Then arose in Brooklyn, quietly at first, a sentiment for annexation. It was felt that two such city governments, under the existing conditions, could not, side by side, maintain amicable relations or possibly work hand in hand for the mutual benefit of their respective cities, and that they would gradually but inevitably drift into more and more pronounced opposition, involving each other, in the end, into countless rash expenditures, perhaps even into a condition of financial bankruptcy. There was no need, for instance, it was agreed, for the cost of two municipal establishments, while under one retrenchment, economy and progress might become practical watchwords. Such were some of the arguments put forth in Brooklyn in favor of annexation. They were indorsed by many in Williamsburgh, but the bulk of the population there was not ready for any such sweeping change as self-annihilation.

On January 1, 1854, William Wall, the head of a local cordage factory, a man who had risen from the ranks by his own industry and shrewdness, became the second and last Mayor of Williamsburgh. He desired to institute a term of rigid economy, and tried to introduce something like business principles in the management of the affairs of the city; but the Aldermen were decidedly practical politicians, versed in all the arts which that phrase implies, and had no patience with such notions. Mayor Wall would not yield to their ways, or their wiles, or their demands, and the number of his vetoes became such as to win for him the attention of almost the entire community, and especially of all interested in municipal progress. Still the Aldermen persevered in carrying on a campaign of spoils, and Mayor Wall, even by the most rigorous application of the powers vested in him, could not wholly arrest their schemes of plunder and extravagance. So, as the only avenue of practical, early, and complete relief that presented itself, he threw himself with all his energy into the annexation movement. Strengthened by this, the advocates of annexation, or consolidation as it was sometimes called, caused a bill to be prepared, which passed the Legislature, and on January 1, 1855, the city of Williamsburgh passed officially out of existence and became simply a section of Brooklyn, and of the history of that city the further story of Williamsburgh is a part. In dealing with Brooklyn we will speak further of this consolidation, but here we may say that the new city not only included Brooklyn and Williamsburgh, but also the whole of the township of Bushwick, and including the section, almost distinct in itself, one time called Cherry Point, but which by that time had been known as Greenpoint, and which now became Brooklyn's Seventeenth Ward.

For many years after the Hessians had simply became ugly memories, Cherry Point pursued the even tenor of its way and floated along the current of life with typical Dutch placidity and evenness. The change to modern conditions and development came about in unexpected fashion and mainly through the tireless energy of one man, and that man not a native — Neziah

Bliss. Bliss was born in 1790, at Hebron, Conn., and his life was that of a typical Yankee adventurer. After some business experience in a store in New Haven, he removed in 1810 to New York City, where he made the acquaintance of Robert Fulton, the pioneer steamboat builder, and won the confidence and friendship of that great inventor. A year later Bliss went to Philadelphia, where, with Daniel French, he became connected with a company that proposed constructing a steamboat to ply on the Schuylkill. At the same time he found employment in a book store and in other clerical work, for, although the boat project proved a mechanical success, there was little money in it. In 1817 he removed to Cincinnati, where he organized a company and built the first steamboat ever seen there, the General Pike. It plied between Cincinnati and Louisville, and proved a money-maker. Mr. Bliss sold out his interest in her in 1819 and went to New Orleans. His business career, however, need not here be closely followed; he had the usual alternations of success and ill luck incidental to all pioneers, and a pioneer he essentially was.

In 1827 he returned to New York, and, becoming acquainted with Dr. Eliphalet Nott, he assisted that gentleman in several of his researches in steam navigation. The result of this was the establishment of the Novelty Works in New York, in 1831, which proposed to construct sea-going steamboats, and of that concern Mr. Bliss was the head. In the following year commenced his connection with Greenpoint, by his purchase, along with Dr. Nott, of thirty acres of the farm owned by John A. Meserole. In 1833 he still further identified himself with the place by his marriage to Mary A., daughter of John A. Meserole. He at once saw that the territory offered great chances for development, and, evolving a project looking to that end, he threw himself into it with characteristic energy and promptitude. He extended his holdings by the purchase, in 1833, of the Griffin farm, and during the following year had the entire territory surveyed and laid out in streets. In 1835 he still further increased his acreage by purchase, expecting that the United States Navy Yard would be transferred to Greenpoint from the Wallabout. But that project fell through, and thereby Mr. Bliss suffered severe pecuniary losses.

However, his fortunes were now fully thrown in with Greenpoint, and, undaunted by the slow progress and serious losses, he applied himself zealously to the immediate development, of the place. In 1838 he built a foot-bridge across Bushwick Creek, and in the following years opened for traffic part of a turnpike road which was subsequently extended to Williamsburgh. In 1839, too, he had the satisfaction of selling some lots to John Hillyer. a builder, who at once erected a house there, and this example was quickly followed by others, Mr. Bliss getting an average at that time, it is said, of fifty dollars for each of his lots. By 1842 a boom in building in Greenpoint fairly set in, and by that time Mr. Bliss began to reap some benefit from the scheme he had so thoughtfully planned some ten years previously and which for a long time had seemed destined to prove utterly barren of results.

But he did not wish to make Greenpoint alone a city of homes; he desired to make it also the center of the trade which was to support the homes. Its unrivalled water front made it a natural center for the coal trade, and the first of a series of coal yards was opened in 1843, at the foot of F street, on a point stretching into the East River, locally called Green Point, and which gave its name to the whole district. In 1850 a ship yard was established by Eckford Webb, and this proved the beginning of a great establishment, for many years the greatest of all local industries. In 1850 Mr. Bliss secured from New York a lease of a ferry to ply between Greenpoint and that city, and it was opened for traffic in 1852. It finally became financially the most successful of all the ferries plying to New York. The Greenpoint Gas Works were incorporated in 1853, largely through Mr. Bliss's influence and advice, and as by that time Greenpoint had thousands of homes, with Episcopalian, Methodist, Baptist and Reformed churches, with a good public school, and several social and literary clubs and societies, it may fairly be said to have progressed toward full development in a most marked manner, and Mr. Bliss had already begun to enjoy the full fruition of his plans and was also venerated as the first citizen and founder of Greenpoint. But its full development was to come with annexation to Brooklyn. When that event took place it found Mr. Bliss still in the lead in the affairs of the ward, as he had been in those of the village, and he was chosen to represent it in the Board of Aldermen of the consolidated city. So the history of Greenpoint merged, January 1, 1855, into that of the city of Brooklyn, of which it then became-, a component part.

Thus it will be seen that the early history of Greenpoint is virtually a part of the life story of Neziah Bliss. This thoroughly typical American citizen died in 1876.

# CHAPTER XXX. GRAVESEND.

The English Town of Kings County — Lady Moody — Early Settlers and Law: A Religious Community with a Sad Closing Record.

Among the towns of what is now Kings county, Gravesend for many years, in one respect, stood alone. It was an English settlement, while the others were Dutch; it was not included in the aggregation known as the "Five Dutch Towns;" its interests seemed always on a different footing from theirs, and yet it was intensely loyal to the Dutch regime. As to the origin of the name archaeologists have widely differed, and many a learned argument has been set forth in favor of some pet theory or -other. Etymologists, more than any other class of students, have been guilty of weaving the most absurd theories, — so much so that a book on etymology ten years old is about as valuable, practically, as an ancient almanac; but they differ from all other classes of theorists by the remarkable good nature and equanimity with which they see their airy creations of words about words quietly thrown down. Considerable time, patience and ingenuity have been spent to demonstrate that the name of this town was derived from 'S Gravesende (The Count's beach), after a place in Holland, but an equal amount of time, patience and ingenuity have been expended in endeavoring to prove that it was simply a transference of the name of the town of Gravesend in England. Which of the two. is right we will not attempt to discuss, for after all the question matters very little, — only we cannot help remarking that a great amount of argument and antiquarian anxiety would have been spared had some one of the early chroniclers quietly jotted down his views on the subject.

Another and more interesting argument among the local antiquaries has been caused by the effort to show that white men trod the soil of what afterward became Gravesend town long before a white face was seen on Manhattan Island or in Brooklyn, or even Flatlands. Indeed, we are told that Verrazano. the Florentine navigator, who came here to explore the coast and "see what he could see" on behalf of King Francis I, of France, in 1527, had anchored in Gravesend Bay; but the evidence on this point is not very clear, and has been the subject of much protracted and learned dispute. Still it is not asserted that he effected a landing. He compared the harbor to a beautiful lake, and describes the boat-loads of red men which darted hither and thither on its surface. He did not investigate further, but seems to have sailed away in a northerly direction. As he passed out he saw natives gathering wampum on Rockaway Beach, and next discovered Block Island, which he called Louise, after the mother of King Francis. In 1542 we read of another visitor, Jean Allefonsee, who reached the harbor after passing through Long Island Sound, and anchored off Coney Island; and we get glimpses of other navigators who seemed to thoroughly content with the beauties of New York's bay that they did not try to institute any acquaintance with the land itself.

In September, 1609, however, Hendrik Hudson arrived in New York Bay and landed a boat's crew on Coney Island or thereabout, and there had a tussle with the natives and lost one of his men. So runs local tradition. Across the bay, on the New Jersey shore, the local authorities have laid the scene of the tragedy at Sandy Hook, and built up a pretty strong theoretical argument in support of their claim. There is no doubt that Hudson landed several parties while in this vicinity and that he did not use the natives either courteously or kindly: and it is just as likely that a boat's crew from the "Half Moon" landed on the shores of Gravesend Bay as on any other place. The whole argument amounts to very little either way, and could the Gravesend theory be sustained, which it certainly cannot — neither can the Sandy Hook story, for that matter — its only result would be to give Gravesend in a sense a degree of superiority over her neighborhood as the scene where the white man made the initiatory steps toward taking up his burden of converting that part of America to his own use and profit. It may he well, however, to recall the name of the hero — perhaps he might be so called — who is recorded as having been the first white man to fall a victim to Indian valor, or treachery, in the waters surrounding New York. He was an English sailor, John Colman, and he was killed, so we are told, by an arrow piercing his throat. His body was buried where it fell, the spot being long known as Colman's Point. But such legends are unsatisfactory at the best, and we must come down to facts.

The earliest patent for land in Gravesend was issued to Anthony Jansen Van Salee, who has already been referred to at sufficient length in our notice of New Utrecht and elsewhere. This patent was dated May 27, 1643. On May 24, 1664, Gysbert Op Dyck, who emigrated from Wesel in 1635 and settled in New Amsterdam, where in 1642 he became Commissary of Provisions for the colony, obtained a patent for Coney Island. From Bergen's "Early Settlers of Kings County" we learn that "the present Coney Island was, on the first settlement of this county, composed of three islands, divided from each other by inlets or guts, now closed. The westernmost one was known as Coney Island, the middle one as Pine Island and the eastern one as Gisbert's Island, so named after Gisbert Op Dyck." Here we run up against another etymological puzzle. What is the meaning of the word Coney? Thompson, who, by the way, identifies Pine Island as the scene of the Colman tragedy, tells us that the Dutch called it Conynen Eylandt, "probably from the name of an individual who had once possessed it." Others assure us that Conynen Eylandt is simply Rabbit Island, and they are probably right. Op Dyck never occupied the land covered by his patent, and seems to have held the property simply for a chance to sell it. This afterward led to pretty considerable trouble, involving the consideration and even the direct intervention of their High Mightinesses themselves.

There were doubtless settlers prior to 1643 in parts of what was afterward included in Gravesend township, but if so their names have not come down to us. That year, however, was a memorable one in fhe annals of Gravesend, for then Lady Moody and her associates first settled there. They were, however, driven by the Indians from off the lands on which they settled by virtue of a patent issued that year, and went to Flatlands, where they remained until the redskins became more peaceable and amenable to reason. When her Ladyship and her friends returned Governor Kieft, on December 19, 1645, issued to them a second patent for the town of Gravesend, the first probably being lost in the turmoil of the times, and the patentees named included the Lady Deborah Moody, Sir Henry Moody, Bart., Ensign George Baxter and Sergeant James Hubbard. This is the real beginning of the English town of Kings county, and Lady Moody ought to be regarded as its founder. She had a most interesting career, being a wanderer in search of civil and religious liberty at a time when aristocratic women were not much given to asserting themselves on such matters outside their own immediate households.

Deborah Moody was the daughter of Walter Dunch, a member of Parliament in the days of "Good Queen Bess." She married Sir Henry Moody, Bart., of Garsden, Wiltshire, who died in 1632, leaving her with one son, who succeeded to the baronetcy. After Sir Henry's death her troubles began. In 1635, probably to hear the Word preached more in accordance with her own interpretation than she possibly could in Wiltshire, and being a stanch nonconformist in religious matters, as well as a believer in the utmost civil liberty, she went to London and stayed there so long that she violated a statute which directed that no one should reside more than a specified time from his or her home. She was ordered to return to her mansion in the country, and it seems likely did so, for the Star Chamber had already taken action in her case and brooked no trifling with its mandates. Probably she became a marked woman, and the watchful eye of the law was kept on her movements so steadily that, to secure liberty of worship and movement, she decided to emigrate. She arrived with her son at Lynn in 1640, and on April 5, that year, united with the church at Salem. On the 13th of May following she was granted 400 acres of land, and a year later she paid £1,100 for a farm. From all this there is every reason to believe that she intended making her home in Massachusetts. But she soon found out that true religious liberty, as she understood it, was not to be found in Puritan New England. A steadfast enquirer into religious doctrine, she became impressed with the views of Roger Williams soon after settling in Massachusetts, and his utterances concerning the invalidity of infant baptism appear to have in particular won her adhesion. Being a woman who freely spoke her mind, she made no secret of the views she held, and her sentiments attracted much attention and drew upon her the consideration of the Quarterly Court. As Roger Williams had been thrust out of Massachusetts because of his views and his ideas on religious tolerance, Lady Moody's position could not be overlooked, and so, after being seriously admonished and it was apparent that she persisted in holding to her convictions, she was duly excommunicated. Possibly in her case this might have ended the trouble, for she appears to have won and retained the personal respect of all her neighbors; but, being a high-spirited woman, she seems to have determined to seek still further to find the freedom for which she longed, and, to the surprise of all, removed with her son and a few chosen and fast friends to New Amsterdam. Here she was warmly received by the authorities. She met several Englishmen in the fort, among them being Nicholas Stillwell, who had, in 1639, a tobacco plantation on Manhattan Island, which he was compelled to abandon temporarily on account of the Indian troubles. He was quickly attracted by the idea of helping to found an English settlement where his fellow countrymen could not only mingle in social intercourse, but could unite to defend themselves whenever any need arose. He is said also to have been a believer in religious toleration and to have suffered persecution on that account in England; but the additional statement so often made to the effect that he had been forced to leave New England for the same cause is not borne out by facts. He never saw New England. Lady Moody, who had ample means (she retained her property in Massachusetts intact in spite of her removal), was regarded, singular to say, by Governor Kieft as a welcome addition to his colony, and he gladly gave her and her associates a patent for the unoccupied lands she, or someone for her, suggested, on which to form a settlement such as they desired.

At Gravesend Lady Moody was the Grand Dame, the real ruler. She enjoyed the confidence of Kieft and of Peter Stuyvesant to a marked degree, and although the latter was not over-fond of seeking the advice of women in affairs of state, he did not scruple to consult her on more than one occasion. He was entertained along with his wife at her house, and Mrs. Martha Lamb tells us that the Governor's wife was "charmed with the noble English lady." It has been claimed that Lady Moody assumed the principles of the Society of Friends when that body first sought shelter on Long Island, but the evidence tends to show that she simply befriended and sheltered some of the primitive Quakers in accordance with her ideas of perfect religious freedom. She seems to have remained at Gravesend until the end of her life's journey, in 1659, the stories of her visiting Virginia, or Monmouth City, New Jersey, or other places, being without authentication. She found in Gravesend that degree of liberty in search of which she had crossed the sea, and was content to pass her days in its congenial atmosphere. Of her son. Sir Henry, little is known. He left Gravesend in 1661 and went to Virginia, where he died.

In many respects the patent issued by Governor Kieft to Lady Moody was peculiar. It was the only one extant in which the patentees were headed by a woman, and it contained such full powers for self-government and for the enjoyment of freedom of religion as to be unique among the patents signed by Kieft or his successor, Stuyvesant.

The only fault to be found with this document was the loose way in which the boundaries were set forth. This was amended to a certain extent in the patent issued in 1670 by Gov. Lovelace, and the limits were still more closely defended in Gov. Dongan's patent, issued in 1686. In the latter document the quit rent to be paid by the town was fixed at "six bushels good winter merchantable wheat," a tax that was felt to be comparatively light, and therefore — as is usual in such circumstances — just and equitable.

On being armed with Kieft's patent Lady Moody and her friends lost no time in proceeding to the land awarded them and beginning operations by laying out a town site. Concerning this the late Rev. A. P. Stockwell wrote:

In view of the natural advantages which the town possessed, they no doubt hoped to make it, at some future day, a large and important commercial center. From its situation at the mouth of "The Narrows," and with a good harbor of its own; with the ocean on the one side, and the then flourishing village of New Amsterdam (New York) on the other, there did indeed seem to be good ground for such an expectation. But unfortunately, as the event proved, Gravesend Bay, though affording secure anchorage for smaller craft, would not permit vessels of large tonnage to enter its quiet waters with perfect safety; and so the idea of building a "city by the sea," which in extent, wealth, and business enterprise, should at least rival New Amsterdam, was reluctantly abandoned.

However, with this end in view, as the work begun would seem to indicate, they commenced the laying out of the village. Selecting a favorable site near the center of the town, they measured off a square containing about sixteen acres of ground, and opened a street around it. This large square they afterwards divided into squares of four acres each, by opening two streets at right angles through the center. The whole was then enclosed by a palisade fence, as a protection, both against the sudden attacks of hostile Indians, and the depredations of wolves and other wild animals which were then common upon the island. Upon one of the oldest maps of the town, on file in the clerk's office, we find a perfect representation of the village-plan as originally laid out. From this we learn that each of the four squares was divided into equal sections, laid off around the outside of each square and facing the outer street. These were numbered from one to ten, in each of the four squares. This gave forty sections in all; and thus one section was allotted to each of the forty patentees. By this arrangement every family could reside within the village, and share alike its palisade defense. In the center of each square was reserved a large public yard, where the cattle of the inhabitants were brought in from the commons, and herded for the night for their better protection. At a later period, if not at this early date, a small portion of each square was devoted to public uses. On one was the church, on another was the school-house, on another the town's hall, and on the fourth the burying ground. The farms, or "planters' lots" as they were then called, were also forty in number, and were laid out in triangular form with the apex resting in the village and the boundary lines diverging therefrom like the radii of a circle * * *. From the fact that the village was divided into forty lots and that forty farms radiated therefrom, we have naturally inferred that there were forty patentees. If this be so, one of them very early in the history of the town must have dropped out of the original number, either by death or removal, or, as tradition has it, forfeiting by his profligate life all his right, title, and interest in the property allotted to him.

It seems, however, from the records that only twenty-six persons up to 1646 had settled with Lady Moody in Gravesend and taken part in laying out the town, and that the full quota of forty according to the plan was filled up by subsequent arrivals.

The first troubles met with came from the Indians, who appear to have held rather obnoxious views as to the settlement from the first.

Every man was ordered to be armed and equipped to meet a possible, even probable, attack at any moment, and was also required to keep a certain part of the palisade surrounding the town in thorough repair. When the palisade was being built in 1646 an attack was made unexpectedly, and the best the settlers could do was to escape to Flatlands. Lady Moody's house, probably because it was the most conspicuous in the settlement, was most frequently marked out for attack, and Nicholas Stillwell, who seems in time of such trouble to have assumed command, had a difficult task in repelling the savage warriors. The townspeople for a time became despondent over the outlook. Stillman himself returned to New Amsterdam and saw no more of Gravesend until 1648, when he bought a town plot, and even Lady Moody had serious thoughts of going back to her property in New England. But a peace was finally patched up between Gov. Kieft and the Indians and Gravesend was allowed to take up the thread of its story without more trouble.

Another Indian incursion, the last on record, took place in 1655, when a fierce attack was made on the town; but although the settlers could not drive the foe away, on account of their numbers, they made a gallant defense behind their palisade and kept the red-skins at bay until relieved by a force of military from New Amsterdam. From the first the settlers, according to their lights, tried to deal honestly with the aboriginal owners of the soil. Even before Kieft 's second patent was issued in December. 1645, they had secured by purchase a deed from the Indians, and in 1650 and 1654 they secured other deeds covering the land on Coney Island. In 1684, when all trouble was at an end. they secured another deed from the red men, for all the lands in Gravesend, in exchange for "one blanket, one gun, one kettle." Surely the principle of fair dealing could go no further!

The municipal history of Gravesend began almost with its settlement. In 1646 the first three "approved honest men" elected as Justices were George

Baxter, Edward Brown and William Wilkins; Sergeant James Hubbard was elected Schout, and John Tilton (who had accompanied Lady Moody from New England) was chosen to be Town Clerk. All these elections were approved by the Governor. Town meetings were held monthly, and at one, held Sept. 7, 1646, it was decreed that any holder of a lot who by the following May had not erected a "habitable house" on it should forfeit the lot to the town. Such matters as the repair of the palisade, registry of what are now called vital statistics, the defense of the town, the morals and habits of the citizens, and the humane care of livestock, were the subjects most generally discussed. All the inhabitants were compelled to attend these town meetings when summoned by the beating of a drum or the blowing of a horn. Infractions of the laws were tried before justices and the penalties at first were fines which were for a time put into the poor fund, but after 1652 were placed in the treasury for general purposes. In 1656 the people passed a stringent liquor law which prohibited entirely the sale of "brandie, wine, strong liquor or strong drink" to any Indian, under a fine of fifty guilders for a first offense and double that amount for a second. No more than one pint was to be sold, at one time, even to white people. This law was rigidly enforced in spite of the difficulty of proving its violation. The laws regarding the preservation of the sanctity of the Sabbath, as might be expected, were very rigid. It seems strange to record the fact that at one time in Gravesend a town meeting ordered a bounty of five guilders to be paid for every wolf killed in the township. The town court attended to all petty criminal or civil causes, but the criminal cases were comparatively few, and slander and assault seemed to be the prevailing weakness of the more demonstrative citizens. In 1650, for these decadents, as well as for petty thieves, the stocks were brought into requisition and continued a favorite mode of punishment until the nineteenth century was well advanced. In 1668 the town received quite a boom by the settlement in it of the Kings County Court of Sessions which had previously met in Flatbush. This body continued to dispense justice in Gravesend until 1685, when it returned to its former home.

It is singular that in an essentially religious community like Gravesend, and a community the earlier records of which are more complete and methodical than those of any other town in Kings county, there should be any dubiety about its first place of worship; but such is the case. An effort has been made to show that a Dutch Reformed Church, or congregation, was established in 1655, and the church now existing of that body claims a history dating from 1693; but both these dates are manifestly wrong. In 1655, and even in 1692, the Dutch was the language used in the service of that body, and we must remember that Gravesend was an English community. In 1657 Dominie Megapolensis, in a report to the Classis of Amsterdam, said that at Gravesend they reject "infant baptism, the Sabbath, the office of preacher and the teachers of God's Word, saying that through these have come all sorts of contention into the world. Whenever they meet together the one or the other reads something to them." These were very probably Lady Moody's own views and show why no early church was founded in the settlement at all. In 1657 Richard Hodgson and several other Quakers reached Gravesend and were kindly received, but there is not the slightest reason for supposing that Lady Moody adopted all of their tenets and became a member of the Society. That would have been a departure from her own First Principles and she was not the sort of woman to make such a change. That the Quakers found a resting place at Gravesend is certain; it was founded for just such a refuge; and in 1672, when George Fox was on his American tour, he also stopped at the town, where he found several of his people and held "three precious meetings." But it was not a Quaker settlement, nor, like Flatbush, a Dutch Reformed settlement. There is no mention in the records of the church at Flatbush of a congregation at Gravesend until 1714, though it is possible that for many years before some of the citizens attended worship in Trinity Church, New York, and that the authorities there, at intervals, sent over a clergyman to hold services in the town. From 1704 there is evidence that the ministers at Flatbush considered Gravesend part of their bailiwick and receipts were formerly extant showing that Gravesend paid a share of the Dominie's salary from 1706 to 1741. In 1714, after Dutch had ceased to be the sole language used in the Reformed churches, an agreement was entered between the people of Gravesend and the church at New Utrecht for a share in the services of the ministers who visited the last named town. It is probable that when this short-lived arrangement went into effect a church building was erected. It seems certain that one was in existence in 1720, when it was called "the meeting-house" and was apparently ready to house a preacher of any denomination who came along. The Rev. Mr. Stockwell, who patiently investigated this subject, did not believe that any separate congregation of any religious body was organized in Gravesend prior to 1763. That body was the Reformed Church, and as the records were kept in Dutch until about 1823 we may readily understand that the English-speaking citizens had little share in its foundation or in its progress.

In 1763 a new meeting-house was built on the site of the first one, a little oblong building with high pitched roof, surmounted by a belfry. Inside was a plain box-like pulpit with a huge sounding board. Underneath one side of the gallery was the negro quarter, reserved solely for the use of the colored brethren. "This old church," wrote Mr. Stockwell, "within the memory of those now living was without stoves or any other heating appliances. The women carried foot-stoves, which, before service, they were very careful to fill at the nearest neighbor's, while the men were compelled to sit during the long service with nothing to generate heat but the grand Calvinistic preaching of the Dutch dominie, or the anticipation of a warm dinner after the service was over!" Whitefield preached twice in this little tabernacle, which continued in use until 1833, when it gave way to a more modern structure, which, with many improvements, is still in use. In 1767 Martinus Schoonmaker became pastor of the little congregations in Harlem and Gravesend, receiving as salary from the last named £35 a year and preaching at frequent intervals. In 1783 he became minister of the Collegiate Church, with his headquarters at Flatbush, and after that held services in Gravesend once in each six weeks, and Gravesend continued to be part of the care of the Flatbush ministers until 1808, when the Collegiate arrangement ceased. It was not until 1832, however, that the Gravesend church acquired a settled pastor, und in that year the Rev. I. P. Labagh was installed. In 1842 he was suspended from the ministry for refusing to recognize the authority of the Classis, and for holding opinions deemed unorthodox, and the Rev. Abram I. Labagh was installed in his place. This pastorate continued for seventeen years, and in 1859 the Rev. M. G. Hanson was called to the pulpit. He resigned in 1871 and a year later the Rev. A. P. Stockwell was called. This gentleman devoted much care to the study of the civil and ecclesiastical history of Gravesend, and to a sketch from his pen the present chapter of this work has been greatly indebted. He continued to minister to this church until 1886 when he retired and devoted himself mainly to literary work until his death, in Brooklyn, in 1901. He was followed in the ministry of Gravesend by the Rev. P. V. Van Buskirk, who still retains the charge, and who has labored most successfully and won the love of his large and steadily growing congregation, as well as of the entire community in which he has ministered so long and so faithfully.

We have seen that in one of the squares in the original plan of Gravesend a place was laid aside as a burying ground, and it was probably used as such when occasion required. The earliest record extant, however, concerning this now venerable God's-acre is contained in the will of John Tilton, dated Jan. 15, 1657, in which he devised land "for all persons in ye Everlasting truthe of ye gospel as occasion serves for ever to have and to hold and to make use of to bury their dead there."' It is thought that the land thus deeded adjoined the original burying ground and Tilton's bequest was in reality an addition and at once incorporated within its boundaries. It was probably part of the original lot, which Tilton received when he settled at Gravesend with Lady Moody. The oldest stone extant now bears the date of 1676, and many of the inscriptions discernible are in Dutch. One plain rough stone, hardly readable, was thought by Teunis C. Bergen to mark the grave of Lady Moody; but this was merely an antiquary's fancy. From the formation of Greenwood Cemetery the Gravesend burial ground began to fall into disuse and interments in it have now practically ceased. There is another burying ground in the township, — Washington Cemetery, — laid out in 1850 and inclosing about 100 acres, which is mainly used by Hebrews.

Regarding the dwellings which early existed in Gravesend, the Rev. Mr. Stockwell said:

It may be interesting to know the style of house which afforded shelter and protection to the early settlers. If the following is a fair specimen, it will not strike us as being too elaborate or expensive, even for that early day. Here is the contract for a dwelling, as entered by the town-clerk upon his record:

"Ambrose London bargained and agreed with Michah Jure for his building him a house by the middle of June nexte, and to paye the said Michah 40 gilders for it — at the time he begins a skipple of Indian corne, at the raising of it 10 guilders, and at ye finishing of it ye rest of the said summ. Ye house to be made 22 foote long, 12 foote wide, 8 foote stoode with a petition in ye middle, and a chimney, to laye booth rooms with joice, to cover ye roof, and make up both gable ends with clabboards, as also to make two windows and a door."

This man, London, was rather a speculator, and soon disposed of this house, and made another contract for a larger and still more commodious one; the contract price for building it being $44. John Hawes was the builder and his contract was to build "1 house framed uppon sills of 26 foote long, and 16 foote broad and 10 foote stoode, with 2 chimneys in ye middle and 2 doors and two windows, and to clabboard only ye roof and dobe the rest parte." The price was no gilders, or instead, "one Dutch cow."

But, if their houses were built more with reference to their comfort and actual necessities than for display, the same was true of their household furniture and personal effects, as will be seen from the following inventory of the estate of John Buckman, deceased, dated in the year 1651, and signed by Lady Moody as one of the witnesses. Among a few other articles appear the following: "1 Kettle, 1 Frying Pan, 1 Traye, 1 Jarre, 1 pair breeches, 1 Bonett, 1 Jackett, 1 Paile, 2 Shirts, 1 Tubbe, 1 Pair shoes, 2 pair ould stockings, 9 ould goats, money in chest, 32 gilders."

The first roads to these houses were mere wagon paths, rough and unkempt, although the roads, or streets inside the palisades in the town square, appear to have been well kept, and were regarded as the best to be seen anywhere. The outer roads were made simply by merely clearing away the brush, and their boundaries were kept defined mainly by the traffic. At times, however, the town meeting took a hand in their improvement, as in 1651, when it was agreed that "every inhabitant who is possessed of a lot shall be ready to go by the blowing of ye horn on Thursday next to clear ye common ways." In 1660 a highway was laid out from the town to the beach. By 1696 Gravesend was connected with Flatbush and Flatlands and New Utrecht by rough but serviceable roads, and the King's Highway, still extant among a wilderness of new streets, was laid out about the same time.

Notwithstanding all its advantages of magnificent soil, a settled community, perfect freedom of conscience and proximity to the even then great commercial center, the progress of Gravesend was slow. It had, it would appear, at one time some pretentions to commercial dignity on its own account, for in 1693 it was declared one of the three ports of entry on Long Island; but even with this distinction it continued to make tardy progress. In 1698 its population was only 210, including 31 men, 32 women, 124 children, 6 apprentices and 17 negroes. By 1738, forty years later, the total number had increased to 368, of which 50 were negroes. In 1790 it boasted 294 whites and 131 negroes. Probably when the Revolutionary War broke out it contained in round numbers a population of 350, white and colored.

That war, as in the case of the other towns in Kings county, may be said to mark the central point of the history of Gravesend. Many of the troops were landed on its ocean front on that memorable morning in August, 1776, when the British movement began. It was supposed that from its English antecedents, Gravesend would be even more pronouncedly Tory in its sentiment than the other towns in its part of Long Island; but the opposite seems to have been the case. In the battle of Aug. 27th the Patriot fighters from Gravesend are said by the local historians to have given a good account of themselves, although their losses were small as their knowledge of the country enabled them to escape from the defeat and return to their homes in safety, while others who escaped in the melee were captured or killed by roving bands of the enemy. The tide of war soon carried the troops away from Gravesend. But during the entire British occupation of the island the town was in a condition of perpetual trouble and excitement. Prisoners and soldiers were billeted upon the people without ceremony, the soldiers robbed with apparent impunity and lawless bands of thieves made frequent descents upon farmhouses and stripped them of their valuables and provender. It was truly a reign of terror for the peace-loving people while it lasted, and Patriot and Tory seemed to have suffered alike from the horrors of military rule. That the people were peaceably disposed is very evident from the fact that several of the Hessian soldiers remained in Gravesend after peace was declared and assumed all the duties of citizenship, and, it is said, with credit to themselves. On October 20, 1789, General Washington, then President, visited Gravesend and held a sort of levee in the town square. As might be expected be was devotedly welcomed and with his visit we may consider the early history of Gravesend fittingly brought to an end.

Having thus presented the leading facts in the opening annals of Gravesend, the story of a particular section which to a certain extent has always maintained a separate history, and the name of which is known throughout the civilized world, even in places where Long Island's Gravesend was never heard of, may here be fittingly considered. This is the famous Coney Island, the first disposal of which to a white man has already been mentioned in this chapter. Op Dyck tried to realize on his purchase by selling his eighty-eight acres of sand dunes, brush and waterfront to the Gravesend people in 1661, but they declined to purchase, alleging that it was theirs already by right not only of their town patent but of a deed of purchase in

1649 from Cippehacke, Sachem of the Canarsies (in which the island was called Narrioch), and also of another deed, dated May 7, 1654, in which (in exchange for 15 fathoms of seawant, 2 guns, and 2 pounds of powder) they obtained from the Nyack Indians, who claimed to be the real owners, not only a conveyance of Coney Island, but a strip along the shore near the old village of Unionville, which afterward involved the town in much vexatious litigation. Failing thus to dispose of it. Op Dyck sold his claim to Derick De Wolf, the transfer bearing date October 29, 1661. In the following year De Wolf, who had obtained from the West India Company in Amsterdam a monopoly for the manufacture of salt in New Netherland, erected his plant on the island and commenced operations. Incidentally he warned the Gravesend folks to cease from pasturing their cattle on Guisbert's Island, or using it for any purpose. This so enraged these usually quiet and peaceable citizens that they marched to the island, overrun the establishment, tore down the palisade and manufactory and made a bonfire of their ruins, and threatened to silence the remonstrances of the man in charge by throwing him on top of the burning pile. This put a stop to the enterprise; and, although De Wolf sent a remonstrance to Amsterdam, and their High Mightinesses ordered Stuyvesant to protect the salt-maker in his rights, the Governor did nothing in the matter. In fact, he openly took the side of the Gravesend people in the dispute, and so the trouble continued until the advent of Governor Nicolls wiped out the monopoly. In Governor Lovelace's charter, or patent, issued in 1671, the right of Gravesend to the island was clearly set forth. Still there seems somehow to have remained a doubt, and in 1684 a new conveyance was obtained from the Indians and the whole was placed beyond any pretense of future question by the terms of Governor Dongan's patent of 1685, and Coney Island continued to be a part of the territory of Gravesend until the town government itself was wiped out of existence by the Moloch-like march of modern improvement. The island's destinies being then so far settled, it was, in 1677, laid out in thirty-nine lots of some two acres each, and so divided among the people. They agreed to fence it in and plant it only with "Indian corn, tobacco or any summer grain," and when not so used it was to be in common a feeding place for cattle.

The Labadist Fathers, who visited Coney Island in 1679, have left the following record: "It is oblong in shape and is grown over with bushes. Nobody lives upon it, but it is used in winter for keeping cattle, horses, oxen, hogs and others, which are able to obtain there sufficient to eat the whole winter and to shelter themselves from the cold in the thickets." It continued to be used mainly for feeding cattle either in common or by lease down to about 1840, when its modern history may be said to begin. The people of Gravesend, however, seem to have been careful to retain in their own hands and for their common use many of the privileges of ownership, such as fishing, hunting, the use of timber and common rights of pasturage to unenclosed places.

The history of Gravesend from the time of Washington's visit until about 1870 might be characterized by the term "reposefulness." In fact, its people might be said to have dwelt by themselves and for themselves and to have let the world roll along, unmindful of how it rolled so long as its commotions did not shake them off. Human nature now and again asserted itself around election times, when the citizens shouted their preferences, but when the election was over the men, then as now, wondered what they really had been shouting for, and what difference the result made to them. There was marrying and giving in marriage, children were born, educated at the Village school to the best of its ability, and then stepped into their fathers' shoes; or if there were many sons in a household each managed to secure a bit of farm land in the township and settled down to start a new branch of the family, and the little cemetery, even with Tilton's pious addition, was steadily being filled up. So far as we have been able to judge, few Gravesend boys, comparatively, left the township to seek their fortunes in the outer world. Within it there was at least an abundance, and if it had no millionaires it had no paupers, and by paupers I mean men or women who have fallen by the wayside in the struggle of life as a result of their own waywardness or worse. Early in the nineteenth century we read of a new road being occasionally opened, making transit to the beach or to the other townships easy, and now and again we come across stories of amateur fishermen from the outside world who discovered its shore and spent a few days now and again, to return to their homes with stories of wonderful success, generally justified in their cases by truth. The court records show an intricate bit of litigation now and again over some boundary question, of little or no interest now that boundaries have been swept away; while the church continued a matter of prime interest in the community and the real center of its civil and social as well as its religious life. These brief sentences really sum up the history of Gravesend for the half century or so that passed from the time the last British troopship sailed out of the Narrows until what might be called the modern awakening set in. A glance at the population returns helps to emphasize all this. In 1800 its figures were 517, and ten years later 520, a gain of 3. By 1835 it had increased to 695, and to 951 according to the State census of 1845.

Some might begin the modern story of Gravesend from around the last date on account of the religious activity which then sprang up. The Third Reformed Church edifice was dedicated in January, 1834, a parsonage was built in connection with it in 1844, and a chapel and meeting house was erected in 1854, covering the site of the pioneer church. In 1840 a Methodist Episcopal Church was organized at Sheepshead Bay, under the name of the Methodist Protestant Church, and although that peculiar designation has long been abandoned it still carries on its work. In 1844 another Methodist Episcopal Church was organized at Unionville.

From the church to the school is an easy transition, for in most of our early records the two almost followed each other so closely that their beginnings might be said to be contemporaneous. In Gravesend, however, it is not until 1728 that we find evidence of a school-house, when a deed shows that on April 8' of that year "one house and two garden spots" were sold for £19 by Jacobus Emails to the freeholders for the use of a school "and for no other use or employment whatsoever." This purpose, however, was not carried cut to the letter, for the site thus laid apart for educational purposes was that on which, in 1873, the town hall was erected. It is hardly to be imagined, however, that no provision for education existed in Gravesend prior to 1728, and it is likely that as soon as the need appeared a teacher found employment and a place for teaching, even although, as elsewhere on Long Island, he migrated from house to house. The building erected on the Emans "lots" served as school-house until 1788, when a larger structure was erected on the same site. This continued to be the local school-house until 1838, when another site, singular to say, from another representative of the Emans family (Cornelius), was purchased and a commodious building erected which afterward was known as District School No. 1, and so continued until annexation. Gravesend is now as well equipped with educational facilities as any section of Greater New York, while its private schools have won many tributes of praise for their high standing and efficiency.

The modern progress of Gravesend may be traced as clearly by the extension of its roads as by any other basis, for its progress in this regard was slow and gradual and strictly in keeping with absolute necessity. It is only within recent years that the construction of public thoroughfares began to be undertaken before there was developed a crying demand for them. In 1824 what was known as "Coney Island Causeway" was laid out from Gravesend to the ocean front, virtually a continuation of an old road through the village, and although somewhat primitive it continued to be a toll road, paying a dividend to its stockholders until 1876, when it was sold to the Prospect Park & Coney Island Railroad. In 1838 a free road was begun from Gravesend to Flatbush, a continuation inland of the road to the sea. In 1875 the road was widened to 100 feet and extended to the Brooklyn city line, receiving the name of Gravesend avenue. It proved from the first the main artery of trade and travel. The Coney Island Plank Road, laid out and partly opened for traffic in 1850, which extended from Fifteenth street, Brooklyn, to Coney Island, was long the principal carriage road to the shore. The planks were removed after ten years' service. In 1871 an effort was made to improve this road, but while the story is one of the most disgraceful in local politics, it is hardly worthwhile to enlarge upon it now. Many other roads were surveyed and several were opened up between 1865 and 1876, but in not a few cases they are still roads only on the map. Ocean avenue, from Prospect Park to the ocean, five miles long and in places 100 feet wide, was opened for traffic in 1876, and was a popular thoroughfare from the beginning. It was an honest piece of work throughout, and showed the citizens how economically an improvement could be effected when undertaken by business men and carried out on business principles.

But all these roads fade into insignificance when compared with that magnificent accomplishment, the Ocean Parkway, which was begun in 1874 and completed in 1880. It is five and one-half miles long, with a width of some 210 feet, and is one of the most perfectly appointed and best equipped roads in the world. Its main purpose is pleasure, and its appearance on a spring or autumn afternoon, crowded with richly appointed vehicles and pleasure carriages of all sorts, bicycles, automobiles, as well as pedestrians, is not to be found surpassed, if equaled in all desirable respects, by the boulevards of Paris. It is one of the many enduring monuments to the late J. S. T. Stranahan, who is generally conceded to be the originator of the idea of constructing such a magnificent parkway.

One feature which added to the material progress of Gravesend was the introduction of horse-racing, which may be said to have commenced in 1868 with the incorporation of the Prospect Park Fair Grounds Association. This body of "horse-lovers" bought a tract of some sixty acres near Gravesend avenue, built a club house and laid out a track. The association afterward removed to Ocean Parkway. Another track was laid out at Parkville. These were comparatively private affairs and did not prove profitable to those who find profit in horse-racing. In 1880, however, a bold bid for public favor was made by the Coney Island Jockey Club, which secured about one hundred and twenty-five acres of land near Sheepshead Bay, laid out a splendid track, adapted the grounds thoroughly to meet the wants of large gatherings of people, built a commodious grand-stand, stables, out-houses, etc., and the enterprise at once sprang into popular favor. It was not long before the "race days" became events, and attracted crowds of all classes from New York, Brooklyn and even more distant places. Since then the Brooklyn Jockey Club has established a course at Gravesend and the Brighton Beach Racing Association another at Coney Island. These have their ups and downs, it seems to us, in public favor, but all manage to secure more or less patronage and more than meet the demand for the "sport of kings," as it is called, in the section of Long Island in which they are located. All these institutions have helped to build up Gravesend and to aid in its financial prosperity. Whether they have aided in moral progress, whether they have brought within its precincts a class of residents such as the fathers of the settlement would have wished, are questions which others may attempt to solve. A historian only at times becomes a moral philosopher.

The introduction of the horse car and the steam railroad, passing through Gravesend and yearly conveying increasing crowds to the seashore, finally brought the quiet settlement to the notice of the outside world and aroused it from its sleep of over 200 years.

Brooklyn, too, was steadily filling up the gaps in its own domain and was annually extending its suburban lines, and so the land-boomers got an eye on Gravesend and began to menace its rural life. All that was needed to inaugurate a new condition of things was a rapid and cheap mode of transit, and that was furnished in time by the trolley, — the "ubiquitous trolley," as the newspaper reporters used to call it in its early days. The population began to grow with amazing rapidity and new streets were Steadily opened in reality or on paper. Old farms were abandoned to the builders, while new settlements, some of them with exceedingly fancy names, sprung into existence that put the older settlements like Unionville for a time far in the background, while Sheepshead Bay, which once might have been called Gravesend's suburb, became in reality the center of its life. The popularity of Coney Island reflected itself on Gravesend. It was the attraction which the land-boomers made most use of to invite settlers, and the closer and more accessible an old farm was to the water front the more quickly was it staked out, its old glory wrecked, and its ancient story wiped out. The new settlers who poured in did not understand the old days, the old methods, and while the shadow of annexation was steadily gathering over the old English town it became the prey of local politicians, some, it is sad to think, claiming, and claiming rightly, descent from original settlers; but most of them of more recent importation, and all of them developing traits of patriotism for "what there is' in it." There is no doubt that in its latter days Gravesend, like Flatlands, became the prey of a gang of political spoilsmen, and their acts, as much as anything else, forced the annexation movement to culminate on July 1, 1894, when Gravesend became a thing of the past and its territory quickly took a place as Brooklyn's Thirty-first Ward.

It is a pity that the last scene in the separate history of Gravesend should be one of riot, bloodshed, contempt for law, and stern retribution. For several years the leading figure in Gravesend was John Y. McKane. The history and character of that man are deserving of critical study. He was purely a product of modern American life, and we question if his type, although plentiful enough here, could be produced anywhere else in the wide world. He was born in county Antrim, Ireland, August lo, 1841, and was brought to this country when a few months old by his mother, his father having preceded them. The family settled at Gravesend, and when sixteen years of age McKane was sent to learn the trade of carpenter. In 1865 he married Fanny, daughter of Captain C. B. Nostrand, of Gravesend, and in 1866 commenced business on his own account as a builder and carpenter at Sheepshead Bay. From his twenty-first year he was active in local politics, quickly gathered around him a number of other local workers whose leadership, by making him master of many votes, not only gave him power and influence, but enabled him to extend his business on all sides so as to make him really independent of political emolument. But he believed in holding office, for that in turn gave him political power, and as Supervisor of the town he had often an opportunity of rewarding politically those who were faithful to his fortunes. His influence was made still greater in 1883, for then he was elected President of the Board of Supervisors for Kings county. At one time he was Gravesend's "Poo Bah," holding the office of Police Commissioner, Chief of Police, President of the Town Board, the Board of Health and the Water Board, — and it is difficult to recall what. His business as a builder continued to flourish, and one could not stand at any point in the old village of Gravesend, at Sheepshead Bay, or along Coney Island without being able, in the new cottages and hotels, to point out his handiwork, and good, honest work he did, — of that there is no doubt. His popularity was unbounded. Everyone spoke well of him, and although most people knew him as a politician, and one who was as well versed in the ways and wiles of local politicians as any man living, it was believed that his own hands were clean. He would stand by a supporter through thick and thin, he never repudiated a bargain, broke faith with a friend, or forgot a service. A stanch Democrat, he professed to have the welfare of Gravesend at heart more than the fortunes of his local ticket; but that ticket he always worked for with all his heart. His private life was pure and happy. He had a pleasant home, and there he spent his pleasantest hours. For years he was an active member of the local Methodist Church and the superintendent of its Sabbath-school. Up to a certain point in his career never a word was spoken against him. He was the "boss;" he ruled with a rod of iron; he was in all sorts of deals, and it was believed he was thoroughly honest personally and that whatever underhand and shady work he did was done simply in the line of business of the political boss. Most people felt that with all his faults things were safer with him than with any boss who would surely be raised to reign in his stead, — seeing that a boss was necessary. As Gravesend grew in population, as Coney Island year after year added to its visitors by thousands, McKane's position grew in importance, and he had to use all the customary accomplishments of the professional politician to maintain his footing.

The key to his power lay in the ballot-box, and for years it was known that the returns from Gravesend at any election were just as McKane wanted them. There were loud complaints at times of irregularity, but nothing was done, for as usual political excitement and indignation generally subsided after each election. Then, too, as election after election passed over, McKane became more reckless and defiant of all law. Respect for the law governing elections was especially forgotten by him and cut no figure in his calculations. There is no doubt that for years the ballots cast in Gravesend were manipulated to suit McKane and his coterie. This in time became so glaring that little more was needed to expose the whole sham and bring it to an end than the zealous protest of some men of determination, and that man came to the front in William J. Gaynor. In 1893 he was nominated for Justice of the. Supreme Court, and when the campaign was on he determined to pay attention to Gravesend, being well aware that McKane was bitterly opposed to him and would stoop to even the most desperate act to accomplish his defeat. He determined to have at least an honest vote in Gravesend, and to that end obtained an order from the Supreme Court compelling the Registrars of Elections to produce the registry books; but the books could not be found. On election day twelve watchers sent by Gaynor went to Gravesend armed with an injunction from the Supreme Court forbidding McKane or anyone else from interfering with them; but McKane, folding his arms behind his back, refused to touch the document, uttering the memorable words, "Injunctions don't go here." Colonel Alexander S. Bacon and the other watchers were arrested, some were maltreated brutally, and all were glad to get back to Brooklyn. Gravesend had 6,000 votes registered, while her population should only have shown some 2,000. The votes cast were 3,500, proving that in spite of all the excitement, fraudulent methods had been at work. American citizens can stand a good deal; they can he plundered, imposed upon and deluded by politicians year out and year in with impunity. Every now and then they arise in their might and "turn the rascals out," but they soon forget their indignation, the rascals return to their plunder, and things go on as before. But there is one thing the people will neither condone nor forget, and that is tampering with the ballot-box, the foundation of all their liberties, and the united voice of a free people. Of the 3.500 votes cast, Gaynor received an insignificant number, but the general returns showed that he was elected to the bench by a large majority. Public attention as to affairs in Gravesend had been aroused, the flagrant tinkering with the ballot-box and the insults and indignities and maltreatment of those who represented the law created a deep feeling of resentment in the community, and a demand arose for the prosecution of the offenders. A fund was raised to bring the matter to an issue, and McKane and several of his prominent associates were indicted. As a result of his trial McKane was convicted of violating the election law, and on February 19, 1894, sentenced by Justice Bartlett to six years in state prison. After a few delays, trying to evade the sentence by legal quibbles, he began his term in Sing Sing on March 2, following, and was there incarcerated, "a model prisoner," the keepers said, until April 30, 1898, having then finished his term less the deduction allowed to all prisoners who behave themselves as behavior is understood in penal institutions. He emerged from prison a broken-down man in every way, and did not even attempt to regain his old-time grip. His once indomitable spirit was crushed beneath the terrible blow which had transformed him from "a useful citizen" into a convict, and he died, brokenhearted, September 5, 1899.

McKane was not the only one who suffered for the "crime of Gravesend," as the reporters put it. Many of his supporters suffered imprisonment and fine, the most noted being Kenneth F. Sutherland, sent to prison for one year and fined $500 on one count and sentenced to another year's imprisonment on a fresh charge; R. V. B. Newton, sentenced to nine months' imprisonment and $750 fine; A. S. Jameson, eighteen months; M. P. Ryan, four months and $500; F. Bader, five months and $500; B. Cohen, four months and $500; and so on down to comparatively petty sentences, for the less conspicuous workers of the gang. Possibly the full extent of the frauds at the ballot-boxes was not realized by the public until the election at Gravesend in April, 1894, when, under honest auspices, only 1,928 votes were cast.

Thus closed in turmoil and gloom the story of a town founded in righteousness and honesty, and distinguished for its uprightness and the even tenor of its ways. It demonstrated the unscrupulousness of politics and die rottenness which can be introduced into our municipal government by a few men who are zealous for power. No one pitied McKane and his fellows, and their fate has been held to be a significant and much-needed lesson to others who might be induced to drift into such methods; and drift is the right word. McKane and his associates were not bad men; in private life most of them were above reproach; but they drifted along the current of low political intrigue until, blind to the results, they "shot Niagara," went beyond the safeguards of law and order, defied these in fact, and landed in prison cells. Their story is a blot on American politics, and it is a pity that the records of Gravesend should close with the details of a political crime and its salutary punishment.

# CHAPTER XXXI. CONEY ISLAND.

For many years after the Revolution Coney Island lay practically dormant. The heirs of the thirty-nine persons referred to in the preceding chapter, among whom most of Guisbert's Island was divided in 1677, held their right for many years in that apportionment, but the property was unproductive. By 1734 most of their claims had been bought by Thomas Stillwell, who in that year started the march of modern improvement by digging a ditch which enabled farmers' and gardeners' boats to reach the market on Manhattan Island much more quickly than formerly. All the arable land was practically on the division known as Guisbert's Island. Pine Island and the original bit of sand known as Coney Island, or Narrioch, made up the rest of the territory, all of which is now known under the one popular name. The sea, then as now, played sad havoc with this stretch of sand. Sometimes the three islands were quite distinct, at other times they were, as now, practically one. The whole territory at one time was little more than the backyard of Gravesend, and at intervals that town enjoyed a little income by letting the privileges not covered by the rights of the original thirty-nine. From time to time other divisions were made of the territory, always in thirty-nine lots, as fresh demands were made by the slowly increasing population, and the last of these divisions was that of 1821. By that time the utility of Coney Island as a "resort" was beginning to be understood, and before the end of that decade the place boasted its first hotel, — the Coney Island House. Wyckoff's Hotel followed, and these two establishments divided the patronage of the place. In 1844 a bathing pavilion, with attachments, was erected at what is now known as Norton's Point, and in 1847 another hotel was built on the island, — the Oceanic. It was burned down at the end of its first season, and afterward rebuilt.

This was the beginning. But it is difficult to say exactly when the modern movement which resulted in making Coney Island famous fairly set in. In one sense, no date can be definitely fixed, for, like Topsey in "Uncle Tom's Cabin," it "just growed." Every year from 1847 witnessed some improvement, some new bathing-houses run up with unplanned lumber and primitive appointments, some roughly constructed hotel or restaurant, cheap saloon, democratic eating-houses where you could bring your own luncheon or eat what was produced on the premises, lager-beer bars, and a show or two, generally of a startling character, such as newly-caught wild Indians, educated pigs, museums, special exhibits of "sole remnants of the ancient Aztec sovereigns of Central America," and the like. Each year more and more of these things seemed to litter the beach, and each year the crowds of visitors increased. It was a democratic resort, and there was plenty of room for all sorts of tastes. If the visitors wanted to be in a throng, the throng was there; if they desired quiet, a short walk among the dunes gave them all the quietness that Lady Moody could have enjoyed in her "bouwerie." Then the crowds became too great and people began to complain that the place was a resort for roughs, and the descendants of the good old settlers of Gravesend held up their hands in horror at the scenes of Sabbath desecration and midsummer riot which had grown up in their midst. The steamboats were carrying thousands of visitors, the railroad had begun its work of transporting people from the outskirts of Brooklyn and from Bay Ridge to the ocean, and even one lumbering horse-car line was established, which was taxed to its capacity during the season. The crowds, however, gave rise to trouble of all sorts; Sundays were seldom passed without exhibiting scenes of riot and debauchery, and by 1875 respectable New Yorkers and Brooklynites began to shun Coney Island and talked of it as having been given over to the mob, the rough element, in their midst, and predicted its early doom to silence and decay. But the mob held on, and recalcitrants were won back to some part of the island at least. By 1876 its fame had spread over the whole country, and in that centennial year it was regarded as one of the sights of New York and one to which all visitors to the commercial metropolis had to be conducted.

In many respects 1875 might be regarded as the opening year of the modern Coney Island. The old divisions of the island by that time had begun to be known by their modern names thus: West End (Norton's Point), West Brighton, Brighton Beach, and Manhattan Beach.

It is almost useless to attempt to describe modern Coney Island in a historical work, for the yearly changes are so many and so kaleidoscopic as to make any outline seem out of date a few months after it has been penned.

It is the great democratic outpouring place of the Greater New York, and although all around the great city new resorts appear to spring up every year, the island seems not only to retain, but to extend its popularity with each recurring season. Somehow it has adapted itself to the wants of the great multitude of visitors. Those who want quiet and exclusiveness can find it in the Oriental Hotel, which is the outpost of the modern Coney Island. At Manhattan Beach, with its theater, music, fireworks and other amusements, there is exclusiveness and pleasure combined. Brighton Beach claims to be a family resort primarily, and to a great extent retains that characteristic. It attracts larger crowds than the places already named, being a center for transit facilities; and, having superb bathing accommodations, it attracts visitors of all classes. It really forms the dividing line between aristocratic and democratic Coney Island. The regular visitors to the Oriental Hotel, or Manhattan Beach, or Brighton Beach, however, would hardly care to admit that they had any connection with Coney Island. That good old name has become somewhat demoralized, too much associated with "the great unwashed," with cheap shows, bawling photographers, Sunday beer and vulgar frankfurters to be congenial to ears polite. So at all three the name of Coney Island is tabooed, and when in these modern days the island is referred to we are supposed to speak of the long stretch of sand lying still further to the westward; Here, however, the island retains all the many peculiarities and types which won for it its first popularity. Its manners are free and easy, its crowds have assembled to have a good time according to their individual ideas, and they have it. One account tells us: "At the West End. or Norton's, the island has been but little improved. Accommodations are provided here for parties with lunch-baskets, and there are numerous unattractive-looking bathing-houses. This part of the island is now being redeemed from neglect by the building of good houses.

The Atlantic Yacht Club has now established its quarters there. West Brighton was formerly known as Cable's, and is the central part of the island. Travelers arrive at the beach by railroad as a rule, and alight in a spacious depot, facing the finest iron pier on the island. To the stranger the scene is suggestive of a great fair-ground. In the center is a broad plaza with green grass and flowers, traversed by wide wooden pavements, and numerous hotels and places of amusement are clustered around. Bands play every afternoon and evening in pavilions, and the beach is brilliantly illuminated at night by the somewhat ghastly white rays of the electric light. A camera obscura here gives charming views of the beach, sharply outlined, delicately toned, and well worth seeing. An observatory 300 feet high occupies a prominent place, and from the top, reached by large elevators, a fine view of the island, the bay and the adjacent cities may be had. Two piers, each about 1.300 feet long, constructed of tubular iron piles, run out from West Brighton. On them are various buildings, used as saloons, restaurants, concert halls, etc., and hundreds of bathhouses. Steamboats from New York land at the piers hourly. Near the piers is the Sea Beach Hotel (this structure was the United States Government building at the Centennial Exhibition). The Concourse, which leads toward Brighton Beach on the east (or left), is a wide drive and promenade about a third of a mile long. Park wagons are continually traversing its length, and there are two rustic pavilions in which pedestrians may rest themselves. It is maintained by the Park Department, and no buildings are allowed between it and the ocean. It has been seriously damaged by storms in recent winters, and has lost much of its former glory, the eastern end of it, nearest to Brighton Beach, having been entirely destroyed." The winter of 1901-2 proved particularly destructive, not only to this section of Coney Island, but to all the others. Several miles of roadway were destroyed by a storm early in the season and a large number of buildings unroofed or blown down. Even Manhattan Beach suffered severely and miles of beautiful lawns were ruined. But all that seems to be a regular winter story in spite of mere human ingenuity, and protective arrangements of all sorts.

But by whatever name its sections may be designated for advertising and business purposes, the historical designation can never be wiped out. Coney Island, in fact, is itself, but the end of the great sand bar, broken here and there by inlets, hurled, twisted and changed by every winter's storm, which extends along almost the entire south coast of the island and bears many names. The bar is the great feature of the south shore and gives to it most of its charms of scenery and climate. It has developed on its course many charming resorts; the surface of the sand has been in places so beautified by turf and flower bed, mammoth hotel and charming cottages as fairly to claim a title to being a summer paradise; but no part has been so beneficial to the toilers in New York or Brooklyn as that which still flourishes under the old name of Coney Island, — the name first given to it by the Dutch pioneers

From the earliest times of its European history vague stories of smuggling and piracy have been rife concerning Coney Island. A good proportion of such stories was either entirely fabulous or was founded on such slim foundation of fact that the foundation itself has disappeared. In its early ante-resort days Coney Island must have been a wild and deserted place, its storms even more terrible than now, and the imaginations of the few visitors were quickened by the wind and desolation, the solemn stillness that prevailed except for the low moaning of the sea in times of placidity, or its terrible howling when the Atlantic, roused to fury, seemed to break in all its anger on the sandy bar. Little wonder that popular imagination and innate human superstition associated the dunes and creeks and bays and points with tales of strange, weird doings, and that such stories gathered in importance and weirdness and tragedy as they sped on from mouth to mouth. Such stories have become too vague to be regarded as history, but it is a pity that some of them had not been preserved. Many of the exploits of Heyler and Marriner, the patriot freebooters, were performed in what may be called Coney Island waters, and one of these was related by General Jeremiah Johnson from the recollections of some of its participants. While here in command of two whaleboats. Captain Heyler saw a British sloop of war lying off the island and determined to secure it. By quietly approaching the vessel in one of the boats Heyler found that no watch was on deck and that the officers were playing cards in their cabin. Signaling for his other boat it quickly came up, and the sloop was at once boarded from each side, and so astonished were those on board at the sudden and unexpected attack that they surrendered without even a show of resistance. The crew were removed as prisoners and the ship set on fire. It was said that $40,000 in cash and many valuables went up in smoke when the sloop was destroyed; but this we may well doubt. Captain Heyler had a warm heart for plunder as well as for his country.

One well-authenticated story of piracy has come down to us, and we give the narrative in the words of Mr. William H. Stillwell, the patient and painstaking historian of Coney Island, who has devoted many years to unraveling the many vexed questions of its boundaries, its early settlers and their descendants, as well as telling the story of its wonderful modern growth.

Coney Island is connected with a tragedy of the sea, well-nigh forgotten by even the older residents of the vicinity, but which was the cause of intense excitement at the time. On the 9th of November, 1830, the brig "Vineyard" cleared from New Orleans for Philadelphia with a cargo of cotton, sugar and molasses, and $54,000 in specie (all Mexican dollars), consigned to Stephen Girard, Esq., of the latter city. The officers and crew of the brig were William Thornby, captain; Mr. Roberts, mate; Charles Gibbs (alias Thos. D. Jeffers). Aaron Church, James Talbot, John Brownrigg and Henry Atwell, seamen: Robert Dawes (age eighteen or nineteen), cabin boy; and Wansley, a young Delaware negro, steward and cook. When the brig had been five days out at sea, and was off Cape Hatteras, the negro steward informed some of the others of the money on board: and, with Gibbs, Church, Atwell and Dawes, planned to kill the captain and mate, and possess themselves of the specie. On the night of March 23rd, between 12 and 1 o'clock, as the captain was on the quarter-deck, and the boy Dawes was steering, the negro Wansley came up on deck, and. obeying a prearranged call from Dawes to come and trim the binnacle light, as he passed behind the captain felled him with a pump-brake, and killed him by repeated blows. Gibbs then coming up, he and Wansley flung the captain's body overboard. Roberts, the mate, who was below, came up the companion way to ascertain the cause of the commotion, and was attacked by Church and Atwell, who failed, however (through nervousness), to accomplish their design upon him. He retreated to the cabin, where he was followed by Gibbs, who, not being able to find him in the dark, returned to the deck for the binnacle lamp, with which he re-entered the cabin, accompanied by Church, Atwell and the boy Dawes; and Roberts, being speedily overcome by their blows, was dragged upon deck and hurled into the sea — still alive, and able for a while to swim after the ship, begging for mercy. Talbot, who, in his terror at what was going on, had sought refuge in the forecastle, and Brownrigg, who had fled aloft, were now called by the conspirators and offered their lives and equal share in the booty if they kept silent. It is needless to say that they joyfully accepted the terms thus unexpectedly offered them. The conspirators then rifled the vessel, divided the specie; and, under direction of Gibbs, who, from his being the only one understanding navigation, assumed command of the vessel, their course was laid for Long Island. When within fifteen or twenty miles off Southampton light the vessel was scuttled and fired, and they took to their boats: Gibbs, Wansley, Brownrigg and Dawes, with about $31,000 of the money, in the long boat, and Church, Talbot and Atwell, with about $23,000, in the jolly-boat. The wind was blowing a gale, and in attempting to cross Duck (or Rockaway) Bar, the jolly-boat upset, and its occupants, with their share of the booty, were lost. The occupants of the other boat were compelled, by fear of a similar fate, to lighten their boat by throwing overboard all but $5,000 of their stealings; but finally succeeded in reaching the shore of Pelican Beach, then part of Barren, now Coney Island. Their first care was to dispose temporarily of the specie by burying it in a hole (dug with an oar) in the sand at a considerable distance from the shore, each taking out sufficient for his immediate wants. Food and lodging were their next most pressing wants, and meeting, on Pelican Beach, with Nicholas S. Williamson, of Gravesend, they told him a pitiable tale of shipwreck, and, getting from him the needed directions, they passed on to Dooley's Bay, on the northwest shore of Barren Island. Here resided John Johnson and wife, and his brother William, who kindly received and cared for the shipwrecked mariners, and gave up to them for the night their own room and beds. Brownrigg and the Johnson brothers thus happened to occupy chairs in the living-room; and as soon as the other inmates of the house were asleep Brownrigg revealed the whole matter to the two Johnsons. In the morning, after getting such breakfast as the place afforded, the pirates desired the Johnsons to take them over to the hotel at Sheepshead Bay, whence they might get a conveyance to Fulton Ferry and New York. This the Johnsons did, and returned to Barren Island without unnecessary delay; and, proceeding to the spot described by Brownrigg (and to which they had gone in the early morning with Wansley to get some clothes left there), they dug up the specie, removed it to another hiding place remote from its first location; and, by walking in the water, effaced all traces of the direction they had taken.

Meanwhile Gibbs and his party were bargaining with Samuel Leonard, the hotelkeeper at Sheepshead Bay, when suddenly, in the presence of all, Brownrigg, declaring that he would go no further with them, denounced his companions as pirates and murderers, and unfolded the whole story of the Vineyard's fate. Wansley incontinently took to his heels to the woods, and Gibbs and Dawes were seized and bound by the inn-keeper and his people; and Justice John Van Dyke was summoned, who promptly issued warrants for the arrest of the pirates. The one constable of the village found his hands full in guarding Gibbs and Dawes: and so Robert Greenwood, of Sheepshead Bay, volunteered to go into the woods and look up Wansley. After an hour's search he found the negro, and presenting a huge pistol, ordered him to fall on his face and cross his hands behind his back. Wansley submitted, and Greenwood, sitting astride of him, tied his hands securely, ordered him to arise, and marched him back to Leonard's hotel. After the negro had been thoroughly secured his captor showed him the pistol (utterly destitute of either lock or load), with the remark that it "was just as good's any other if you knowed how to use it." Gibbs, Wansley and Dawes were then lodged in the county jail at Flatbush.

The Johnsons had been none too quick in securing the $5,000; for, scarcely had they regained their home when Squire Van Dyke, with Brownrigg as guide, appeared on the scene, and going right to the spot where the money had been deposited the day before, found it gone! Brownrigg was then sent to join the others at Flatbush; and from thence they were remanded to New York Bridewell. Indictments being found against Gibbs and Wansley, they were tried and convicted on the testimony of Brownrigg and Dawes; and on the nth of March, 1831, were sentenced to be hung; sentence being carried into effect on the 23rd of April following.

John and William Johnson, apprehensive of further search being made for the money, made no haste to get it home. In a day or two they were visited by agents of the insurance companies and an officer, who not only searched for the money on the beach, but thoroughly ransacked the Johnson abode from garret to cellar, without success. Having, finally, as they thought, eluded the vigilance of the law, John Johnson and wife planned to get possession of it without the assistance of William. Accordingly, one night, while the latter was asleep, they stole out and unearthed the treasure, and reinterred it in two parcels, one of $3,400, the other of about $1,600. Knowing how closely William would scan the beach when he discovered his loss, they made only the slightest mark to designate the new place of deposit on Pelican Beach, by tying knots on the long sedge-grass, which could be seen only by the closest scrutiny. William's indignation, when he discovered the loss, was intense; his suspicions fell upon his brother, and going to New York he informed the insurance companies, who entered suit against John for the recovery of the money. The trial, which was held before Judge Dean, in the Apprentices' Library, in Brooklyn, ended in John's acquittal, for want of sufficient evidence. He then moved to Brooklyn, and William to Canarsie. But when John went to look for his deposit, he found only the larger sum. A high tide had swept over the site of the other; the action of the waves had loosened the knots in the sedge-grass, and the $1,600 was lost to him forever.

In 1842 the Skidmore family, living on "Ruffle Bar," concluded to remove their house, in sections, to a new site on the shore of Dooley's Bay, Barren Island. The house was accordingly taken down piecemeal, and most of it carried across the bay and piled up near its future site. The moving was not quite completed on the day appointed. On the foundation of their old home had been left the wooden ceiling of an upper chamber, in one piece or section. During the night a violent storm drove the tide up to an unprecedented height; and, in the morning, when Jacob Skidmore arose, he was surprised to find that his chamber ceiling had been brought over by the tide from Ruffle Bar to Dooley's Bay, without injury. Anxious to learn whether any other of his property had gone farther west, he proceeded along the northerly, or inside, shore of Pelican Beach, which then had become separated by a small inlet, shallow enough to be forded at low tide, but at high tide floating skiffs through it from the ocean to Dooley's Bay. The eastern part of Pelican Beach then had a ridge of sand hills, while the western was as fiat and level as the whole of it is now. Arrived at these sand hills, from whence to get a view of the surrounding country, he saw none of his lumber; and, acceding to the suggestion of his companion, Mr. Loring, hurried back so as to cross the inlet before the tide got too high. Taking a last look, as they did so, they noticed the shore or ocean side of Pelican Beach much washed away, and also saw his neighbors, Willett Smith and Henry Brewer, approaching. Smith and Brewer came on easterly until they reached the spot where John Johnson and wife had last buried the $1,600; and here, by the storm over night, the silver dollars had been uncovered, and lay scattered along the beach. The two men lost no time in filling pockets and boots, and carried away all they could; but they could not keep their good luck to themselves, and in a day or two business was almost entirely suspended in Gravesend. and every man who could got to Pelican Beach. The intense excitement only gradually subsided when a succeeding storm placed the location of the "find" so far to sea as to be absolutely beyond further search.

# BROOKLYN

## CHAPTER XXXII. THE STORY OF BROOKLYN VILLAGE TO THE BEGINNING OF THE REVOLUTIONARY MOVEMENT.

Standing at the junction of Fulton street and Flatbush avenue, and looking in the direction of the City Hall, the modern Brooklynite can cast an eye over the site of the first settlement out of which grew the present magnificent metropolitan borough. Standing there, looking at the throngs of all classes of society passing and repassing on the streets, the crowded cars, the loaded teams, and the elevated railroad crashing overhead, one can hardly realize the little village of the middle of the seventeenth century with its few scattered houses nestling as closely together as possible so as to afford mutual protection from bands of predatory or murderous Indians, with fields of growing grain giving a golden tinge to a landscape whose prevailing color was green, the color of luxuriant nature. Even in its early stages the red man found much in Breuckelen to incite his cupidity, and a twentieth century marauder, standing on the spot here indicated, might well exclaim, as Blucher is said to have exclaimed on visiting London, "What a place for loot!"

If we were asked to describe in a word the progress and end of Brooklyn, we would answer, Annexation. That has been its crowning feature all through. The place we now designate as the borough of Brooklyn was no less the result of annexation than was the city of Brooklyn prior to 1855, the date of its first most noted extension, when Williamsburgh and Bushwick joined their fortunes with it, Old Breuckelen really waxed in strength and dominated the other towns with which it started, and which started under more auspicious conditions than it, by absorption of outlying villages from time to time. The Wallabout, for instance, was one district, Gowanus another, the Ferry another, Bedford another, — all of which, one after the other, fell in with the group of houses which found the central village on the rich agricultural plateau. The first purchase within the old limits of Brooklyn City — the pre-1856 limit — was at Gowanus, where in 1636 William Adriaense Bennet, an Englishman by birth and a cooper by trade, and Jacques Bentyne, another Englishman, — an important man in the colony, for in 1636 he was Schout Fiscal of New Amsterdam, and for several years a member of Governor Kieft's Council, — bought 936 acres from the Indian proprietors. Three years later Bentyne sold out his interest in the property to Bennet, who resided on it until his death, about 1644, when it passed to his widow. This purchase is regarded by Dr. Stiles as "the first step in the settlement of the city of Brooklyn;" but there are indications of earlier settlement.

In 1637 Joris Jansen (Rapalye) obtained a patent for some 334 acres of land at the Wallabout, and so began that historic settlement. About 1640 a ferry was established which plied between the present Fulton street and Peck

Slip, and around the Fulton street end arose a small settlement to which the name of "the Ferry" was given.

By reference to the map on page 97 of this volume, where the context gives an account of this ferry and vicinity, one will notice that at the time the map was drawn the name of the village was spelled Brookland, at least by some parties; that Rapailie was one of the many ways in which that name was spelled, that being before the days of spelling-books and dictionaries, and even before the era when correct orthography was thought a very important matter; and that the road to Jamaica, running southeastwardly, was the main business street or thoroughfare of the village.

The prospects of greater things led the mind's eye of the resident to a vague and distant future, with scarcely any correct idea of what the place would be at the end of a hundred or two hundred years, and life was comparatively monotonous. The initial improvements or any new country are necessarily very slow, as the first settlers are not wealthy and are obliged to work laboriously up from small beginnings, with many losses by experimentation, accident, etc. For the time being there does not seem to be any definite promise of great things soon to come. The capitalists arrive after a long time, the small capitalists first and gradually the larger ones afterward, and improvements are correspondingly more and more rapidly effected.

The essential features of those pioneer times have in many important respects been duplicated in all the Western States. Not until recently have capitalists felt like pushing railroads out into unsettled districts in order to develop their resources and invite settlement; and this movement has indeed been a great blessing to the public, notwithstanding the general dissatisfaction with railroad grants of lands. Of course, both in the enterprise of extending railroads into unsettled portions of the country and in the legislative grants of lands in aid of railroad construction, there would be, in keeping with the characteristic weaknesses of human nature, many mistakes, — in excessive grants by one party and excessive railroad building by the other.

Bit by bit, as recorded in another chapter, the shore front was occupied by farms right down to Red Hook, where in 1643 Wouter Van Twiller assumed proprietorship by virtue of a patent afterward forfeited. At Gowanus and Wallabout as well as at the Ferry small settlements quickly sprang up. Between Gowanus and the Wallabout lay a level stretch of territory which the aborigines, as it was exceedingly fertile and easy of cultivation, used for. growing their maize. To this tract they gave the name of Mareckawieck. Through it lay the road or trail that led from the Ferry to Flatlands, and it was on this trail, and on this fertile tract right between the present Court House and Flatbush avenue, that the village of Breuckelen had its beginning.

To the early settlers reference has already been made, and we may here take up the story by saying that the pioneer white dwellers on the trail located their homes in proximity to each other, quickly availed themselves of the policy outlined by the West India Company that the settlers should "establish themselves on some of the most suitable places, with a certain number of inhabitants, in the manner of towns, villages and hamlets," and held a meeting at which it was determined to form a town. Governor Kieft was at once notified that they had organized a municipality at their own expense, to which they had given the name of Breuckelen, after the village of that name on the Vecht, in the home province of Utrecht. The proceedings which led up to this seem to have been promptly indorsed by Kieft and publicly ratified in the following proclamation, issued in June, 1646:

We, William Kieft, Director General, and the Council residing in New Netherland, on behalf of the High and Mighty Lords States-General of the United Netherlands, His Highness of Orange, and the Honorable Directors of the General Incorporated West India Company, To all those who shall see these presents or hear them read, Greeting:

Whereas, Jan Evertsen Bout and Huyck Aertsen from Rossum were on the 21st May last unanimously chosen by those interested of Breuckelen, situate on Long Island, as Schepens, to decide all questions which may arise, as they shall deem proper, according to the exemptions of New Netherland granted to particular Colonies, which election is subscribed by them, with express stipulation that if any one refuse to submit in the premises aforesaid to the above-mentioned Jan Evertsen and Huyck Aertsen, he shall forfeit the right he claims to land in the allotment of Breuckelen, and in order that everything may be done with more authority, We, the Director and Council aforesaid, have therefore authorized and appointed, and do hereby authorize the said Jan Evertsen and Huyck Aertsen to be schepens of Breuckelen; and in case Jan Evertsen and Huyck Aertsen do hereafter find the labor too onerous, they shall be at liberty to select two more from among the inhabitants of Breuckelen to adjoin them to themselves. We charge and command every inhabitant of Breuckelen to acknowledge and respect the above-mentioned Jan Evertsen and Huyck Aertsen as their schepens, and if any one shall be found to exhibit contumaciousness towards them, he shall forfeit his share as above stated.

This done in Council in Fort Amsterdam in New Netherland.

It may not be inappropriate here to refer to the ancient town after which the new settlement was named, and to this end we quote from the able monograph on "Origin of Breuckelen," by Mr. Harrington Putnam:

Amersfoort, Breuckelen, and Utrecht have many historic associations. To the politician and reader of Motley, they are forever linked with the career and tragic end of Barneveld. In 1619, he fell a martyr to the cause of state rights and local self -government. Such an event, comparatively recent in 1646, and still appealing to the sense of individual liberty, may have been recalled by the settlers in America. While the liberties of Utrecht had been the cherished objects of Barneveld's solicitude, he proudly proclaimed his birth in Amersfoort. In moments of arduous public labor he looked hopefully forward to an honorable and calm retirement from the tumults of party strife to his beautiful estate at Guntersteijn in the village of Breuckelen.. Breuckelen, however, was an ancient village three centuries before the settlement in New Netherlands. Located between Utrecht and Amsterdam, it was early noted for its healthfulness, which soon made it a desirable residence region. The surrounding fields and foliage are strikingly green and luxuriant, even for Holland. Castles grew up about it along the banks of the beautiful Vecht, which all the successive tides of war have not quite destroyed.

In the Dutch records, Breuckelen had various spellings, as Broklede, Broicklede, Brackola, Brocklandia, and Broeckland. Hence some say that the name came from its brooks and marshes — van de drassige en broekactige veenlanden — meaning a brook or marsh land. It is mentioned as an important place in the year 1317. There were two parishes on opposite sides of the Vecht. These are BreuckelenNijenroide, from the castle of Nijenrode, and Breuckelen-St. Pieters. The small river Vecht dividing these towns may be considered an outlet of the Rhine, which parts in two channels at Utrecht. The Vecht turns to the north and empties into the Zuider Zee. It is navigable for small vessels, and at Breuckelen is a little over two hundred feet wide.

The old country-seats along the Vecht, once set in the prim, geometric gardens of the last century, are now represented by modern villas, half hidden by trees, which to-day form bits of unmatched rural scenery. Eminent landscape painters of the modern Dutch school have loved to make studies amid these gentle windings, and the celebrity of the Vecht in art bids fair to surpass the forgotten fame of the neighboring castles. Old drawbridges of wood cross the sluggish river. Trees come close to the tow-path, bordered by quaint gardens. Along the garden edges, looking out upon the stream, are Koepels or tea houses and over all this abundant foliage rises a church spire.

Jan Evertsen Bout is generally regarded by local historians as the founder of Brooklyn, and as such deserves somewhat more than merely passing notice. According to the record in Bergen's "Early Settlers in Kings County," he was born in the Province of Gelderland in 1603 and entered the service of the West Indian Company. In 1634 he emigrated to New Netherland and we find him, four years later, settled as a farmer at Pavonia (Jersey City, N. J.). In 1643 he was chosen one of the eight men then selected to represent the people in the days of Gov. Kieft's extremity and became a member of the Council by Kieft's appointment in 1645. That same year he secured a patent for fifty-six acres of land on Gowanus Kill, and when the town of Breuckelen was organized he was chosen as the first of its Schepens. In 1660 he was enrolled as a member of the Reformed Dutch Church in Breuckelen. He was twice married, first to Tryntje Symons de Wit, and secondly to Annetje

Pieters. No children blessed either union, and after his death, in 1670, Annetje married Andries Janse Jurianse and appears to have brought him, as a dower, Jan's Brooklyn property.

The year 1646, in view of Kieft's proclamation, already given, may therefore be accepted as the beginning of Brooklyn's municipal history. The measure of local self-government then awarded to the community was as limited as was possible. The magistrates were in office and clothed with honor and authority, but they had no one to carry out their orders; so they at once petitioned Kieft, and the nature of their petition can easily be inferred from that dignitary's answer, which was as follows:

Having seen the petition of the schepens of Breuckelen, that it is impossible for them to attend to all cases occurring there, especially criminal assaults, impounding of cattle, and other incidents which frequently attend agriculture: and in order to prevent all disorders, it would be necessary to appoint a schout there, for which office they propose the person of Jan Teunissen. Therefore we grant their request therein, and authorize, as we do hereby authorize, Jan Teunissen to act as schout, to imprison delinquents by advice of the schepens, to establish the pound, to impound cattle, to collect fines, and to perform all things that a trusty schout is bound to perform. Whereupon he hath taken his oath at the hands of us and the Fiscal, on whom he shall especially depend, as in Holland substitutes are bound to be dependent on the Upper Schout. Schouts on the Bailiff or Marshal. We command and charge all who are included under the jurisdiction of Breuckelen to acknowledge him, Jan Teunissen, for schout. Thus done in our council in Fort Amsterdam in New Netherland, the first December, Anno 1646.

With the appointment of this terror to evildoers the municipal government of Brooklyn may be said to have been made complete as far as it could be under the circumstances. It does not seem likely that the Schout was much exercised over the degenerates from within the village, and that his income from Breuckelen was mainly derived from what might be called legal fees, such as drawing up writs, petitions, certificates and the like. During the remainder of the Dutch regime the story of the young town passed on so placidly that really there is little for the general historian to tell, and what little there is gathered around the fantastic figure of Peter Stuyvesant. Soon after that potentate "of uncertain reputation, impetuous, high tempered, energetic and persistent," as Henry Cabot Lodge has described him, succeeded Kieft in 1647. the whole of New Netherland felt the benefit of the change. But his paternal notions were at times carried too far, and in the protests against his assumptions of power the people of Breuckelen were ever active and were represented in all the conventions which so often aroused the wrath of the paternal "Silver Legs," as the Indians called Stuyvesant, on account of the silver bands which strengthened and adorned his wooden limb.

In 1660 a palisade was erected around the settlement of homes, and in that year also Henricus Selyns began preaching in Brooklyn, thus marking the beginning of the great factor in the city's subsequent fame. The palisade proved a source of comfort during the Indian outbreak of 1663. But in spite of the general success of the colony as a whole under Stuyvesant, the progress of Breuckelen in the matter of population continued very slow, as may be understood from the fact that when the Director and Council decided that the village should contribute eight or twelve men to the common defense of the Dutch towns, a meeting of the inhabitants voted to the effect that such a proposition was outrageous, that it really called for more men than the place should or could provide. But then Breuckelen was constantly giving the Director trouble by not complying with his wishes and tamely submitting to his notions. On his arrival he ordered an election of nominees for membership in his Council, retaining the final selection from those elected in his own hands. New Amsterdam, Breuckelen, Amersfoort and Midwout were among the places thus honored by a taste of popular government. Out of the eighteen thus chosen by public vote the Governor selected nine as his advisers, and his choice from Breuckelen fell upon Jan Evertsen Bout. In 1653, at the unauthorized convention of representatives of New Netherland towns held in New Amsterdam, Breuckelen was represented by Frederic Lubbertsen, Paulen Van der Beeck and William Beeckman. Probably Bout did not attend because of his official position. The meeting apparently accomplished nothing. Stuyvesant was bitterly opposed to such things and he emphatically told the delegates to go home and not to assemble again on such business; but there is no doubt the convention indirectly led to an increase of municipal privileges all round. In Breuckelen the number of Schepens was increased from two to four and it got a Schout all to itself in the person of David Provoost. The latter official was one of the early settlers in New Amsterdam, arriving there in 1639, and he afterward held several official positions. He received his appointment as Schout in 1654 and in 1656 was succeeded by Pieter Tonneman. It is difficult to understand why Provoost resigned so soon, for he appears to have been an inveterate office-seeker, and it was not until 1665 that we find him in another position, that of Clerk of the local courts. Probably the fees attached to the Breuckelen appointment were too small to suit his views or his ambition. Tonneman held on until 1660, when he was appointed Schout of New Amsterdam and then Adrian Hegeman became Breuckelen's Schout, with a fixed salary in addition to what seems to have been for the time quite generous fees.

Shortly after the unauthorized meeting of representatives of the people which Stuyvesant so ruthlessly put down, Bout again comes under our notice. In 1654 he declined to serve any longer as one of the Schepens, declaring he would rather return to Holland than venture on another term. However, says Harrington Putnam, "no excuses regarding his private business were accepted [by Stuyvesant]. Though the Schepen-elect had served for previous terms, and filled other colonial offices, he was not now allowed to retire. The Sheriff was formally ordered to notify him of these summary commands of Gov. Stuyvesant: 'If you will not accept to serve as Schepen for the welfare of the village of Breuckelen with others, your fellow-residents, then you must prepare yourself to sail in the ship King Solomon for Holland, agreeably to your utterance.' This appeal to the civic conscience of one who had been prominent as a reformer, coupled with the grim threat of deportation, was irresistible. No further declinations in Breuckelen offices seem to have troubled the Council." Bout did not go to Holland, but continued in public life until at least 1665, for he was then one of the representatives of Breuckelen at the Hempstead convention; after that he passes from our view.

In spite of his paternal methods and domineering tactics, there is no doubt that under Stuyvesant's rule the Dutch towns steadily advanced in self-government. He was virtually as one man standing like a barrier between two forces of progress, for the home authorities in New Amsterdam always showed themselves, when appealed to, to be in favor of the fullest measure of local self-government and the liberty of the subject, while the Dutch pertinacity never permitted an aim to be lost sight of once it was believed to be a right. There were frequent quarrels between the Dutch towns and Stuyvesant, and these there is no doubt drove him to seek the support of the English settlers at Gravesend and elsewhere much more than possibly he cared to admit. But his arbitrary will kept alive a certain measure of discontent which even he had to reckon with, and it is a singular fact that it was under Stuyvesant that the acceptance of the theory that the people were the source of power and the arbiters of law found its earliest acknowledgment in what is now the State of New York. The first principles of union were also instilled into the minds of people and ruler when, in 1664, the Director felt impelled to call a meeting of representatives chosen in each community to consider various matters of common interest and indirectly to repair the damage done by his own misgovernment. At that meeting Breuckelen was represented by William Bredenbent and Albert Cornelysen Wantanaer, two of its Schepens. It is of little moment what that meeting did: its importance lies in the fact that it was called at all and that it had been called at the direct behest of such a ruler as Stuyvesant. It met in April in the fort at New Amsterdam, and five months later the English flag waved over that stronghold, an English Governor held sway and the indomitable Pieter troubled the lieges no more.

So far as Gov. Nicolls was concerned, the chief feature of his administration, the chief feature that is of interest in the history of Breuckelen, was the granting to it of a charter which has been reproduced in facsimile, while of the events of the six years' administration under his successor, Gov. Lovelace, only the beginning of the village of Bedford need be recorded. The second Dutch regime was barren of incident, so far as concerns the history of Breuckelen, and when, in 1674, the English Government was resumed the village seems to have accepted the charge again with placid equanimity. Governor Dongan in 1686 gave it a new patent, which served the purpose of helping his administration with a fee and fixing some disputed boundary questions.

But amid all these changes in rulers Breuckelen continued to make definite progress, and by 1676 it had assumed its place at the head of the five Dutch towns. Its taxable rate was adjusted on a valuation of £5,067, while that of Middlewout was £4,872, Boswyck £22,960, New Utrecht £3.024, and Amersfort £3,966. Gov. Dongan fixed the town's quit rent at twenty bushels of wheat. In 1698 the population of Breuckelen (it had then become Brookland) was given at 444, not including 65 slaves, while its nearest neighbor, Flatbush, rejoiced in 405 whites and 71 slaves.

Much of the early history of Breuckelen that has come down to us is in regard to boundary disputes, for it does not seem that in the political troubles of the commonwealth, such as the Leisler excitement, or even in the charges of the ruling powers, its people took any very profound interest. The matter of their boundaries, however, seems to have been a vital question and was the cause of much trouble between them and the good folks of Flatbush and Bushwick, while the rights in connection with the ferry were also a source of standing and perpetual worry with New York. In these troubles and complications and claims, however, the Brooklyn people seemed to want no more than might be considered their just right, and an instance of their conscientious regard for this may be found in the following excerpt, showing in the way in which they adjusted their own internal boundaries at a public meeting of the citizens:

At a Town meeting held the 25th day of February, 1692-3, at Breucklyn, in Kings County. Then Resolved to divide their common land and woods into three parts, in manner following to wit:

"1. All the lands and woods after Bedford and Cripplebush, over the hills to the path of New lotts shall belong to the inhabitants and freeholders of the Gowanis, beginning from Jacob Brewer and soe to the uttermost bounds of the limits of New-Utrecht.

"2. And all the lands and woods that lyes betwixt the abovesaid path and the highway from the ferry toward Flattbush, shall belong to the freeholders and the inhabitants of Bedford and Cripplebush.

"3. And all the lands that lyes in common after the Gowanis. betwixt the limits and bounds of Flatbush and New Utrecht shall belong to the freeholders and inhabitants of Brooklyn, fred. neck [Frederick Lubbertsen's Neck], the ferry and the Wallabout."

In 1702 Fulton Street was laid out and except near the water front provided a fairly good thoroughfare out to Bedford Corners, and in a measure to Flatbush. This road was so highly regarded that it received the name of the King's Highway, and jealous eyes were kept upon it to guard against encroachments upon its width and usefulness. However, at that time Brooklyn and its then suburbs — Gowanus, Wallabout, Bedford, Red Hook and Cripplebush and the Ferry — were tolerably well supplied with roads, at least with roads which made communication between them comparatively easy. Still the whole territory grew slowly in point of population, much more slowly than might be expected considering the opportunities for settlers and the wide extent of fruitful land that lay fallow awaiting the cultivator. Even in 1738 the population of Brooklyn and what we have called its suburbs did not exceed 725, yet even these limited figures placed it far in advance of the other Dutch towns.

Of the internal history of the people little is known until almost the beginning of the century, for the records of the town prior to the close of the Revolutionary War have mainly been lost or destroyed. A few incidents might be chronicled, such as the meeting of the Colonial Legislature in a house on Fulton street in 1752, owing to the fear of small-pox, which then raged in New York; but as a rule such details as we have are hardly worthy of being incorporated in a general history, however useful some of them may be for assisting the historian to arrive at conclusions on matters of purely local interest. In fact Brooklyn was a municipality in name but only a community in reality until after the nineteenth century had begun, and although by that time its population had increased to nearly 1,700 it was almost unknown outside of Long Island and Manhattan. Tytler's Gazetteer, published at Edinburgh in 1781, in its account of Long Island did not think Brooklyn worthy of even being named, while Moore's American Gazetteer, issued in 1798, briefly describes it as having "some elegant houses, which He chiefly on one street."

Whatever history the district had, centered at the Ferry. Some means of transit between Manhattan and Long Island was necessary from the time the first house was erected on the latter, and the ferry therefore may be regarded as the first of the local institutions. When it originated, however, we know not; but for two or three years the little traffic there was, was done by private boats owned on the Long Island side by the farmers and on the Manhattan side by the usual boatmen who plied along the waterfront. The journey was a long and tedious one, for the currents were strong and were also treacherous enough to infuse a sense of danger into the ideas of whoever meditated the voyage.

Transit across the river was not long, however, to remain a matter of chance, for in 1642 we find Cornells Dircksen (Hoogland) acknowledged as ferry man. Probably there was no formal appointment. Cornells kept a tavern in connection with his little farm at what afterward became Peck Slip, and he owned a piece of land and a house near the present site of Fulton ferry on Long Island. Very likely he set up a tavern there, too, and so the ferry came into being from the trade between the two points. Certain it is that the first ferry was between the points above named. Ten years later, after it had passed from Cornelis's hands, the ferry trade had become so important that the New Amsterdam authorities considered it 'should be made to return them some revenue; but Gov. Stuyvesant refused to entertain the idea, although afterward he admitted the public character of the service by permitting it to be placed under certain regulations. These included a fairly regular service, some requirements for the comfort of passengers and a scale of charges, and in return for observing these rules, or rather for accepting them, the Ferryman enjoyed a monopoly of the traffic. The arrangement was certainly a very liberal one all round for the boatman, but then there seems, it is mortifying to say, some reason to believe that he had quietly to hand over a proportion of his earnings to Stuyvesant. This new arrangement, in spite of the Governor's "rake-off," proved so profitable that competition for the privilege became excited, and in 1655 Egbert Van Borsum, who came here as skipper of the ship Prince William, leased the ferry from the Governor, agreeing to pay him 300 guilders per annum. He also got a patent for two lots on the Long Island waterfront, and there erected a structure which long served for both ferry house and tavern. Under him the place seems to have become quite a resort for the "roving blades" of the period. Egbert died about 1670, and for several years the tavern was run by his widow, while his son Hermanus attended to the ferry business. The house erected by the elder Van Boersum continued to serve its varied purposes until 1700, when a new building was erected of stone. This structure was destroyed by fire in 1748, and was succeeded by the historic ferry-house which was in existence during the British occupation in 1776. The ferry itself became a part of the municipal property of New York City under the Dongan charter of 1686. The legality of this charter was subsequently disputed, and led to interminable lawsuits, but the charter was confirmed by royal warrant in 1692. It was run, with varying success and on short leases (generally seven years) by private individuals, farmers and tavern-keepers mostly, as a separate holding; but the rent paid advanced steadily so that by 1710 it brought to the corporation of New York an annual rental of £180 — the largest single source of income over which the local treasury rejoiced. But the fact that it was a New York institution was rather galling to the Brooklyn settlers and a cause of complaint from a very early period. Their complaints evoked no change, however, and the New York corporation in 1694 actually bought sufficient ground at the Brooklyn end and built the ferry-house.

In 1707 Cornelius Sabring, the owner of a farm in what is now known as South Brooklyn and member of Assembly for Kings county from 1695 to 1726, and therefore a man naturally possessing much local influence, tried to get permission from Gov. Cornbury to establish a new ferry, and his request was backed up by quite a number of influential indorsers; but the New York corporation stubbornly contested what they regarded as a movement both "unreasonable and unjust," and their opposition prevailed. This claim at ownership of the Ferry was one that became the more bitterly contested by Brooklyn as time went on and more stubbornly upheld by New York as the income increased. Even in 1745 they denied the rights of residents of Brooklyn to cross the river in their own boats and so transporting friends, or produce, and when one of these boatmen, Hendrick Remsen, appealed to a jury to establish his claim to such an apparently inalienable privilege, the New York authorities contested the case bitterly. The jury before whom the action was tried found in Remsen's favor, and after a long interval the Supreme Court finally awarded him £118 14s 10 ½d for damages and costs. The New York corporation appealed the case to the King and Council, and somehow the matter there rested, for a final decision had not been rendered when the Revolutionary War broke out. It was alleged, however, that Remsen was quietly pacified with a gift of a house and parcel of land near Coenties Slip, in New York City. It is a matter of little interest now to go into all the details of the struggle against what used to be called the usurpation, by New York, of rights to the Long Island shore: it has no more interest to the reader of history at the present day than the disputes as to boundaries waged by some of the five Dutch towns so fiercely against each other; indeed, in a sense it was in reality simply another form of boundary dispute and as such has had its meaning, virtue, and force removed forever by the inexorable march of modern progress and the soothing influence of consolidation. The income from the ferry steadily advanced, and while we read of one or two of the lessees losing money it proved a steady source of revenue to the New York corporation. In 1750 it brought £455, and in 1753 £650.

"In May. 1766," writes Dr. Stiles ("History of Brooklyn" vol. III, page 527), "it passed into the hands of Samuel Waldron for five years at a yearly rent of £660, and in May, 1771, was renewer to him for another three years, at £550 per annum. At the expiration of his lease in 1774 it was determined by the corporation that three ferries, viz., one from Coenties Slip to the landing place of Messrs. Livingston & Remsen [foot of present Joralemon street: this ferry's buildings were burned during the Revolutionary War and it was then abandoned]; the second from Peck's Slip to land at Jacob Brewerton's wharf, or landing place, at Brooklyn ferry; and the third from the Fly Market (foot of Fulton street, New York) to the same landing place at the Brooklyn Ferry. Accordingly, on the 12th of April, 1774, three several leases were duly executed for the term of two years, viz., to Elisha De Grushe, for the first-named ferry, and to Samuel Balding for the second-named ferry, at an annual rent of £20, and to Adolph Waldron for the third at an annual rent of £430. * * * In May, 1776, the whole ferry came under the control of Adolph Waldron, for two years, at £450 per annum. Waldron, being a Whig, left New York with the American army in 1776 and did not return until the close of the war. During the British occupation of New York and Long Island the ferry was let by Mayor Matthew and Gov. Try on to two of their Tory friends. Van Winkle and Buckett, probably for their joint benefit. Van Winkle is described as a very important-feeling man, who was accustomed to walk about in a silk morning gown. They raised the fare to 6d, not so high a charge when we remember that wheat was then selling in New York at the ordinary rate of one guinea per bushel. After the evacuation Capt. Adolph Waldron, by a lease executed June 23. 1784, resumed the ferry for five years at the yearly rent of £500. During the severe winter of 1783-4 it is said that he and his sons made considerable money by purchasing wood in Brooklyn and selling it in New York, where it was quite scarce."

In 1789 Waldron tried to have his lease renewed, but the corporation thought more money could be made by leasing the ferry building and licensing a number of boats to carry passengers and freight across the river. In 1795 a ferry was established by the corporation between Main street, Brooklyn, to Catharine street, New York (long known as the New Ferry), and leased by William Furman and Theodosius Hunt, and with the mention of that transaction we may fittingly close this chapter.

# CHAPTER XXXI. BROOKLYN.

Close of the Revolution to the Incorporation of the Village — Preeminence of the Ferry — The Beginning of the Navy Yard.

In the chapters of this work dealing with the Battle of Brooklyn and the events antecedent and subsequent to that landmark in American history, the story of Brooklyn from the beginning of the Revolutionary movement until the British flag passed out of New York Harbor as an emblem of possession is fully told.

On March 7, 1788, Brooklyn was duly recognized by the State Government as a town, a proceeding which was virtually a confirmation of the old royalist charter by the new republican order of things. There is no doubt that the changes caused by the Revolution and British occupation and evacuation had caused much havoc in the town, had brought all its real business interests to a standstill and laid waste much of the property of its residents. Hence some time, after peace was restored, was occupied in putting matters in order, in counting up losses and calculating future chances. The fact that in 1785 a fire department was organized shows that the beginning, at least, of the upbuilding movement was not long delayed. That it had fairly recovered itself by 1800-1 was evident from the fact that the history of land-booming in Brooklyn was about that time inaugurated by the Sands brothers placing their once famous Olympia on the market, — a scheme which has already been fully detailed in this work. Quite a large accession to the population was received from the tide of Irish immigration, which had even then set in to this country.

A still more significant evidence was the establishment, in June 26, 1799, of the first newspaper ever printed in Brooklyn, "The Courier and New York and Long Island Advertiser," by Thomas Kirk, a bookseller and printer. It was not much of an effort, either in its literary or news aspects, its publication being prompted probably more to advertise its owner's business than anything else; but it was a beginning. It lasted some four years, issuing weekly from its office at the corner of Fulton and Front streets. Kirk was also the printer of the first book issued in Brooklyn, a pamphlet containing General Lee's oration on Washington, in 1800. In 1806 (May 26) the condition of the journalistic field in Brooklyn was tested by a new venture — "The Long Island Weekly Intelligencer," issued by Robinson & Little. On June 1, 1809, Kirk tried a fresh adventure, — "the Long Island Star;" but in 1811 he sold it to Alden F. Spooner, who may be regarded, if not as the real father of journalism in Brooklyn, as at least its first successful exponent.

It is not a little singular that the first great industry to feel the benefit of the new national progress in Brooklyn was that of shipping and shipbuilding. In 1788 the Sarah, belonging to the Sands brothers, opened the eyes of the local merchants to the advantages of Brooklyn as a port, and thereafter many larger vessels, mainly in the West India trade, began to lie up at her wharves, while the connection with the coastwise trade steadily increased. From the Ferry to the Wallabout many wharves were built well out into the stream so as to permit large vessels to dock. Warehouses were erected close to the water-front, and other commerce sprung up in the same section. In 1798 a large trading ship was built on its water-front and in 1799 the frigate John Adamis, thirty-two guns, was launched at the Wallabout, right in the territory now included in the United States Navy Yard.

In a directory for 1796 we find in addition to the usual array of grocers and what may be called domestic vendors and tavern-keepers, livery-stable men, loading houses and carpenters, shoemakers and other tradesmen and storekeepers, such industries represented as rope-making, chair-making, gunsmithing, also a land-broker, a master builder, a copperplate printer, a lumber merchant, a brewer and a dyer, showing that by that time Brooklyn was prepared to meet any requirement of the existing requirements of civilization. Later a floor-cloth factory and a cotton-goods mill were established. Other evidences of this civilization's requirement may be gleaned by the thoughtful from these facts: In 1806 the cage or watch-house was the object of consideration at a town meeting at which a regular night watch was organized, and in 1808 $1,500 was voted for the erection of a new poorhouse. In 1809 a visitation of yellow fever led to Brooklyn's being quarantined for a couple of months by New York, and in 1812 it was nearly wiped out by a fire which started on Main street, near the ferry.

The extent to which the yellow fever epidemic spread led to considerable feeling among the local physicians. With these professional healers the city was well supplied, and among them Drs. Ball, Wendell, Lowe and Osborne were probably as well equipped as any of their brethren in New York. Dr. Lowe, who was a brother of the Rev. Dr. Lowe of the Dutch Reformed Church, possibly had the largest private practice in the town for many years. In 1815, when there was an epidemic of smallpox, Drs. Ball and Wendell announced their willingness to vaccinate all who so desired free of any charge, that is, we take it, all who were too poor to pay a fee, thus forestalling one of the most beneficent provisions of our modern Boards of Health.

In 1811 the circle of practitioners of the healing art in Brooklyn received quite an -addition in the person of the "Rain Water Doctor," although he was never recognized as belonging to the circle. This curious charlatan, for charlatan he undoubtedly was, although he seemed to understand some matters of vital importance in combating disease better than his legitimate brethren, believed, or professed to believe, in the copious use of rain water as a remedial agent, and used a wide range of herbs in his treatment of diseases, believing them to be the natural correctives of all human ills. He seemed to have no faith whatever in what were commonly called drugs and was credited, according to popular Tumor, at all events, with effecting some remarkable cures. These stories quickly spread and attracted large throngs of patients to Brooklyn, not only from various parts of Long Island but from New York and New Jersey, and his headquarters at the Black Horse Tavern, where is now the junction of Fulton and De Kalb avenues, became thronged with patients. All reports agree that his charges were exceedingly moderate, and it was said he even returned large fees handed him by grateful patients who regarded themselves as cured of their ailments by his treatment. Nay, more, he even, it is said, placed a marble monument over the grave of one patient who had come to him too late for any earthly remedial methods to be effective. A wonderful physician, truly! But we fear that in the stories we have concerning him a good .deal of current rumor is dished up as solemn fact. He continued in Brooklyn for about a year (1811-12) and then, probably because his methods were becoming stale and trade was falling off, removed to Providence, R. I., where he died in 1815.

During the time covered in this section, too, a great change was taking place in Brooklyn, — the first of a series of similar changes which had often puzzled land speculators and set real-estate prices in a kaleidoscopic whirl. The center of trade was shifting from the plateau on which old Breuckelen itself stood down toward the Ferry. Around that spot there had long clustered a collection of taverns, but now houses of entertainment and business establishments of all kinds struggled to get as near to the foot of Fulton street as they possibly could. It was in the Ferry district that the new comers who were steadily increasing the population settled, and the overflow, instead of stretching back in the direction of the present City Hall, pressed along the water-front until it reached Catharine Ferry. It has been estimated that in 1815 three-fifths of the total population of Brooklyn lay between these two points. There were congregated the stores, and the professional men, while the rest of the town maintained its rural character. Old Breuckelen became, for a time, a suburb of the Ferry, just as were Bedford and Gowanus and Cripplebush and Red Hook. Even the most aristocratic dry-goods store was kept at the corner of Fulton and Front streets, and there Abraham Remsen discoursed of the latest fashions in gowns and bonnets, ribbons and laces, until the neighborhood itself began to become unfashionable. Remsen's establishment was the pioneer of the retail dry-goods business in Brooklyn, a business which now in point of magnitude is said to exceed that of Manhattan borough itself.

But while the Ferry district was thus predominant an event occurred during the time covered by this chapter which was destined not only to preserve the name of the Wallabout section but to keep it distinct and prosperous no matter what other changes might come. On the water-front of the bay was the shipbuilding establishment of John Jackson, surrounded by about a dozen houses where his workmen resided. He did a large, although somewhat intermittent business. In 1801 the United States Government bought Jackson's establishment and thirty acres of land, and thereon proceeded to lay out a navy yard. It is said that the price Uncle Sam paid for the property was $40,000. It was not until June 1, 1806, however, that the Government fairly commenced work on the land, for then Lieutenant Jonathan Thorn was appointed Commandant and began putting the place in order for its new mission. He was retained there only for a year, being succeeded July 13, 1807, by Capt. Isaac Chauncey, who continued in control until May, 1813, when he was ordered to the Great Lakes and there entered upon that series of naval maneuvers which made his flag ship, "The Pike," one of the best known boats in the American navy. Chauncey was followed at the Navy Yard by Capt. Samuel Evans, who held the office of Commandant until 1824. These three men were brilliant officers and have left enviable records in the Navy Department, and the annals of the country and their appointments show that from the first the government. fully appreciated the importance of its Brooklyn property. Lieut. Thorn was killed on the Oregon coast many years after he left Brooklyn while in command of one of John Jacob Astor's trading ships.

The war of 1812 found Brooklyn not only determined to resist any recurrence of British occupation but united in the desire to uphold the position of the country without regard to the poor politics which had rendered a recourse to arms necessary. The story of Brooklyn's share in that conflict (bloodless so far as. she was concerned) has already been told and can here be dismissed with this passing reference. But we may here be permitted to say that, worthless and needless as that war was in many respects, it was important in that it really united the country into one grand and actual Federation. Before it the states were little other than a union on paper; they formed a nation, it is true, but it was a nation only in name; but the events which followed the declaration of war in 1812 made them a nation in reality. Thereafter the Government at Washington was recognized as pre-eminent and the necessity for its solidity, strength and effectiveness was recognized even by the most virulent upholder of the theory of State sovereignty. Some of the lessons of the war were speedily forgotten, notably that of the necessity of a strong navy; but the imperative need of the central Government being powerful enough to meet every emergency and to direct the country amid the policies and jealousies of the nations of the world was never afterward lost sight of or ignored.

It was not until the middle of February, 1815, that the news that peace had been proclaimed reached Brooklyn, and as soon as the excusable paean of joy over that event was ended the town resumed its forward march, and the march seemed more blithesome than ever before. It was not all work and no play any longer; life was not taken so seriously as formerly; tea houses were opened in every direction; "gardens" where people could regale themselves with music, wine or beer in the open air were set out in all the main thoroughfares, the wharves took on new life and the market at the

Ferry, beside the great liberty pole, the grand emblem of what had been won, was a daily scene of business excitement. Every occupation appeared to "boom;" an "era of prosperity" had arrived, and looked as if it had settled down for a long stay; all the local horoscopes seemed to promise that the town had a bright future before it, and all that could be dreamed of as wanting was a form of local government which would work harmoniously and bring about quickly the best results. No time was lost, for in December, 1815, a meeting called to consider the advisability of seeking a charter of incorporation as a village. The sentiment at this meeting was so completely in favor of this step that a general meeting of the citizens was called, and at that gathering, Jan. 6, 1816, the matter was heartily indorsed and a committee was appointed to draft a bill for incorporation and present it to the Legislature. This committee comprised Thomas Everitt, Alden F. Spooner, Joshua Sands, John Doughty and the Rev. John Ireland. The bill was laid before the Legislature within a few weeks, on March 13 it passed the Senate and on April 12 the Assembly assented. The territory thus incorporated under a village government was described as "beginning at the Public Landing south of Pierrepont's Distillery, formerly the property of Philip Livingston deceased, on the East River; thence running along the Public Road leading from said Landing, to its intersection with Red Hook Lane; thence along said Red Hook Lane to where it intersects the Jamaica Turnpike Road; thence a northeast course to the head of the Wallaboght Millpond; thence through the center of the Millpond to the East River; and thence down the East River to the place of beginning." The village was to be governed by a board of five trustees, who with three assessors were to be elected by popular vote each year. The board, when elected, was to select its own officials. To facilitate matters the first trustees were named in the act, — Andrew Mercein, John Garrison, John Doughty, John Seaman and John Dean, and these held their first official meeting on May 4, 1816. That meeting may be said to mark the beginning of the modern history of Brooklyn.

# CHAPTER XXXIV. THE VILLAGE OF BROOKLYN.

It will have been noticed that what was incorporated as the Village of Brooklyn formed in reality only a portion of what had been grouped together as the town, and comprised little more than what formerly used to be spoken of as "the Ferry." It even left outside in the cold the old Breuckelen itself; and the Wallabout and Bed-, ford and the rest of the suburbs of the old Dutch town were permitted to get along as best they might. The trade was concentrated round the Ferry district, the population concentrated there, and from there the expansion was destined to flow that was to bring all the scattered sections under one rule again, that was once more to link all their fortunes together. But while the Village of Brooklyn was thus only a part of the whole, it was the part in which local history was made for the eighteen years during which the village charter remained in force.

Yet to all of what afterward became the extended city of Brooklyn the forces then at work in the village were big with import, for on the progress there made depended ultimately the welfare of all the other sections. It was as if the sturdiest brother of a family assumed the care and responsibility of the interests of all the rest, and started out to win enough capital which, if wisely garnered, would in time benefit him and equally all the others. During these eighteen years, therefore, while we speak of Brooklyn, we have to forget the other members of the family and think only of the old section close to the East River, which had come to the front and was making such a bid for position and wealth.

How the new departure aided in the prosperity of the place may be understood from the fact that while in 1816 the population of Brooklyn was 4,402, by 1820 it had increased to 7,475, and most of this increase was counted within the limits of the incorporated village, for outside of it there was very little to attract new-comers. By 1825 the figures had increased to 10,791, and by 1830 to 15,295; but by that date the ferry district had really overflown its old limits and was making its own prosperity felt all over the old town.

In 1818 the incorporated village was surveyed and sign-posts were erected on the various street corners. Sands street, which was then a fashionable thoroughfare, was paved in 1822, and Fulton street was provided with a sidewalk, both of these being regarded as wonderful improvements. The year 1824, however, witnessed the outbreak of a desire for public improvements, somewhat astonishing in its scope and intensity. Streets were graded and improved in all directions, a new market was built, the fire department was nearly doubled and new buildings began to rise all over the village, generally of a more pretentious style,' architecturally speaking, than those which had hitherto contented the citizens. The streets, too, were kept clean by dint of a series of local ordinances, and the night watch was strengthened and made more effective than ever. It is said that no fewer than 164 new buildings were erected within the village during that year. A Board of Health was also then organized. In 1825 a stone walk had been laid from the Ferry to Water street, and the comfort of this caused a general desire for the introduction of such sidewalks on all the principal streets. The people had really begun to take a pride in their city and also had acquired wealth enough to pay for the improvements they desired without inciting any more than the average amount of grumbling which is the inherent right of every taxpayer.

Certainly trade was most prosperous during these years of the village regime. Every season seemed to find a "new industry added, and all the while the old ones were strengthened. The shipping industry made particularly rapid strides and an evidence of this is found in the fact that in 1823 the United, States customs authorities erected on the water-front near the foot of Cranberry street a three-story warehouse, — an immense structure for those days. On July 1, 1824, there were moored to the village wharves, by the count of a local statistician, eight full-rigged ships, 16 brigs, 20 schooners and 12 sloops, altogether representing a great amount of trade and commerce. In 1828 Dr. Stiles tells us the village contained "seven churches, eight rope-walks, seven distilleries, two chain-cable manufactories, two tanneries, two extensive white-lead manufactories, one glass factory, one floor-cloth ditto, one card ditto, one pocket-book ditto, one comb ditto, one seal-skin ditto, seven tide and two wind-mills, an extensive establishment for the preparation of drugs, and articles required for dyeing and manufacturing, conducted by Dr. Noyes, late professor of Hamilton College, seventy grocery and dry-goods stores, two printing establishments, lumber and wood-yards, master masons and carpenters. The rope-walks manufactured 1,130 tons of cordage, annually at an expenditure of $260,000, and employed 200 persons. The distilleries consumed, on an average, 780 bushels of grain per day, at an expense of $368,200 per annum. The sealskin factory employed 60 men; pocket-book factory, 40 persons; comb factory, 20; the card factory, 300 persons; and other branches in all 400 to 500 persons. Immense quantities of naval stores, hemp, cotton, India goods, hides, provisions and lumber, were stored at Brooklyn."

The reason for so much naval stores being in Brooklyn lay in the fact that the Government was beginning to make full use of its property .it the Wallabout. In 1817 work was commenced on the line ship Ohio, and it was launched May 30, 1820. In 1820 the then Secretary of the Navy (Samuel L. Southard of New Jersey) recommended that a navy yard of the first class should be established on the Wallabout property, and as the recommendation was adopted the work was begun of putting the place in serviceable condition. Capt. Isaac Chauncey was again placed in charge and so continued until 1833. Under him the property was enclosed and an earnest of its future importance was given in the order for the construction of the sloop of war Vincennes, which was launched April 25, 1826, followed by the building of three other sloops, — the Lexington, the Fairfield and the Peacock, an armed schooner — the Enterprise — and the revenue cutter Morris. All these were constructed during the continuance of Brooklyn's village charter, and incidentally helped considerably also in the upward movement of. the municipality. It should be mentioned that another vessel, the Fulton, the first steam warship, was built at the Wallabout by the Government in 1815 from plans prepared by Robert Fulton himself; but she never proved of any value and exploded while lying at anchor, in 1829, causing a loss of forty-eight lives. The Wallabout never returned to the jurisdiction of Brooklyn, and so when the time of reorganization came a certain amount of territory, a town within itself in fact, was lost to the city; but the benefit of the establishment of the navy yard to Brooklyn has been more than can easily be estimated.

The year 1824, besides being memorable for its internal improvements, is deserving of being prominently remembered in local annals for many other reasons, and the most notable of these was, perhaps, the establishment of the first bank, — The Long Island Bank, with Leffert Lefferts, Jehiel Jagger, John C. Freecke, John Vanderveer, Jordan Coles, Silas Butler, Fanning C. Tucker, Jacob Hicks, Henry Waring, Nehemiah Denton, Elkanah Doolittle, Thomas Everitt, Jr., and George Little as its first directors. An insurance company, "The Brooklyn Fire," was also established in 1824. Before the city charter was issued several other banks were organized and the increase of such institutions amply demonstrates the steady rise of the local and general business interests.

But wealth does not obliterate misery and we are reminded that even in those prosperous times the poor in Brooklyn asserted themselves. On March 30, 1824, there were in the almshouse 11 men, 16 women, 5 girls and 8 boys — a total of 40; and during the winter of that year ninety-three loads of wood were distributed from the institution among the poor throughout the village. The need for enlarged facilities for poorhouse purposes were then so apparent that some nineteen acres of land near Fort Greene were purchased from Leffert Lefferts, for $3,750, on which to erect a new shelter for those who fell by the wayside, by poverty, disaster or disease, in the struggle for existence. This property was outside the village limits, lint it was proposed to erect on it a building sufficient to meet the needs of the whole of the old town. The establishment of a poor farm in 1830 at Flatbush helped to lessen the extent of the village expenditure for the poor, as it removed from its care what might be called county cases, cases which should hardly have been thrown upon the people of the village at all.

While spending money lavishly for the development and improvement of the village, it is amusing to read in how simple and unpretentious a fashion the Trustees, the City Fathers of the day, conducted its business. They held their meetings in a room over a grocery store within a few yards of the entrance to "the Ferry," and while the meetings were on public business the

Trustees declined to allow a newspaper reporter to be present or even to permit the minutes of their meetings to be copied for publication. What was done, however, was readily learned, the refusal of the minutes being due more to a sense of official dignity than anything else. They seem to have been a jolly lot of mortals, these early trustees, and conducted their proceedings on a conversational rather than an oratorical basis, and so got through with the consideration of any knotty point more quickly than through formal speeches had been the rule. Probably, not being lost in rhetorical fogs, they appreciated each detail clearly. They also understood each other better, and to help this understanding it was their custom, as soon as the meeting was called to order, to send for a supply of bread or biscuits and cheese and a bottle or two of brandy or gin, and then proceed to business. At the end of their official term they enjoyed an oyster supper and pledged each other heartily. All this, it should be noticed, was done at their own expense, the modern official junketer had not been evolved.

Under such auspices the village flourished and even acquired a measure of fame. It was not forgetful in the higher things that make for the good of a community and give it character. In 1823 what was known as the Apprentices' Library was organized with the view of supplying reading matter for apprentice mechanics and in fact working people of all classes. Within a year this library had a collection of some 1,200 volumes, all presented by citizens, and 100 regular readers. It proved such a success that in 1825 a new building was erected for it in Cranberry street, and there in 1826 the Board of Village Trustees removed their meetings, although whether the conveniences for cracken and cheese and drinkables were as accessible as at "the Ferry," history is silent. The cornerstone of the library was laid on July 4, 1825, by the Marquis de Lafayette, then on his memorable tour through the country for which he had fought in the days when it was struggling for existence. Up to Lafayette's visit, Brooklyn had not been much disturbed by the sojourn of great men in its midst. It had seen Washington in war and welcomed him in peace. President Monroe crossed to Brooklyn in June, 1817, and two years or so later Andrew Jackson paid it a flying visit, although on what particular business the Hero of New Orleans crossed the East River we have no means of accurately knowing. Talleyrand lived in Brooklyn for some time, and so did Tom Paine, the agnostic. These were all the great men — the men of National fame — who had walked through Brooklyn since its famous battle until the appearance of Lafayette, and that the illustrious veteran received an ovation goes without saying.

An admirable picture of how Brooklyn looked in 1820 has been preserved for us on the canvas painted in 1820 and representing a part of the city in its winter dress. The picture is now in the Brooklyn Institute. The painter, Francis Guy, was a native of England, who came here in 1796. After many vicissitudes he settled in Brooklyn in 1817 and devoted himself to landscape painting. As might readily be understood, he did not prosper exceedingly, the taste of Brooklyn not having by that time reached such a stage as to care for art for art's sake. Guy was reckless in money matters and had other failings, which prevented his gathering and keeping much of this world's goods, and he died in poverty in August, 1820. His widow sold sixty-two of his landscape paintings at public auction in New York and realized thereby $1,295.50. The bit of Brooklyn represented in the "snow scene" lay just before the windows of his house, 11 Front street, and the figures introduced were all drawn from life from among the artist's neighbors. The canvas was exhibited in Brooklyn as soon as it was completed, and for the correctness of its drawing and its characteristic portraits was pronounced a masterpiece by the local connoisseurs, who must be regarded as the best judges of the value of such a work as a reproduction of a scene with which they were familiar. The picture has been often engraved, but gives so clear an idea of the place represented at the time that it is here reproduced, along with a keyplate, which was printed in Dr. Stiles' "History of Brooklyn."

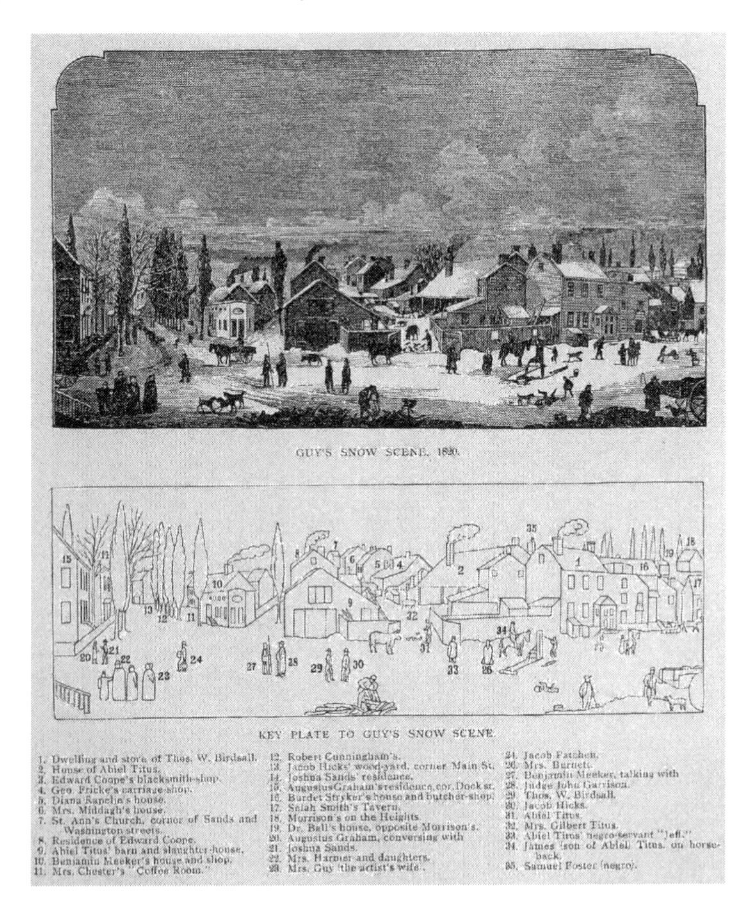

GUY'S SNOW SCENE, 1820.

KEY PLATE TO GUY'S SNOW SCENE.

The church influence in Brooklyn was steadily extending itself during the period now under review and so far as educational facilities went there was no lack of opportunities for the young American to grow up with all the advantages of a liberal training. There were, even before the village was organized, private schools in abundance, and in 1813 a number of ladies organized what they called the Louisian Seminary, where, free of cost, poor children were to be instructed in reading, writing and arithmetic, and in addition the girl pupils were to be taught such practical accomplishments as knitting and sewing. This establishment was really the beginning of the free educational 'system of Brooklyn. The Louisian school was a success much more emphatic than its projectors had anticipated and the claims upon its facilities soon threatened to swamp, by their very extent, the well thought out scheme of the ladies. In 1816, as a result of this experience, a public meeting was held with the view of bringing about a free public school. This was agreed to and the Louisian school was taken over under the new movement and the ladies were released from their embarrassing position with regard to it. A frame building was erected for the use of this free school on the corner of Concord and Adams streets, and the cost was defrayed by a tax. Pupils whose parents or guardians could pay for their tuition were expected to contribute to the support of the institution, but to others its advantages were free. In 1829 a Collegiate Institute for young ladies was opened' on Hicks street; but it did not prove a success. It was a step in the right direction, but the stride was too long for the time. In 1816 a Sunday school was opened in Brooklyn. It was mainly for negroes and seems to have been secular as well as religious in its aim; but bit by bit the secular features were eliminated and the movement grew so rapidly that when, in 1829, the Kings County Sabbath-school Union was formed, it had jurisdiction over no fewer than twenty-three schools.

Another movement for social betterment was inaugurated in 1829, when a temperance society was established. The old hard and deep drinking habits had by that time lost their hold upon the community, excessive indulgence was no longer fashionable, and drunkenness was not even regarded as excusable. Yet in that year, with a population of some 12,000, Brooklyn had 160 places where intoxicating liquor was sold at retail. Little wonder that a temperance wave set in and an effort made at improvement, of which the Temperance Society was one of the weapons. The movement had markedly a successful result, for by 1835, when the population had increased to 24,310, the number of retail liquor establishments had decreased to fifty.

While so much progress was going on it is disappointing to be obliged to chronicle the fact that Brooklyn lost a chance of one magnificent improvement in 1826, which, had it been carried out, would to-day have placed her in possession of a most valuable piece of property, almost unique for its beauty and usefulness. This was the rejection of the suggestion of H.

B. Pierrepont and others that the lands on the heights overlooking the bay should be bought by the city and converted into a public park. The lands were then used for agricultural purposes, when they were used at all, and as it was not thought possible that they could ever be utilized for building purposes they might have been secured at a comparatively trifling cost. But the opportunity was lost. The public took, apparently, no interest in the matter. The value of public parks was not then clearly understood, and even many who favored such a park thought that the land indicated was too difficult of access ever to become of much use to the people.

Another matter to be deplored is the apparent ease with which, in spite of the excellence of the local physicians, the watchfulness of the Board of Health and the evident effort at local cleanliness, imported diseases played sad havoc in the village. In 1822, as in 1803 and 1809, there was an outbreak of yellow fever, when nineteen cases were reported, of which ten proved fatal. The disease, however, was confined to the neighborhood of Furman street, where it was first noticed. In 1832 cholera made its appearance and from June 20 until July 25, when it was reported as stamped out, there were ninety-five cases, thirty-five of which terminated fatally. The cholera, however, at that time was on one of its apparently periodic rounds and New York and other cities suffered terribly. In these circumstances it was thought unlikely that Brooklyn should escape. Indeed, but for the excellence of its medical service the mortality list would have shown sadder figures.

When the prosperity of the village seemed assured and everything bespoke a glowing future, it was inevitable that a great rise should take place in the value of its lands and that the inevitable speculator should take advantage of this to boom sales and create on the solid substratum of actual success and need a fictitious value and speculative demand. In our favorite year of 1824 the real estate within the bounds of the village was assessed at $2,111,390; and building lots contiguous to the old Ferry, when they came into the market, brought fancy prices. In 1826 Dr. Evans successfully turned one of the heights. Mount Prospect, into a private residence reserve. Within it he erected several cottages and laid out the grounds around them with such taste that the place became one of the most attractive in Brooklyn. Although almost three miles from the ferry, lots around this improvement so quickly advanced in price as to be significant of the impending change. In 1833 a land mania, or something akin to it, set in and values advanced almost daily. The rise was by no means confined to the village: all parts of the old town felt the change. A piece of land used as a pleasure resort (The Parmentier Garden) at the junction of the Jamaica and Flatbush roads was purchased for $57,000 and at once surveyed, cut up into lots and sold at auction for some $70,000. A farm at Gowanus of twenty-six acres brought $25,000 at auction, and ten acres at Red Hook realized $47,000. A couple of speculators from New York bought a farm and laid out on it a wide avenue, intending to restrict it to private residences of the best class. The lots were large (80 x 100 feet) and the venture seemed a dangerous one, but its complete success was assured when, in 1835, Trinity Church (now St. Luke's) was erected upon it. Now, as Clinton avenue, it ranks as one of the most beautiful and fashionable of the residential sections of Brooklyn. Even some of the remote, outlying sections of the old town had begun to feel the prosperity of the village and to share it. .A new settlement sprung up on the old Cripplebush road, and along what is now Flushing avenue many houses were being erected, generally in small colonies convenient to ropewalks or other works, while the employees of the navy yard, at times, needed more house accommodation than could readily be found. On the other side of the Ferry improvements even began to assert themselves on the heights, — the territory deemed absolutely useless but a few years before, — while further away lay another settlement, for which in 1833 a new water route to New York was opened almost at the foot of the slope, and to this was given the name of South Ferry. In fact it was seen that the village had burst through its legal boundaries and was pressing out into the old township in every direction, and the conditions which resulted from all this expansion slowly but surely became the reverse of satisfactory in various important respects. It had early been seen in the history of the village that it was laboring under some of these disadvantages: it was apparent even then that its boundaries were too circumscribed and its municipal powers too limited, and in 1825 a public meeting was called to consider the advisability of applying to the legislature at Albany for a city charter. But matters were not then ready for that, and the meeting voted against such an innovation, much to the chagrin of the promoters, who thereupon duly adjourned the meeting, and with it, as they thought, the project, for twenty-one years.

In the following year the legislature passed several acts amendatory of the government of villages and under the provisions of one of these Brooklyn elected ten trustees instead of five, without, however, any further real or supposed benefit to the community than the exaltation of five more citizens into places of honor; but even this did not silence the movement which was making steadily for a change. In 1833 the movement for increased local powers had increased so far that a bill was introduced in the Legislature for the incorporation of the City of Brooklyn, and though it passed the Assembly it was killed in the upper house. There seems to be no doubt that the influence of New York City was inflexibly directed against any attempt to create a strong municipality on the opposite shore of the East River from Manhattan Island. It is difficult to understand nowadays why such should have been the case, but unfortunately the sentiment of opposition existed. There is no room for doubt on that point. Possibly the idea that a city should have something more to say with regard to ferry rights and perquisites than was possible for a village, had much to do with it. But there were other and more valid reasons. The ease with which Brooklyn could be reached from the then heart of New York's business and manufacturing districts aroused the fear of the real-estate manipulators on Manhattan Island, and it was inevitable even to the sodden brains of the New York Aldermen of the period, that if Brooklyn should become the city of homes — homes of New Yorkers — another big drop in tax receipts would be the inevitable result. New York could only grow in one direction — northward — and the journey thither was slow and uncertain, even in the best of weather, while a pleasant trip by ferry landed the dwellers in Brooklyn, within a short ride of pleasant, semi-rural streets, where comfortable homes could await them. Then in all such matters as shore and river jurisdiction a city government might speak with greater emphasis than could the trustees of a village or the representatives of half a dozen sleepy and forgotten little communities, mainly agricultural. So bitter was the opposition, so pressing became the need for a change, that, despairing of bringing about the improvement in any other way, at one time a proposition was actually broached that instead of seeking a separate charter Brooklyn should ask for annexation to New York! That notion did not find much favor, however. It was not only humiliating to the local feeling of civic pride that had sprung up, but it was felt that the river itself furnished a barrier that could not be crossed even by an act of Legislature; that nature's boundary line could not be obliterated.

So the agitation for a new charter was kept up with unflagging interest, and, at last, by an act which passed all the usual legislative perils, the struggle was won and Brooklyn became a city on April 10, 1834. The charter was a most comprehensive document and brought together again under one government the scattered sections of the old town of Brooklyn. It divided the city into nine wards. The first included the famous Ferry district, which had created the modern Brooklyn and had been the legal village for some eighteen years; the second embraced what had been Olympia and to it was also given the New (Catharine) Ferry; the third was the old Breukelen; the fourth was another part of the village territory; the fifth lay around the Wallabout; the sixth extended to Red Hook; the seventh contained Cripplebush and Bedford; the eighth reached to Gowanus; while the ninth carried the line of the city cult to the territory which belonged to Flatbush. It was a comprehensive scheme, compact and well thought out. So far as could be seen' it fully met all passing needs and promised plenty of scope for the future, and in its possession Brooklyn rejoiced except for the grip which New York still managed to retain on her ferry system and its feudal hold upon the river which washed with equal impartiality the shores of Long Island and of Manhattan.

The ferry interests had yearly been assuming greater proportions. When we last referred to their history they formed quite a respectable item in the resources of the old city of New York and they had been steadily growing. For some years the Old Ferry and the New had shared the business, but the yellow fever epidemic of 1809 having its seat near the Brooklyn termini of these two water routes, a change was made and a ferry established between Joralemon street, Brooklyn, to Whitehall street, New York. This inconvenient arrangement was abandoned as soon as public confidence was restored and we hear of no more ferry changes until 1817, when a boat was run between Little street, Brooklyn, and Walnut (now Jackson) street. New York. This was never a popular route and was abandoned about 1850.

Prior to 1814 the means of transit across the river were sail or row boats, the journey was long and the wind and tide and ice and snow played sad havoc very frequently with the time and tempers of the travelers. Then even in the best of times, the trip was too often uncomfortable, for the passengers were mixed up with cattle, sheep, garden and farm produce and all and sundry sorts of baggage. The ferrymen generally tried to wait for a full load before starting and that meant time wasted at the ferry house, which, however profitable it might be to the tavern nearby, was not conducive to the equanimity of the wayfarer. Then when the weather was rough or "thick" it was impossible to say when or where the voyage might end. Perhaps the current would force the boat up to Hellgate and run it ashore on Astoria, or it might be forced into a contrary direction and give one a close look at Governor's Island or effect a landing finally at Red Hook instead of Manhattan Island. Upsets were of frequent occurrence. Sometimes a horse took it into his head to suddenly change his position and so caused the loaded boat to keel over; sometimes a number of sheep played the game of "follow your leader" into the river and the effort to stop them brought about disaster. Drunken boatmen were often the cause of serious accidents, and if we can credit the newspaper reports and current gossip a boatman who was not rude and unmannerly was unknown. We are, however, inclined to disbelieve in another piece of current gossip, which had it that whenever a Long Island man made the voyage to New York (apart from dwellers at the Ferry) he invariably made his will, adjusted all his earthly affairs, and set out amid the tears and prayers of his household and friends!

In 1813, after having successfully operated two steam-ferry services between the New York and New Jersey shores, Robert Fulton made the corporation of New York the offer of a similar service between that city and Brooklyn, and on January 24, 1814, the negotiations were settled and a lease signed giving control of the ferry between "Old Ferry, Brooklyn," and Beekman's slip. New York (the previous landing place had been at the Fly Market), for twenty-five years to Robert Fulton and William Cutting. They were to pay an annual rental of $4,000 for the first eighteen years of the term, and $4,500 for the remainder, and on or before the 24th of May following, they were to place a steamboat on the route to run daily every half hour from sunrise until sunset and in addition were to run the full complement of barges as then was in the service. It was provided that a second steamboat was to be placed on the route by May, 1819. Under the lease the rates of ferriage were to be increased, and when this part of the arrangement became known there was a furious outcry in Brooklyn. A town meeting was held to protest against the increase, and New York City was roundly denounced. A remonstrance to the corporation of the latter produced no effect, an offer on behalf of Brooklyn to lease the ferry on the same terms and run it at the old rates was promptly rejected, and finally an appeal was drawn up and forwarded to the Legislature. Somehow the document mysteriously failed to reach that august body. In the midst of all the din, Messrs. Fulton and Cutting pushed ahead with their plans, organized "The New York and Brooklyn Steamboat Ferry Association," and on May 10, 1814, the first steam ferry-boat on the East River, the Nassau, commenced operations, making some forty trips during the day. The innovation was regarded on all sides as a complete triumph. Fulton did not long enjoy the success of this experiment, for he was laid to rest in the Livingston vault in Trinity churchyard in 1815, and his partner, Cutting, died in 1821.

It was but a short time before the service proved inadequate and a demand for increased carrying capacity arose. Instead of the additional steamboat a horse-boat (the machinery propelled by horse power instead of steam) was provided in 1818, when the fare was fixed at four cents a trip for either steam or horse boat, with certain commuting privileges. A horse boat had also been established at the New (Catharine) Ferry, but there, as soon afterward at the Old Ferry, it was found to prove an expensive arrangement, and the introduction of steam all round became merely a question of time. Even when the long-looked-for second steamboat was added it did not meet all the requirements, and the establishment, in 1836, of a new service at the South Ferry did little to relieve the business at the foot of Fulton street. Improvements were slow, feeble and paltry, and although it had long been urged, it was not until September 28. 1827, that an all-night service was introduced. The great trouble was that the stockholders were not united under any directing head or animated with any real view of accommodating the public interests, especially the interests of Brooklyn, which were those most concerned in the development of the ferry service. To remedy this, if possible, most of the stock was purchased in 1835 by a committee of Brooklyn capitalists, who intended to run the Fulton and South ferries until the expiration of the current leases on both in 1839, so as to promote the interests of their own city. The committee did their best and accomplished much in the way of improvement, but lost money by their public spirit. When the time came for the leases to be renewed it was felt that the only way out of the difficulty, and the only way which the interests of Brooklyn would be conserved, was by the formation of a new company of citizens, who should run both ferries on a business basis and at the same time with an eye to the wants and requirements of their own city. The company was formed and a lease signed on May 3, 1839, giving the New York & Brooklyn Ferry Company a lease of the water routes for five years, at an annual rental of $12,000, and, under other financial restrictions and stipulations, which were soon found to be very oppressive.

# CHAPTER XXXV. THE FIRST CITY

The act constituting the City of Brooklyn went into effect April 10, 1834, and the elevation of the old town occasioned at first much rejoicing all over its territory, and some of it found expression on April 25 in a grand procession, which wended its way through a number of the principal streets, and the inevitable oration, which was delivered in the First Presbyterian Church, in Orange street (on the present site of Plymouth Church), by William Rockwell. There was every reason for pride in the new municipality. It covered an extent of territory nearly twelve miles square, with thirty-five miles of streets, had a population of 27,854, twenty churches, three business and one savings banks, two markets, efficient fire and police departments and all the accessories of a well governed and progressive city, a clearly defined future, a host of public-spirited citizens and an ambition to press onward. Its people loved the city, honored its past and revered its memories. It was of course but as a village yet compared with New York, but then it possessed, what its big neighbor did not possess until many years afterward, a sense of civic pride. Still there were a few pessimistic people, mainly those living in the outlying parts of the old town, and who had escaped the modernizing influences at work all around them. The village of Brooklyn, among the other modern improvements, brought as one of its contributions to the new city what seemed to many of the simple country farmers like an unsurmountable load of debt, $22,000, and a lawsuit involving about as much more. The rest of the component parts of the new city had not only steered clear of such an appendage, but had brought to the new partnership some valuable real estate. The city, of course, had to assume the village indebtedness and it was felt by those pessimistically inclined that this was a theme for mourning. The simple-minded Dutch farmers had not become civilized enough to "regard a public debt as a blessing," nor did they appreciate any system of financiering that was not based on hard cash. But they soon had their eyes opened: their education was not long delayed. The first election for aldermen was held on May 5, and so far as we can see it was conducted strictly on local issues and with an eye to facilitating the business of the new community rather, as is so common nowadays, than with any ulterior views as to the relation of the candidate to state or national politic. The result was the return of the following:

1st ward — Gabriel Furman, Conklin Brush.
2d ward — George D. Cunningham, John M. Hicks.
3d ward — James Walters, Joseph Moser.
4th ward — Jonathan Trotter, Adrian Hegeman.
5th ward — William M. Udall, Benjamin R. Prince.
6th ward — Samuel Smith, William Powers.
7th ward — Clarence D. Sackett, Stephen Haynes.
8th ward — Theodoras Polhemus, John S. Bergen.

9th ward — Robert Wilson, Moses Smith.

It is questionable if Brooklyn in all her history from then until now, ever rejoiced in a really abler or more thoroughly representative body of City Fathers. They were all men of standing in their respective communities, most of them were men of substantial means and wide business interests and all had considerable influence in local affairs. They were animated by a single desire to promote the welfare of the new municipality, and they set about doing it at once and to the best of their ability. We cannot agree with all that this first Board of Aldermen did, but that its members were devoted with rare honesty of purpose and strict fidelity to the prosperity of the young city and of their constituents, is beyond question.

The first and most emphatic evidence of this occurred on their opening meeting, where they elected George Hall as first Mayor of Brooklyn. No man in Kings county had a more intimate acquaintance with local affairs or more practical experience in their administration. He had served as a trustee of the old village and was its last President, holding that office when the law which brought the city into being went into effect. Born in New York, September 21, 1795, of Irish parents, he grew up an American among Americans, and in time became one of the local leaders of the old Know-Nothing party, a party whose merits have been forgotten in the modern unscrupulous rush for "votes." Whatever opinions he held he never concealed, and he followed the line of policy he deemed the best with the utmost zeal, regardless of personal consequences. A thoroughly brave man, as his work during the cholera epidemic showed, he had the courage of his convictions in all his public doings. He was a stanch advocate of teetotalism and was especially proud of having been the first man in Brooklyn to sign a temperance pledge. So determined was his aversion to intoxicating liquor that he refused to swallow a little on his dying bed, even when it was prescribed by his physician. That was a characteristic trait of the man. No one could be more determined than he upon any point after he believed it to be right. Nor was any man more generous. In business life he acquired more than a fair measure of success, yet his charities kept him poor. He was always giving, and giving in such a way that no one, not even himself, knew the extent of his bounty. In all local institutions for helping the poor, the distressed, or encouraging youth, or promoting the welfare of the people, he was for years a foremost figure. His administration of the first mayoral term of Brooklyn was a successful one in every way, and he was a candidate for the office in 1844 and again in 1845, but went down each time with, his ticket. In 1854, when Brooklyn, Williamsburgh and Bushwick were consolidated, he was the successful candidate for the votes of the united territory, and so became the first Mayor again in another chapter of Brooklyn's history. In 1861 he was the Republican candidate for the office of Registrar, but was defeated, and after that took no active part in politics and spent his days quietly at the home which many years before had been presented to him by his fellow citizens, at 37 Livingston Place. There he died April 16, 1868, regretted by the entire community, and the funeral oration was delivered by Henry Ward Beecher, who well knew and thoroughly appreciated the many sterling qualities of him who had served Brooklyn so faithfully and so long. Mr. Beecher on this occasion made one of his most eloquent public utterances, one of those addresses which won for him praise as a citizen, apart from his eminence in the pulpit.

The other Mayors elected during this section of our history were:

Jonathan Trotter 1835-1836
Jeremiah Johnson 1837-1838
Cyrus P. Smith 1839-1841
Henry C. Murphy 1842
Joseph Sprague 1843-1844
Thomas G. Talmadge 1845
Francis B. Stryker 1846-1848
Edward Copeland 1849
Samuel Smith 1850
Conklin Brush 1851-1852
Edward A. Lambert 1853-1854

The Mayors were chosen by the Aldermen until 1840, when a new act of the Legislature gave the people the privilege of electing their local chief executive, and so Mayor Cyrus P. Smith entered upon his second term under really popular auspices. Most of these men were of more than ordinary ability and fully deserved the pre-eminence they received at the hands of their fellow citizens. Only three of them — Johnson, Murphy and Stryker — were natives of Brooklyn. Samuel Smith was a native Long Islander. Trotter was born in England, and the others hailed from various parts of the Union. Trotter was a leather dresser and acquired considerable means, but was "caught" in the financial panic of 1837 and compelled to retire from politics to build up anew his business connections, and so continued until his death, in 1865. Of the long and varied career of Mayor Johnson full details have already been given. Mayor C. P. Smith was essentially a self-made man, and was graduated from Dartmouth College in 1824, after paying his way through its classes with his own earnings. He then studied law and settled in Brooklyn, in 1837, where he quickly built up a splendid practice. From 1835 until he was chosen as Mayor he was the city's Corporation Counsel. The chief feature of his whole career was, however, his devotion to the cause of popular education, and he was connected with the Board of Education for thirty years, during twenty-one of which he presided over its deliberations.

Joseph Sprague, who was elected Mayor in 1843, was a native of Leicester, Massachusetts, and he led a rather adventuresome and disappointing business life until, in 1811, he married a member of the Debevoise family and settled at Bedford, Brooklyn. He made considerable money during the war of 1812.

From that time he became prominently identified with Brooklyn and was President of the village from 1827 to 1832. He was one of those who secured a charter for the Long Island Bank and was one of the founders of the Long Island Insurance Company. In 1834 he was chosen President of the Long Island Insurance Company and carried that institution safely through the panic of 1837. As Mayor he worked incessantly and honestly for the welfare of Brooklyn, and although at first he encountered strong opposition from those hostile to him in politics his sterling honesty and high administrative qualities slowly but surely overcame all factious opposition, while his action in causing the arrest of several members of the Board of Aldermen for misdemeanor, based on their neglect of public business, demonstrated to all concerned that though a man of placid. Christian character, he was not to be trifled with. He was, almost from the beginning of his connection with Brooklyn, a worker on behalf of its religious interests, and was one of those who, in 1822, founded the First Presbyterian Church. He was also prominent in Masonic circles and in 1826 was elected Master of Hohenlinden Lodge, No. 56. He was re-elected Mayor in 1844 and may be said to have continued in public life until his death, December 12, 1854.

T. G. Talmadge, who was elected Mayor in 1845, was a native of New Jersey who settled in Brooklyn in 1840 and at once, seemingly, became prominent in its public life. Although successful as a business man, he was a politician clear through, a Democrat "dyed-in-the-wool," as they used to say, and he carried his political ideas — his party dogmas and cries — into everything he said or did. He took a most active interest in the development of the Gowanus district, in which he held considerable property and developed an enlightened public policy as President of the Broadway Railroad Company. He acquired much influence in the national councils of his party, being at one time chairman of its General Committee, but he was not called upon to hold any elective position outside of Brooklyn, and he died there May 4, 1863. At the election for Mayor, in 1846, Talmadge was again a candidate, but was defeated by his Whig opponent, Francis Burdett Stryker.

Stryker was a worthy, but at the same time a curious, product of American political life. When he received the mayoralty nomination he was working as a journeyman carpenter, but had previously held the elective office of Sheriff, showing that he had built up a strong following among the people. He was re-elected Mayor in 1847, and again in 1848, each time in face of strong opposition; and although his administration of the office could not be called brilliant it was eminently safe, while his practical knowledge of the wants of the people and his devotion to them in many trying times won him hosts of supporters, independent of party. Yet he was a strict party man at all times, and every office he held came to him as a reward for his political zeal and as a result of his political influence.

His successor in the Mayoralty, in 1849, was also a zealous Whig, Edward Copeland. He was a graduate of Columbia College, a scholar, a good business man, and a safe administrative official. For many years he was a member of the Board of Education and it was probably in connection with that body his best work was done. He was succeeded as Mayor by a Democrat, Samuel Smith, who, however, only served from April, 1850, to the close of that year, an amendment to the city charter making subsequent official terms begin with the calendar year. His opponent for the civic prize was J. S. T. Stranahan, whom he defeated only by some 300 votes. Stranahan was at that time comparatively a stranger in Brooklyn. Smith belonged to an old Long Island family, and had carried a musket during the War of 1812 as a member of the Washington Fusiliers. Originally a cooper by trade, Smith had managed to acquire some real estate near what is now Fulton street, afterward added to it by extensive purchases around the present Schermerhorn and Smith streets, and went into farming to hold his property together, and earn his living and pay his taxes while waiting for the rise in value, which he saw was inevitable. When it came he found himself wealthy, and all through his life he continued to be a shrewd but honest dealer in Brooklyn real estate. He was elected Mayor with the view of introducing economy in local affairs, and this he certainly succeeded in accomplishing, as far as his limited term of service gave him opportunity.

The whirligig of politics at the following election gave him a Whig successor, in Conklin Brush, who held the Mayor's office for two years, and also gave the city a good business administration. To his exertions and business instinct Brooklyn was largely indebted for the successful establishment of the Atlantic Docks, of which he was elected a Director at the formation of the company, in 1840; and as President of the Mechanics' Bank, of Brooklyn, he judiciously used the resources of that institution in furthering the commercial interests of the city at large.

At the election of 1853 politics see-sawed again and a Democrat was chosen to the executive office. Edward A. Lambert, the last of the Mayors of the first City of Brooklyn, as it is commonly called, was a native of New York City, but removed across the East River at an early age. As Mayor he strove to reduce the expenses of the municipality and certainly succeeded in introducing several reforms in the way of economy, while at the same time, with the financial blindness of the period, he gladly granted charters to such organizations as street railroad companies practically for minimal considerations. Of course at that era in municipal history the value of such franchises were decidedly unknown quantities, and as by their bestowal the general public was supposed to be primarily benefited, such franchises were generally freely given away, not alone in Brooklyn, but in all other cities. Yet a little of the shrewdness shown by private citizens in buying and holding real estate might have been applied to estimating the future value of these gifts and made them of considerable practical value to the treasury of the municipality. Certainly in the case of the street car lines, and their multiplicity in the main arteries of Brooklyn, nothing contributed more to the upbuilding of the city outside of the ferry system, and in that way the community was benefited; but had such public franchises been awarded from the first on a business basis, it would have saved many hard feelings and harsh words in the future. Mayor Lambert's term was distinguished by the inauguration of several public improvements, to which reference will be made in the course of this chapter; and it was also marked by plague and riot, the latter the result of the bitterness of political feeling mainly between the citizens of Irish birth and the local Know-Nothings, both of which parties, or factions, or classes at the time proved irreconcilable as the famed Kilkenny cats. When the rioting broke out Mayor Lambert was enjoying a trip across the ocean for the benefit of his health; but on his return he quietly put down the open turbulence and his firm hand guided local affairs into their usually calm current. He continued active in public life after his retirement from the City Hall, and during the Civil War was prominent in local measures undertaken on behalf of that great conflict and especially in the memorable Sanitary Fair of 1864.

In recalling those citizens who presided over the destinies of Brooklyn in what was beyond a doubt the most critical period in her history — the period of her development — the name of the fourth Mayor, Henry Cruse Murphy, has been reserved to the last for more special mention, as he was not only the most richly endowed, intellectually, of all his predecessors and successors in that office, but because he became a figure of national importance, and much of the higher intellectual development that distinguishes Brooklyn at the present day is due to his initiative and example. A gifted man in every respect, a public-spirited citizen, an able and accomplished lawyer, a man of sterling honesty and purity of purpose, inflexible in his pursuit of the right, yet warmhearted, generous and sometimes impulsive, he was the very type of man most Americans desire to see lifted up into high public station, but who seldom are ambitious for such honors, or care to be associated with active politics.

His grandfather, Timothy Murphy, emigrated from Ireland in 1766 and settled in Monmouth county, New Jersey. Timothy prospered in his new abode and saw active service on the Patriotic side during the Revolution. He grew rich as his years advanced, married into a good family, and left four sons and four daughters. The second of these sons, John G. Murphy, settled in Brooklyn in 1808, engaged in business as a millwright, held several public offices, was the patentee and coinventor of the "horse" ferryboat system, and acquired a comfortable competence. He died in 1853; leaving four daughters and two sons. The eldest of the latter, Henry C. Murphy, was born in Brooklyn, July 5, 1810, was educated for the legal profession and after he was graduated at Columbia College entered the office of Peter W. Radcliffe, in New York. In 1833 he was called to the bar and at once entered upon practice in Brooklyn. Success came to him quickly. He was even then well known in literary circles, and the local Democratic leaders had found him a brilliant speaker, a quick debater and a zealous partisan, whose loyalty was beyond question; one who possessed, in fact, all the qualities that promised future leadership. In 1834, within a year after he had "hung out his shingle," he was appointed Assistant Corporation Council, and at the Democratic State Convention that year, to which he was a delegate, he received the honor of the Chairmanship of the Committee on Resolutions. In 1835 Mr. Murphy formed a professional partnership with John A. Lott, and not long afterward Judge Vanderbilt was added to the alliance, which as Lott, Murphy & Vanderbilt was for many years afterward not only the leading legal firm in Brooklyn but the heart of its political life, the local headquarters of the Democratic party, the abiding place of "the machine," as we would call it nowadays. Mr. Murphy devoted himself mainly to the legal business of the firm, retaining his activity in politics, however, and seeking relaxation in literary work. In those days he was recognized as one of the busiest men in Brooklyn, and the calls upon his time were many and incessant, for his personal popularity was unbounded.

In 1842 he was selected by his party as its candidate for the Mayoralty of Brooklyn and was elected. His platform was the old and well-worn one of "retrenchment and reform," and he started to make good his promises of an economical administration by reducing his own salary and by instituting many judicious changes which led to other economies. His administration was of rare value to the city, and was conducted on lines which advanced its present and future interests, for he had an abiding faith in the future of Brooklyn. As Mayor he added greatly to his personal popularity and this caused him to receive, in 1843, the Democratic nomination for congress from the Second District. He was elected and served one term, but was defeated when he presented himself for re-election, owing to dissensions in his party's ranks. In 1846, however, he was again returned, and on the expiration of that term he declined to be a candidate for re-election. His legal business then demanded his entire attention and he devoted himself to it, leaving politics for the time to take care of itself. In 1852, however, he came to the front again, in the public eye, for at the Democratic National Convention, held in Baltimore that year, he found himself a prominent candidate for the Presidential nomination. That honor fell, however, to Franklin Pierce and in the contest which ended in the latter's election Mr. Murphy took a prominent part and then returned to his law practice. In 1857 President Buchanan appointed him Minister to The Hague. One of his biographers, Mr. L. B. Proctor, writes:

As he had long been identified in the work of rescuing from oblivion the early history of our State, particularly that part which relates to our first colonization by Holland, there was something in the opportunity which this appointment offered eminently congenial to his historic and literary taste, and this was the paramount reason for his accepting the position. Before leaving for this new sphere of action, a farewell banquet was given him at the Mansion House, Brooklyn. It took place August 5. 1857. A large number of his fellow citizens of all parties were present to testify to their high respect for him. The occasion will long be remembered as one of the happiest social events that ever took place in Brooklyn. In response to a sentiment he made a brief, touching, farewell address, in the course of which he used the following prophetic language, which recent events have proved singularly true: "It requires," he said, "no spirit of prophecy to foretell the union of the two cities, of New York and Brooklyn, at no distant day; the river which divides them will soon cease to be a line of separation, and, bestrode by the Colossus of Commerce, will form a link which will bind them together."

During his absence of three years at The Hague, he found time to communicate a series of thirty-five most interesting letters upon Holland and other parts of Europe, to The Brooklyn Eagle, many of which were extensively copied in other papers. As happens in most cases of eminent jurists and statesmen occupying places of commanding influence, Mr. Murphy became a subject of invidious comment, by which dull or prejudiced men seek to disparage those gifts, and that influence, which is beyond their own reach; and there were those who sought to injure Mr. Murphy, in attaching blame to certain acts of his while at The Hague, and even launching the arrows of detraction at him while at home. But these were of short life, and his fair fame emerged from them, and he continued to exercise great influence, much of which was exerted in behalf of his native city.

Recalled from The Hague by President Lincoln in accordance with political usage, Mr. Murphy strained every effort to aid in the preservation of the Union he loved and the Constitution he revered. He was zealous in promoting enlistments, used his purse freely in sending men to the front and was mainly instrumental in equipping two regiments. During the conflict between the States he was a member of the State Senate and every war measure in the Legislature found him an unwavering and liberal supporter. In 1866, and again in 1868, he was prominently mentioned as a candidate for Governor, and in 1875 he entered the lists for a seat in the United States Senate, but after a long and somewhat acrimonious contest he was defeated by Francis Kernan.

While, in a certain sense, Mr. Murphy failed of success in his aspirations for a place in National politics, there is no question of the eminent success of his position as one of the upbuilders of Brooklyn. As Mayor he carefully watched over the entire interests of the city, safeguarded its treasury, and fostered improvements. Such schemes as the improvements of the water-front, the Atlantic Docks, and the opening of great thoroughfares, like Myrtle avenue, were zealously promoted, and in later life he procured the appropriation which built the dry docks at the Navy Yard. He interested himself particularly in the development of Coney Island as a popular summer resort, believing that Brooklyn itself would be benefited thereby, and he rendered practical assistance to this end as President of the Brooklyn, Flatbush & Coney Island Railroad. In the advancement of the ferry system he was also an ardent worker, and the union of the cities of New York and Brooklyn by means of a bridge capable of carrying all sorts of traffic was one of the dreams of his early manhood which he lived to see fully realized. When the plans for such a scheme were first submitted he threw himself into the project with all the enthusiasm of his nature, and whether as President of the company which first launched the plans for spanning the East River, or afterward as one of the Trustees representing the City of Brooklyn in the work, he never wearied in rendering watchful assistance or practical direction and advice while the work progressed in the face of countless and unforeseen obstacles.

To a certain extent it may be said that Modern Brooklyn is Senator Murphy's greatest and most enduring monument. But time brings about a strange forgetfulness of municipal achievement and there is no gainsaying the fact that his name will longer be recalled for his literary work than for anything else. A man of scholarly attainments, he was all through his life a diligent student, and history, especially local history, had a deep, unwearying fascination for him. He gathered together in early life a valuable library of books relating to early American exploration and story of which in later years he was justly proud, and he was hardly settled in practice before he began an investigation of the early history of Brooklyn, which finally placed him at the head of all local historians. He delighted also to study the records of the early Dutch settlements, and for this study he found ample scope during his official residence at The Hague. His work as a student of history, however, found its richest fruits in the aid he rendered in the organization of the Long Island Historical Society, and in the circular which first called that institution into life his name appeared as the leader. To its library and collection he proved a liberal contributor, and in all its work — publications, lectures, discussions, as well as building and collecting — he was from its institution in 1864 until his death an unwearied worker. All through his career he was a diligent contributor to the local newspaper press and for a brief period was editor of The Brooklyn Advocate, the precursor of the Brooklyn Daily Eagle. Of the latter paper he was at one time proprietor, and many of his most charming essays and interesting historical letters and monographs appeared in its columns from the day it was first issued almost until he laid aside his pen forever.

Many of Mr. Murphy's most valuable papers, such as translations from the Dutch of early voyages to America, etc., are entombed and forgotten in the printed "Transactions" of the New York Historical Society, of which he was long a most active member. He died in 1882, leaving behind him a memory for a life of good deeds and noble aspirations which ought ever to keep his name at the very head of the long roll of distinguished citizens of which Brooklyn is so justly proud.

Having thus, as in duty bound, paid our respects to the Mayors, we may now consider the progress of the city under their respective reigns. As has been said, they all filled, and most of them filled well, their appointed places in the community; and, this much premised, we may proceed to speak of the community without much reference to the nominal leaders. The time has gone by when the history of a nation is considered as told in a series of biographies of its rulers; and Mayors, like even greater potentates, must be relegated to the background when we speak of The People.

With the inauguration of the new city, as was to be expected, an active era of public improvement set in. A movement to purchase some waste land at the Wallabout for a public park was instituted by the corporation and a survey of the entire territory under the charter was ordered and begun; but it was not until 1839 that the Commissioners completed their labors and were able to submit a report. Then a scheme for a permanent water line, from Jay street round to Red Hook, was prepared by General J. G. Swift, and adopted, although its suggestions were not fully put into effect for quite a number of years, and in fact were not carried out at any time in full details as the desire to encroach upon the river as much as possible by filling in the shore line necessitated constant change in the adopted plans.

But the glory of the new city, the outward and patent sign of the new order of things, was to be the projected City Hall, which before a stone was laid was regarded as certain to prove an architectural wonder, the Taj Mahal of America. Building on the foundation work was begun in the fall of 1835 and on April 28, 1836, Mayor Trotter laid the corner-stone, with the usual ceremonies and amid much speech-making and rejoicing. An idea of the intended magnificence of the edifice may be gathered from the following contemporary description, which is quoted from Prime's "History of Long Island:"

"Brooklyn City Hall, now erecting, is situated at the intersection of Fulton, Court, and Joralemon streets, occupying an entire block, forming a scalene triangle of 269 feet on Fulton street, 250 on Court street and 222 on Joralemon street. The exterior of the building is to be constructed of marble, and to have porticoes on the three fronts, with columns thirty-six feet 6 inches high, ornamented with capitals of the Grecian order from the design of the Tower of the Winds, resting on a pedestal base seventeen feet high, which when completed will be sixty-two feet from the ground to the top of the cornice. The angles are to be surrounded by domes, and rising from the center of the building will be a tower of one hundred and twenty-five feet in height, which will be enriched with a cornice and entablature supported with caryatides standing on pedestals. The whole will have a most splendid and imposing appearance when finished. The interior will be finished in the most chaste and durable style of architecture, calculated to accommodate the different public offices, courts, etc."

For a time all seemed well; but the work had not progressed very far when the Brooklyn folks began to understand that they had not fully reckoned with the question of cost, and after beginning operations, as usual, "with a rush," the bills began to pour in upon the city with equal celerity. Contractors had to be paid almost as soon as the foundation work had been completed, and then almost every fresh course of stone called for a payment to the builder. The public treasury was by no means very plethoric, so before the walls were on a level with the street payments began to be intermittent, the work began to flag, the initiatory rush was over, interest in the possession of an architectural wonder weakened, and finally the financial panic of 1837 forced a cessation of all work. Little was said regarding a City Hall for several years, but during these years of reflection the Brooklyn authorities had a chance to abandon the hankering after architectural glory. While the building lay thus unfinished and neglected, Historian Prime endeavored to make the melancholy situation useful by pointing a moral. He said: "This stupendous undertaking, although arrested in its commencement by uncontrollable circumstances, not only constitutes an important item in the early history of the city, but is fraught with instruction to individuals and communities. And as corporations as well as individuals often learn wisdom by dear-bought experience, should these massive walls never rise higher the expenditures may not be wholly in vain. They will stand as a friendly beacon to warn the future guardians of the city of the mistakes and errors of by-gone days."

But useful as the moral might have been, such a memorial of municipal miscalculation could hardly be permitted to endure indefinitely, no matter how many important lessons it might present. In 1845 the plans were revised and modified, all the Grecian porticos but one were cut out, the caryatides were left severely alone, the extent of the structure was abbreviated and simplicity everywhere took the place of ornament. After these changes work was resumed and by 1849 the City Hall was completed as we have it to-day. Although shorn of its intended gorgeousness it is a beautiful structure, and its elegant proportions always delight the eye. Although, architecturally, it cannot compare with the beautiful edifice which is the headquarters of New York's Civic Government, there is much about it to admire, — perhaps more than if the original designs had been carried out in their entirety, for it seems to us these designs attempted to accomplish too much, and their completed results would have given us an architectural atrocity which would have been laughed at instead of eliciting the anticipated praise.

The financial panic which finally sealed the fate of the original designs for the City Hall was felt all over the country. Into its general causes we have no need here to enter: its origin and its story of disaster belong to the general history of the United States. So far as Brooklyn was concerned its results were mainly felt in a more rigorous safeguarding of financial resources than in any great excess of local business failures. Certainly the consequent dullness of trade was felt, and felt keenly, in Brooklyn: the prices of the necessaries of life rose sharply and as usual in such crises the poor suffered severely, but the local stringency and depression were but the reflex of what the country was experiencing. On May 10 the banks in New York City suspended specie payments, and on the following day, as the result of the advice of a hurriedly called public meeting of citizens, the Brooklyn banks adopted a similar course. It took exactly a year for matters to right themselves, and during the continuance of the commercial disturbances the people were taught two very valuable lessons: First, that the administration in Washington was at the head of the financial interests of the nation, and that paper stamped or printed and circulated as money was not money.

But the disaster of 1837, having no local foundation, soon lost its effect in Brooklyn and the march of improvement and development was again taken up. The most notable feature in this was the inauguration of the Atlantic Docks enterprise already referred to. In 1840 Daniel Richards organized a company with a capital of $1,000,000 and bought some forty acres of what was practically waste land along Buttermilk Channel from Red Hook northward — a tract of marsh, inlet, low, idle, washed fiats and mud banks — with the view of turning the property into a gigantic basin with a series of warehouses, so that the largest merchant vessels might there discharge or receive their cargoes. The project was pushed forward vigorously and many of the brightest business men of Brooklyn became connected with it. Work began on June 1, 1841; cribs of piles were built, ponds were deepened and a stone bulkhead outlined the water's front. The soil removed to make the main basin was used to fill in shallows and inlets behind the bulkhead and on the solid ground thus formed the first of the warehouses was commenced in May, 1844. Four years later the splendid line of warehouses half a mile long presented a magnificent unbroken front to the bay except in the center, where a passage some 200 feet wide permitted vessels to enter the basin. All this work drew renewed attention to the section in which it was situated and so the prosperity of South Brooklyn, as it came to be called, had its real beginning. In 1848 Mr. Richards petitioned the Common Council for permission to open thirty-five new streets in the vicinity. Other improvements followed and the commercial success of the enterprise made most of these improvements permanent. The Atlantic

Docks have proved a great factor' in Brooklyn's business life. The main basin has an area of forty acres and a depth of twenty-five feet, and can be entered at any state of the tide. The total wharfage is about two miles, and the pier head facing Buttermilk Channel is 3.000 feet long. The warehouses are substantial two to five-story structures of brick and granite, and now cover an area of twenty acres, while beside them are nine steam grain elevators, one of which can raise 3,000 bushels an hour. Such facilities have caused the Atlantic Docks to become famous in shipping circles the world over and have made Brooklyn one of the leading grain depots of the world.

Another improvement, one of even more direct public utility, was the development of the system of public transit throughout the city. In 1840 a line of omnibuses was run between Fulton Ferry and East Brooklyn, and in 1845 a similar service was established between Fulton and South Ferries. In 1854 the Brooklyn City Railroad Company was incorporated and by July of the following year several of its routes were opened, notably those of Fulton street, and Myrtle avenue and Flushing avenue, with the Ferry as their starting points. It was not long thereafter before omnibuses became a thing of the past; even Montgomery Queen's stage line between the Ferry and Wallabout, splendid service though it rendered in its day, had to give way to the street car.

Several efforts to provide an adequate water supply for the city were made during the time covered by this section, but without avail. In 1853 several streams and ponds necessary to a supply of water were purchased by the authorities, at a cost of $44,000; but when the question of taking steps to bring about an ample and complete supply was submitted to the taxpayers as the law demanded, the matter was invariably voted down. There is no doubt that in this as in some other things Brooklyn was decidedly slow, and slow in defiance of her own best interests. For instance, it was not until 1848 that gas was introduced into the city, over twenty years after it had been successfully introduced across the river, where its success as an illuminator could readily have been seen. Still gas was a luxury, and its introduction into the dwellings of the people was apt to be attended with so much "muss" and discomfort that it is not to be wondered at that the citizens, unaccustomed to its comfort and convenience, were apathetic concerning it. But we cannot conceive why they were so strangely indifferent to the absolute necessity of a full and unfailing water supply, even were it for no more than the protection of their own lives and property from fire. That scourge had several times asserted itself a sufficient number of times to have served as a significant assurance that additional protection was absolutely needed.

The most memorable of these illustrations was that given on the night of September 7, 1848, when flames were seen to burst out of a frame building on Fulton street, near Sands street. The wind was high and with incredible swiftness the flames spread until the whole block back to Henry street was a seething, hissing mass. Then the flames leaped across Middagh and Fulton streets. Sands street to Washington street was quickly doomed, and so was the territory between High street and Concord street on one side, and Middagh and Orange across Fulton street, as well as both sides of Fulton street from Poplar street to Pineapple. In fact between Henry and Washington streets and Sands and Pineapple and Concord streets but little was left standing. Brooklyn's fire force could do nothing to stop the progress of the flames and twenty-five engines which went to the scene from New York were powerless to render much aid, if any, on account of the scarcity of water, and it was only by the seamen and marines from the Navy Yard blowing up the houses in the line of the fire that its progress was finally checked. The loss was estimated at $1,500,000, and among the buildings destroyed were three churches, — Sands street Methodist, the Baptist, and First Universalist, — as well as the Post Office and the offices of "The Star" and "The Freeman" newspapers. The details of this disaster should have proved a salutary lesson as to the immediate need of an abundant water supply, but it failed in this regard, although the widening of Fulton street along the line of destruction was one beneficial result that came from the calamity. Two years later another serious warning came, when several warehouses in Furman street went up in smoke and involved a loss of some $400,000. Then it began to be apparent, even to the most close-fisted taxpayer, that a water supply was a prime necessity, as it had long been evident to the thinking part of the population, and serious efforts were made to hit upon a scheme that could meet with popular favor. But when the question of cost presented itself, the desire again died out, and plan after plan was suggested without the slightest success. Even the spectacular effect of the destruction of Colonnade Row, on the Heights, on Dec. 20, 1853, did not arouse the people anew to a sense of their danger, for when on June 1, the following year, a plan was submitted for a full water system with a reservoir at Cypress Hills, it was rejected by 6,402 votes out of a total of 9,015 cast. Still it was only too evident that some complete system was bound to come, and those who most keenly realized the danger did not lose sight of the project until, as we will see in a subsequent chapter, it was successfully accomplished. One result of the conflagrations named, and many less conspicuous or disastrous ones, however, was the organization of the various hose companies into a Fire Department, in 1855, under a central board. Up to that time and indeed for some years afterward a fire company was more of a political machine than anything else.

There was another direction in which the pressing need of a plentiful water supply was indicated, although at that time the need was not so well understood as it is in our more enlightened days. That was its great helpfulness in fighting zymotic diseases. Of visitation from such diseases Brooklyn had its full share in the past, and even under the enlarged powers of city government the visits continued. In May, 1849, it was announced that cholera had broken out, a case being reported from a house in Court street; but as the disease had been raging in New York for some time its appearance in Brooklyn did not occasion much surprise. It continued its ravages until near the close of September, causing 642 deaths. Most of these fatal cases were from, overcrowded neighborhoods, where filth, poverty and drunkenness abounded, or from houses on low ground where stagnant water filled the cellars or lay in deep pools in front on the highways, or in the rear yards. Many fatal cases came from dwellings on the river front; and could the story of the visitation have been rightly interpreted it would have been perceived that a plentiful supply of water and a proper regard for sanitary conditions would have lessened the death rate by a half or even more. Another visit of the same dread scourge in the summer of 1854 swelled the ordinary death figure for the year by 656.

Such outbreaks undoubtedly represented either a lack of knowledge on the subject, or popular disregard, or both, as to the means by which they might be prevented or their consequence mitigated; and such remarks might also be made of another episode in the history of the time now under consideration, which was not creditable to the city government or to the mass of its citizens.

This was the riot of April 4, 1844, between native American citizens and citizens or residents of Irish birth in the vicinity of Dean and Wyckoff streets, and which was only ended by calling out the militia. It was a part, in fact, of a long series of irrepressible conflicts caused by the bitterness engendered by the Know-Nothing movement and which then raged all over almost all States. But the presence in Brooklyn of a large Irish contingent and of such a big majority of native-born citizens ought to have kept the authorities on the alert to prevent any outbreak such as that which did occur. So excited was popular feeling in this instance that the militia had to remain under arms all night patrolling the district.

There were many companies of militia then in Brooklyn, — the Light Guards, City Guard, Continental Guard and others. In fact there had been no lack of martial spirit since the days of the War of 1812, but in most cases we fear it was the uniform that attracted the recruits rather than any burning desire to aid in the maintenance of harmony or the preservation of the State. Each company was a separate organization, each had its own uniform, and considerable rivalry was shown as to which would secure the most gorgeous. Discipline in all of them was lax, drill was confined mainly to marching so as to be ready for a parade, and rifle shooting was rather regarded as a pastime than a serious business. It was seen that all these conditions should be improved, and that the city ought to have a military arm which should at once be worthy of it and prove of practical use should the occasion arise. The riot of 1846 and the various lesser conflicts between the civil authority and the citizens showed how useful an efficient military force could be. In 1844 several of the separate companies were organized into a regiment — the Fourteenth — but as each company wore its own uniform and made and interpreted, to a great extent, its own laws, the regimental institution was mainly a paper one. In 1856 the Thirteenth Regiment was similarly formed out of separate companies, the first of which had an existence since 1827. It was not until the outbreak of the Civil war that Brooklyn really had a trained military force among her resources.

The police force was a semi-political machine, and, while it is not to be inferred from that that it did not do its full duty to the best of its ability, still its political complexion prevented it from acquiring a full measure of efficiency. Then it should be remembered that the force was small and the extent of territory under its care was wide and the population somewhat scattered. When the city came into existence J. S. Folk was at the head of the force, which consisted of 247 men, some of the outlying districts retaining small forces of their own. In 1850 a fully equipped police department for the entire city was formed and this continued to preserve the peace until as the result of a villainous act of political chicanery, Brooklyn in 1857 was merged into the Metropolitan Police District, and the police control virtually fell into the hands of New York City politicians. It got rid of that iniquitous political scheme in 1870, passed again under local control and continued as a separate institution until the final stage of consolidation — when Brooklyn as a city ceased to exist.

But enough has been said of fires and cholera and the police, and attention may now be turned to the directions in which the city was making real progress to metropolitan greatness. In 1844 the Association for Improving the Condition of the Poor was organized, mainly through the efforts of Senator Murphy. In 1848 the City Hospital, by a gift of $25,000 from Mr. Augustus Graham, was put in possession of an endowment fund, while a few years later! Mr. John B. Graham provided the city with an Old Ladies' Home. The Brooklyn Athenaeum was started in 1852 and the Packer Collegiate Institute for Girls, organized in 1854, carried on the work of the Brooklyn Female Academy. The value of real estate steadily advanced year after year and the city continued to spread out in all directions. In 1835 its population was 24,310: in 1840 it had increased to 36,233; in 1845 the figures were 59.574, and in 1853 they had swelled to almost 120,000. Brooklyn then had all the elements of trade to insure its continued prosperity. Its docks were, in 1853, the wonder of America, and some of its industries, notably that of white lead, in which the philanthropic brokers, Augustus & J. B. Grah.am, were leading factors, far exceeded in the value of their annual output that of any other place in the world. In 1853 taxable property amounted to $12,000,000, it had fifteen public schools, and libraries in abundance. Nine carriers, however, sufficed to deliver the mail from the post office at 337 Fulton street,

— a small number indeed; but it must be remembered that people wrote less frequently then than now, that the age of the advertising circular had not arrived and that people were more in the habit of calling for their mail than in these later days.

That Brooklyn was extending and growing there was no question. Hardly a month passed that some farm did not find itself transformed from bearing crops into city property bearing houses, and it was then that Brooklyn first applied to itself the title of City of Homes, the right to which it disputed with Philadelphia until it assumed the more dignified epithet of the "City of Churches." In connection with the steady increase in the population it was even then admitted that the cause of this was the steady migration of men doing business in New York to homes in Brooklyn. Even Mr. Prime noticed this fact and expressed some fear lest such citizens should neglect the duties which they owed as citizens to their place of residence. But the very opposite proved to be the case. A man's heart is generally in his home, and while for a time such new-comers might regard themselves as New Yorkers they soon came to look upon themselves as Brooklynites pure and simple and to become among the most devoted of its citizens. The old gibe that Brooklyn was New York's bedroom was never used by a resident of Brooklyn but by some disappointed inhabitant of Gotham who was unable to change his environment from circumstances which very likely in his heart of hearts he regretted. In Brooklyn a man could own a home, could live amid all the influences of wholesome surroundings and pleasant society and at the same time be within as easy reach of his office, or store or factory as though he had no ferry to cross. At that time, 1853, Brooklyn's means of transit, poor as they were in comparison with those now existing, were far superior to those in its twin city.

No better test of the progress of a city can be found than in its newspaper press, and it is fitting that some reference should here be made to that of Brooklyn. Mention has already been made of Printer Kirk's journalistic ventures and the connection of Alden Spooner with the "Long Island Star" beginning with 1811. "The Long Island Patriot," issued in 1821 by George L. Birch, an Irishman, was carried on under that title until 1833, when it was changed to "The Brooklyn Advocate" and published by James A. Bennett. Under his regime Senator Murphy was its principal editorial writer, finding in the opportunity thus afforded (there was no money in it) an excellent sphere of practice for his pen. In 1835 its title was again changed and it became "The Brooklyn Advocate and Nassau Gazette," which lengthy cognomen it retained until its suspension in 1839. In 1834 a new candidate for public favor appeared in the "Brooklyn Daily Advertiser." It became an evening paper within a few months, then sought support as a morning issue and finally resumed its position as an evening paper, and as the "Native American Citizen and Brooklyn Evening Advertiser" became the organ of the Know-

Nothings. It fell into the newspaper morgue with the decline of that political sentiment. "The Brooklyn Daily News" was commenced in 1840 and after a brief career was merged with the "Long Island Daily Times," but the combination failed to win popular support and the effort ceased in 1843. "The Brooklyn Evening Star" was issued by Col. Spooner in 1841 (after two previous unsuccessful efforts, in 1827 and 1834) and continued to figure in Brooklyn journalism until 1862, when it was compelled to suspend, the following year, 1863, witnessing the suspension of Spooner's once popular sheet, the "Long Island Star." Long before that happened, however, Alden Spooner had ceased from his labors, having passed away Nov. 24, 1848. The other journalistic ventures in Brooklyn of this period are hardly worthy of being even mentioned; they were merely "poor sons of a day" and retain an interest only for the local antiquary, and but a passing degree of interest even for the most enthusiastic of these. The literary merit of those fleeting sheets was most conspicuous by its absence.

To all this, however, an exception must be made in favor of what is now, and has been almost since its first issue, the most successful and influential paper published on Long Island, — the Brooklyn Daily Eagle. Lately indeed it has boldly wandered forth from its insular domain and demanded a place among the great metropolitan dailies, and its demand in that respect has been very generally allowed. Indeed it is difficult to see how it could be denied. A perfect and complete epitome of the news of the world its matter well edited, its news stories clear and logical, and its editorial page bristling with clear cut comment on events of the day, — comments which carry a vast amount of weight into the political and' social life, not alone of Long Island but of Greater New York and the nation; a newspaper that is at once literary, scientific, religious and social, every issue of which is a reflex of all that is going on at home or abroad, of all that interests a farmer, a preacher, a professional man, a merchant, a mechanic, which appeals with equal force and renders equal service to the teacher in his sanctum and the man about town, — it renders a faultless service and fully deserves the honorable position it has won and holds. Its origin was very humble. The first number was issued October 26, 1841, with the primal purpose of serving as a campaign sheet for the local Democracy, and, secondly, with the view of testing public opinion and sentiment as to the prospects for a daily newspaper devoted to that party. Senator Henry C. Murphy was its real proprietor and editor, although in the latter capacity he shared the work with the once celebrated author of the "Moon Hoax," Richard A. Locke. Its success was immediate, and this, coupled with the triumph at the polls of the policy it had espoused, seemed to warrant its continuance as a daily institution.

Throwing off its campaign features, it commenced its career as a daily newspaper Dec. 27, 1842, under the editorial care of William B. Marsh, who won for it an enduring measure of success prior to his death, in 1846. Before that, the paper had been purchased by Isaac Van Anden, who continued to publish it until 1870, when he sold the property to an association of leading Brooklyn citizens, who turned its proprietorship into a joint stock company, and so it remains. Under such editorship as that of Henry McCloskey, Walt Whitman, Thomas Kinsella, William Wood and its present head, St. Clair McKelway, its course has been one of uniform success; and its policy, while honestly and purely Democratic, has ever been maintained free from party dictation o the influence of any political machine. National, State or Municipal. For many years its office on lower Fulton street near the old ferry was one of the landmarks of Brooklyn, but the changes caused by the opening of the bridge rendered that location undesirable, and since 1892 it has occupied a magnificent building erected for its own use on a site which for half a century prior to 1868 was that of the St. John's Episcopal Church, and in 1871 was occupied by the ill-fated Brooklyn Theatre, which was destroyed by fire, Dec. 5, 1876, under most appalling circumstances.

Although, as we have seen, bountifully supplied during the period covered by this section of its history. with newspapers, Brooklyn could not be described as having much literary distinction. Most of her best work in that department belongs to a later period, and such literary souls as she did produce had to search elsewhere for their bread and butter, which things are as essential to literature as to mechanics. Oliver Bell Bunce, once known as a novelist whose most popular book was a little work entitled "Don't," pointing out mistakes "in the use of the English language, is sometimes regarded as belonging to Brooklyn; but on what ground, beyond that of temporary residence in it, seems difficult to point out. So, too, with John G. Saxe, the poet, who certainly resided in Brooklyn for a time and wrote much of his verse there, but never somehow became identified with it. For a time it might be said he was in Brooklyn, but not of it.

It seems hard to have to put a native Long Islander and a poet of world-wide renown in the same category, but it seems to be that which fits Walt Whitman the most truly. Born in West Hills, Suffolk county, May 31, 1819, he was educated mainly in Brooklyn. After a time of wandering, during which he learned the trade of printer, he returned to that city where he for a time was editor of the "Eagle," and engaged in business as a printer. It can hardly be said that he was a success either as an editor or as a business man, or that he identified himself much with Brooklyn. He speaks of its "beautiful hills," but its central point of attraction for him was the ferry, and his heart was more in the Manhattan than on the Long Island shore. Still there seems no doubt that it was in Brooklyn he wrote the twelve poems which in 1855, in a small quarto of ninety-five pages, made up the first edition of "Leaves of Grass;" and it was in Brooklyn also that much of the additional verses under that head that were contained in the second edition, which appeared in the following year. Both editions were published in New York, and soon after their publication Whitman ranked only as a visitor to the island of his birth, — "Paumanok," as he liked to call it.

Gabriel Furnam, to whom every writer on Brooklyn's history is under a deep debt of gratitude, might have attained a considerable position in the world of literature had he so applied himself. He was a man who naturally possessed vast industry, wonderful capacity for research, a keen and critical judgment, and no one can read the manuscripts he has left without admitting that he was a most zealous worker. His literary style was clear, nervous, and sometimes exceedingly graphic, and as a public speaker and lecturer he never failed to charm his audiences. On the history and the antiquities of Brooklyn and Long Island he was a perfect encyclopedia, and his vast stores of what might be called "local learning" were at anyone's service. He was born in Brooklyn in 1800 and died in that city in 1853. In early life he studied law and in 1827 was appointed a Justice in the Municipal Court, serving for three years. In 1837 he was chosen to the State Senate and remained a member of that body until 1842, when he ran for the office "of Lieutenant Governor on the Whig ticket and was defeated. Then he retired from public life and devoted himself to his books. He had, however, in some way, acquired the opium habit, and indulgence in that cursed weakness crushed out whatever ambition he originally had and gradually left him physically and financially a wreck, and that result was only too evident at the very time when he ought to have been in the zenith of his powers. It deadened his brain, exhausted his power of initiative and capacity for work, even for thought; and his death, in the Brooklyn City Hospital, was a sad end to a career that was for a time so useful, and seemed so full of promise. In 1824 Furman issued his only book, — "Notes, Geographical and Historical, Relative to the Town of Brooklyn." It was reprinted in 1875. along with the contents of a manuscript volume, "Long Island Antiquities and Early History," which was picked up in a bookstore by Frank Moore, a well-known historical student, who edited the volume and gave it to the world.

# CHAPTER XXXVI. CHURCH DEVELOPMENT.

Taking it all in all. the purely literary life of Brooklyn in this epoch is hardly worth recalling. But its intellectual development then centered in the church and in its hands nothing was neglected of those very influences which have led to lasting results in literature, in art, in science, and in all the amenities which call out the higher and richer phases of intellect and character and which makes society nobler and purer and life better worth living. The era covered by this section was one of rapid development and growth among the churches of all creeds or denominations. It saw the Roman Catholic body so increased as in 1853 to entitle Long Island to be constituted into a diocese with the late Bishop Loughlin at its head, antedating by several years the advent of a Protestant Episcopal bishop; for it was not until 1869 that that body attained that dignity.

As might be expected, the old Dutch Reformed Church was the strongest religious organization in Brooklyn, and it maintained its hold even in the midst of what men then called "Liberal discussion" and "modern thought." To the old First Church, which in 1835 was settled in its third building, on Joralemon street, there was added in 1837 the Second, or "Reformed Dutch Church on the Heights." Two years later that congregation built a church on Henry street, near Clark street; but in 1850 a more imposing structure was erected on Pierrepont street and over that society, from 1847 until 1859, the Rev. George W. Bethune presided as pastor, and by his eloquence in the pulpit, his activity in passing affairs, his eminence as a scholar and his originality as a thinker, writer and poet, made it become the first of Brooklyn's churches to acquire a measure of national fame. Dr. Bethune, more than any man in that era, could have invested Brooklyn with a literary reputation, or raised up within it a literary cult; but such of his writings as were given to the public while one of Brooklyn's pastors, he published elsewhere, sought as it were a different public for the fruits of his pen, while the work of the church itself engrossed his daily life in the city in which for so many years his lot was cast and which yet holds his memory in reverence. His later years were clouded by ill health, and he died at Florence, in 1862. His remains, however, were brought across the Atlantic and laid in Greenwood beside those of his father, Divie Bethune, the first of New York's merchant philanthropists, and his famous grandmother, the sainted Isabella Graham.

The Dutch Reformed Church steadily reached out all over the city limits during the period now under notice, engaged as it were, in active missionary work, in marked distinction to its old centralizing and conservative spirit. In rapid succession it had more or less flourishing congregations at Gowanus, the Wallabout, East New York, as well as in other points where the population was growing.

But in missionary work the Episcopal Church showed equal strength and energy with the pioneer Dutch body. When this period now being reviewed opened in reality Protestant Episcopalianism regarded Brooklyn as but one parish, with two churches, St. Ann's and St. John's. By the time the period closed it had organized and housed — generally in splendid temples — no fewer than fifteen new congregations, including the palatial Trinity. Into the story of these congregations we cannot here enter into detail; but three may be selected for brief mention, mainly because they illustrate, in more or less degree, the progress of all the others. The early history of St. Ann's Church has already been referred to. In 1835 it was under the rectorship of the Rev. Benjamin Clarke Cutler, and gradually gathering around it all the usual agencies for active church work, a Sunday-school, library, orphan asylum, etc. Dr. Cutler's pastorate continued until his death, in 1863. The Rev. Lawrence H. Mills was chosen as his successor and under him the church left its old house of worship on Washington street (the terminus of the Brooklyn bridge now runs across the site) and worshipped in its chapel at Clinton and Livingston streets. The Rev. Dr. Noah H. Schenck succeeded Mr. Mills in 1867, and in 1869 the present magnificent building used by the congregation was completed. The old burial ground of the church on Fulton street, near Clinton street, after being unused for many years, was abandoned altogether in 1860, the human remains in it were disinterred and a suite of business premises — St. Ann's Buildings — was erected on the site. Dr. Schenck died in 1886, and the present rector, the Rev. B. F. Alsop, was called. As a condition of a gift of $70,000, made in 1878 by Mr. R. Fulton Cutting, the seats in St. Ann's are free. This gift removed all the indebtedness of the church and enabled it to begin a new era of active zealous Christian work. Its revenues are large, its field of activities broad, its methods liberal and its work has been singularly blessed. The Church of the Holy Trinity might in a sense be regarded as one among the many daughters of St. Ann's, as its founders, Edgar J. Bartow and his wife (Harriet C. Pierrepont), were long associated with the latter, the husband as an officer of and worker in the Sabbath-school, and the wife as an active instrument in the charitable field which has ever been a feature of St. Ann's. Mr. Bartow was descended from an old Westchester family and took up his residence in Brooklyn in 1830. In business life he was a paper manufacturer, but not a little of his once immense wealth came from his shrewdness in taking advantage of the rising tide of Brooklyn real-estate values. Blessed with riches and animated by a sincere desire to add to the spiritual blessings of Brooklyn, Mr. Bartow and his wife in 1844 selected a site for a new church at Montague and Clinton streets, engaged the services of Minard Lefever, the most noted ecclesiastical architect of his day, and erected a building which for beauty of design and general adaptability far surpassed any structure at that time in the city. Its cost when completed was estimated at $175,000, but no one ever knew the exact figure, for every dollar was met by Mr. Bartow. The church was opened for Divine service April 25, 1847, and the Rev. Dr. W. H. Lewis became the first rector. The entire property unfortunately continued in Mr. Bartow's hands, as it had been his intention to complete it according to the original designs. But in 1856 the embarrassed condition of his affairs forced him to realize on all his available estate, and to his deep regret it became necessary to dispose of the church property, along with the rest. It was offered to the congregation for $100,000 and the offer was accepted. Starting out anew, as it were, under a heavy load of debt. Dr. Lewis continued his pastorate with much success until 1860, when he resigned and was succeeded by the Rev. Dr. A. H. Littlejohn, afterward first Protestant Episcopal Bishop of Brooklyn. For a long time the financial condition of the church was one of the wonders of Brooklyn. It seemed so burdened that relief appeared an impossibility and rumors were frequently heard that the congregation would be compelled to abandon its princely edifice and seek a humbler shelter. But wise counsels prevailed, the people held on, able heads managed the finances, and slowly but surely the debt gradually disappeared, the building was completed according to its original designs, with its beautiful spire; the rectory, abandoned in the time of despair, was repurchased, and its financial ability for aggressive church work was placed on an equal footing with any in the city. In 1869, when Bishop Littlejohn was consecrated, he was succeeded as rector of Holy Trinity by the Rev. Charles H. Hall, whose ministry was one of the most practically successful of any in the fruitful story of Brooklyn's churches. He remained in charge of the parish until his death, Sept. 12, 1895. The present pastor is the Rev. S. D. McConnell. The membership is now over 1,100, and the church property is valued at $400,000, while not a penny of debt rests upon it.

The third church selected tells us another story of advancement and illustrates a different method of Christian work and church upbuilding, and it brings before us a zealous laborer in the vineyard, one whose name and works are not, it is to be feared, as widely remembered in Brooklyn as they ought to be. Until the day of his death, in 1865, no personality was better known or more kindly regarded in the city than that of the Rev. Evan Johnson. He was born at Newport, R. I., June 6, 1792, and was there ordained in 1813. After a brief service as curate in Grace Church, New York City, he became rector of the Episcopal Church at Newtown, Long Island, in 1814.

The same year he married Maria, daughter of John B. Johnson. Through her he acquired some property, and for a number of years he not only attended faithfully to the duties of his church but managed successfully the affairs of a large farm which he owned. After his wife's death, in 1825, he determined to remove from Newtown, and, selling his farm for $4,000, he settled, in the following year, 1826, in Brooklyn, where at his own expense he bought land and erected St. John's Church. To the congregation he gathered there he ministered for twenty years, seeing it steadily growing in membership and usefulness, but all the time declining to accept a cent for his services. Indeed it was his boast in his latter days that he had preached and filled all the duties of a pastorate for forty years without any monetary remuneration! In 1847, finding that St. John's was self-supporting, he sold the building and ground to the congregation and with the money thus received proceeded to put in operation a project he had long cherished, — the erection of another church in a section of the city where poverty abounded and religion did not. Hiring a room in Jackson street, he commenced holding Divine services in that small apartment in September, 1847. This was the beginning of St. Michael's. The congregation grew so rapidly that in a few months he was able to lease the old Eastern Market building, on High street. There the church and parish were duly incorporated and in time a self-supporting and vigorous congregation was added to the list of the successful Episcopal Churches in Brooklyn. It now occupies an elegant building erected for its use on High street, and this, with the adjoining rectory, is estimated as worth $100,000. The church has 480 members, no indebtedness, and raises annually about $16,000 for church work.

During the period covered by this chapter the Reformed Church added seven churches to its number, the Lutherans four, the Methodist Episcopal twelve, the Baptists twelve, the Congregational nine, the Presbyterians eight, while the Roman Catholic Church added sixteen. These figures indicate a vast amount of activity, and practically every section of the city found itself more or less fully covered by church influence. The field was large, the workers were many, — so many in fact that it is beyond the scope of this work even to attempt to recall their names. Almost any selection that could be made would be unjust to those omitted, but it may be said that there was not a better body, a more self-denying body, a more energetic body of earnest, devoted Christian workers to be found anywhere than might be found in the list of Brooklyn's preachers during this division of its story. We read of little troubles bothering a few of the congregations, we read of efforts made in the course of Teaching out bemg unfortunate on account of an error in judgment as to location or an error, in calculation of resources on the part of enthusiastic workers, and now and again we read of a pastor being compelled to stand aside on account of his health breaking down under the unceasing strain of his work. Such errors, such drawbacks, such sorrows, however, were unavoidable, and had but little effect on the general result: and so, as we read the story of Brooklyn church life during the years between 1834 and 1854, we see a strong body, a nervous force, steadily reaching out in all directions and leavening the whole into a Christian community, a lighted lamp set as it were upon a hill and shedding its rays over all the land. For it was in this period that Brooklyn in reality became generally known as the "City of Churches," and its churches acquired a measure of national fame.

Three men were conspicuous in bringing all this about; and as they have all three passed beyond the veil and the value of their services was so preeminent as to be beyond cavil, we may close our study of the church life of the first City of Brooklyn by recalling some of the prominent features of their careers.

John Loughlin, the first Roman Catholic Bishop of Long Island, was born in county Down, Ireland, in 1816. Early in life he came to America, settling for a time in Albany, N. Y., and was educated for the priesthood at Mount St. Mary's College, Emmittsburg, Aid. In 1842 he was ordained priest and became attached to St. Patrick's Cathedral, New York, of which, in 1844, he became Rector. He was subsequently appointed Vicar General of the New York diocese, and was consecrated as Bishop of Brooklyn October 3, 1853, by the Papal Nuncio, the Most Rev. Cajetan Bedini, Archbishop of Thebes. Bishop Loughlin named St. James's as his cathedral church and thenceforth his life was bound up in the history of his diocese. Under him the Church steadily extended, new parishes were opened up in rapid succession, and schools and charities quickly followed. The Bishop was a consistent believer in active religious work, in, work outside the pulpit, in the homes and the social circles of his people. To aid in such endeavor he introduced into his diocese, in 1855, the Sisters of St. Joseph and the Sisters of Mercy, and he crowned, as he believed, his church building work in 1868 when he had the corner-stone of a cathedral and diocesan establishment laid by Archbishop McClosky, on a splendid site at the junction of Carlton and Vanderbilt avenues. It was designed to be the finest group of ecclesiastical buildings on Long Island, — to rival in fact anything of the kind in America. But he did not live to see the work completed. The buildings remain uncompleted even to this day, although a part of the cathedral has been opened for service and a palace for the Bishop's residence has been completed, a beautiful structure in keeping with the importance and dignity of the office. Bishop Loughlin continued sedulously to advance and protect the vast interests committed to his care, quietly and unostentatiously, but none the less effectively, until his death, Dec. 29. 1891. It may truly be said that on assuming the Bishopric he gave himself up wholly to his work, and that the full story of his life in Brooklyn would he but the story of the marvelous progress of his Church from 1853 until 1892. On May 2, 1892, the Rev. Charles E. McDonnell was installed as his successor. In writing of the personal career of such a man as Bishop Loughlin, the biographer is necessarily limited as to its details. A true leader in such circumstances is essentially the head of a force, and while his life is spent as the representative of that force, and the leading director of its movements, he more or less completely sinks his personality in its direction. Such self-abnegation, in fact, has been one of the causes of the modern success of the Roman Catholic Church. But in dealing with the career of such a man as the late Rev. Dr. Storrs, his individuality not only stands out in bold relief all through his career but that individuality reflects its own characteristics upon the church with which it is associated and gives it not merely local but national importance, an importance which generally passes away with its creator although the church to which he ministered may remain intact. To illustrate perhaps a little more plainly, it may be said that the Church of the Pilgrims was better known as Dr. Storr's Church during that gifted man's life-time than by its official designation.

Richard Salter Storrs was descended from a long and illustrious line of New England clergymen. His father, Richard S. Storrs, was for sixty-two years pastor of the First Congregational Church of Braintree, Mass.; his grandfather, who also bore the name of Richard Salter Storrs, was pastor of a Congregational Church at Long Meadow, Mass., for thirty-three years, and his great-grandfather was a Chaplain in the Patriot army during the American Revolution.

Richard S. Storrs was born at Braintree, Mass., Aug. 21, 1821. He was graduated at Amherst College in 1839, and for a short time was engaged as a teacher in Monson Academy. It was apparently his idea at first to prepare himself for the bar, for he entered the office of Rufus Choate as a student. He abandoned law for theology, however, and entered Andover Seminary, where he was graduated in 1845. He became pastor of a Congregational church at Brookline, Mass., in that year, and in the following year was called to the Church of the Pilgrims, and was installed as pastor on Nov. 19, 1846. It had been organized only two years before, and Dr. Storrs was its first minister.

The corner-stone of the present edifice of the Church of the Pilgrims, at Henry and Remsen streets, was laid in 1844, and the building was dedicated in 1846, several months before Dr. Storrs was installed as pastor. Many changes and improvements have since been made in the building.

Dr. Storrs was a Commissioner of Parks of the City of Brooklyn from 1871 to 1879. He was elected President of the American Board of Commissioners for Foreign Missions in 1887 and continued in that office for ten years, and was one of the leaders of the old Manhattan Congregational Association, which seceded from the main Congregational Association after the Beecher-Tilton trial. In 1881, on the occasion of the thirty-fifth anniversary of his pastorate. Dr. Storrs was the recipient of a purse of $35,000 from parishioners and friends.

From 1848 to 1861 Dr. Storrs was associate editor of The Independent. Much of his attention was given to the Brooklyn Mission Society, and for a quarter of a century he was President of the Long Island Historical Society. He also served as First Vice President of the Brooklyn Institute of Arts and Sciences, and as a member of the Amherst College Board of Trustees.

Dr. Storrs was married in October, 1845, to Miss Mary Elwell Jenks, granddaughter of John Phillips, the first Mayor of Boston, and a niece of Wendell Phillips. Mrs. Storrs' father was a clergyman. She died in 1898, leaving two daughters, Mrs. L. R. Packard and Mrs. E. B. Coe, wife of the Rev. E. B. Coe of the Dutch Reformed Church, New York.

The Rev. Dr. Richard S. Storrs was a historic figure in the ecclesiastical world of America. "His death," says a writer of one of the many biographies issued after his death, "removes from the American ministry one of its most scholarly lights, and by it Brooklyn loses a citizen honored and beloved for more than half a century. The last of an extraordinary group of Brooklyn ministers, he was not alone a local force spiritually and secularly, but a man of recognized importance in the entire Christian world. He was a scholar, orator, man of affairs, and a historian of authority, as well as pastor.

"Dr. Storrs represented in Brooklyn for fifty-three years the tradition of the conservatism and the rhetorical elegance of the Puritan pulpit of New England. During much of that period, in a neighboring church — Plymouth Henry Ward Beecher stood for the opposites of these pulpit ideals, the radical thought, the reforming impulse, and the genius for impassioned oratory.

"In all his preachings Dr. Storrs kept in touch with the Scriptures, and their teachings were the foundation of his utterances. New England born and bred, he lived according to the precepts of the Pilgrims, and he preached as he lived. His greatness lay in broad and humane scholarship. Possessed of an alert and vigorous mind, he treated his themes with a delightful thoroughness and clothed his thoughts in beautiful and fitting speech."

Dr. Storrs's fiftieth anniversary as pastor of the Church of the Pilgrims — his golden anniversary — was celebrated in 1896 by a week of general public rejoicing, in which many prominent men took part.

Dr. Storrs delivered what is regarded as his greatest oration on June 1, 1865, on the impressive theme of the death of Lincoln. He was a most prolific worker and the large number of his works which have been published give some idea of the energy and industry of his life. The titles of some of his published lectures and addresses are as follows: "Congregationalism; Its Principles, and Influences;" "Obligation of Man to Obey the Civil Law;" "Christianity: Its Destined Supremacy on the Earth;" "The Relations of Commerce to Literature;" "Colleges, a Power in Civilization, to be Used for Christ;" "Constitution of the Human Soul;" "Character in the Preacher;" "The Puritan Scheme of National Growth;" "The Bible, a Book for Mankind;" "Declaration of Independence, and the Effects of It;" "John Wyckliffe and the First English Bible."

Feeling the approach of his end, and suffering greatly from enfeebled health, Dr. Storrs formally resigned his pastoral charge Nov. 19, 1899, but retained his connection with the church as pastor emeritus. His last appearance in the pulpit was in April 22 following, when he conducted the services in company with the Rev. H. P. Dewey, of Concord, N. H., whom the congregation, at his suggestion, had decided upon as his successor. His health continued to fail in suite of his relief from his pastoral duties and he gradually grew more infirm until the end came, June 5, 1900, at his home. No. 80 Pierrepont street. Three days later his remains were interred in Greenwood Cemetery. The news of his death caused many regrets in Brooklyn; it was truly felt that the last of a race of Princes in Israel had truly fallen, and several movements for some tangible memorial of his life and public services were proposed and discussed. But these seemed to awaken little practical response, and the memory of this good man is likely to be enshrined only in his own works.

A still more famous, more popularly famous, preacher came to Brooklyn in this era, the Rev. Henry Ward Beecher. It is difficult to compress the story of the life work of this gifted man into the few paragraphs which the compass of this work necessitates, and yet a history of Brooklyn without mention of Beecher's work would necessarily be incomplete. He was one of the sons of the Rev. Lyman Beecher, who in the course of a busy life of eighty-eight years spent some fifty years in the active work of the ministry and became one of the intellectual leaders of the country. Lyman Beecher, "stood unequalled," writes one, "among living divines for dialectic keenness, pungent appeals, lambent wit, vigor of thought and concentrated power of expression." This sentence might also have been applied to Henry Ward, the most gifted of his sons, at whose home in Brooklyn he died in 1863. All of Lyman Beecher's children became famous for their genius or noted for their usefulness. Most of them were in some way connected with Long Island, where, at Easthampton, Lyman Beecher preached for several years.

Henry Ward Beecher was born at Litchfield, Conn., June 24, 1813. After being prepared for the ministry under the direction and instruction of his father, he was settled as minister of a Presbyterian Church at Laurenceburg, Ind. While there, living mainly on his hopes, he married Eunice White, who survived him after the close of his life's journey. In 1839 he removed to Indianapolis, where he labored until 1,847, when he received the call to become pastor of the newly formed Plymouth Congregational Church, Brooklyn. He accepted, entered upon that memorable pastorate October 10, 1847, and continued to be identified with Brooklyn — its world famous citizen — until the end of his career. In his opening sermon he announced that he would preach of Jesus "not as an absolute system of doctrines, nor as a by-gone historical personage, but as the ever living Lord and God," and added that he included anti-slavery and temperance as parts of Christ's teachings. That brief system of theology continued ever after to rule in Plymouth. When, many years later. June 30, 1883, he received the congratulations of his fellow citizens in Brooklyn's Academy of Music, on the occasion of the celebration of his seventieth birthday, he enlarged upon it as fellows:

"The inspiration which has made the force of my whole life I found in a vision of the lovie of God in Jesus Christ. It has grown larger and larger with the sympathy which is natural to my constitution, compassion of God, manifestations of God in Jesus Christ, that side of God which is great, holy, beautiful, showing Him to have compassion on the ignorant, and on them that are out of the way. I have tried to have compassion like Christ. The less worthy the object, the more it was needed. I went right upon the side of the dumb and needy, without consideration. I think it most heroic for a man with standing and influence and ability to give himself to them. I thank God I had a desire to work for His glory, when to do it was to earn scoffings and abuse and threats. When Kossuth brought Hungary to us, my soul burned. The wrongs of Greece made my heart kindle. Nearly all the nations of the world, all under the sword of the soldier or the ban of harsh governments, have aroused my sympathy and effort. I did not go into these because they were humanities or specious philosophies, but because it was Christian: that's all. I did it for humanity because I loved Christ. In my preaching it has been the same. I have attacked governments, institutions, anything; never a denomination or a body of ministers. I have preached against the principles involved in all, and in my own denomination as much as in others. I have preached for the deliverance of souls, for clearer light, for a plainer path, that the stumbling blocks might be removed. These things I have changed in only to grow more intense and emphatic: first, the universal sinfulness of mankind, so that it is necessary everywhere for men to be born again by the Spirit, necessary for a life to be given to human nature above its animal nature, and this only by the Spirit of God; second, I believe in conversion and the effectual influence of the Spirit of God; third. I believe with ever-growing strength in the love of God in Jesus Christ. I know that Christ loves me, and that I shall go where He is. By grace am I saved, say I. The feeling has grown in my later years, and when under great pressure and sorrow that raised a strong sea, my strength and courage all came from this view — Christ loves me, He will hide me in His pavilion till the storm is passed. The sweetness of life is as much dependent on the love of Christ as the landscape is on the sun to bring out its lights and shadows. I never believed so much in the Gospel as to-day. My faith in it has never been shaken, except in the ideals. I was never so sure as now of its truth."

From the first, Beecher's ministry in Plymouth was a triumphant success. As the late Benjamin J. Lossing said: "It has no parallel in the history of pulpit oratory and pastoral labors. Thousands were brought into the church during his ministry. Its audience room, always full, would accommodate 3,000 persons. At times more than that number have been packed within its walls. The membership of the church averaged about 2,500. Its contributions to benevolent and charitable purposes have been munificent." Beecher was not what many would have called an orthodox preacher. He believed that smiles should follow a sermon as well as tears; he thought happiness as appropriate a theme for contemplation as sorrow; he believed in describing the joys of heaven rather than in painting the horrors of hell; in fact he did not believe in the doctrine of eternal punishment, and openly declared himself on that point in a discourse preached in 1878. His manner was dramatic, his illustrations were drawn from actual life, mainly from his own reading and observation, and h:' treated every theme from the standpoint of common sense, attempted in short to interpret the life to come by the life that now is. Creeds and dogmas, especially as the years grew upon him, he had little use for, and, starting out in life as a disciple of Calvinism, he so developed, as he said himself, that in 1882 he and his congregation threw off even the loose and pliant bonds of Congregationalism and withdrew from association with that body. In his church Beecher was singularly beloved and well understood, and his word was law. He made it famous, and from its pulpit he not only spoke to three thousand or more auditors at every service, but to an outer audience of many, many thousands more, for his sermons, carefully reported, were printed weekly in a publication called "Plymouth Pulpit," and so were circulated and read all over the civilized world. Most popular preachers have, singularly, to meet a crisis during their careers; and Beecher's personal crisis came in 1874, when he was openly charged with immorality, the lady in the case being Mrs. Tilton, wife of Theodore Tilton, a brilliant figure in the literary world of that day but now forgotten excepting for the history of this charge, which developed into one of the *causea celebres* of American jurisprudence. The case first came up in Plymouth Church, and there, after investigation, the charges were dismissed as without foundation. A civil suit followed, Tilton figuring up his heart losses at $100,000. The trial of the action, which continued for some six months, was watched with intense interest and at the close much regret was expressed when it was learned that the jury could not. agree, nine of the members being in favor of a verdict for Beecher and the remaining three disagreeing with their view. But Beecher was acquitted at the bar of public opinion. The worst that could be said of him was that his own innocence of wrong-doing or wrong intent had sometimes placed him in positions from which rumor and slander might easily raise up flimsy tissues of falsehood, while his liberality of thought and disregard of conventionalities had brought him into contact with a class of people, some of them fanatics, some of them literary and social curiosities, and some of them people who, to put it mildly, had wits and lived by them. New York at that time was full of curious people, and Beecher, generous, open-hearted, always zealous in his search for truth, was sometimes too apt to listen openly and seriously to their vagaries. After the excitement of the trial had spent itself his influence in Plymouth Church became greater than ever, while he himself emerged from that dark cloud with his thoughts broadened and mellowed, and more intensely than ever before preached of the infinite love of Christ.

Apart from his pulpit the life of Henry Ward Beecher might be divided into two parts, — his work as a citizen and as a man of letters, over both of which, however, it should be remembered to his credit, his pulpit work predominated, or rather both contributed to its requirements. When in the height of his fame as a public lecturer, commanding $500 a night, he had to decline many engagements when they seemed likely to interrupt his pastoral duties. He kept a close watch over the passing events of the day and spoke of them freely and unreservedly from his pulpit. On the slavery question his abolitionist views were as a part of his Bible, and in that cause he was one of the most tireless workers. When the Civil War broke out he threw himself heart and soul into the task of defending and strengthening the position of the Northern States. Plymouth someone has said, virtually became a recruiting station for the Northern Army and raised a regiment of its own which went to the front, one of its officers being the pastor's son.

In 1863 Beecher went to England to recuperate his health, but the condition of public opinion which he found existing there compelled, him to try and correct an erroneous impression as to the origin and meaning of the war, which caused a great deal of sympathy to be thrown away, both in England and Scotland, on behalf of the States then fighting for secession and slavery. The story of the triumphant progress of his self-imposed mission forms one of the most interesting chapters in his biography.

As a platform orator Beecher was unapproached even in that day of great orators, and his oration on "Robert Burns" has been conceded to be the most brilliant which the worldwide celebration of that poet's centenary called forth. In the field of letters Mr. Beecher was a diligent worker, and we can only wonder at the industry which produced so much in the midst of occupations that constantly called him from his library and his desk. Shortly after settling in Brooklyn he began writing for "The Independent," and he edited that still influential organ, from 1861 to 1863. Afterward, from 1870 to 1880, he edited the "Christian Union." His separate writings are too numerous to enumerate here and it may briefly be said that they run from sermons to politics, lectures and essays, and take up all sorts of themes, from a "Life of Christ" to "Norwood." a novel of New England life.

Mr. Beecher's later years from 1874 were truly years of peace and were fruitful of good works and profitable to all. He died suddenly March 8, 1887, when Dr. Lyman Abbott, who succeeded him as editor of the "Christian Union," was called to fill the pulpit of Plymouth. This he did, keeping the great congregation intact until, feeling the weight of years, he resigned, in 1899, and was succeeded by the present pastor, the Rev. Newell Dwight Hillis, who preached his first sermon in that capacity March 19, 1900. A magnificent bronze statue of Mr. Beecher has been erected in front of the Brooklyn City Hall, as a result of a popular subscription. One wall of Plymouth Church is graced with a memorial tablet, and his body rests beneath a massive monument of Quincy granite in Greenwood, where, too, lie the remains of his noble-hearted wife who on March 8, 1898, joined him beyond the veil.

Churches and church-yards used to be associated in the olden times, and although in our modern system they are widely separated in our cities this seems a fitting place to write of what an after-dinner speaker in New York with grim humor once called "Brooklyn's noted industry, its cemeteries." The first of these great "Cities of the Dead" in point of formation as well as foremost for its costly memorials and beauty of situation, was due, probably more than that of any other individual, to the initiative of Mr. Henry E. Pierrepont. The gradual increase of population in New York and Brooklyn had not only caused many of the old God's-acres to be abandoned, but, in numerous cases, had necessitated what many thought the desecration of the graves by opening them up, removing the bones and bodies, and turning the land into practical use for business purposes. Mr. Pierrepont proposed the selection of a large tract of ground which would serve as a place of burial, for New York as well as for Brooklyn, a veritable necropolis, a garden set aside forever as a Testing place for the dead. His observations while on several visits to Europe had confirmed his sense of the practical utility of some such scheme, and his intimate knowledge of Brooklyn had prompted him to turn to the historic hills of Gowanus, the heart of the site of the Battle of Brooklyn, as presenting an ideal place for such a shrine. The matter was thoroughly ventilated and discussed, and met with a ready response, but it was not until 1838, some years after it was first talked about, that a company was formed and about 200 acres of land purchased, the property extending from what is now Twenty-first to Thirty-fourth street and from Fifth avenue to the old city line. It required a good deal of manipulation to secure all of this land, although most of the owners agreed to receive in payment stock in the proposed cemetery, and to obtain the necessary state and local sanctions for its future preservation and amenity and the unalterable restrictions to its sole use for burial purposes. These preliminaries of land and regulations duly arranged, the subscription books to the stock of the company were opened November 3, 1838. All through that winter work on the grounds was vigorously pushed and much progress was reported. In 1839 an amendment was secured to the deed of incorporation which practically made the institution become a public trust, for by the amendment none of the gain or profits from the operation of the cemetery goes into the pockets of any one, but all money realized over and above necessary working expenses is devoted to the preservation and beautifying of the grounds. It is this feature which has made Greenwood rank first among our local "Cities of the Dead." The plan proved a popular one from the first, and the work of adaptation proceeded so rapidly that lots were advertised for sale in 1840, and the first burial was on September 5, that year, when John Hanna was laid in a grave at the base of Ocean Hill to await the coming, one by one, of a vast host of silent neighbors.

For several years, in spite of the success of the enterprise, the corporation had to stagger along under a load of financial troubles. That it emerged unscathed from these, carried on unceasingly its expensive scheme of improvements, and met all its obligations, was due to the zeal, energy and financial ability of the late Joseph A. Perry, who was one of its original incorporators and became its comptroller and manager in 1842, devoting thereafter his entire life to its service. Under him the usefulness of the entire scheme soon became more and more adequately appreciated, and the daily increasing beauties of the enclosure were made thoroughly known among the people. Greenwood's walks and hills and dales quickly became so popular that there was danger of the cemetery becoming a "resort" rather than a place of seclusion and mourning and where the bitter memories of bereavement might be soothed by solitude and by the appealing beauties of nature, supplemented by the artifices that humanity and love and thoughtfulness could suggest or provide. But stringent rules were enforce to prevent this tendency from spreading, and all fear of it has long since passed away. The success of the undertaking and the popularity of Greenwood were so assured that even in 1845 Dr. Prime could write of it as follows in his history: "It was purchased by a company incorporated April 18, 1838, with a capital of $300,000, in shares of $100 each, for a public burial ground. The surface is admirably diversified by hill and dale, while every now and then a beautiful little lake is spread cut in the valley. The greater part of the area is deeply shaded with dense forest trees, without underbrush, which give to the whole scene the somber aspect of the habitation of the dead. The grounds are not cut up into squares and parallelograms. No such figure is seen throughout the whole extent. But spacious avenues, neatly graveled, wind through every valley, encompassing numerous hillocks and intersecting each other at every turn. The main avenue, called "the tour," in numerous windings forms a circuit of three miles. You might travel for hours within this hallowed enclosure with a fleet horse and yet at every turn enter a new road. The work of appropriation seems to have just commenced. Though the grounds have been in the market more than seven years and many have availed themselves of the opportunity of providing a narrow house for themselves and their families, and many have already been deposited here, yet they are so extensive and diversified that it is only here and there you meet with a solitary vault in the side of a hill or an occasional monument on its summit. But here is an assembly that will never diminish and is sure to increase, which it will probably do until bone and ashes mingle with ashes in kindred dust."

The original purchase was soon found to be too limited for the future growth of the place, and steps were taken to acquire as much contiguous property as was desirable and could be secured, two notable additions being sixty-five acres on the southwesterly side and eighty-five acres on the eastern side, which made the property extend into the old town of Flatbush. It now encloses 474 acres, and in that respect has reached its full possible growth with the exception of a few small parcels which it is expected time will make available and which will cut off a trifling irregularity in its boundary line. Up to October 1, 1930, the number of interments was 309,000.

From the beginning the story of Greenwood has been one of constant, almost daily, improvement, and for beauty of location, artificial adornments, scrupulous care in maintenance, magnificence of many of its tombs and monuments, it is far ahead of any public necropolis in the world. Space is not available to follow here in detail the story of its development further than to say that its most striking improvement, the main entrance, with its sculptured gateway on Fifth avenue, was completed in 1861. The time is coming when the disposal of single graves will be a thing of the past and when even the sale of lots will be at an end, and many changes and improvements will then be effected which will still further add to the beauty of the enclosure. To provide for this a reserve fund has been slowly maturing which now amounts to $2,500,000, so that when the time comes that no further income is obtainable from the sale of the lots the welfare of the cemetery will be amply guarded.

The success of Greenwood inspired several movements in a similar direction. The first of these, Cypress Hills Cemetery, was laid out by a company incorporated in 1847, and which purchased 125 acres of land, which have been added to until the cemetery now encloses 400 acres. The first interment was made in 1848, and its silent population was quickly built up by its receiving bodies from the old churchyards of New York and Brooklyn, the sites of which were being turned over to the uses of the living. Its location is beautiful, but up to within a recent period it was so difficult of access that its success, from a financial point of view, was much retarded; but now, with increased facilities in that respect, it is yearly yielding better returns to its stockholder. It is steadily being improved and many of its monuments rank as splendid specimens of such art. One feature of Cypress Hills Cemetery is the number of special plots it contains. The most notable of these is that known as "the Soldiers' riot," which contains in its center an imposing monument, and the whole enclosure is under a distinct management from that of the rest of the cemetery. The Actors' Fund has also a fine plot, and so has the Press Club, while such organizations as the St. Andrew's Society, the St. David's Society and the St. George's Society have here plots where they bury such of their country people who may die friendless or poor, or both. A small plot contains the graves of soldiers of the war of 1812, but unfortunately these graves are not marked by any stones. The cemetery is a fitting resting place for such heroes, for it was itself once placed in order for battle, and on its slopes General Woodhull, prior to the

Battle of Brooklyn in 1776, prepared to meet an attack, while several cannon balls fired from British cannons have been dug up in the course of making improvements.

In 1849 the Cemetery of the Evergreens was incorporated and 112 acres were acquired by its stockholders, since extended to 375 acres. It also occupies ground which may be classed as historic, for over it many of the soldiers in General Howe's army marched in August, 1776, when executing that strategic movement which brought such havoc to the Patriot forces. Its Chinese section, situated on a bleak hillside, separated from the cemetery proper, is the scene at times of many strange ceremonies.

While on this subject brief mention may be made of other cemeteries which lie within the Long Island division of the Greater New York, and which caused some sections, such as Newtown, to be spoken of as one vast burying ground. There is little to be gained by detailing their history or describing their memorial or scenic beauties, but most of them are as trimly kept and made as attractive as a liberal expenditure of time. thought and money can achieve. Such cemeteries as Calvary, with over 700,000 bodies lying in its graves and vaults, and Lutheran, with 300,000, are vast cities of the dead and contain the ashes of many men and women once famous in local annals, while Mount Olivet, Mount Nebo, Most Holy Trinity, St. Michael's, Salem Fields, Mount Zion, Holy Cross, Cedar Grove and Methodist are the best known among the smaller ones. At Fresh Pond, in Queens Borough, is the public crematory, where those who prefer that form of disposing of their dead to burial can have their preference put into quick effect. It is generally held that cremation in the time to come will be the general mode of getting rid of the body after its spirit has passed, and that cemeteries will then be turned into public gardens or opened up for building purposes; but if so the idea of cremation does not seem to be attaining its destined popularity very quickly. Fresh Pond crematory has now been in operation since 1884, and up to October, 1900, only 3,795 incinerations had taken place in its furnace. But the number seems to be growing slowly each year. In 1899 there were 540, and in 1900, 610.

During the years covered by this chapter the ferry system of Brooklyn made considerable progress, and was extended as fast as the growing demands of the various sections seemed to warrant. In fact, so far as Brooklyn is concerned, she has always been alive to the necessity of perfection in her ferry services, and but for the handicap imposed by the claims of Manhattan that service would have advanced with more rapid strides than it did. In 1836 what is known as South Ferry was opened, in 1846 the Hamilton Ferry was established, and the Wall Street Ferry in 1853. These, as well as the older ferries, were run by different companies, and except at Fulton Ferry the service was poor, for the cost of maintaining each was considerable and the financial returns to the owners were meager, —when there were any returns at all.

The first really upward step looking to general improvement was taken in 1844, when the Brooklyn Union Ferry Company was formed. The president was N. B. Morse, and Henry E. Pierrepont was vice-president, as well as a trustee, along with Jacob R. Leroy. These gentlemen formed the directorate, along with George Wood, Joseph A. Perry, John Dikeman, Joseph Ketchum, John B. La Sala, Seth Low, C. J. Taylor, L. Van Nostrand, Walter N. De Grauw, H. R. Worthington, C. N. Kiersted, C. P. Smith, John Dimon, A. G. Benson, Charles Kelsey, James E. Underbill, Ezra Lewis, S. E. Johnson, E. J. Bartow and George Hurlbut. There were some features attending the formation of the company which were regarded with surprise at the time, it being even alleged that one or two of these directors bought their stock and obtained their seats with the view of selling out the lease of the Fulton and South Ferries, control of which the corporation had secured, to outside parties. But if any such purpose was entertained it was balked by the public spirit of Messrs. Leroy and Pierrepont, in whose names the leases of the two ferries had been made out and whose sole aim in the matter was to promote the interests of Brooklyn. Practically the lease they held was accompanied by no reservations, and so whatever scheme may have been concocted to defeat the public-spirited purposes of the incorporation was easily defeated before it had time to mature. The corporation at once proceeded to manage its property so as to add to its financial prosperity by effecting improvements in its service. The landing stages and ferry houses were rehabilitated, new and larger boats were placed on each route, the running schedule was quickened and the utmost regularity introduced, while the fare was gradually reduced until, from four cents on Fulton Ferry and three cents on South Ferry in 1836. a uniform rate on both of one cent was established in 1850. The corporation, despite these changes, made money, and the business at the other ferries dwindled rapidly, so much so that there were rumors that some of them would be abandoned.

In 1850 a new lease of the Fulton and South Ferries was secured for ten years by Messrs. Leroy and Pierrepont, and their company, in addition, secured the Hamilton Ferry, which at once began to feel the beneficial effects of the change. The business, especially at Fulton Ferry, which the street railroads made their terminus because it was the most popular, steadily assumed larger proportions, — so much so as to give rise to ideas of danger in the mere handling of such crowds as passed over it morning and evening. The movement, too, of the street railways tended to increase the traffic at the one point and helped to demoralize the service at the ferries which the corporation did not control. A change of some sort became imminent: either the outside ferries should be purchased by the company, or two at least would have to be abandoned. The latter contingency was to be regretted, it was felt all round, as Brooklyn needed all the outlets possible. The results of a long series of private conferences was that the owners of Roosevelt, Gouverneur, Catharine, and Wall Street Ferries agreed to sell out to a new company which should be incorporated and to take their purchase money in stock. When all the negotiations were completed what we would now call a trust was called into existence. A new company was formed, virtually the old one under the slightly altered name of the Union Ferry Company of Brooklyn, and complete possession of the entire system was entered upon. Being now thoroughly protected against private interference, Messrs. Leroy and Pierrepont at once surrendered their leases of the Fulton, South and Hamilton Ferries to the new corporation, which henceforth controlled these routes, as well as the Roosevelt, Gouverneur, Catharine and Wall Street Ferries: and although the financial results of the deal were at first disappointing the clouds soon cleared away and the entire system was placed on a footing satisfactory both to the public and the stockholders.

The Navy Yard during this period was steadily extending its size and importance. Through the exertions of H. C. Murphy, then a member of Congress, a splendid dry dock was constructed at the yard. It was commenced in 1841, and was completed some years later, at a cost of over $2,000,000. Business, however, was at no time rushing at the yard, and the records only show the construction of the following Government ships:

Brig Dolphin, commenced in 1836, launched June 17, 1836; schooner Pilot, commenced in 1836 (for the Surveying and Exploring Expedition), launched September, 1836; steamer Fulton (second), commenced in 1835, launched May 18, 1837; sloop of war Levant (second class), commenced in 1837, launched December 28, 1837; sloop of war Decatur (third class), commenced in 1838, launched April 9, 1839; steamer Missouri, commenced in 1840, launched January 7, 1841; brig Somers, commenced in January, 1842, launched April 16, 1842; sloop of war San Jacinto, commenced 1837, launched April 16, 1850; sloop of war Albany (first class), commenced in 1843, launched January 27, 1846; steamer Fulton (third), rebuilt, commenced in 1850, launched August 30, 1851.

It was seriously discussed about this time whether the Navy Yard really was of any practical benefit to Brooklyn and whether the city would not be much better off were the Government to take its outfit somewhere else and leave the Wallabout to aid in the development of the commerce of the city. It was felt, however, that the location of the Navy Yard where it had so long been not only added to the importance of Brooklyn, but that it promised to be one of the city's best means of defense should a foreign invasion ever be threatened. Mr. Murphy's dry-dock scheme, when inaugurated, put a stop to whatever idea the Government may have held of relinquishing its hold in Brooklyn's historic bay, and the notion was abandoned on all sides. The Navy Yard, it was felt, was a fixture and its location was an ideal one for every conceivable purpose. Indeed, the question of change has long since been relegated to a place among the many dead issues we meet with in the history of Kings county which arc only worth, from a historical point, a reference of a line or two simply to show that they really existed, but are no longer worthy ut consideration or discussion.

It was, however, this national occupation of the Wallabout and the consequent failure of Brooklyn to extend in its direction that proved one of the leading arguments against the utility of the consolidation of Brooklyn and Williamsburgh when that subject came up for serious consideration. It was easily seen by reference to any plan or map, or even to the eye of the observer on the East River, that the two cities were quite distinct and separate from each other, and that the Navy Yard had prevented a complete line of dwellings and warehouses and workshops being erected along the water front, which would of a certainty have been formed and made a chain connecting the two municipalities had the way been clear. But there the Navy Yard lay, completely blocking, as it were, municipal progress, and back of it rolled a stretch of wild and mostly unoccupied territory which the most optimistic fancy could not see, even if parceled out into streets and squares and avenues by the surveyors and map-makers, filled up with residential or business establishments. But the fiat had gone forth, the politicians and official spoilsmen had practically wrecked Williamsburgh; and although many thought that while the union must inevitably come, it should be deferred in the interest of both municipalities for a quarter of a century or thereabout, those in favor of it craved immediate action. The bill ordering the consolidation became a law in April, 1854, and with the passing of the 31st of December following Williamsburgh and Bushwick lost their identity and became part and parcel of the city of Brooklyn, which then entered upon another phase of its own history. The first Mayor of the first city of Brooklyn was George Hall, singularly enough chosen to be the first Mayor of the new city, and on assuming the office January 1, 1855, he delivered a most interesting reminiscent address, and this chapter cannot be more appropriately closed than by an extract from it:

It is now twenty-one years since I was called by the common council to preside over the affairs of the late city of Brooklyn, then first ushered into existence. The population of the city, at that time, consisted of about 20,000 persons, residing for the most part within the distance of about three-quarters of a mile from Fulton Ferry. Beyond this limit no streets of any consequence were laid out, and the ground was chiefly occupied for agricultural purposes. The shores, throughout nearly their whole extent, were in their natural condition, washed by the East River and the bay. There were two ferries, by which communication was had with the city of New York, ceasing at twelve o'clock at night. There were, within the city, two banks, two insurance companies, one savings bank, fifteen churches, three public schools and two weekly newspapers. Of commerce and manufactures it can scarcely be said to have had any, its business consisting chiefly of that which was requisite for supplying the wants of its inhabitants. Sixteen of its streets were lighted with public lamps, of which number thirteen had been supplied within the then previous year. The assessed value of the taxable property was $7,829,684, of which $6,457,084 consisted of real estate and $1,372,600 of personal property.

Williamsburgh was incorporated as a village in 1827. Its growth was comparatively slow until after the year 1840. At the taking of the census in that year it was found to contain 5.094 inhabitants, and since that time it has advanced with almost unparalleled rapidity, having attained a population of 30,780 in 1850. It was chartered as a city in 1851. Within the comparatively short period of twenty-one years Bushwick, from a thinly settled township, has advanced with rapid strides, and yesterday contained within its limits two large villages, together numbering a population of about 7,000 persons. Williamsburgh, from a hamlet. become a city of about 50,000 inhabitants. Brooklyn, judging from its past increase, yesterday contained a population of about 145,000 persons, and on this day the three places consolidated into one municipal corporation, takes its stand as the third city in the Empire State, with an aggregate population of about 200,000 inhabitants. The superficial extent of area included within the city limits is about 16,000 acres (or twenty-five square miles). The extent in length of' the city along the water front is eight and one-half miles, along the inland bounds thirteen and one-half miles, and between the two most distant points in a straight line seven and three-fourths miles, and its greatest width five miles. Within these limits 516 streets have been opened for public use. * * * Thirty miles of railroad tracks, exclusive of those of the Long Island railroad companies, have been laid and are in use upon the streets of the city; besides twelve lines of stages or omnibuses. The city, to a great extent, is lighted by gas, supplied by the Brooklyn and Williamsburgh Gas Light Company, using ninety-five miles of pipes along the streets. The streets are lighted with public lamps, numbering in the aggregate 3,766, of which 2,609 are gas lamps. Thirteen sewers have been constructed, extending in length five miles. There are 157 public cisterns and 547 wells and pumps. There are two public parks, one of which will rival in magnificence, as respects its natural position and commanding prospect, that of any other city in the Union.

Reference was then made to the formation of Greenwood and Evergreens Cemeteries; to 113 churches within the city; to 27 public schools, containing 317 teachers and about 30,500 scholars; to the Packer Collegiate Institute, the numerous private schools, the Brooklyn City Hospital, the Orphan Asylums, the Old Ladies' Home, industrial schools, dispensaries, etc.; also to nine banks, four savings institutions, eight insurance companies, five daily and two weekly papers, etc. The assessed value of taxable property during the previous year was estimated: In Brooklyn — of real estate, $64,665,117; of personal property, $8,184,881; Williamsburgh — of real estate, $11,242,664; of personal property, $11,614,559; Bushwick — of real estate, $3,106,864; of personal property, $109,000; making the aggregate in the whole city, $88,923.085.

Thirteen ferries, keeping up a constant communication with the city of New York, and the almost continuous line of wharves between Greenpoint and Red Hook, as well as the commercial facilities furnished by the Atlantic Docks, and the expensive ship building at Greenpoint, were also alluded to. The police of the new city, under Chief John S. Folk, comprised seven districts, with an aggregate of 274 men; the Eighth, Ninth and Eighteenth Wards not being included, they having a special police at their own expense. The fire department was also on a good footing, the western district having twenty engines, seven hose-carts and four hook and ladder companies; the eastern having ten engines, four hose-carts, three hook and ladder, and one bucket companies.

## CHAPTER XXXVII. THE ERA OF THE CIVIL WAR, 1865-1870.

In this division it is proposed to treat of the history of Brooklyn — the Consolidated City — as it was generally called from the date of that consolidation (January I, 1855) until the beginning of 1870. That period may rightfully be called the era of the Civil War, for although that terrible conflict lasted only during four years out of the fifteen years thus included, yet the time of preparation and recuperation ought to be included. While it cannot be said that the preparatory events leading to that war had much more than a passing influence on the progress of Brooklyn, it must be admitted that, in keeping with all loyal, slavery-hating communities in the North she saw the dark clouds settle out of which was to issue that bolt which was to strike Fort Sumter, and felt the need of ample preparation to meet the storm. She had to grope in the darkening atmosphere for a while, not knowing exactly what might be required of her, where the storm would break, or how far it might spread. She kept on as calmly as could be in the even tenor of her way, extending her boundaries, effecting improvements in her internal economy, and then, when the time did come, taking her full share with the Northern cities in the grand work of preserving the Union of the States.

During this period Brooklyn had five occupants of its civic chair, all men of marked individuality and in every way worthy of the honors heaped upon them by their fellow citizens. Of Mayor Hall mention has already been made and there is no need to dwell upon his career during the new term 1855-6 further than to say that he was elected upon a temperance and religious platform and zealously kept every plank in place. Possibly one of the proudest moments of his life was when, July 31, 1855, he broke ground for the reservoir of the Nassau Water Company on Reservoir Hill, Flatbush. That company had been chartered earlier in the same year and in June the Brooklyn Common Council had subscribed for $ 1,300,000 of its stock, thus giving the city a controlling interest in its management. Mayor Hall zealously put in operation all the laws he could find on the statute books which aimed at preserving the amenity of the Sabbath, and in the poorer quarters of the city he aroused a strong feeling against himself by the determined manner in which he enforced the regulations requiring the closing of all sorts of stores on the day of rest, while his determined refusal in spite of many urgent and influential appeals to permit the street cars to run on Sundays added to his unpopularity with the masses, although most of the old residents thoroughly approved his policy, so far as these public vehicles were concerned.

But long before his term was up he found himself decidedly a most unpopular personage among all classes, — particularly among the very classes who were most zealous in their use of the ballot-box. His rectitude and loftiness of purpose were unquestioned, but it was felt that his many peculiar views on public morals were not in keeping with the spirit of the times, — were too paternal and Puritanic for the nineteenth century.

His successor, who entered upon office with the advent of 1857, was Samuel S. Powell, a native of New York City. Mr. Powell had resided in Brooklyn since 1838, and for many years was engaged in business as a clothier. In 1845 he was elected for a term to the Common Council, but declined reelection and held no other public office until he was elected to the Mayoralty. He was a religious man, but not so strict in his notions as his predecessor, so he permitted the street cars to be run on Sundays and winked at' Sunday store trading so long as it was kept within bounds and was not only necessary to' the comfort of the poor, but Was demanded by public opinion. As a result his popularity steadily increased, and he was triumphantly re-elected when his first term expired. Afterward, in 1871, he was again called to the Mayor's office and served a third term, and he was chosen Comptroller in 1874, a Park Commissioner in 1877, and County Treasurer in 1878, holding the latter office at the time of his death, February 6, 1879.

Mayor Powell was what would nowadays be called an independent Democrat, and had received the Mayoralty nomination in spite of "the machine" of the party, which then had its headquarters in the law office of Lott, Murphy & Vanderbilt. His successor, Martin Kalbfleisch, however, was elected in 1861 by more "regular" Democratic management, and as the War Mayor of Brooklyn deserves to be held in loyal and kindly remembrance. Mayor Powell, it should be said, had proved himself devoted to the national cause, and aided the Government to the best of his ability and the extent of his influence, but it was Mayor Kalbfleisch's fortune to be in office shortly after the storm broke, and he continued to direct Brooklyn's loyal aspirations during what may be called the darkest period of the awful struggle. In him, a native of the Netherlands and a naturalized citizen, the Union had no more stanch advocate or the National Government a more single-hearted adherent. He could not understand for a long time, it was said, exactly what the contest was about, but he enjoyed the advantage of his citizenship, had found wealth and friends and home in the land of his adoption, and looked upon the schism — any schism — as a crime. He had settled at Greenpoint in 1842, and there built up a splendid business as a manufacturer of colors. He at once took a deep interest in local affairs, organized a school so that his own children and those of his neighbors might have the advantages of a good education, and paid the teacher's salary out of his own pocket for a considerable time. In politics he became quite an active figure, and he was soon recognized in the local Democratic party as an indefatigable worker, being, as a noted Brooklyn politician said, "One of those Dutchmen who never let go until they have carried their point, and don't know when they are beaten." In 1851 he was elected Supervisor of the old town of Bushwick and held that office until Bushwick was "consolidated," of which project he was a stanch advocate. In 1855 he was chosen Alderman of Brooklyn's new Eighteenth Ward, and held his seat in the Common Council until he became Mayor. While he held that office it may be said that war measures occupied his whole time, and he proved indefatigable in his efforts to strengthen the hands of the Government and at the same time fulfill all the active duties incumbent upon him as the head of a municipality which, in spite of the civil commotion, was extending" itself in all directions and almost daily entering upon improvements and new enterprises all of which were adding to its reasons for civic pride. After a term in Congress he was again elected Mayor, in 1867, and held that office until 1871, two years before his death.

Mayor Kalbfleisch's successor to that title, in 1864. was one of the local heroes made conspicuous by the war, — Colonel Alfred M. Wood. This man of many brilliant parts was a native of Hempstead, and what might be called a politician by profession. He was engaged in business in Brooklyn for a short time early in life, but was unsuccessful, and in 1853 was elected Collector of Taxes, and re-elected in 1856. In 1861 he was elected to the Board of Aldermen and was chosen as its president. When the war broke out he was the senior officer of the Fourteenth Regiment of militia, and, resigning his civic office, he devoted his entire time to filling up the ranks of the regiment and led it to the front. At the first battle of Bull Run he was conspicuous for his bravery, and was severely wounded just as the panic among the Northern troops began. While being removed from the field in an ambulance. Colonel Wood found himself forsaken, for the driver had cut the traces from the horse which had been hauling the vehicle and ridden away. With the help of some of his own men, whom he happened to fall in with. Colonel Wood contrived to reach a bit of woods, where they lay concealed for four days, when the little party was captured by some Southern soldiers. On partially recovering from his wound, Colonel Wood was sent to Richmond and there ordered to be executed; but the sentence was not carried out, and after a time he was exchanged. Returning to Brooklyn, he was received with all the acclaim due to a hero, and on October 20, 1863, received the nomination for Mayor and was elected by a rousing majority, his leading opponent being Mayor Kalbfleisch, who certainly deserved better treatment at the hands of the voters. But it. was a time when war heroes were the idols of the public and could get anything they sought from an admiring populace. Although he did not go to the front, Kalbfleisch probably accomplished a thousand times the service that his rival could have claimed credit for, but then "the consecration of battle," as the orators used to call it, did not figure in his record. Wood made a good Mayor, devoted himself to the best interests of the city, and after his term was over filled several minor offices in the gift of the National Government, and then went abroad.

Samuel Booth, in 1866, succeeded Colonel Wood as Mayor. Mr. Booth was born in England in 1818, but was brought here while yet an infant, and had resided in Brooklyn from the tenth year of his age. He learned the trade of carpenter, and in 1843 started in business on his own account, steadily pressing upward until he was at the head of a flourishing establishment. After a long and honorable record in various public offices, and winning much personal popularity as chairman of the local Bounty Committee, which disbursed some $3,800,000 to the soldiers and their relatives, he found himself, on entering upon the office of Mayor, in 1866, in the awkward position of having the Board of Aldermen mainly made up of political opponents, and presumably, for party purposes, ready to defeat any policy upon which he might enter. This position of things lasted during his entire term, but his own sterling honesty safely carried him through and he retired with the good will of the citizens generally. Afterward he became Postmaster of Brooklyn, and when he quitted that office, in 1874, enjoyed many honors as a private citizen, — honors which came to him willingly from all classes of his townspeople.

The succession to the Mayoralty again brought Martin Kalbfleisch to the front, and that sturdy Hollander held the reins of power when the period allotted to this chapter came to a close. He proved as safe and successful an administrator of the city's affairs in time of peace as he had during the eventful years of his previous administration when the issues of the war dictated everything, and in 1868 he had the satisfaction of seeing Brooklyn advance with greater strides than ever before to queenly rank among the cities of the country.

One of the most significant movements of this period was that tending to consolidation with New York, although consolidation itself was hardly more than broached in public. Much of this arose from the fact that Manhattan Island was so overwhelmingly Democratic that those opposed to that party could see no way of thwarting its influence other than by legislative enactment. In 1855 Fernando Wood was elected Mayor of New York City and held that office until 1858, when he was defeated by a fusion candidate, Mr. D. N. Tiemann. On the conclusion of the latter's term Wood again became a candidate and was elected, serving until the close of 1862, and afterward entering Congress. He was a man. of strong personality, a natural leader of men, and brim-full of ideas, progressive in his own way, determined to achieve his own purposes and overcome opposition, and without any of those nice scruples which sentiments of honor and honesty inspire in lofty or even well-trained minds. Like so many other "local statesmen," Wood began political life as a reformer and ended as a partisan with all the qualities which that designation implies in American politics. He had no broad views on any subject, he was not a statesman; nothing but a politician, and that, too, of a purely local type. He saw nothing beyond New York, and took no interest in the Nation, except as events in it affected his bailiwick, with a firm and united Democratic majority behind him in New York, he cared little for outside affairs, and it was this sentiment more than any real approval of the threatened Southern secession that led him, when the crisis became acute, to publicly suggest that New York City should secede from the Union and become an independent State, dragging with her into her loneliness Brooklyn and Staten Island. Afterward public opinion, the only thing he feared in this world, showed him he had gone too far, and he slid down from his top-lofty position with all the skill he could command. It was this steady and crafty manipulation on the part of Wood and his followers to increase and solidify the Democratic strength, of Manhattan Island that led the opposition party to concoct measures calculated to offset his schemes, and one of the first of these was to take the control of the local police out of his hand, for it was only too clearly self-evident that that force was being used by him as one of the most effective agents in perpetuating and strengthening his local party, and, as has been said, a strong local party was all that he cared about at that time. Accordingly, in 1857, a bill passed by the Legislature became law, under the signature of Governor J. A. King, which united the police of New York, Kings, Westchester and Richmond counties and the towns in Queens county into what was called the Metropolitan District, and which was to be governed by a board on which .the Mayor of New York had only an ex-officio seat, as well as had the Mayor of Brooklyn, while the real power over the entire force was vested in the appointed commissioners, the most notable of whom was the late J. S. T. Stranahan. For a long time Mayor Wood tried to defy the Legislature and endeavored to retain intact the old municipal force in his immediate jurisdiction, thereby giving to the world the spectacle of two sets of Dogberrys doing exactly the same work and often coming into actual collision in doing it. In the long run Wood was forced to bow to the superior authority of the State and yielded ungraciously, but Brooklyn from the first loyally accepted -the mandate. It was this union that was generally regarded as the first actual step toward consolidation, and it was his experience as a Commissioner that led Mr. Stranahan to become impressed with the view which governed his later years that the destinies of Brooklyn and New York were one and the same, were inseparable, in fact, whatever they might be in name, and that neither could reach the full fruition of metropolitan greatness until they were united into one compact municipality. It must be said that under the Metropolitan Police law, bad as it was, Brooklyn was much better protected than under her former independent force; but the enforcement of the measure led to another unexpected and unbearable evil. Like New York, Brooklyn was a Democratic stronghold, although its type of Democracy was purer and less identified with municipal scandal than had been prevailing for some time on Manhattan Island. But the police law demonstrated the ease with which local affairs could, when occasion required or party exigencies demanded, be directed from the headquarters of the State Government, and as a result of the devious ways of politics Brooklyn for a long time, — virtually during the period covered by this chapter, — was deprived, on many and important occasions, of the privilege and right of home rule which had hitherto been her boast. But the system of meddling in purely local affairs on the part of the State was discovered, after a few years of practical test, to be a bad one for both parties, equally dangerous to both, and Republicans as well as Democrats proclaimed against it with gratifying results when the Tweed gang obtained a foot-hold in State politics and ran things to suit themselves in a manner that finally aroused the people to action irrespective of party.

That the Metropolitan Police act proved a benefit to Brooklyn was due more than all else to the energetic and public-spirited labors of Commissioner Stranahan, who then began to acquire that degree of public confidence and personal popularity which later won for him the unquestioned title of "First Citizen of Brooklyn." Mr. Stranahan was born at Peterboro, New York, in 1808. In 1832 he became associated with Gerrit Smith in business in Oneida, and in 1838 was a member of the State Legislature. In 1840 he took up his residence in Newark, New Jersey, where he remained four years, engaged in railroad promotion and the actual building of railroads. In 1844 he settled in Brooklyn, which continued to be his home until the time of his death.

Mr. Stranahan at once took an active part in local affairs, ran for Mayor and was badly defeated, and from 1854 to 1857 was a Representative in Congress; but his first real work for the city was accomplished on the Police Commission, of which he was a member. Thenceforth until laid aside by the weight of years his life story was really a part of the history of Brooklyn. It was in 1860 that he began his association with the public improvement with which his name is yet closest connected and which accomplished the most lasting good, — the inauguration of the movement which gave to the city its famous Prospect Park.

That beautiful enclosure now contains some 516 acres, and is not only a park for health and recreation, but a memorial of the famous battle of Brooklyn, for that sanguinary episode of the War of the Revolution was fought mainly within its boundaries and those of the adjacent Greenwood. At Prospect Hill, or Lookout Hill, a stately shaft was erected by the Sons of the American Revolution in 1895, in memory of the 400 Maryland soldiers who fell in that battle while defending the retreat of the American army to the Brooklyn fortifications, when it was seen that the day was to end in the defeat of the Patriot cause. This memorial helps to remind the visitor that he is treading historic ground. The first Board of Commissioners appointed by the act to "lay out a public park and parade ground for the city of Brooklyn" comprised J. S. T. 'Stranahan, T. H. Rodman, E. W. Fiske, R. H. Thompson, Thomas G. Talmadge, Stephen Haynes and Cornelius J. Sprague; but it is no disparagement to the services of the others to say that the leading spirit among them all, the most persistent and indefatigable worker, the one who was least disheartened at delays and annoyances, was Mr. Stranahan.

As soon as the commission was organized Egbert L. Viele, who had prepared the plans for the laying out of New York's Central Park and saw them carried through their initiatory stages, was appointed chief engineer of Prospect Park and drew up the original plans on which work was commenced, the park territory being then bounded by Ninth avenue, Douglass street, Washington avenue and. the Coney Island road. The outbreak of the Civil War summarily arrested this great public improvement. Allele resigned his office and hurried to the front, and until the conflict was over little could be done with the scheme but to watch and plan and wait. With the return of peace came renewed effort, and in 1865 a revised plan for the enclosure was prepared by Olmsted & Vaux, the most famous firm of landscape architects then in the United States. This plan suggested the addition of new lands and the abandonment of some parts of the original scheme, and by successive legislative enactments the suggestions were all given practical endorsement and accomplishment by 1868, and in 1871 most of the general improvements were completed and the grand people's garden and playground was dedicated to public use. Mr. Stranahan continued to act as president of the Board of Commissioners until 1882, when a new board was appointed by the Mayor, of which Mr. William E. Kendall became chairman, and that body continued to direct its fortunes until it was placed in charge of the Commissioner of Parks, when the entire system of Brooklyn's breathing places was ruled as a department of the municipal government.

Since 1865 the story of Prospect Park is one of continuous improvement, beauty added to beauty, and the work is still going on, every year developing some fresh charm, seeing the completion of some .design, and the whole being carried on with a liberal expenditure which speaks volumes for the tastes of the city; for the history of the park belongs to the city, the now existing borough merely carrying on and maintaining the work. The principal entrance, the Plaza, is on Flatbush avenue, where stands the magnificent arch erected by Brooklyn in memory of those of her sons who fought in the Civil War. This pile is now surmounted by a bronze quadriga by Macmonnies, the Brooklyn sculptor whose home has been in Paris for many years, and the whole structure is one of those artistic achievements which give distinction wherever they are seen. Beside this memorial is one of the modern wonders, — an electric fountain, — and across the Plaza is a splendid bronze statue of General G. K. Warren. The whole surroundings of the park at the Plaza arc most artistic and a constant source of delight to the eye. Beside the entrance stands a bronze statue of Mr. Stranahan, erected during the lifetime of that most estimable gentleman as an evidence that Brooklyn was not ungrateful for the many years of toil .and thought he had given to her best interests. The park contains several other memorials, notably the bronze statue of Abraham

Lincoln, erected on the Plaza in 1869 by a popular subscription, but afterward removed to its present site beside the lake, busts of Beethoven, Mozart, Washington Irving, Thomas Moore and John Howard Payne, and a pair of bronze panthers which guard the entrance at Third street. There are within the enclosure some eight miles of drives, fourteen miles of pedestrian roadways and a lake covering about sixty-one acres, while from the top of Lookout Hill is one of the most interesting panoramic views to be seen in or around the Greater New York. Flocks of sheep nibble the grass on the meadows, swans and other water fowl make their homes on or beside the lake, a deer paddock and a bear garden add to the interest or amusement of visitors, while on the top of a low hill is preserved sacredly an old Hebrew burying ground placed there long before the park was thought of. As it stands to-day Prospect Park is eminently a people's popular resort. It is used for games, rambles and rest, and in summer music is provided twice a week to lighten the hearts of the multitude. In the park all tastes are gratified. One can mingle with the passing throng or find solitude as deep and as quiet as though a thousand miles away from a busy, bustling, prosperous city, with its accompanying noises and distractions.

Thanks to the forethought and public spirit shown in the acquisition and development of Prospect Park, Brooklyn possesses a magnificent variety of such resorts, some of which are even yet only in course of preparation for the public needs. Forest Park, for instance, some 550 acres, mainly of woodland, on the heights between Ridgewood Park and Richmond Hill, will be a source of delight to all lovers of the artistic and beautiful when the plans now in process of unfolding are completed or nearly so, and Dyker Beach Park, 144 acres, at Fort Hamilton, will be prized as a beach resort. Bedford Park is now contained in four acres of the Spanish Adams estate and boasts an old colonial mansion, and Tompkins, City, Winthrop, Ridgewood, Canarsie Beach, Cooper, and a dozen others all scattered through the borough, as well as open spaces innumerable, show that the builders of Brooklyn have been thoroughly mindful of a city's necessities in the way of breathing and recreation places.

To describe these in minute detail would be going beyond the province of this work, but a few lines may be devoted to Fort Greene Park (sometimes called Washington Park).

We have already mentioned the acquisition of a Fort Greene Park, a portion merely of the present enclosure. In 1847 the people petitioned the Legislature for the necessary authority to purchase all the land generally spoken of as Fort Greene, so that it might be re-served as a park, and as soon as this authority was obtained the land was secured and laid aside for public uses. It contains thirty acres and has cost the city, for land, improvements and maintenance, something like $2,000,000;

but even this great expenditure has proved a splendid investment, for with the exception of Prospect Park Fort Greene has become the most frequented and generally used of the city's pleasure grounds. It is at once a memorial, a tomb and a playground. It was one of the central points in the line of defense at the battle of Brooklyn. It was before that crisis thickly wooded, but when the issue came the wood on its crest was hurriedly cleared and a fortification was constructed on which five guns were mounted. It then received the name of Fort Putnam. During part of the battle of August 27, 1776, General Washington stood there and watched the progress of the conflict with an agonized heart as he realized only too surely as soon as he learned that the line of defenses had been turned, that victory was not to rest with his force is. In the War of 1812 it again formed a link in the chain of defenses, and was then christened Fort Greene. In one of its slopes is the tomb in which lie the bones of the Patriots who died in the prison ships in the Wallabout during the Revolution and were originally buried with scant ceremony, or rather with brutal lack of ceremony, in the sandy soil of its shore. The park is now handsomely laid out in walks, lawns, terraces, and is completely enclosed by a stone wall. From its highest point a splendid view may be obtained, while for nine or ten months in each year it affords a pleasant place of quiet relaxation for all classes of promenaders.

Brooklyn's entire system of public parks, now under a single head — a Park Commissioner — has a combined area of 1.649 acres. In addition many of the driveways, such as Ocean Parkway, Eastern Parkway. Fort Hamilton avenue, Bay Ridge Shore Drive, Eastern Parkway, Bay Parkway and others are virtually to a great extent public parks and are used as such. These driveways are in the care of the Park Commissioner, and form an aggregate of roads and drives, including all varieties of scenery, of some forty miles.

As the city extended the street railways continued to multiply and push out in all directions, sometimes indeed anticipating the line of progress by pushing their rails into what seemed a wilderness. In 1862 the Coney Island Railroad from Fulton Ferry to the beach was completed, covering a distance of eleven miles and forming the longest car line in the city. In one particularly important detail the Brooklyn street cars were far superior to those of New York at that time, the former .being heated by small but sufficient stoves which maintained a comfortable degree of heat even in the bleakest weather. But in most other respects, in frequency, regularity and what might be called ubiquity, Brooklyn's system of transit was then far superior to that prevailing on Manhattan Island.

Brooklyn, however, had need of all such facilities, for her business was extending in all directions and homes were springing up in all sorts of suburbs, in spite of the war-cloud which hovered over the land all through the years covered by this chapter. In fact while private enterprise may have to some extent hesitated, and undoubtedly did so, the city itself seemed to press forward with conceivable improvements. On December 4, 1858, a water supply from Ridgewood was first used, although it was four months later, April 27 and 28, 1859, before the people found time and opportunity to appropriately celebrate the improvement, which they did by a monster parade, listening to orators and illuminating the city. Before the close of the next year a site was secured on Montague street, at a cost of $41,000. and the erection of the Academy of Music was begun by a corporation with a capital of $150,000. The building was opened in January, 1861, and has since been the scene of many a brilliant and historic gathering.

The intellectual interests of the city were not forgotten. In 1857 the Mercantile Library Association was formed; and the Young Men's Christian Association, organized in 1853, was soon noted for the success of its work. In 1855 the number of churches was computed at 113, with several in course of construction, and indeed it would be a curious year in the story of Brooklyn that could pass without several such edifices being erected. The steadily increasing rise in the value of land on Manhattan Island and the difficulty of access to its remoter parts, which then practically meant all of it north of Thirty-fourth street, made many of her manufacturers take advantage of the cheap land in Brooklyn or its immediate vicinity, where there was also excellent transit facilities much more moderate than in Manhattan. Land could be bought in the neighborhood of Brooklyn, in extent enough whereon to erect a factory and surround it with a group of workers' houses, for less than such a block could be rented on Manhattan within an hour's team travel of the City Hall. So in and around the city, notably in Greenpoint and Williamsburgh, factories of all sorts began to spring up, steel works, shipbuilding works, sugar works, printing offices, breweries, chemical works, color works, oil refineries, — it is difficult to enumerate them all, — and each of course had an influence not only in attracting new residents but in developing the city in their respective sections. As fast as population increased the system of street transit kept pace. Even the Wallabout district, swampy, unkempt, and ill-favored in many ways, felt the influence of the tide of manufactures and enjoyed a share, and the result was that as a manufacturing city Brooklyn, even before the war cloud had been dissipated, felt impelled to claim no mean rank among the beehives of the Union. The policy of the city was to attract such additions to its midst and to make the most liberal arrangements possible to retain them. It also realized the immense advantage it possessed in its water-front and was slowly but surely utilizing it so as to attract as much commerce as possible. The Atlantic Basin had already proved a financial success and had of itself opened up for use a section of the city which had previously been known only to the lone fisherman, the farmer, and the market gardener.

Shortly after the beginning of the period we are treating in this chapter the Erie Basin on Gowanus Bay was begun and in spite of the perilous times and several unavoidable delays was pushed through and completed, and opened for business October 13, 1866:. It is a magnificent shelter, covering now 100 acres and protected by a semi-circular breakwater measuring about a mile. It includes ten piers of various sizes, grain stores with a capacity of 3,000,000 bushels, and stores for saltpeter, chloride of potash and other chemicals as well as general merchandise. Several floating grain elevators are always found in it and each winter about 700 canal boats are laid up in its shelter and many of our yachting devotees keep their crack boats there when the racing season is over. It was of course built by private enterprise but the enterprise was primarily brought about by a desire to aid in the development of the city, a desire which seems to have inspired, to more or less degree, the life of every one who has resided in Brooklyn long enough to rank as one of its citizens. The Erie Basin was a commercial success from the beginning and so continues, although it has shared in the evil fortunes of the Brooklyn Wharf & Warehouse Company, to which its ownership was transferred when that unwieldy and badly managed trust was formed in 1895. On Jan. 9, 1901, a disastrous fire occurred at the Erie Basin, destroying one of its piers and two vessels, besides a great quantity of stores, involving a financial loss, it was estimated, of about $500,000.

Another notable improvement in the same direction was accomplished by the Gowanus Canal Improvement Commission, which was called into existence by act of the Legislature in 1866. Under it the historic creek, widened and deepened, became a genuine water highway, a mile long in its main line with several branches, carrying what might be called the sea-power right into the city. Along this canal brick, lumber, coal and other yards were soon located, the moderate cost of the land as well as the ample loading and docking facilities commending the whole line of the improvement to those dealers in bulk who could handle their goods either in the way of receiving or shipping by a water route. A boat could leave a brickwork on the Hudson, for instance, and carry its load right ta Baltic street, Brooklyn, whence it could easily be transported to any part of the city, saving time and money in transporting and handling. In 1867 a similar improvement was effected in the Wallabout district, and it may be said that Brooklyn is as well supplied with internal waterways as any city on this side of the Atlantic.

From 1866 to 1870 was a time of marked development in the history of Brooklyn. The war was over, it was a time of upbuilding, rebuilding everywhere, sometimes a little feverish and uncertain, it is true, but in the main healthy and in the direction of repairing the damage and the waste and the delay brought about by four years of disunion, war, hate, and waste of blood, brain, and treasure. In 1867 3,539 new buildings were erected, and in 1868 3,307, a lesser number certainly than that of the previous year but many of the structures of a much more costly character. In 1867 sixteen miles of water pipes were laid and fourteen miles of sewers, giving the city 210 miles of water pipes and 134 miles of sewers. In 1869 there were 150 miles of sewer pipes and 224 miles of water pipes. In 1864 the assessed valuation of the real estate in the city was $103,593,072; in 1865, $106,470,308; in 1866, $113,941,366; in 1867, $122,748,954; in 1868, $131,271,141; in 1869, $179,064,130; and in 1870, $183,822,789. It must be remembered that the assessed valuation was about one-half of the real market value. These figures are more eloquently illustrative of the material progress of the city than any words could possibly be.

But the city had its drawbacks. On the map it had about 500 miles of streets, but on only about half of these were there any houses, and on little more than a quarter was there sewage provisions. Around the ferry the population was congested, — far too much for health, and on the less crowded streets the sanitary arrangements so necessary for the public welfare were absent. A house might be found standing on a street, the only dwelling on a block, and besi.de it would be a swamp, while the water for domestic purposes was procured from a well, without the slightest thought as to where the water came from or what it passed through. Even in the heart of the city sanitation in the poorer dwellings was almost unknown, or at best deemed only a luxury for the rich. It has already been seen how easily from this cause Brooklyn had received several dread visits of cholera, and in 1860 it found itself in the grasp of an epidemic of yellow fever, which, it was claimed, was brought to the port by some ship or ships from the South. How it did originate, however, is not very clear; but there is no doubt of the stern fact that forty-six cases of the disease were reported and of these thirty-four were found on Congress street. In 1866, however, there came an even more dreaded visitor, cholera, of which there were reported 816 cases. Of these 573 ended fatally, and there were also reported 142 fatal cases of what was described as cholera morbus. The greatest number of cases and of deaths occurred in the Twelfth ward, between the Atlantic Basin and Gowanus Bay, where there was a total absence of sanitary provisions, of abundance of wells and a scarcity of water mains. That the disease did not spread over a wider territory and with even more terrible results was due to the heroic exertions of the medical profession, whose labors during the anxious months of July, August and September were beyond all praise. Through the demands of the physicians a hospital for the treatment of cholera patients was opened at the corner of Van Brunt street and Hamilton avenue, and later a second one, in the City Park. Brooklyn had already become conspicuous for the excellence of its medical service, and during this period it came to the front with remarkable brilliancy. In 1856 the Central Dispensary was established, and in 1858 the Long Island College Hospital and Dispensary was organized, the St. Peter's Hospital Dispensary in 1864, St. Mary's Hospital in 1868, and several other institutions having for their primal object the care of the sick were started on their mission of practical charity and love during the period.

# CHAPTER XXXVIII.
# INTELLECTUAL AND SPIRITUAL LIFE.

In literature the city made little progress as a producer, although as a reading center its importance was everywhere recognized. Such of its sons and daughters as displayed literary ability found the best and readiest market for their wares in other places, and those of its residents who were practically active in literary work belonged in reality to Manhattan Island or were simply birds of passage temporarily in Brooklyn. This was the case with John G. Saxe, one of the most popular American poets of his day but whose memory, since his death, at Albany, in 1887, seems to have been gradually receding into the dark mist of time, where so many bright and fragrant memories become forgotten. It cannot be said that Brooklyn showed any sign of the possession of a literary cult then any more than it does now. It has been held that Oliver Bunce Bell wrote his "Romance of the American Revolution" and his "Bachelor's Story" in Brooklyn; but both of these are now hardly regarded as literature as time has robbed them of the popularity they once enjoyed. Still Bell could hardly be claimed as having done anything to confer literary eminence on Brooklyn. His interests centered in New York. Frederick Saunders, too, wrote most of his "Salad for the Social" and his earlier "Salad for the Solitary," as well as several of his other books, in his home in Brooklyn, but he carried the manuscript to New York, where his days were spent and where his real work was done. Brooklyn contained only his "bedroom." Much of Alden J. Spooner's best work was done during this period, and he and Senator Murphy and Gabriel Furman and Gabriel Harrison and a few others might, had they so desired, have won some measure of literary fame for the city they loved so well, but either they did not so desire or the fates were unpropitious, or they wanted a leader and those who might have' been leaders like Beecher, or Murphy, or Storrs, were too busy with other matters to attempt to found a literary forum.

In a literary sense the greatest of all these names, the one who might have formed and attained leadership in a literary guild and so given Brooklyn some degree of individuality in the world of letters, was the last named,— Gabriel Harrison, — a man of many and brilliant parts but whose every effort seemed destined to lead to financial failure. Born in Philadelphia, in 1825, he settled in New York in 1831 with his father and early conceived a passion for becoming an actor, inspired in that direction by seeing a performance by Edwin Forrest at the Park Theatre in 1832, it is said, although children of seven years of age are not generally bothering much about a vocation to carry them through life. However this may be, he made his first appearance as an actor in Washington in 1838, taking the part of Othello in Shakespeare's famous tragedy. For some time he was interested in photography by the Daguerre process and did work which won the praise of the inventor himself;

but there was no money in it. In 1845 he became a member of the Park Theatre Company in New York and in that position lent effective support to Charles Kean. Mr. Furman's active connection, publicly, with Brooklyn dated from 1848 when he first appeared at the Garden Theatre in a round of characters, and so endeared himself to many of its best people that he was persuaded to make it his home. In 1851 he organized the Brooklyn Dramatic Association, and, with the exception of a year or so when he managed the Adelphi Theatre in Troy, Brooklyn henceforth continued to be his home and the constant scene of his labors. In 1863 he opened the Park Theatre, when he produced most of the popular operas and high-class dramas of the day with a conscientious regard for the correctness and completeness of every detail, as well as the ability of every actor, in a manner that was far ahead of the usual run of such things in America. This endeavor, while praised on every hand, involved a degree of expense which the returns did not warrant, and he was compelled to retire from the management under a cloud of indebtedness. Thereafter he acted as manager of the Brooklyn Academy of Music and in that capacity contrived to struggle along for a time. From his early years Harrison had excelled as an artist and his interest in art had led to his appointment as secretary of the Brooklyn Academy of Design, for which institution he raised enough money to free it from a load of indebtedness and to put its art schools on a satisfactory footing. His own artistic work was then winning recognition and he was enabled to dispose of as much of it as he cared to finish and put on the market, but his conscientious scruples of only sending forth the very best of which he was capable or which seemed to him to come nearest to his high ideals, kept him from realizing all that his brush might have brought him. As an artist his best known work is a portrait of Edwin Forrest as Coriolanus, although some of his landscapes are worthy of a generous need of praise. But his main business from the time he left the Academy of Music was that of a man of letters. In 1872 he organized the Forrest Club of Brooklyn, with the idea of its becoming a literary and dramatic society of some influence, but it passed away after an existence of a few years sans accomplishment. In the same year he published "The Life and Writings of John Howard Payne" (Albany, 1872), and it is to his efforts that Brooklyn is indebted for the bust of that author which now adorns Prospect Park. He adapted Hawthorne's "Scarlet Letter" for the theatre and wrote "Melanthia," a tragedy, as well as a number of dramas, most of which were produced on the stage but failed to obtain any hold on the public and are now forgotten. After doing a good deal of literary work of one kind or another his health failed and he was laid aside for several years by nervous prostration, during which he accomplished little except a graphic chapter on the drama in Brooklyn for Dr. Stiles's work, the "History of King; County." In 1887 he became a teacher of elocution in Brooklyn and so continues.

The story of the newspaper press during the period was about as barren of incident as the general literary field was barren of living results. The Eagle had obtained a standing as the leading local newspaper in point of circulation and influence and zealously and worthily strove not only to increase its grip but to strengthen it. In this it succeeded to a greater extent than even its owners probably anticipated. There was a constant issue of new literary street and family papers which fluttered for a brief time and then disappeared, filling during their existence no felt want and passing away without leaving any sign. There were, too, several attempts made to establish new daily or weekly newspapers without capital or connection or public purpose, and meeting with the usual fate. "The Signal," in 1855, ran a brief course of six weeks as an evening paper and then ceased; and the same year saw the beginning and end of "The Brooklyn Independent," a weekly organ which was to proclaim the views of men who were bereft of a party and wanted to find shelter somewhere again. "The City News," begun in 1859, for a time was looked upon as a successful competitor of "The Eagle," but whatever measure of success it had was of but brief duration, and in 1863 it was consolidated with "The Union." That paper was first issued Sept. 14, 1863, as a Republican organ and had a marked measure of success while the war lasted. After that it began to decline and in 1870 its original owners disposed of it to Henry C. Bowen, and Stewart L. Woodford (afterward Minister to Spain) became its editor. In 1872 the proprietorship again changed hands and Theodore Tilton became editor. In 1866 "The Brooklyn Argus" appeared, as a weekly, becoming a daily in 1873, and it continued to be published until 1877, when it was merged in the "Union," which then became the "Union-Argus."

One literary development of moment in Brooklyn was the increase in the number of public libraries. The Mercantile Library Association, organized in 1857, got together a large collection of books and its classes and lectures were for years features of the higher social life of the city. In 1867 the Brooklyn Library was housed in its commodious building in Montague street, where it now has a collection of 150,000 volumes, including a special collection of 3,000 reference works. The Library of the Long Island Historical Society dates from 1863 and now numbers 62.3.40 volumes. Brooklyn of the present day, while it contains no single institution which can take rank as a great library, is abundantly provided with institutions of a thoroughly practical sort, so that the citizens so inclined can really command the world's current literature free of any cost. The free library of the Packer Institute has 67,906 volumes, and there are quite a number of smaller institutions the uses of which are free or available by payment of a small sum.

In Brooklyn, too, is one of the latest and most effective developments in the way of a really useful public library which, while it is still in the experimental stage, seems certain of success in application and rich success in results. The Brooklyn Public Library has for its object the development of a municipally controlled institution on the lines of the largest possible free circulation of books, and under the new regime has progressed rapidly. Its municipal control gives to Brooklyn the honor of proclaiming as her own the only municipal library in Greater New York. The Long Island City Library, while being conducted upon the same lines, is much less extensive, and the New York Free Library is still to some extent under corporative control. The definition of a free library, as given by the State Board of Regents, voiced by Mr. Melvil Dewey, is "one owned and controlled by the city."

In February. 1899, the library came under municipal authority, and Mr. Arthur E. Bostwick, who was formerly chief librarian of the New York Free Circulating Library, was placed at its head. Mr. Bostwick is a graduate of Yale College and has taken the degree of Ph. D. He is well known in library circles, beings extensively affiliated with library interests. He has twice occupied the Presidency of the New York Library Club, and is now President of the Long Island Library Club.

The library is the product of the Brooklyn Public Library Association, the association in turn being the outcome of the interests in free library extension, as upheld and proclaimed by the Woman's Library Association, of which Mrs. Mary E. Craigie was chief pioneer.

At the time of the city's assumption of the library it consisted of the main branch, at 26 Brevoort Place, and the Bedford Park branch. Since that time there have been added five branches: Williamsburgh, 380 Bedford avenue; East, 29 Pennsylvania avenue; South Brooklyn, 1147 Fourth avenue; and Flatbush, 5 Caton avenue, opened as Flatbush Free Library, and transferred to Brooklyn Public Library in January, 1899. The latest branch established is Prospect Branch, at Litchfield Mansion, Prospect Park, used at first as a station for the traveling library department: it later became of the same character as the other branches. The situation of this branch, which is an important one, is but temporary, the site chosen for its permanent quarters being at Sixth avenue and Third street.

Originally the library contained some 20.000 volumes; to-day there are 50,000 volumes. The library's worth is best judged by the city's recent appropriation of $80,000 for its next year. This is twice the amount appropriated in 1899. To this $20,000, conditionally available, may be added, to be used for maintenance of established free circulating libraries, when they shall be acquired as branches of the Brooklyn Public Library. The libraries alluded to are New Utrecht, Fort Hamilton, Bay Ridge, and Union for Christian Work.

Throughout the library the open-shelf system prevails, and is considered by the librarian to be the most desirable method, particularly where the borrower's interest is concerned. The loss, in his estimation, which is a natural outcome of such a plan, is in every way compensated for by the actual good accomplished.

At the main branch, which is also the building of administration, there is a most successful children's department, situated on the ground floor. The building is modern in its appointment and most attractive. Each branch, in so far as possible, is conducted, especial requirements of localities being considered, upon the model of the main branch, the children's department included, even when it is only possible to reserve a corner of a room for them.

The Traveling Library Department, which is at the main branch, is under the direction of Mrs. Mary E. Craigie, Assistant Librarian.

The privileges of this department for schools, literary clubs, etc., are just beginning to be realized, and will be more used by them as the advantages become known.

It is the directors' object to co-operate more and more, not alone with schools, but with all institutions of learning and progress. It is a matter of great encouragement that the reception of the library branches has been most enthusiastic, the borrowers being all the time on the increase; and whereas ordinarily in the establishment of a free institution gifts of money, etc., are a proof of progress, the greatest possible evidence for the future success of the library lies in the ability of the people to appreciate their own needs; the consequent demand being best supplied and strengthened by one who, having already been helped by the institution, in turn becomes interested. An actual gift of money from one not appreciative of the library's privileges does not voice to the same extent the people's progress in culture. Mr. Bostwick is an advocate of complete organization in the administration of the library.

The apprentice class in connection with the library, while it is under the control of the librarian, is more directly under the supervision of Miss Theresa Hitchler, the library's chief cataloguer. It is an institution of merit. Six months' free service to the library entitles the applicant, after passing civil service, to take competitive examination for entrance on the force of the Brooklyn Public Library.

Beginning with the main branch, each library will eventually contain an art and a music department. Unity of purpose and determination in pursuit of the highest interest of the institution committed to their charge is upheld to the entire force of the Brooklyn Public Library by its chief librarian.

The aims and scope of the Brooklyn Public Library have been treated at some length bene because they are so perfect and far-reaching as to make the institution a model one and worthy of careful consideration by all engaged in such work or planning a similar design of municipal usefulness. Just as this volume is about to go to press, however, the munificent gift of $5,000,000 by Andrew Carnegie to establish a group of popular libraries throughout the Greater New York has been announced and the problems occasioned by the princely donation are being thought over by the local leaders in library work. So far, as seems likely the main policy to be adopted will be a unification of all existing public libraries under the management of one central body and the erection of what may be termed "Carnegie library" buildings throughout the municipality. Brooklyn, of course, getting her share. Manhattan's great libraries — the Astor and the Lenox — are already united, and with the money left by Samuel J. Tilden as a perpetual endowment, will have their headquarters in the New York Public Library Building now in course of erection by the city (and at the cost of the city) on Fifth Avenue and Forty-second street. This will likely be the heart of the entire library system of the Greater City, and when these details are perfected the work of the Brooklyn Public Library may be changed somewhat, but meantime it carries on its beneficent mission to the best of its ability and present resources, regardless of what the future may have in store, or rather confident that the future will only bring progress and improvement.

It is impossible within the limits of this work to attempt to follow with any degree of detail the progress of its churches during the time covered in this section. It was a time of great spiritual activity in all directions and the churches were represented in every movement. Pastors and people were drawn together in all walks of life and in all pursuits, and the clergy were no longer a class who dwelt apart, but men who boldly grappled with all the questions of the day, questions concerning local and National government, the war, the claims of peace, and the regeneration of the Republic after its baptism of fire. In this Henry Ward Beecher led the wav and set the fashion, and it was his intense, throbbing sympathy with men around him and in measures of even passing moment that made the platform of Ph-mouth Church become a forum of the people as the pulpit had not been since the days when John Knox thundered from that in St. Giles' Church in old Edinburgh and denounced and defied his sovereign Queen — the unfortunate Mary Stuart. The activity of the clergy in all that pertained to the war was most marked, and especially so in all the measures tending to brighten the lot of the boys at the front or to alleviate the sorrow and hardship of those they left at home. To rehearse even that story, to chronicle even those deeds of active interest and loving charity, would alone require the space of a large and portly volume. In these circumstances we must be content with selecting three representative names as illustrative of the rich array of preachers who in this era made the words spoken in Brooklyn pulpits literally ring throughout the world.

In 1860 the Rev. Theodore Ledyard Cuyler was called to the pastorate of the Park Presbyterian Church, then but recently organized. He was born at Aurora, N. Y., in 1822, was educated at Princeton and was minister of the Market Street Dutch Church in New York when he accepted the call to Brooklyn. There his success was immediate and the congregation had to erect a new structure on Lafayette avenue to carry on the work, and even that had to be enlarged. Dr. Cuyler's success was remarkable in that, while not unmindful of the stirring events of his time, he never forgot that he was first of all a minister and that his first duty was to win souls to Christ. His services were purely evangelistic, and all the work of the church, and a royal working church it was, was directed to that prime duty. But he used the religious press to show his standpoint on passing events and especially upon such matters as temperance, charity and missions. He was a graceful and ready writer, one who could plead with his pen as effectually as with his tongue, and denounce shams and hypocrisies and evils with a degree of force which he would not have been thought proper in the pulpit. He wrote many books, mainly religious, all of which enjoyed a large sale and made his name known throughout the land, throughout the religious world in fact. In 1890 he retired from the active pastorate, but has continued to reside in Brooklyn and maintained his literary work so that he is still an active power for good. He preaches occasionally in various churches in whose midst he may be sojourning, but his life is spent mainly in his study where he keeps a close watch on the parsing events of each day and never fails when the occasion demands it to issue a note of warning or of approval or point a fitting moral to any story which strikes his fancy.

The second representative selected was a man of different stamp but whose name was even more popularly known — in time — than that of Dr. Cuyler. Indeed for many years his name was popularly bracketed with that of Beecher as a leader in the local church world. In 1834 a Presbyterian church was organized on Schermerhorn street — the Central. It dragged on, doing good work in a quiet way, until 1869, when it issued a call to the Rev. Thomas DeWitt Talmage, who accepted, and with his advent the church became a power. He was born at Bound Brook, N. J., in 1832, and his first charge was the pastorate of the Reformed Dutch Church at Belleville in his native state. From 1862 he was pastor of a church in Philadelphia, but while his ministry there was a successful one it was not startlingly so. Someone has said that Talmage needed the environment of Brooklyn to bring out the qualities which won for him his preeminent position. However that may be, there is no question of his immediate success in Brooklyn. Within a year the Central Church became too small to hold the throng of worshippers, and in 1870 the congregation built a new edifice, with a seating capacity of 3,400. Even this proved too small and so it was enlarged to accommodate 500 more. This edifice was burned Dec. 22, 1872, and a new structure rose from its ashes, a magnificent Gothic building with a seating capacity of 5,000, the largest Presbyterian church in the country. It, too, was destroyed by fire, on Oct. 27, 1889. Another new "tabernacle" was erected for Dr. Talmage, but it in turn was consumed by fire, May 13, 1894, and with it ended his pastoral labors in Brooklyn. The regular congregation seemed unwilling to enter upon the burden of erecting a fourth "tabernacle," and the story of the negotiations showed that not one of these buildings for the congregation had ever been a paying investment; that Dr. Talmage had for years received no salary; that there was a heavy load of indebtedness. The regular members were comparatively few, and while each service was crowded with worshippers the collection baskets were poorly filled, and, as one puts it, "the church could not get along with a weekly income of a penny a seat." So the church was abandoned. Dr. Talmage subsequently accepted a call to Washington and that city has since been his home. His popularity as a preacher is undiminished, while as a literary worker the demands made upon him and successfully responded to, indicate that his inordinate capacity for such labor does not weaken with the advance of years.

A typical Brooklyn citizen, an Irishman, a Roman Catholic priest, a Republican in politics, and a loyal American clear through, may be spoken of about here as our third representative Brooklyn clergyman. The Rev. Sylvester Malone was born in Trim, county Meath, May 18, 1821, and came to America in 1839 and at once entered on a course of study to qualify himself for the priesthood, and was ordained August 15, 1844. He was then assigned to the pastoral charge of the little congregation at Williamsburgh. His ministry was a success from its very beginning. Within two years he had filled the benches in the little church building with worshippers, paid off a heavy burden of debt which lay upon it and had started a movement to erect a new and more fitting place of worship. He was a most active man in those early days, his parish was the most extensive, in point of territory, of any near New York, he attended closely to all its parochial needs, and he lectured, visited and planned for the good of his people continually. He early became known as a man of liberal spirit, a sturdy adherent of his own church, but at the same time an admirer of all churches which had for their purpose the salvation of souls. A doubting, an agnostic, "a modern thought" community he had no patience with, then or thereafter. His first principle next to faith was sincerity, and when he found a man sincere he had no trouble in honoring and respecting him, no matter how far their views as to church questions might diverge. These sentiments early won him the love of all classes in the community and that love deepened into reverence as time went on.

In his own congregation he was decidedly popular long before the people of Williamsburgh understood him, and this popularity found tangible evidence in the rapidity with which his plans for erecting a new church was carried out. The corner-stone of the new edifice was laid May 30, 1847, and on May 7 in the following year the building was opened for worship. To it was given the name of the Church of Sts. Peter and Paul, and it at once became a center of religious and educational activity. It had a congregation numbering 5,000, a parochial school with capacity for 1,000 scholars, a religious library and various church societies, all engaging with enthusiasm in various details of religion and missionary work.

Thereafter his life was bound up with his church, and his devotion, his eloquence, his sterling Americanism, made it one of the most talked of congregations in a city that has had more famous churches than any other in America. Perhaps the most significant honor paid him was in 1894, when he was selected as one of the Regents of the New York State University. He was equally the friend of Beecher and Storrs, of Mayors Low and Schieren, of Theodore A. Havemeyer and Silas B. Butcher, of Rabbi Gottheil and Dr. Charles Cuthbert Hull. He retained his popularity to the end of his life's journey and much genuine grief was expressed throughout Brooklyn when it became known, on Friday, Dec. 29, 1899, that Father Malone had passed to his rest at an early hour that morning.

The cause of Father Malone's popularity may best be understood by citing a few extracts from some of his public utterances. Speaking of the New England Pilgrims at a public celebration of Forefathers" Day in 1877, Father Malone said:

The Puritans were the representatives of the principle which forms the nucleus of our present civilization. I remember paying a visit to Plymouth, in company with two Catholic priests. We had not long to stay and it was raining when we arrived at that spot. In spite of that fact we went to the rock and I remember, in all the wet, we knelt down and reverently kissed that blarney stone, thinking that it would do us good to pay that tribute to the memory of the founders of this country. The spirit of liberty which imbued the Pilgrim Fathers has built up the country to what it now is. That same spirit was manifested when we asserted the independence of the nation at large, shaking off the fetters of oppression. It was that same spirit which called us to preserve our liberty during secession. But for the New England element during the late Civil War. we would never have preserved the Union. But for the New England element the Pacific coast would have gone in with the secessionists. It is my honest conviction that it was the Puritan spirit which carried the struggle to a successful ending. Of course, all other nationalities aided us, but their struggles would not have amounted to anything had it not been for the energy of the Yankee. As a lover of that liberty which imbued these patriarchs and imbues our present Government, I am delighted to be present with you to-night. I thank you for the warm reception you have given me and I thank you that I have had the opportunity of expressing my sentiments.

An ardent lover of his native land, he had no tolerance for some of the forms which love of Ireland assumed in this country. Speaking with reference to St. Patrick's Day parades, he once said: "What insanity is it that brings St. Patrick from his niche in God's temple to the streets to be made the subject of laughter and derision? Silver-tongued orators fire your enthusiasm; but, harken ye, you are no better nor worse than the people of any other nation. It is true that the Irish have as their characteristic a love even to death of their faith. It seems, in God's good providence, that they are the instruments He uses to counteract the effects of the work of the Reformation in England; for go the world over, where the English tongue is spoken, and there you will find Irishmen. Does this apply to the Irish Catholic politicians, who for their own preferment bring their religion and their race into politics? If you are politicians be American politicians. Your religion and its saints and the apostles of the land dear to you and your ancestry do not need street pageants. Flock to your church, for there alone is the place to give honor to St. Patrick, and there alone you will gain the strength to walk through this world with honor to yourself, your religion and Ireland."

In his "jubilee" meeting, October 16, 1894, surrounded by a host of the brightest men in Brooklyn, men of all shades of religious faith, political complexion and social class, he turned aside in the course of his address from an acknowledgment of the many tributes paid him to eulogize the American volunteer soldier: "It was the American soldiers who won for us the proud pre-eminence of being the safest and most trustworthy civil organization as a free nation that the world has ever known. Let, then, the American citizen soldier be forever honored who has done his work so well, and, in doing so, has left to posterity an example of self-devotion and patriotism which will ring joyous notes down the ages, so that American patriotic citizens may always be relied on to do good and faithful services for fatherland in times of war as in times of peace. The American citizen being the shield in war and the industrious, peaceful member in a great and prosperous nation in times of peace, we can always trust this citizen soldier who takes to war because it is in the line of duty, and is at home in peaceful pursuits just for a similar reason. Duty in both spheres of activity gives the citizen a place in the warm affections of the family, in the confidence of the community and in the admiration of the country for which he feels and bleeds. There may be degrees in my charity, but I am not ashamed to say it, that, all peaceful as is my natural disposition, and is also the nature of my calling, my soul awakens to the highest regard for the soldier of the Union who laid down his weapons of war when peace was proclaimed and went back to the plow and his counting house and the other pursuits which were in his line of duty before he answered the summons to shoulder his musket and be drilled for the terrible conflict."

Perhaps no man ever more truly painted his own character than Father Malone delineated his own in the words with which he closed the address from which the above quotation was made, and with these few words from his own lips this all too brief record of a lovely life may fittingly close. He said:

"I give you an inside view of the workings of my soul for the last fifty years. It labored for God and revealed religion; and in doing so the children of God were never for a moment forgotten and the children of God with me would include even Ingersoll. No one can be beyond my most earnest sympathy. I love to do the most good where it is most needed. Such has been my life in the past — the same it shall be in the future. And while a merciful Father will bless me with health and understanding, I will ever be with Him, always showing mercy, blessing the. weak and strong alike, the Jew and the Gentile, the Protestant and the Catholic, the Democrat and the Republican. And you, dear friends, and all who have taken an active part in this celebration, will be remembered by me in time and in eternity."

# CHAPTER XXXIX. THE CIVIL WAR.

In the beginning of 1860 the military resources of Brooklyn included a little over 1,150 officers and men, with vague notions of discipline and rather picturesque ideas of drill and duty. They were good men, most of them, in a fighting sense, but for many years all ideas of fighting had been abandoned, real war was something that might only be encountered in picture books, and the principal aim of the soldier was to wear an original sort of uniform: the more original and outré the more gallant a soldier was he. The Thirteenth Regiment had 250 men on its roll, the Fourteenth had 150, the Twenty-eighth had 400, and the Seventieth 350.

The Thirteenth was in point of years a historic command, for, although only organized in 1847, it was a gathering together of several military companies, some of which could trace a descent, more or less direct, to commands which were ready to do battle on the earthworks in 1814. They included the Brooklyn City Guard, the Pearson Light Guard, the Washington Horse Guard, Oregon Guard, Jefferson Guard, Williamsburgh Light Artillery, and the Brooklyn Light Guard. All wore different uniforms: some had white coats, some had red, and one was rigged up in facsimile of the old Continentals when the latter were on dress parade. In 1858, when a gray uniform was ordered by the State to supersede the various fantasticalities, it nearly disorganized the command and the strength of the regiment was greatly reduced. The Fourteenth Regiment came into existence in 1846, and was also made up of a number of separate companies each wearing its own uniform. It was originally known as the Brooklyn Chasseurs, probably for no other reason than that the name sounded much more heroic and dignified than light infantry would have done. In 1861 it adopted the zouave dress, which it wore during the war. This garb won for its wearers the title of "Red-legged Devils," a compliment to the fighting qualities they constantly and gloriously exhibited. The Twenty-eighth Regiment was organized in 1860, when it seemed certain that war was about to be the outcome of the trouble between the States, and when war was inevitable and the North began to put its military force in order it was deemed advisable to disband the Seventieth Regiment. It was a nondescript body, half artillery and half cavalry, and in that form not easily handled. But the men were not lost to the State. The artillery portion organized what was known as the First Battalion of Light Artillery, and rendered good service in manning the forts in the harbor, while the cavalry formed the nucleus of a regiment of horse.

The news from Fort Sumter and President Lincoln's call for troops aroused the utmost excitement and enthusiastic patriotism throughout Kings county. The existing regiments at once began recruiting, and found no difficulty in swelling their ranks. Money began to be poured out from every quarter to help those who proposed to do the fighting. The city government appropriated $75,000 to assist the families of those who volunteered.

Plymouth Church gave $1,000, Pierpont Street Baptist Church $1,077, and others in lesser degree. The Stars and Stripes were floated from every pinnacle, one Roman Catholic priest, Father Rafina, raising the emblem of union and liberty with his own hands on the top of his church, and military companies were being daily formed and nightly drilled. On April 20, — five days after receipt of the President's proclamation — General Duryea was ordered to send two Brooklyn regiments to the front and selected the Thirteenth and the Twenty-eighth, and three days later (April 23, 1861) the former marched from its armory under Colonel Abel Smith 600 strong. leaving 200 men behind awaiting equipment. The regiment went to Annapolis, and afterward was stationed in Baltimore. The Twenty-eighth, under Colonel Bennett, went to Washington, and was on active duty until the end of the term of three months for which the enlistment of both regiments in the national service had been made. Both commands returned to Brooklyn when that time expired, although it was then beginning to be understood that the war had barely begun.

Writing of the history of the Thirteenth Regiment during the war, General Horatio C. King said: "Many of its officers and men there (on the return to Brooklyn after the three-months term) entered the volunteer service, and it is said that the Thirteenth furnished a larger number of officers from its ranks than any militia organization except the Seventh (New York City). One entire company of the Fifty-first New York Volunteers (Colonel Ferrero) was recruited by Captain Samuel H. Sims, formerly Lieutenant in Company B. Colonel Abel Smith raised the Eighty-seventh New York, and was killed by accident while superintending the organization. Captain' Joseph Morgan, of Company C, afterward became Colonel of the Ninetieth New York Volunteers, in which Captain John Sullivan, of Company A, was a Captain. Captain Morgan also raised and commanded the One Hundred and Forty-eighth New York Volunteers. John Manly was made Captain in the One Hundred and Fifty-ninth New York Volunteers, and was killed at Irish Bend, Louisiana. The Third New York Volunteers, Colonel Abel Smith, Jr.; Fifty-first New York, One Hundred and Thirty-ninth New York. Seventy-ninth New York (Highlanders), Forty-seventh New York. Fifth New York Artillery, and Thirty-seventh New York were indebted to the Thirteenth for many excellent officers. Major John H. Walker. of Rankin Post, No. 10, G. A. R., was taken from the ranks of Company D by General Scott, and made an officer in the regular army. But it is impossible to follow the names in detail. At least 600 of those who were connected with the Thirteenth entered the army and navy and served their country with zeal and fidelity.

"Upon the retirement of Colonel Smith, Lieutenant-Colonel R. B. Clark was elected Colonel, with John B. Woodward as Lieutenant-Colonel, and S. K. Boyd as Major. May 2, 1862, the regiment again responded to the call of the Federal Government, and proceeded to Baltimore, where, after a march of four miles, it encamped just outside of Fort McHenry. The camp was christened 'Camp Crescent.' June 6th four companies of the regiment embarked for Fortress Monroe, thence to Norfolk. The remaining four companies, which left Baltimore June 7th, went direct to Portsmouth, Virginia, and the entire regiment a few days later arrived at Suffolk, Virginia. Here it was brigaded with the Second, Fourth and Twenty-fifth New York and the First Delaware, General Max Webber commanding, relieving veteran regiments, which were sent at once to the Peninsula. The country around was held by the Confederates, and the duty was both arduous and fraught with danger. The camp at Suffolk was called 'Camp Crooke,' after the commander of the Fifth (New York) Brigade, General Philip S. Crooke, recently deceased. It formed a part of the extreme left wing of McClellan's army, and rendered very effective and valuable service. At a review by General Dix, commanding the corps, accompanied by General Mansfield, the division, and General Webber, the brigade commander, General Dix complimented the organization as a 'superior regiment.' Picket duty and the usual accessories of war, except actual collision with the enemy, occupied the time until the expiration of the term of service, when, on August 31st, the men turned their faces homeward, and again received a most cordial welcome.

"Again, in June, 1863, and for the third time, the regiment was called into active service, and, with other New York militia, was hurried to the front. Colonel John B. Woodward was in command, with W. A. McKee as Lieutenant-Colonel. The presence of the militia organizations in Pennsylvania enabled veteran regiments to go to the immediate front, and, although no one of them was under fire, their service was of incalculable benefit to the Union cause. They had many weary marches, and suffered privations hard for unseasoned troops to bear. The overwhelming defeat of the Confederates at Gettysburg, and their final retirement across the Potomac, rendered the services of the militia no longer indispensable, and, in consequence of the draft riots in New York, in July, 1863, the Thirteenth was ordered home, and during August did guard duty in the city while the draft proceeded, preventing further outbreak."

Many of the members of the Twenty-eighth Regiment also volunteered at once upon their return for active duty at the front, but the regiment as such did not leave Brooklyn again until 1863, when it was ordered to Harrisburg, Pennsylvania. It was home again in July to aid in the suppression of the draft riots.

But gallant as these two regiments proved themselves, and ready for any sort of service as the officers and men undoubtedly were, there is no doubt that the fighting glory of Brooklyn was more fully maintained by the Fourteenth, — "the red-legged devils," which won a record that for endurance and accomplishment is second to no other during the trying years of the great conflict. It was mustered into the service of the United States at first for the term of three months, and afterward for three years. Its story is in brief that of the Civil War, from the time it marched away under Colonel Alfred M. Wood until it was mustered out June 1, 1864. Those who then had not completed their term of enlistment were at once transferred to the Fifth New York Volunteers. and gave abundant evidence that the fighting tradition of the Fourteenth had not suffered by the change of number.

On leaving Brooklyn May 16, 1861, the regiment, under Colonel Wood, went to Washington, and on the 23rd of the same month it was mustered into the service of the United States. Then, with its strength increased to 960 men by recruits from Brooklyn, it entered Virginia and suffered much loss in the first battle of Bull Run. There Colonel Wood: was wounded and taken prisoner, and Lieutenant-Colonel E. B. Fowler assumed command. Then its war record commenced in stern reality, and it took part in the battles of Manassas Plains, Chantilly, South Mountain, Antietam, Chancellorsville, Gettysburg, Wilderness, Laurel Hill, Spottsylvania Court House and a host of others, great and small. It was always on the move, always ordered to the front wherever was the danger line, and it could always be depended on to perform whatever task was assigned to it. Under such circumstances its glory was great, but its losses were heavy. At South Mountain it lost thirty per cent, of its fighting force; at Gettysburg it lost half its available strength, and so on the story of destruction went through the entire service. Needless to say that when, in 1864, the bulk of the regiment was honorably discharged and returned to Brooklyn, the survivors of a hundred fights met with a reception at the hands of their townspeople that certainly. repaid the veterans for many a weary march and three years of hardship and peril. When the war was over the regiment was reorganized under Colonel Fowler, who continued as its commandant until 1873, when he was succeeded by James McLeer, now Brigadier-General in command of the Second Brigade, New York National Guard.

On the outbreak of the war, as has been .already said, the military fever in Brooklyn rose to a high pitch and separate companies were voluntarily formed in nearly every section of the city, the Brooklyn Grays, the Carroll Hill Guards, Guard Lafayette, Relief Guard, City Guard and the like. When the -war was fairly on a number of these organizations determined to unite in the formation of a regiment, and so in 1862 was started the Twenty-third. That command had a brief but honorable experience at the front. The Forty-seventh Regiment was organized the same year and after pretty much the same manner, but was recruited mainly from the military companies in the Eastern District. In May, 1862, under Colonel J. V. Meserole, it was ordered to assist in the defense of Washington, and remained in the service of the Nation until, with the Twenty-third and other regiments, it was ordered back to assist in stopping the draft riots. The Forty-seventh afterward performed another tour of duty at the front in 1863. In 1864 it was housed in its -own armory, the first structure of the kind in Brooklyn.

The other regiments in which Brooklyn's sons took their share of fighting at the front included the 15th, 31st, 48th ("The Continental Guard," recruited by Colonel Perry), 50th, 51st, 56th, 67th (First Long Island, "Beecher's Pets"), 73rd, 87th, 90th (organized at East New York), 132rd, 139th, 158th, 159th, 164th, 165th, 173rd, 176th, 5th Artillery, and the 15th Engineers. Besides these there were many companies of Brooklyn men to be found all through the service, as in the First Engineers, Duryea's Zouaves, Fourth and Fifth Cavalry and several others.

Having thus discussed as largely as need be here the force which Brooklyn directly sent into the field to defend the Union, it is proper to turn to the consideration of what was done at home to help the fighting arm. Besides the call for troops, one of the earliest things that brought the war right home to Brooklyn was an alarm (in the early part of 1861) from the Navy Yard over a rumor (rumors were rife in those days) that an attempt was to be made to destroy it by fire. In some way news of the rumored attack reached Captain Foote, then in charge of the yard, and he at once laid the matter before flavor Powell, stating that he only had a force of seventy-five or eighty men, — too few to defend the Navy Yard, — and requested assistance so that the property of the Government might be protected. According to the news received by Captain Foote, the plans of the conspirators had been fully made, and made with so much thoroughness that the utmost exertions were necessary, — immediately necessary, — to avert what promised to be a terrible catastrophe. Many at the time doubted the existence of a plot at all, — dubbed the incident "The Navy Yard Scare," and ridiculed the story generally; but afterward it was fully confirmed that a plot to destroy the Navy Yard had really been concocted, although the exact details, so far as known, are not so ample as were those furnished by rumor. However, Captain Foote was thoroughly convinced that a plot was in existence, and fortunately so impressed Mayor Powell with a sense of the seriousness of the situation that the latter at once placed the Thirteenth Regiment and Colonel Graham's artillery under arms ready to appear at a moment's notice, while an extra force of police (1,000, it is said) thoroughly patrolled the boundaries of the yard, on the river as well as on the land side, watched the ferries for suspicious gangs, or followed any loiterers near the scene of the proposed outrage. The rest of the militia in the city was ordered to be in readiness to take up arms in quick order. Nothing unusual occurred, however, the extraordinary precautions warning the conspirators against making any attempt, and the scare passed over as quickly as it had arisen.

There is no doubt of Brooklyn's entire loyalty to the Government during the crisis of 1861. Doubtless some of the traitorous element which seemed to infect New York had an influence on a few in Brooklyn belonging to the lawless and discontented class, a class seemingly inseparable from all large communities, in the poorer districts, but even of these the number who had any sympathy with the objects of the rebellion was very few. Brooklyn was a loyal city, and it gave many unmistakable evidences of it. Money was liberally subscribed, the Common Council doing its full share, and even the banks agreeing to make loans on terms which at other times would have been rejected, churches and societies voted money, private subscriptions were abundant, recruiting for the army was easy, and more than one corporation followed the example of the Union Ferry Company, which promised to pay the salaries of such of its employees as volunteered to those dependent upon them and to hold their positions in its service open until their return from the front. The members of the Kings County Medical Society promised to render to the families of the volunteers free of cost such medical services as might be needed.

The public interest was also manifested in many and unmistakable ways. On April 22, 1861, a mass meeting of citizens was held at Fort Greene, at which it was estimated that 50,000 persons were present, and every Union sentiment was wildly cheered. A Union salute of thirty-four guns was fired, and the gathering demonstrated that clergy, politicians, business men and men of all ranks and shades of opinion had thrown down all the barriers which marked out their folds and come right out into the open with the single idea of supporting the national administration at Washington. As Father Malone said, it was no time to talk about mistakes having been made, of this one to blame or that one to blame, to denounce politicians or even to anathematize those who had brought about the crisis. The crisis had come, the flag of the United States had been ruthlessly pulled down, and all should be forgotten until restoration had been accomplished, and the only way to accomplish that was to support loyally and without reservation or question the Federal Government. It was a grand meeting in every way, and resulted in a generous outpouring of money as well as a marked impetus in the enrollment of volunteers for duty at the front. It has been estimated that from April, 1861, until July, 1862, 10,000 Brooklyn men went into the military service of the Government. It should be remembered that no one anticipated the magnitude of the struggle on which the country had entered, and all had underrated the tenacity of purpose with which the Southern States would cling to their Confederacy.

The enlistments for active service in Brooklyn, as in most other places where the loyal spirit predominated, were rapid at first; but when it began to be realized that three months were really to cut no figure in the settlement of the disturbance and that the end promised to be a matter of years, volunteering began to fall off at a most alarming rate. This is not to be wondered at. This is a nation of business men and business is too complex a concern to be easily laid aside for three or four or an uncertain number of years and then taken up again, while even those holding situations could hardly expect them to be kept open indefinitely awaiting their return. Under these circumstances there was little cause for surprise that the active war spirit should fag a little. The country was in the position of a traveler who finds himself at the bottom of a very steep bit of road. To get over it quickly he gathers up his strength, discovers it to be steeper than he imagined and that he had used up all his energy in the first rush; so he has to wait a little until he recovers a little of what he has wasted, and then, wiser than before as a result of his first experience, he carefully and stolidly plods upward until he reaches the top and finds himself on level ground once more.

But while the enlistments fell off in Brooklyn there were no suggestions heard anywhere in the city that the war should cease except as a result of submission on the part of the seceded States, and every effort was made to encourage the military arm. It was felt that the work entered upon had to be completed. All sorts of inducements were offered to stimulate recruiting. Money continued to pour in to various committees organized to help the families of those who were in the tented field, and subscriptions to provide equipment for new regiments or companies Starting for the front were liberally responded to. The Common Council, the Board of Supervisors and corporations of all kinds generally regarded as soulless, gave liberally and promptly. There is no need of going into details or to quote examples. The patriotic liberality of Brooklyn at this juncture was beyond all praise, and the credit belongs to the city at large rather than to the individual givers.

Brooklyn aided in the defense of the Union very effectively also in another way. It was in one of her shipbuilding yards, — that of A. J. Rowland at Greenpoint, — that Ericsson's famous Monitor was constructed. It was launched January 30, 1862, just 100 days after the keel had been laid, a marvel of rapidity, and the strange vessel, almost every line of which evolved a new idea, was completed with equal haste, but without any sacrifice of essential qualities, so that she was put in commission on February 25th. On March 9th she had concluded her virgin voyage to Hampton Roads, and at once engaged the Confederate ironclad, "Merrimac," which was playing havoc with the wooden ships belonging to the United States Government. The success of the "Monitor" was so immediate and complete that the Government ordered quite a fleet of similar vessels, no fewer than seven additional ones being constructed at Rowland's establishment. Long before the war closed a large number of war vessels of various grades had been constructed in different yards at Greenpoint.

Greenpoint, during the whole of the war period, was an exceptionally busy place, thanks to its shipbuilding industry. The "Brooklyn Union," of March 17, 1864, in referring to this, gave the following summary, after speaking of the succession of monitors built in Rowland's yard:

Though Brooklyn has had to bear its full share of the responsibilities and burdens of the war, its natural advantages and the enterprise of its people have proved equal to any exigency; and the course of our city has been as prosperous and as progressive as in more auspicious times. A satisfactory attestation of this fact may be had by a walk through, the outskirts of the city, where costly structures rear their lofty heads, and the busy hum of industry may constantly be heard. The large manufacturing interests of our city, — which exist to an extent that but few of our citizens have any conception of, — are all highly prosperous, and are employed to their fullest capacity.

But it is in that portion of our city known as Greenpoint where the greatest evidences of progress and prosperity are to be seen. Within the past year a dozen or more streets in the Seventeenth Ward, which promise to become the most frequented and important thoroughfares, have been opened, graded and paved, thus enormously enhancing the value of the property in that district. In the same ward there has been erected within the past eight -months not less than loo first-class dwelling houses and stores, and yet the demand is greatly in advance of the supply. Besides these buildings, there have been erected in the same locality docks, ferry houses and factories, which have largely increased the traffic and importance of the neighborhood.

But, perhaps, the most encouraging feature of Brooklyn enterprise is to be found in the unabated prosperity of the shipbuilding interest. The estimated value of the vessels now building at Greenpoint, including those for the Government, is upwards of ten million dollars, and the number of persons employed thereon is between two and three thousand. * **

A. J. Rowland has two iron monitors under way. One, the "Puritan," a sea-going vessel (length, 340 feet; breadth of beam, 50 feet; depth, 23 feet), is the largest of the monitors yet built, and is justly regarded as a perfect marvel of naval architecture and strength. She is so nearly finished that she will be ready for launching early in May. The other iron vessel under way at this yard IS the "Cohoes," a light draft monitor for coast service. She is 300 feet long, 42 feet wide, 28 feet depth of hold, and 2,800 tons burden. The number of hands employed at this yard will average about 500.

The Dry Dock Iron Works is a young rival of Mr. Rowland's establishment, and was opened last fall by Mr. J. S. Underbill. At this establishment is being constructed a light draft monitor, to be called the "Modoc," and in all respects similar to the "Cohoes," building in Mr. Rowland's yard.

Mr. Henry Steers, at his yard, is building for the Government the sloop "Idaho," a vessel of 3,000 tons, 300 feet long, 44 feet wide, and 27 feet depth of hold. The "Idaho" will be launched within a month from this time. She is built with an express view to speed, will be furnished with two propellers, and contain engines of 3,000-horse power, and will prove a splendid addition to the United States Navy.

A large number of ocean and sound steamers (both side-wheel and propellers), ferry boats and wooden vessels were also being constructed in the various yards.

The Navy Yard was, as might be expected, continually busy during those days of conflict. Besides repairing many existing vessels, the following were constructed at this great establishment between 1861 and 1864:

Sloop "Oneida," launched November 20, 1861.

Steamer "Octorora" (paddle-wheel, double ender), launched December 7, 1861.

Screw steamer sloop "Adirondack," launched February 22, 1862.

Screw sloop "Lackawanna," launched August 19, 1862.

Screw sloop "Ticonderoga," launched October 16, 1862.

Steamer "Shamrock," launched March 17, 1863.

Steamer "Mackinaw," launched April 22, 1863.

Steamer "Peoria," launched October 9, 1863.

Steamer "Tullahoma," launched November 28, 1863.

Steamer "Algonquin," launched December 31, 1863.

"Miantonomah," ironclad, double turret, launched August 15, 1863.

Screw sloop "Maumee," launched July 2, 1863.

Screw sloop "Nyack," launched October 6, 1863.

Screw sloop "Madawaska," launched July 8, 1865. (Engines, boilers, etc., built by John Ericsson).

Screw sloop "Wampanoag," launched December 15, 1864.

# CHAPTER XL. THE DEATH GRAPPLE OF THE STRUGGLE.

Before the middle of 1862 had passed President Lincoln and his cabinet felt that a fresh crisis had to be faced, and in view of the falling off in the enlistment a call was issued August 4th for a draft of 300,000 troops to serve for nine months. The quota assigned to Kings county under this call was 4,294. By that time the first glamor of the war was over, the ideas of a short and glorious campaign had been dissipated and the certainty of a long and bitterly waged contest had taken possession of the people. In other words, the conflict was no longer a fad, but a life-and-death struggle, and the sadness of the outlook induced an apathy that seemed inconsistent to thoughtless minds when considered in the light of the previous enthusiasm. It was, however, merely the natural relaxation which comes to nations as to men in times of over-excitement, and that may be regarded as the real solution of the apathy which Brooklyn, and so many other centers of genuine patriotism, showed to this third call of the Government for troops. The response certainly was disappointing. But a public meeting held at Fort Greene on August 15th to consider the situation changed all that. so far as Brooklyn was concerned, and again aroused the same enthusiasm which had marked the opening story of the war. On the day following the Board of Supervisors offered a bounty of $50 for volunteers, and this in many cases was supplemented by private bounties. Recruiting stations began to present again a lively appearance, tents were pitched in the public parks, recruits were seen in all directions, the funds for the relief of those at the front were liberally replenished, and it was not long before Kings county's quota was secured and equipped, without any need at that time of the dreaded draft. More men, in fact, had volunteered than were asked for, and recruits were sworn in faster than they could be equipped. From then on Brooklyn had no dubiety about answering every demand from Washington. The financial end of all this enthusiasm was fully met in the long run, although the bounty paid by the authorities before the end of the war rose to as much as $300 for substitutes for those drafted who had families entirely dependent on their daily earnings. The spirit of patriotism, the bounty, the aliment allowed in certain cases to family, the generous work of the relief boards, — all contributed tó make men willing to lay down their peaceful avocations and go to the front. At times, indeed, the city looked more like a military rendezvous than a place of peaceful trade and barter, and from the outlying camps, such as at Union Course, parties of armed men were, for a time, constantly marching through the streets on their way to the ferry en route for the front. In June, 1863, came another call for troops, and six Brooklyn regiments responded, the Thirteenth, Twenty-third, Twenty-eighth, Forty-seventh, Fifty-second and Fifty-sixth, and before the close of the month every command in the city excepting one, — the Seventieth, — had gone to the front.

In July the extreme peril of the Nation was felt at Brooklyn's own doors, for on the 13th of that month the famous, or infamous, "draft riots" commenced in New York. There was little trouble expected in Brooklyn from its own residents, but the stores at the Navy Yard offered a tempting prize to the disaffected on Manhattan Island and much private property along the water front was practically unprotected against any attack by rioters in quest of plunder. As usual in such moments, there were hundreds of wild rumors circulated which tended needlessly to magnify the extent of the danger. The force at the Navy Yard was strengthened and the armories and all other points where danger was anticipated were zealously guarded. The Seventieth did good service and special volunteers rallied to meet the crisis. A part of Brooklyn's defensive force was sent over to New York to assist the authorities in the protection of public property, and the police remained on duty day and night ready to answer any call. The Mayor showed himself the right man for such an emergency and was constantly at his post, advising, directing and planning, as long as the danger seemed acute. That danger did exist in Brooklyn, — that the forces of disorder were waiting an opportunity to accomplish something, — was realized on the night of the 15th, when two grain elevators in the Atlantic Basin were put on fire by a mob, causing a loss of over $100,000. The mob even charged the firemen when the latter were engaged in their duty, but were routed by the police. This was practically the only outbreak in Brooklyn of the spirit of disorder which was then widespread in the neighboring city. As soon as possible, however, troops were sent to Brooklyn in sufficient number to quell any further trouble which might arise, and the citizens resumed their ways without the haunting specter of red riot confronting them day and night,— a specter that for a time seemed plainly visible to the dwellers on Manhattan. But it was a sharp and significant lesson as to what might be the result should the force of ignorance and discontent and poverty, which makes for riot and disorder, gain a foothold, even for a brief period.

From that time private generosity fully vied with that of the municipality in equipping troops, increasing bounties and the like, and money was raised in all sorts of ways and with a most generous hand. Perhaps the most notable, certainly the best remembered, outcome of this spirit was the Sanitary Fair of Brooklyn, which was opened February 22, 1864, and by which $402,943.74 was raised. It was one of a series of similar schemes for raising money undertaken in several of the larger cities, but with the exception of New York, whose fair yielded about $1,000,000, Brooklyn was far ahead of her sister cities, for Chicago only raised $60,000 and Boston $140,000, to give a couple of instances. These fairs were undertaken at the request of the United States Sanitary Commission to aid in its remarkable work among the soldiers in the field, and were only suggested when it was thought impossible to secure more money as a result of further appeals to churches, societies. or committees. A great fair was naturally looked forward to as a certainty in New York, and it was first intended that Brooklyn should unite its energies with the good folks of Manhattan in the matter: but after a time, when the movement began to gather a little enthusiasm, the ladies of Brooklyn considered their city big enough and wealthy enough to support a fair of its own. and so the matter was left in the hands of the War Fund Committee of Brooklyn and Kings county and the Woman's Relief Association of the city of Brooklyn. Both of these organizations had already performed grand service in the charitable work made necessary by the war, the Woman's Association in one year alone turning in to the Sanitary Commission clothing and supplies to the value of $50,000.

The plan of having an independent fair, rather than devoting their time and energy to what would be simply an annex to that in New York, was starting at a meeting of the Women's Association, over which Airs. J. S. T. Stranahan presided, and to that lady is due the credit for much of the success which was ultimately achieved. The project at once commended itself to the ladies and was almost at once adopted. The executive committee of their association was thereupon enlarged, the aid of the War Fund Committee was solicited and that body at once heartily endorsed the plan and appointed a committee of sixty to co-operate with the women. This committee at once met and organized by electing Mr. A. A. Low as president. Many meetings were held: Henry Ward Beecher and many of the ministers and political and social leaders of the city entered heartily into the plan, and a splendid spirit of enthusiasm was quickly developed. It was determined that the fair should be, for the honor and the good name of Brooklyn, a grand success; but when one enthusiast. Dr. Spear, mentioned $150,000 as the sum to be aimed at, he was regarded as a visionary. On December 18th the Women's Association sent out notices, all over Long Island asking contributions for the fair. On the following evening the War Fund Committee held a meeting, and after a careful study of the situation and hearing reports on the plan, scope and success of the fair then open in Boston, addresses were delivered by Dr. Cuyler and several others, including Mr. John D. McKenzie, who spoke most effectively from a practical standpoint, and closed by tabling a subscription of $1,000. Thus incited to immediate effort, a subscription paper was drawn up and passed around, with the following results:

A. A. Low $2,500
S. B. Chittenden 1,000
George S. Stephenson 1,000
Peter C. Cornell 1,000
H. E. Pierrepont 1,000
Henry Sheldon 1,000
Josiah O. Low 1,000
George B. Archer 1,000

Joseph Ripley 500
S. B. Caldwell 500
A. W. Benson 500
R. W. Ropes 500
John Frothingham 500
T. S. T. Stranahan 500
Richard P. Buck 500
Henry Sanger 500
Henry K. Sheldon 500
Ambrose Snow 500
S. M. Beard 500
Sidney Green 500
R. H. Manning 500
James P. Wallace 500
Cornelius J. Bergen 500
Cornelius Adams 500
Amos Robbins 500
Seymour L. Husted 1,000
J, B. Wellington 500
John Bullard 500
James C. Wilson 500
Charles Storrs 500
E. B. Place 250
H. G. Reeve 250
Thomas T. Buckley 250
H. K. Worden 250
S. E. Howard 500
W. H. Lyon 250
C. R. Marvin 250
James Humphrey 500
E. T. H. Gibson 1,000

A total of $26,000. Then the enthusiasm over the plan rose to fever heat and was maintained at that point until the fair was over. Air. Chittenden offered. besides his subscription, a pair of Devon steers, which he promised to fatten on Yankee corn, and there were promises of other donations.

By the end of December the subscriptions exceeded $50,000, and the committee began to be burdened with the extent and variety of the contributions in goods. It was intended that the fair should open on February 22, the day fixed for the opening of that in New York; but the management in the latter city found it necessary to postpone their opening until March 28th. When this was announced Brooklyn determined to adhere to the original date, so that any lingering connection even in name between the two movements was clearly severed. The more emphatic this distinction became the more loyally did Brooklyn's citizens rise to the occasion, and the local enthusiasm spread all over the island. Meetings were held in Flatbush and almost every town in Queens and Suffolk, and the scheme rapidly developed into one in which all Long Island had an equal interest. The Academy of Music was secured for the main display, and arrangements were made for the use of other buildings should they be found necessary, while the Board of Aldermen gave the requisite permission for the erection of whatever temporary structures might be desired. A public meeting in the Academy of Music on June 2, 1864, gave the citizens for the first time an adequate idea of what had been accomplished and of what was expected, and seemed to crown the efforts of all concerned with the assurance of success. Then followed a busy time receiving and arranging contributions of every conceivable sort, devising this and that surprise, discussing one novel feature after another, putting plans in operation and getting everything in readiness. It was an anxious season, too, for the committee, for there was so much to do, so much to prepare and arrange for, that the days and nights all seemed to become too short. In fact, even before it was opened the fair had far exceeded the early anticipations of the workers. The Academy was found to be too small, and a temporary structure was erected on its west side on a vacant lot, the use of which was given by Mr. A. A. Low, while a similar structure was raised on a lot across the street belonging to Mrs. Pierrepont, who gladly gave the fair the use of it. On the Low site the building was named Knickerbocker Hall. It was beautifully fitted up and the whole of the material and decorations used in it were presented to the fair and sold by auction for its benefit after all was over. On the ground owned by Mrs. Pierrepont was the New England Kitchen, which proved to be one of the most attractive features of the affair. The Taylor Mansion, No. 119 Montague street, had to be called into service and was turned into a museum of arts, with war relics and other attractive features; and even with all this additional accommodation the contributions so poured in upon the committee that it was difficult to classify and exhibit them properly.

Only two troubles seemed at the close of the season of preparation and just before the opening to cause any discord, and these were in connection with the sale of liquor at the refreshment stands, and the raffling off of any of the articles contributed. Many of the contributors were opposed to liquors, especially the ladies, and quite a number looked upon the usual style of raffling in vogue even at church fairs as being a mild form of gambling. These objections led to quite a discussion, but in the end it was decided that as the fair was to be held for a holy and patriotic purpose it were best that it should be conducted on lines that should be free from -reproach even by the most fastidious and straight-laced, and so it was decided that neither should liquor be sold nor raffling be permitted.

The fair opened on February 22, at 7 o'clock in the evening, and from then until its close the huge enterprise was managed without a hitch, everything proceeding smoothly, so far as the management was concerned, and the public evidently becoming daily more and more enthusiastic over it. But even the ease with which the business of the fair proceeded bespoke incessant and vigilant care and supervision on the part of the committee, and it may be fitting here to recall the names of those who were most active in it, — most of whom have now passed away. Indeed, it was thought that the care and responsibility thrown upon her by this great local undertaking of love and patriotism hastened the death of Mrs. J. S. T. Stranahan, who died August 30, 1866.

There is little need now to enter into any details of the fair, all that were interesting at the time have by the passage of the years lost their significance, and except in importance of results it differed little from similar fairs which had preceded and have followed it. Perhaps we might recall such labors as that of Dr. Storrs and Mr. Francis Williams in editing "The Drumbeat," the daily newspaper which recorded the story of the enterprise and added largely to its funds, or describe the New England Kitchen, where an old-time interior was disclosed with ladies in attendance who were dressed up in the style of their grandmothers, where the spinning-wheel was seen in operation, where the huge open fire, fed by logs, not only diffused warmth and thawed the most careworn face but cooked great pots of chowder and of mush and lent its heat to side ranges where were prepared huge dishes of pork and beans, brown bread, puddings and pies all "such as mother used to bake." But these are glimpses: to tell the story of the fair it would be necessary to use a volume, and it is only in the nature of things to confess that the telling would not repay in interest the reader, who would be wearied and certainly net much edified.

But we have to deal with the. results. The fair closed on March nth; and, when the returns were footed up and it was learned that $402,943.74 had been realized, it is safe to say that there was not a man or woman in Brooklyn who did not feel proud of their city. Of the money thus realized $300,000 was at once paid over to the Sanitary Commission, and in acknowledging it the president of that body. Dr. Bellows, wrote: "As this is by far the largest amount ever put into our treasury at one time by any community, I feel that it deserves the most marked expression of our gratitude and wonder. * * * Brooklyn, by the only thoroughly approvable kind of secession, has henceforth declared her independence of New York. She has indicated her right and power to lead, and we shall no longer hear her spoken of as an appendix to the metropolis. She is, at least, entitled to be the second volume of that great work, the Commercial Capital, of which New York is the first." Certain it is that Brooklyn was no longer considered by the county at large as merely an annex to the city on Manhattan Island.

The idea of cutting away from New York City fund another expression a few days after the fair closed. Up to that time the Brooklyn contributions to the United States Christian Commission were paid through the New York branch of that organization, an organization that was doing a grand work among the soldiers and sailors in the front as well as in hospitals, forts and camps throughout the country. On March 10 a meeting was held for the organization of a branch of this body for Brooklyn, and in this movement the following were active: Revs. James Eels, D. D.; R. S. Storrs. Jr., D. D.; John H. Raymond, D. D.; W. I. Budington, D. D.; J. B. Waterbury, D. D.: J. E. Rockwell, D. D.; Elbert S. Porter. D. D.: E. H. Canfield, D. D.; Samuel T. Spear, D. D.; Charles S. Robertson; L. H. Mills; C. D. Foss; R. M. Hatfield; Theodore L. Cuyler; Wilbur F. Watkins; William S. Karr; E. Mills; Robert Lowery; Samuel B. Caldwell; Thomas H. Messenger; Livingston K. Miller; S. B. Chittenden; Reuben W. Rogers; Henry Sheldon; Edward Cary; William J. Coffin, Edward A. Lambert; William A. Armfield; James C. Southworth; John D. McKenzie; David Wesson; Lewis Morris; A. D. Matthews; R. L. Wyckoff; John G. Fay; Richard H. Cornwell; Benson Van Vleet; Dwight Johnson; Walter S. Griffith. Before the close of the month these men had fully organized the branch, and chosen Walter S. Griffith, president; Rev. Dr. Eels, vice president; Rev. Dr. Waterbury and William J. Coffin, secretaries, and Samuel B. Caldwell, treasurer. It is difficult to estimate the amount of good accomplished by this organization, which was held to be representative, not alone of Brooklyn but of all of Long Island. It was liberally sustained by gifts of money, books, newspapers, the work of sewing circles and by suitable gifts of all sorts; it supplied ten chapel tents, at a cost of $5,000, each with a library, and it forwarded large collections of books to many of the hospitals; it sent Christian workers to the front and on the battleships, and carried the reputation -of Brooklyn as a Christian community right into the very fields where her sons had made the name honored for their gallantry, and it continued its magnificent work with unflagging zeal until the central body deemed the time had come that its labors should end.

Then there were many charitable agencies at work, showing how profoundly the local spirit of generosity was touched and how, as the war progressed, and men — under the impulse of patriotism, large bounties, liberal 'hand" money and public as well as private payments to substitutes, and rewards even to those bringing in recruits to the recruiting stations — were being hurried to the front to meet the demand for drafts, the apparently insatiable demand of the Government for "more." the public benevolence seemed to become month after month stronger and more generous and impulsive. The Woman's Relief Association continued its beneficent work with undiminished zeal. The Female Employment Society performed a rare service among the widows and orphans of deceased soldiers or among families made destitute by the removal of the bread-winner to the front, the

Soldiers' Home Association also carried on a work of mercy and love, and in most of the churches were organizations — sometimes more than one — to aid the fighting man in some way to relieve the distressed, and to comfort those who mourned.

But it is no disparagement to the work of all such organizations, to the splendid achievements of the Women's Relief Association, to say that the greatest and most inspiriting power in all the charitable work of the time was the War Fund Committee. It was organized on Sept. 11, 1862, and continued for three years or so after the war was over. The first members of this committee were J. S. T. Stranahan (president), A. A. Low, Hon. John A. Lott, H. E. Pierrepont, Isaac H. Frothingham, Cyrus P. Smith, William Marshall, J. D. Sparkman, Nathaniel Briggs, Martin Kalbfleisch, John A. Cross, Walter S. Griffith, Conklin Brush, Seymour L. Hasted, Abram B. Baylis, S. B. Chittenden, John H. Prentice and Alexander McCue. This body was afterward somewhat changed by the passage of time, but as a whole those who were active in it at the beginning remained so to the end. Its aims were most comprehensive; its results were most effective. It raised regiments, aided distress, fanned the flame of local patriotism, collected pensions, bounties and soldiers' pay and handed the money to the proper parties, forwarded letters to the soldiers and sent them nurses; it aided widows and orphans, the sick and needy; it was practically an association formed to second the efforts of the Government, to assist the soldier and to help those dependent on him, and it nobly accomplished all that work. The committee may be said to have fittingly closed its mission by the erection, on the plaza in front of Prospect Park, of the statue of Abraham Lincoln, which now adorns a fine site elsewhere in that beautiful pleasure ground.

The news of the assassination of Lincoln, on April 14, 1864, coming so soon after the intelligence of the surrender of Gen. Lee's army at Appomattox on April 9 and the virtual closing of the war had roused a jubilant spirit in Brooklyn, plunged the community into the deepest gloom. It was fully realized that another and most unexpected crisis had arisen, and all classes, all shades of political belief, joined hands in a common sorrow. Flags were everywhere lowered, public offices, courts and theatres were closed and mourning emblems were displayed on every side. On April 15 a mass meeting of citizens was held in the Academy of Music under the auspices of the War Fund Committee, when the public sorrow and horror and indignation were fittingly voiced, and on the 26th a vast procession of citizens honored in spirit the obsequies of the nation's martyr.

But the keen edge of the sorrow passed, and soon the country was busy repairing in the new era of peace the ruin and havoc, the loss and sorrow, which the war had brought. In this grand work Brooklyn was as conspicuous as in the crisis she had been conspicuous in sending men and treasure without stint into the arena. Soon the war became nothing but a hateful memory, except to those from whom it had taken near and dear ones and with whom the bitterness of the fateful years between Sumter and Appomattox remained until the end of life's weary journey. But the story of the war was to furnish in Brooklyn one more ceremony, in this case a gratifying one, and with it we may close this glorious, if tragic, section of our history.

On October 25, 1866, the city presented to each of its surviving heroes of the army and navy a simple silver medal, a trifling but significant emblem, which is now treasured as an heirloom in many a home all over the land. The presentation ceremonies were made the occasion of a grand military parade; and the entire proceedings, conducted by Mayor Booth on the historic slopes of Fort Greene, called forth all the enthusiasm of a people who in time of conflict and peril, of gloom and foreboding, did at least what they could to aid in maintaining the honor of the Stars and Stripes and preserving the work of the fathers of the Republic. On the occasion of the presentation of these medals, three thousand veterans were "decorated" in the sense that French soldiers are decorated when they receive the ribbon of the Legion of Honor, — an idea neatly conveyed by Mayor Booth when he said: "The medal we present bears with it that which money cannot purchase. It represents the heart and voice of 300,000 people; The small ribbon worn by the French soldier as a mark of heroic deeds is prized as highly as life itself. It bears evidence that the wearer has done something for the glory of France. The testimonial we present you to-day bears evidence that you have done very much for the cause of liberty and good government throughout the world." It was a day of triumph for the old soldier when he was thus honored by his fellow citizens through their Chief Executive and in the presence of the Governor of the State (R. E. Fenton), Admiral Farragut and a host of men famous in national and local story. Dr. Storrs delivered the inevitable oration, but it was a masterpiece of oratory, and ex-Mayor Wood, himself one of the veterans, made a fitting response on behalf of his comrades in acknowledgment of the praises which had been heaped upon them.

Gradually the war took its place in history and its public memories were confined to the ceremonies of Decoration Day, when in the various cemeteries the graves of the veterans who had passed away were decorated with flowers and the events of the days which followed the fall of Fort Sumter were recalled by orations in public places or less labored speeches beside many a little mound marked by a flag, beneath each of which rested one who had joined the mighty army above. On one of these occasions, in Greenwood, Mayor Seth Low suggested that Brooklyn should erect a memorial which should at once honor the dead soldiers of the Civil War and be a permanent reminder of Brooklyn's gratitude for the men who left her streets in the course of the conflict to fight for the Union. The suggestion was heartily taken up; but after several plans were talked over the matter seemed to be dropped. Finally the idea of a monumental arch struck the popular fancy and designs for such a structure were prepared by Mr. John D. Duncan, and approved. The money was readily raised, the corner-stone was laid in the Park Plaza in 1800, and the completed structure was dedicated to the memory of the dead in 1892. That is to say, the arch proper was then completed, for since then it has been adorned by sculpture, notably figures by MacMonnies, until it now stands as one of the most beautiful memorials of its kind in the world. The Plaza, too, has been adapted to add to its effectiveness, and the scene of which it forms the most striking feature is not equaled in artistic beauty in any city in the old world, not even in Paris itself, — a city which prides itself on its wealth in stone and line and its architectural triumphs. Brooklyn truly has not proved ungrateful to or forgetful of those who represented her in the tented field or on the battleship when the fate of the Nation was at stake.

Many years have come and gone since the wage of battle between the States, but, although slowly dwindling, the number of survivors of the terrible struggle who are still with us is considerable, and as members of the Grand Army of the Republic wield a great influence not only on the well-being of those themselves to whom have come age and poverty, or on the well-being of the widows of those who have passed away, but upon the community in general.

The Grand Army of the Republic was founded at Indianapolis, in 1866, in the spirit of fraternity, charity, and loyalty. These continue yet to be its watchword. The first Post in New York State was organized at Rochester, in December, 1866, and the fourth, Wadsworth Post, at Brooklyn, a few days later. In Brooklyn the Army has had a most beneficent influence over the fortunes of the old soldiers, procuring them employment, voting them into office, and standing by them in seasons of trouble; and, although at times the cry has been raised that the organization was lending itself to politics, it has never betrayed its watchwords to a comrade, no matter what his politics might be; and while it has certainly sought to influence legislation the influence has been exerted simply on matters pertaining to itself or its members. On two occasions it has come prominently before the public. The first was in the movement which culminated in the founding of the Soldiers' Home at Bath, which was started when Corporal James Tanner pledged his word that Brooklyn would raise towards such a home $10,000, and Brooklyn made good the pledge, with some $4,000 to spare. The second was in connection with the funeral of Gen. "U. S. Grant, when Post 327 of Brooklyn received his name and was part of the guard of honor beside his bier at Mount McGregor and held the most honorable place around the casket containing the hero's remains as they were escorted through New York to the temporary tomb in Riverside Park. There are now thirty-three posts of the Grand Army in Brooklyn Borough, six in Queens county, three in Nassau county, and nine in Suffolk, making fifty-one in all on Long Island. The charitable works of these organizations are well supplemented by those of the Woman's Relief Corps, of which there are sixteen on Long Island, and which render material aid to the aged and poverty-stricken wives, mothers or widows of those New York men who fought in the Union armies, and to the army nurses who rendered the Boys in Blue grand and never fully requited services in the, hospitals and camps.

# CHAPTER XLI. THE SPLENDID CLOSING RECORD.

The story of Brooklyn from 1882 until it assumed its place as one of the boroughs of the Greater New York is one that should be discussed in a volume rather than summarized in a chapter. It presents us with many details which are deserving of thoughtful and extended study. To students of municipal government it shows the steps by which the principle of direct responsibility was carried to its highest and clearest practical demonstration, and the progress of the struggle between that principle and the efforts, unseen but unceasing, of the political machines to undo it. It shows a constant growth of a community in wealth, in culture, in art, in science, in education, in trade and commerce, a vast aggregation of people — the population increasing annually at a rate that seemed certain to make it in time exceed that of the "neighboring city" of New York — and yet without any of the excrescences in the shape of open vice and looseness of morals which is generally such a blot on all great centers. A great commercial city without a stock exchange; a splendid water-front — large enough to serve a world's commerce and yet neglected except in sections. A vast storehouse of Government property without any military or naval aristocracy, a city of churches, of shops, and of homes, a city of splendid distances, splendid buildings, honest aspirations, and yet preserving much of the characteristics of the old village life; a city which was full of politicians, but whose local affairs as a general rule were honestly managed; a city whose marvelous extension was immediately followed by a generous outlay, irrespective of immediate returns, so as to bring the extensions as soon as possible under city conditions, a city which could boast of all the concomitants of the higher civilization, — all these things present themselves for consideration along with a hundred others as we survey the closing twenty-five years of Brooklyn's civic history.

And yet over all as we read the record now, there pointed the inexorable finger of fate pointing to consolidation with the Island of Manhattan and so welding into one grand corporate body the two cities which had grown up side by side an I which, even in spite of oldtime bickerings and jealousies had been helpful and necessary the one to the other. By consolidation the city of Brooklyn disappeared and assumed the lower status of a borough, so did the city on Manhattan Island and the Greater City — the boroughs of Manhattan, Brooklyn, Bronx, Queens and Richmond formed a united community — a city destined to become the greatest in the whole world. Henceforth the story of Brooklyn is merged in that of the Greater New York, but its people believe that in the destinies of that grand city it will be the leading factor, the greatest of the boroughs in population and influence.

So we resume our study of the old city, taking up the story with the advent to power of the victor in the mayoralty campaign of 1881.

Seth Low stepped into the Mayor's office Jan. 1, 1882, after one of the most strenuously contested elections of which even the political history of Brooklyn has record. He was born in Brooklyn, Jan. 18, 1850, and belongs to a family which for over a century had held a leading place among the merchants of New York and the public-spirited citizens of Brooklyn. He received a thorough education, commencing with his entry into the Juvenile High School on Washington street and closing with his graduation at Columbia College in 1870. Then he entered the firm of A. A. Low & Brothers, of which his father was then senior member, and in 1875 was assumed as a partner. Like so many of his family, he became deeply interested in the working out of municipal problems as they presented themselves in the local affairs of the city, and his naturally kindly heart led him first of all to try to effect some improvement of the work of charitable administration which was not only corrupt but inefficient and had for its real sufferers the poorest of the poor — the very class least able to help themselves. By his work and influence the Bureau of Charities was established in 1878 which strove, as it still strives, to systematize the work of charity all over the city, to prevent deception, to aid the really deserving among the poor, to provide temporary employment, to send visitors and nurses among the indigent, to investigate reports of cases of distress and to promote a spirit of co-operation in charitable work among the various churches and benevolent organizations of the city. Its beneficent work is being extended year after year, it has its own lodging houses, day nurseries, wood-yards, laundries, and other accessories and in 1900 it attended to 9,544 cases and expended on its work $21,858. It was while engaged in establishing this great experiment in charitable work that the name of Seth Low first became prominent in Brooklyn; and the straightforward way in which he conducted all the proceedings, the clear and logical manner in which he presented all the details and the business-like way in which the entire subject was handled commended him to the favor of all good citizens of all shades of politics, for it was seen that one of the main issues of his plan was to separate charity from politics altogether. In other walks of life Mr. Low had given marked evidences of his business ability and tact, notably in committees of the New York Chamber of Commerce, and so when a desire arose in Brooklyn to take the affairs of the city out of politics and to run the municipality as a business institution and on a business basis it was felt that he of all men should be chosen to lead the movement to carry such ideas into effect. He accepted a nomination as Mayor on the distinct understanding that if elected he was to administer the office without regard to politics, and simply as a business man would run any trust committed to his care. The circumstances of the time were favorable for such a change and the canvas proceeded with much enthusiasm, its peculiar conditions making the calculations as to its result merely wild guesses on both sides until the ballots had been cast and counted. Mr. Low certainly fulfilled all his pledges and gave the people not only a purely business administration but showed how the application of that principle meant honesty and economy all through the administrative bureaus even to the work of the humblest clerk. He was responsible to the city for his appointees and they in turn were directly responsible to him for the manner in which they conducted their offices, and that sense of personal and direct responsibility governed his entire administration with splendid results. Of course his plain policy was criticized, criticized somewhat bitterly at times, especially by the "war-horses" in both parties, but he held on in his own course and when, in November, 1885, he presented himself as a candidate for re-election, asked the people by their votes to pass judgment on his official course, he was again returned and during his second term still further illustrated the benefits of his non-partisan ideals. The high level he set in municipal administration still remains a beacon to those who are striving to perpetuate his methods in Brooklyn and introduce them elsewhere. To a great extent it was his four years' experience in Brooklyn that guided the framers of the Greater New York charter in much of their work; but they overlooked the fact that instead of a man being appointed Mayor that honor might fall to a mere hub in a machine wheel, and that the hub would have to go just as the machine was directed by the more or less invisible hand at the lever.

Mr. Low was re-elected Mayor at the close of his first term, again by a narrow majority — 1,842 — receiving 49,934 votes as against 48,092 for Joseph C. Hendrix. When he retired at the close of 1885 he went to Europe and then took charge of the business of A. & A. Low, which he desired to close up. This he accomplished with success and tact. His marked success in public life and his rare executive ability had however marked him out for high office, but he steadfastly refused to enter into the vortex of politics and so never proved an available man in the eyes of the party managers. He was a Republican in politics in national issues, but in local affairs he believed in being guided by business considerations. However, in 1890 he was elected president of Columbia College, and after much hesitation he accepted the office and threw himself at once into it with its varied and responsible duties with characteristic zeal. The work of the various institutions which made up Columbia was grouped under a single council, and it soon took a place among the great universities of the country. The management of the negotiations which resulted in the purchase of the splendid site on Morningside Heights and the removal there of the university was another task which he managed with consummate skill, and he further showed his deep interest in the institution by presenting it with $1,000,000 from his private fortune for the purpose of erecting a library building on the new site, now the most conspicuous of the many buildings on the university grounds. His work in this connection was stopped in the fall of 1897, when he became the candidate for Mayor of the Greater New York on an independent ticket.

After his defeat he resumed his labors in connection with the university, but he has held many public appointments, such as membership in the peace conference which met at The Hague in 1899.

It may be noted here, although beyond the limit of time laid down for the scope of this work, that in the fall of 1901 Mr. Low again received the nomination for the Mayoralty of Greater New York, this time from all parties except the regular Democratic forces. On accepting the nomination he resigned the presidency of Columbia and entered on a vigorous civic canvass, which resulted in his election, together with that of his entire ticket. He entered upon the duties of the office of Mayor of Greater New York on January 1, 1902.

As Mayor of Brooklyn Mr. Low held himself completely free from party control and became the foremost exponent of the "business man in politics." His progress was watched with curious eyes by the managers and by the people. While it cannot be said that the latter endorsed him much more strongly than the machine was able to find votes opposed to him, it should be remembered that every interest was arrayed against his success that had been accustomed to regard municipal government as a matter of dicker and deal, a scheme for spoils, soft jobs and various rewards for faithful party service. As Mayor he was in supreme control of the city's affairs, but he gathered around him as heads of departments a group of men in whom the public had confidence, and who, while responsible to him as the executive head of the municipality, were also directly responsible to the people for the departments committed to their care. The late John Fiske, the famous historian, whose death on July 4, 1901, was a terrible blow to American letters, said in his work on "Civil Government in the United States:" "This Brooklyn system has great merits. It assures unity of administration, it encourages promptness and economy, it locates and defines responsibility, and it is so simple that everybody can understand it. The people, having but few officers to elect, are more likely to know something about them. Especially since everybody understands that the success of the government depends upon the character of the Mayor, extraordinary pains are taken to secure good Mayors, and the increased interest in city politics is shown by the fact that in Brooklyn more people vote for Mayor than for Governor or President. * * * The Brooklyn system seems to be a step toward lifting city government out of the mire of party politics."

But it can not be said that the Brooklyn idea in practice continued after Mr. Low retired from the office of Mayor. Toward the close of his second term the candidates put forward for the office were zealous and pronounced party men, General Isaac S. Catlin being at that time a Republican and Daniel D. Whitney a stanch Democrat, the "independent" in politics being ignored, although Mr. Whitney, who had had a most successful career as a merchant, was a good example of the "business man in politics." The contest, however, was conducted on strictly party lines, but Catlin's party seemed to have a splendid advantage in Mr. Low's splendid Mayoral record. The result, however, was the election of Whitney by 49,002 votes to 36,905 given to Catlin, a majority of 12,097. Mr. Whitney was born at Oyster Bay in 1820. When he was ten years of age his parents settled in Brooklyn, and when ready to go to work he found employment in a grocery store; afterward he went into the wholesale grocery trade on his own account. Previous to taking his seat as Mayor he had served as an Alderman and for a time was President of the Board. He gave the city a clean administration, but the old charm of the Low administration was gone. Mr. Whitney was, after all, the nominee of one of the local machines, and that machine was on its good behavior. But with the election of Alfred C. Chapin as Whitney's successor the machine began to feel it could do as it liked. His opponent. Colonel Andrew D. Raird, the nominee of the Republican party, with a splendid record as a business man, a large employer of labor and a veteran of the Civil War, made a splendid run against him, and was defeated by 882 votes, the figures being Chapin, 52,753; Baird, 51,871; but even this narrow majority gave satisfaction to the victor and his friends. However, it made the latter feel cautious for a while. Mr. Chapin had been prominent in Brooklyn's politics since settling there in 1873, the year after he had been admitted a member of the New York bar. He became president of the Brooklyn Young Men's Democratic Club, and through the influence thus acquired was elected a member of the Assembly in 1881, and re-elected the following year. Possessed of a large fortune, he paid little attention to the practice of his profession and devoted himself solely to politics, having set before him as the goal of his ambition the Governorship of the State. His election and re-election as State Controller he regarded as steps in that direction, and his election to the Mayoralty of Brooklyn over such a candidate as Colonel Baird he regarded as a stride. During his first term he gave the people a good administration, and strengthened the police system, increased the park area and in many ways proved that he fully appreciated the opportunities for improving civic conditions and effecting improvements. The people endorsed his work, too, in a most flattering manner, for they re-elected him by a majority of 9,012 over Colonel Baird, who was once more his opponent. Someone said that Chapin's first term was for the people, his second was for the Governorship. He became simply a tool of the local politicians, with his mind set on the Governor's chair. Somehow stories of scandals and deals began to crop out, but nothing substantial was proved against him or his associates until he and his Board of Aldermen had entered into an agreement to buy out the Long Island Water Supply Company, a New Lots concern, for $1,250,000. There was loud grumbling all around at this manifest misuse of public money, and William Zeigler and his counsel, William J. Gaynor, came to the front in a torrent of denunciation. The deal was in fact one of the most barefaced in the history of municipal government since the time of Tweed. The water company was a half moribund concern even in its best days, its plant was practically worthless and its franchises of small value to the community. Its stock had been a drug in the market at $25 a share, and found few purchasers at that. It was shown afterward that before the city had closed its deal they were eagerly bought up, even $70 being paid willingly. When it was learned that the city was to pay $300 a share the reason of the demand for the stock among the politicians was not difficult to discover. The whole concern was worth, at the outside, it was claimed, not more than $62,500, and yet the city had agreed to pay a million and a quarter for it. Zeigler and Gaynor stopped the deal by an injunction. As a result of continued litigation the deal did not get through and was ultimately abandoned. Its story, however, aroused a widespread feeling of disgust and by it Mr. Chapin's political story came to an untimely end. He even asked for a renomination to the Mayoralty, but that was refused, for the simple reason that it was felt his defeat was a certainty. So when the time came Mr. David H. Boody, a well-known New York stock broker and member of Congress from the 20th (Brooklyn) district, was put forward in the fall of 1891 and was elected, securing 73,366 votes to 67,895 cast for Henry A. Meyer, the Republican candidate. Soon after Mr. Chapin received a sop in the shape of an election to Congress from the district vacated by Mr. Boody, but his hold on the machine was loosened, his political end was at hand and he has long since ceased even to reside in Brooklyn. Mr. Boody was born at Jackson, Maine, in 1837, and was educated for the law. After being admitted to the bar he settled in New York and entered the banking house of Boody & McClellen as clerk, the head of the firm being his uncle. There he made rapid progress, was made a partner and the stock exchange member of the firm, and acquired a fortune. Before becoming Mayor he had served in Congress, and had been active in Brooklyn's Democratic circles, and in the Thomas Jefferson Association, the Brooklyn Institute, the Montauk Club and several other organizations, literary and financial. Mr. Boody made a good Mayor; his administration was clean, but when he presented himself as a candidate for re-election the people rejected him and chose Charles A. Schieren, the Republican candidate, by about 30,000 majority. Mr. Schieren was born in Dusseldorf, Prussia, in 1842. He was educated in his native land and came to this country with his parents in 1860. In 1863 he became employed in a leather manufactory in New York's famous Swamp, and five years later started in business on his own account, and in the leather trade, with a capital of about $1,000, — his own savings. Soon he established a trade that extended all over the country and controlled several extensive tanneries. Mr. Schieren has resided in Brooklyn since his arrival in this country, and has taken an active interest in its religious, charitable and political affairs. He is, and has been for years, prominently connected with the Y. M. C. A., the Union for Christian Work, the Society for the Prevention of Cruelty to Animals, and the Young Women's Christian Association. He lent effective aid in the raising of funds for the erection of the statues of Henry Ward Beecher and J. S. T. Stranahan. He was one of the chief organizers and has always been vice-president of the Hide and Leather National Bank of New York. He is also a member of the Chamber of Commerce, and trustee of the Germania Bank of Brooklyn. Of the career of Mr. Schieren or of his successor, Frederick W. Wurster, the last Mayor of the city of Brooklyn, this is not, however, the place to speak in detail. Both proved acceptable executives, but both are still prominent workers in the local Republican ranks, and in neither of their cases is the record of party activity closed. It is sufficient to say here of Mayor Wurster that he was born in North Carolina in 1850, but has resided in Brooklyn since he was seven years of age. Under Mayor Schieren he held the office of Fire Commissioner, and he has long been prominent in Brooklyn's financial circles, including the Nassau Trust Company, of which he was one of the organizers.

During the opening years of the period now under notice the great subject of interest was the bridge. As has already been told, it was finally opened amid great éclat on May 24, 1883, and public curiosity drove thousands to become acquainted with its wonders. The excitement was not over by May 30, the first holiday following the opening, and the structure was thronged. In the afternoon a woman fell on the steps near the New York end, carrying with her several persons near, and a cry was raised that the whole concern was tumbling into the river. Then ensued a wild panic, which, before it subsided, caused the death of about twelve persons, while about fifty were more or less badly hurt. It did not take long for order to be restored, but the incident showed how easily, even in an enlightened community, a senseless yet death-dealing panic could spring up.

But although the bridge was open and free to anyone who chose to invest a cent, one had to walk over or indulge in the luxury of a ride in a private carriage, unless, indeed, one was able to negotiate a ride in a democratic and friendly truck. But even in these few opening months of primitive locomotion the bridge proved most popular, and thousands made the journey across twice a day, while at night, lighted up brilliantly with electric lamps, it formed a most agreeable promenade. On September 24, in the opening year, the cable railroad across was opened to the public, and then it seemed as if the power of the structure was being worked to its fullest extent. The returns for the first year seemed to fully justify a hope for the financial success of the enterprise. Up to November 31, when the books were closed, 4,250,000 passengers had used the promenade and 1,082,500 had been carried on the trains, and the bridge had earned $138,773. Five years later, in 1887, the figures were 2,664,415 promenade passengers, 27,940,313 on trains, and the earnings had increased to $850,724. After a while the promenade on the bridge was declared free, the railroad fare was cut to five cents for a couple of rides, and even less if one is capitalist enough to invest twenty-five cents for ten passage tickets.

When this went into effect it was again felt that the bridge was being used to its fullest capacity, but the surface and elevated railroad managers thought differently. Their ambition was to cross the bridge, but every effort in that direction had been balked by the trustees. After consolidation, however, when the structure became a part of the political equipment, the use of the bridge was extended to the trolley lines and to the elevated roads, and became in effect a part of their system. The result of this great addition to traffic, — in the face of warnings uttered by Colonel Roebling and others, — was evident in ugly rumors of the stability of the structure. Several times it was reported by passengers that something was wrong, but what it was no one who had experienced the something had engineering knowledge sufficient to explain what it was, and the officials spoke glibly about "simple cases of buckling." But on July 24, 1901, traffic on the bridge was peremptorily stopped by the police when it was discovered that twelve of the cable bands on the north side had parted and that there was other damage, the extent of which was not known. For a day or two traffic was continued solely on the north roadway.

The success of the Brooklyn Bridge led to others being projected, and at the date of this writing a second bridge is approaching completion, crossing the river from a point between South Fifth and South Sixth streets, Brooklyn, to the foot of Delancey street, Manhattan. The towers are completed, the approaches are being prepared and a beginning has been made with the work on the cables. A beginning has also been made with a bridge which is to cross the river at Washington street, Brooklyn, to Peck Slip, Manhattan, and is to be much longer than the others, for the structure with its approaches will cover a distance of two miles, and the cost will be a "little" over $15,000,000. Yet another bridge will in time cross the river with a central tower resting on Blackwell's Island, so that ere long, between bridges and tunnels, communication between New York and Brooklyn will be easy from almost any point.

The success of the big bridge and the conveyance to it of almost the entire system of travel have reduced the old Union Ferry system to a subordinate place in the economy of the city, and it may be said that since the opening of the bridge all efforts to improve the service have been abandoned. Even on the ferries least affected by the bridge the service and conditions have remained in statu quo, and the expectation is that bridge or tunnel traffic will make their patronage so fall off that their stockholders will abandon them, or most of them. Indeed, there is even a suggestion in the press that if their continuance is to be assured they will require to be taken over by the city and become a corporation asset, or a means of showing a corporation deficit.

In 1885 the Brooklyn Elevated Railroad commenced running, and in 1888 the Kings County Elevated Road began operations. Bit by bit pillars were run up in all directions until by one or other of the existing five divisions one can ride from Park Row, Manhattan, to Coney Island, or to Jamaica, or Ridgewood without once leaving the road. The elevated railroad system in Brooklyn has not proved a financial success. The great cost of construction, the determined opposition of the property owners in many of the streets pre-empted, the vexatious variety of lawsuits and a number of details which will easily occur to those acquainted with the inner workings of joint stock companies in their earlier stages, watered stock, etc., prevented the golden returns which the promoters so confidently predicted. Of course it was held, as usual in such cases, that time was on their side, that the city was extending steadily, that the roads were built so as to benefit by the extension, that the population was increasing, and everything was satisfactory so far as the outlook was concerned. But many averred that if the roads could only be conducted on a basis of honesty the present would be as comfortable as the future was rosy. But the future in reality only deepened the gloom and made matters worse. In 1892 the trolley system of street-car propulsion was introduced. The permission to erect poles and string wires had been granted on January 23; the Brooklyn City Railroad Company doubled its capital, to $12,000,000, in order to buy the necessary outfit to change all its cars from horse to electric power, and on November 7 the new motor vehicles were placed in service on Third avenue. The innovation was a success from the start, and within two years horse cars in Brooklyn had virtually disappeared, while new routes were constantly being opened up. This success, of course, militated against the elevated roads and seemed to threaten the continued existence of at least some of the lines and the virtual bankruptcy of them all. Most of the surface roads were flourishing, such as the Brooklyn City Railroad, '"Deacon" William Richardson's Atlantic Avenue road, but others, from one cause or another, — in only a few cases failed from lack of public patronage. When, however, the power of the trolley and the great potentialities of the system began to be seen, a series of financial "arrangements" began to operate in Brooklyn's passenger transit circles, which slowly, by due process of evolution, effected a great change in the aspect of affairs. In 1893 a corporation called the Long Island Traction Company bought out the Brooklyn Heights Company and in the following year the Brooklyn, Queens County and Suburban. In 1896 the Traction Company was merged in the Brooklyn Rapid Transit System. In 1893 the Nassau Electric Company was formed, which took over the Atlantic Avenue road, the Coney Island, Fort Hamilton & Brooklyn and the Coney Island & Gravesend. As a part of the financial juggling the elevated roads were united into two companies. In 1898 a grand coup was effected by which the Brooklyn Rapid Transit Company controlled the Brooklyn Heights Railroad,

Brooklyn City Railroad, Brooklyn, Queens County & Suburban Railroad, Nassau Electric, Prospect Park, Coney Island Gravesend Railroad, Brooklyn Union Elevated Railroad Company and the Kings County Elevated Railroad Company.

This is virtually all the roads which pass out of the old city of Brooklyn, with the exception of the Long Island Railroad and what is known as the Coney Island & Brooklyn Railroad Company. The latter is really also an aggregation and includes the De Kalb Avenue, the Smith Street, the Van Brunt and Erie Basin and several other less important lines. Truly Brooklyn is abundantly provided with cheap and rapid transit.

In 1880 Brooklyn had a population of 566,663, and of these 389.000 were natives of the United States; by 1890 it had been increased to 806.343; in 1895 it was reported at 1,055,378, but by that time it had added to its fold Flatbush, with 14,905; New Utrecht, with 10,778; Gravesend, with 9,939; and Flatlands was practically in with 5,000, so that the entire city then had an estimated population of 1,096,000 and an area of 765 ¾ miles. In 1896, when consolidation was effected, its population was estimated at 1,180,000.

## CHAPTER XLII. "THE END OF AN AULD SANG."

But we must turn away from statistics. Though necessary, they are by no means interesting and are apt to become tiresome. But those we have presented form a splendid and significant synopsis of the great progress which Brooklyn made during its last quarter of a century. It was a metropolitan city in fact if not in name, and while growing in wealth was almost daily adding to its possessions in all that an educated, progressive and hospitable city holds most dear.

In literature the first place as representative of the city was still held by the newspaper press. "The Eagle" still sustained its supremacy, and in 1892 vacated its old premises which so long had been a landmark at the bottom of Fulton street and moved to a palatial structure at the corner of Washington and Johnson streets, the site of the ill-fated Brooklyn Theater. The "Standard" was first published in 1884, but after some three years it consolidated, and "The Standard-Union" as such commenced in 1887, and was in reality a survival of several papers, including "The Argus."' In 1886 the "Brooklyn Citizen" commenced its issue, and under the editorship of Andrew McLean soon became noted for its literary ability and won a recognized place as a family newspaper. During the time here treated the publication of weekly papers continued to be a part of the privilege of every man who had a cause to advocate or money to waste; sometimes, it must be told, the amusement of men who had neither. Hardly a month passed without a new weekly being "established," but as a rule the careers of these organs were brief. When the city became a borough, however, there were twenty-nine of these weekly publications in Brooklyn, as follows: Baker's Journal and Deutsche Amerikanische Baecker Zeitung, Bedford Home News, Blade, Life, Courier, East New York Advertiser, Flatbush Press and Kings County Gazette, Greenpoint Independent, Greenpoint Weekly Star, Kings County Journal, Ledger, Nordiske Blade, Nordisk Tiende, Oesterns Haerold, Post, Record, Reform, Reporter, Review, Revue, Saturday Journal, Siirtolainan Supervisor, Svenska Amerikanska Pressen, Transcript, Uptown Weekly, Weekly, and Williamsburgh Democrat.

In 1893 an effort was made to establish a new daily, — the "Chronicle," — but the effort ended in failure in three months, — a few days more. It was organized apparently to "boom" the consolidation scheme, but the people did not need any special organ to enlighten them on that point and so "The Chronicle" came to an untimely end. Since then no real effort has been made to establish a new daily in the City of Churches, and the Eagle, Times, Standard-Union, Citizen and Freie Presse (German) have the field to themselves and meet every requirement ably and well.

But in the higher walks of literature, Brooklyn continued to be as little of a center to the end of her separate history as she was when her position in the world was only that of New York's bedroom. Her story had been written by Dr. Henry R. Stiles and written with a degree of thoroughness that made the work a model in the way of local histories and every line seemed penned with a degree of patient care and loving industry which has made it the text book of all who have since studied the subject, and Thomas W. Field had written an account of the battle of Long Island, while Spooner, Onderdonck, Murphy, Bergen and others had treated of the past with the unwearied carefulness of typical antiquaries and sometimes with the infinite grace of the man of letters, but these things, useful and valuable and inspiring as they are, are not literature; rather are they the foundations for literature. Shakespeare wrote his "Macbeth" with a story in Holinshed's "Chronicles" as a basis. "Macbeth" is part of our literature. Holinshed's "Chronicles" is not, but we could ill afford to lose it. So far as reading, study and the literary gift were concerned Brooklyn might be regarded as a literary producer; but the trouble was that as soon as a man began to acquire eminence in letters he found it necessary as a result of his calling to move across the river or to some other place where the maker of books could weave his thoughts or arrange his fancies or ideas, or formulate his theories or his dogmas with all the processes and agencies at hand for reaching the public. A case in point is that of Prof. John Bach McMaster, whose "History of the People of the United States" promises to rank as an American classic. That work is printed in Brooklyn, but is published in New York, and people speak of him as "the eminent Pennsylvania writer," although he is a native of Brooklyn and in Brooklyn received the educational training which fitted him for the honored position he now holds among the country's historians. Rossiter W. Raymond was long regarded as among the most industrious of Brooklyn's professional litterateurs, and in Brooklyn much of his life work was done, but the world generally regarded him as a Manhattan worker. Will Carleton, the poet, whose "Betsy and I Are Out" has perhaps been as Widely popular as any production of its size that has appeared in recent years, is never spoken of as a Brooklyn poet although his home has been in it for many years; and the same might be said of Wallace Bruce, a man with an international reputation as a lecturer and poet, who set up his home in Brooklyn when he returned to America after representing the United States as Consul at Edinburgh for four years. Henry George, the publicist whose "Progress and Poverty" has proved a new gospel to a large group of earnest, thoughtful men and women who are trying to improve life by removing poverty and laying bare its cause, is never regarded as having had any connection with Brooklyn, although his home was at Fort Hamilton for many years before his death in 1897 during the contest for the mayoralty of New York in which he was one of the candidates. Dr. John D. Ross, who has made a special study of the life and works of Burns, his great poet and countryman, does his literary work in his Brooklyn home, but Brooklyn is never heard in connection with it. It seems a pity that the literature that really ought to be rightly credited to the city, be regarded as a part of its work for the world, should find its sponsors elsewhere.

Possibly one exception might be made to this in the case of the Ford brothers, whose literary work somehow, no matter where printed, has always been associated with the city of Brooklyn. Their father, Gordon Leicester Ford, was a resident of Brooklyn for over 40 years, and as a collector of internal revenue, as business manager of the "New York Tribune," as well as in various other important capacities, was one of its most widely known citizens. A man of many grand qualities, an active and conscientious citizen, a fearless supporter of whatever he deemed to be right, a sturdy partisan yet tolerant of the views of others, he carried with him in his "daily walk and conversation" the hearty good wishes of an ever increasing circle of personal friends. In all the literary and higher social life of Brooklyn he was particularly prominent; and in the affairs of the Historical Society, the Brooklyn Library and similar institutions he was particularly active and helpful. His own collection of books, manuscripts and autographs was in itself a wonder, and long before his death, in 1891, it was regarded as the largest private collection in Brooklyn. It was especially rich in Americana, and for over half a century he had been patiently collecting books, pamphlets, manuscripts, portraits — anything in fact that threw even a slender side light on the story of the land. At his death he bequeathed his literary and artistic treasures to his two sons and they have largely added to them and turned them to practical value in their literary work.

The eldest, Worthington C. Ford, who was born in Brooklyn in 1858, edited "The Writings of George Washington"' in ten volumes, and several other works treating of the "Father of his Country," while his younger brother, Paul Leicester Ford, born at Brooklyn in 1865, has issued the Writings of Thomas Jefferson, also in ten volumes, and quite a host of books from such pamphlets as one on "Who was the Mother of Franklin's Son," to solid contributions to historical study and works of fiction which have been sold by the thousands on both sides of the Atlantic.

Brooklyn has been, and is rich in book collectors and in some of its homes are to be found the largest and choicest collections of rare books to be found anywhere in America. To mention the contents of such collections as that of Mr. Daniel M. Tredwell, author of "A Plea for Bibliomania." "Literature of the Civil War," and a number of other interesting monographs, or that of Norton Q. Pope, or that of Prof. Charles E. West, or that of William Augustus White, or that of C. H. Moser, would be to enumerate a succession of gems enough to fill a goodly sized volume.

But we may here recall one noted collector who certainly turned his treasures to practical use before his death on Feb. 2, 1900. This was James A. H. Bell, who in June, 1899, presented several thousand of his rarest volumes to the Brooklyn Library. He was born in New Orleans on June 4, 1817, and when three years old his parents died of yellow fever. The boy was discovered between the bodies of his father and mother, and was taken to a hospital, but he never contracted the disease. He was subsequently sent by the Mayor of New Orleans to Brooklyn, where his uncle, Augustus Graham, resided. Mr. Graham was the founder of the Graham Institute, which became the Brooklyn Institute, and is now the Brooklyn Institute of Arts and Sciences. Mr. Graham cared for his nephew for some years and eventually he was adopted by his housekeeper, a Mrs. Taylor.

Mr. Bell was for some years engaged in the brewery business in Manhattan. When only 14 years of age he began to take a great interest in books and this interest never lagged. During the last forty years he had been a devoted collector. When his collection had grown too large for him to care for, owing to his advanced age, Mr. Bell presented the most valuable books in it to the Brooklyn Library. This collection is kept in a separate room and is distinct from the regular library. One of the interesting parts of the collection is the index which comprises thirty-six volumes. The index is ii; detail and is all in Mr. Bell's handwriting.

After he made this present to the Brooklyn Library Mr. Bell found that he had too much time to himself and he began to make another collection. At the time of his death he had succeeded in getting about 2,000 volumes for his new library.

Mr. Bell's home at 4s Sands street had been occupied by him and his family for over a half century. When he first took possession of it the house was one of the handsomest in Brooklyn.

Possibly the nearest approach to a literary cult in Brooklyn was due to the establishment of the Long Island Historical Society, but with the passing away of its founders that institution seemed to lose much of its earlier inspiration. For a time its publication fund promised to enrich local literature and did enrich it with four volumes, three of which are of great importance as contributions to the story of Brooklyn and of the American Revolution, and one of interest to the students of the personal life of Georg-e Washington. But with the publication of the last named, in 1889, that branch of the society's usefulness has apparently come to an end. It is housed in a handsome building at Clinton and Pierrepont streets, which it had erected for its own use in 1880, it has a library of 43,000 volumes which is steadily being added to and its museum is a marvelous storehouse of curiosities, — birds, stones, Indian relics, manuscripts, deeds, pictures, — relating mainly to Long Island. Its literary and other treasures are freely placed at the service of all who are interested. The other Brooklyn libraries have already been referred to and it is needless to enlarge upon any of them at this writing as the entire system in the Greater New York is steadily undergoing radical changes.

The literary tendency of the people has shown itself in the great number of literary clubs which have flourished in the city. The Writers' Club, organized in 1895, is mainly composed of professional people: the Brooklyn Catholic Historical Society, founded in 1891, explains its purpose clearly in its name, which is more than can be said of most of the others. But many and varied as are these coteries they are far outstripped in numbers and extent of membership by the musical organizations. The Oratorio Society of Brooklyn, founded in 1893, has a membership of 250; the Arion Singing Society, 600 members; the Harmony Glee Club, 250 members; the United German Singers, 1,400 members; Amateur Musical Club, 200 members, and so on through a list of about 100 organizations. The most prominent composer associated with Brooklyn is Dudley Buck, for many years organist in Holy Trinity Church and who resigned in 1902. In 1871 he became organist in the Music Hall, Boston, and attracted the attention of Theodore Thomas, and he was associated with that famous musician and leader for several years. Many of Buck's best compositions were first produced at Mr. Thomas' concerts, notably the music for Sidney Lanier's centennial cantata, which was given at the opening of the Philadelphia Exposition in 1876. In 1878 Buck became choirmaster and organist of Holy Trinity and resided in Brooklyn until the end. His religious compositions have been much admired and are to be found in all modern books of praise. As a teacher of music he stands at the very head of Brooklyn's instructors.

From music to art is an easy step; but a large volume might easily be written on Brooklyn's artists and art collections. It has long been the home of J. M. Hart, the famous landscape and cattle painter, of Wedworth Wadsworth, whose illustrations to Shakespeare, Cooper, Tennyson and others, as well as his water-color sketches have been highly praised; of Carleton Wiggins, and of E. H. Blashfield who studied under Gerome, won a medal at the Salon in Paris and was one of the decorators of the Chicago Exhibition. The famous "Gibson Girl" might also claim to be a Brooklyn lass, for her designer, W. Hamilton Gibson, has been a resident of Brooklyn more or less steadily since he was a child and was educated at the Polytechnic.

But the painter who has done most to depict Brooklyn and Long Island on canvas is Charles Henry Miller. In reviewing an exhibition of his works given in 1901 a well-known New York critic wrote as follows:

Mr. Miller has followed the adage that beauty lies about one, and need not be sought afar. As Whistler painted and etched the Thames before his Chelsea house, so Miller found his pictures on Newtown Creek and at Hell Gate at Creedmoor, and Roslyn. The mill belonging to the famous local bard. Bloodgood Cutter, appears in two of his compositions. Sometimes he went as far as the Hudson and penetrated the Highlands even into Peekskill; and again he would make a tour of his beloved and always grateful Long Island and paint the "graveyard of ships" at Port Washington, or visit the marshy solitudes of the Great South Bay, linger near the Shinnecock Hills, and reach the. remote hamlet of East Hampton — when East Hampton was not only remote but a hamlet. There is evidence that he has trod the soil of New Jersey; for here is a grove of tall trees at Weehawken with a glimpse of New York in the deep distance.

But for the most part his own little corner is his world, where he paints with evident gusto such townscapes and landscapes as "The Queen's Church," "Springfield Road at Queens," "A Gray Day on Long Island," "Landscape at Queens Park," "Queens Barnyard at Sunset," "Queenlawn Homestead." "Sunset at Queens," "The Queens School." "Queens Corners," "Oaks at Creedmoor, Queens." Like the old Dutchman, like Constable, and some of the French landscapists of 1830-1860, he is a philosopher on the question of novelties, preferring to give all his strength to an endeavor to paint what is at his doors, instead of roaming abroad for the stimulus that new scenery might bring.

At the same time he has not lacked foreign travel. He has studied at Munich and visited other countries besides Holland and Germany. He has been an Academician since 1875, and won medals at expositions in Philadelphia, Boston, and New Orleans. In the course of time his paintings has changed very considerably. Where it was muddy and without sunshine it has become alive. If he has not reached great skill in rendering the delicate differences in atmosphere, some of his later works show the effect of modern struggles with the problem of sunlight and air. Take as an instance No. 56, "A Frosty Day on Long Island." The remains of a cold fog are indicated well by the trees and by the cattle coming into sight in the hazy air, down the level road, toward the observer. This is a very different style compared with his earlier work like "Manhattan from Long Island," where the painting is dull and turbid. "A Cloudy Day in Spring," which was part of the American exhibit at Paris last summer, has a quiet truth to nature that is often lacking in older work. "New York from Newtown Creek," painted in 1876, and "High Bridge from Harlem Lane," are pieces for a historical society rather than for a museum of art; for the value lies in the subject rather than their artistic force.

About a score of paintings here, about one in four, hold one through the beauty of their coloring and the sturdy value of their composition. Easily first stands the big canvas, "Autumn Oaks at Creedmoor," a serious and even grand landscape, large in composition, simple and impressive as to mass, and fine in coloring. A number of landscapes in this style, but not quite so impressive, indicate the strongest vein of the painter.

In 1882 Brooklyn possessed an educational department that was justly regarded as a model. Its resources were ample, its teaching staff was able and enthusiastic and its school rooms were even better appointed than those on Manhattan Island. Its school board comprises 45 members and its system of primary, grammar, evening and industrial schools was complete. In 1882 William H. Maxwell was appointed Associate Superintendent, and

Superintendent in 1887, and from then onward until the close of 1897 he was the real administrator of the affairs of Brooklyn's public school system and administered them well. The city in 1896 voted $2,564,263 for the maintenance of the schools. Possibly no department of the city government was regarded with more pride than this, but somehow since consolidation that feeling is not so generally apparent.

As has already been remarked Brooklyn has never managed to have a recognized university in its midst, but the opportunities for what is called the higher education have been liberally provided even since the days when it was thought that education should consist of something more than a knowledge of the three r's. The Polytechnic, however, is in reality a college and in 1890 received from the Regents of the State University a charter which conferred on it "all the rights, powers and dignities given by law and the ordinances of the Regents to the college." The Polytechnic, however, had an existence since 1854 and as early as 1869 its work was of such a high standard that the Regents gave it the authority to confer the degrees of Bachelor of Science and Bachelor of Arts. Its present building was completed in 1890 and not only has commodious class rooms, studies, laboratories and gymnasiums but ample accommodations for the splendid Spicer library, a collection for reference works collected by Capt. Elihu Spicer at a cost. of $35,000 and presented to the Polytechnic as a memorial of his son who was one of the pupils. It is a technical and commercial school and has about 700 students each year and 50 instructors.

The Packer Institute is the successor of the old Brooklyn Female Academy which was destroyed by fire in 1853. Mrs. William F. Packer then offered to establish with a gift of $65,000, a new school for girls, as a memorial to her husband, and the property of the old school was transferred to the corporation which established the Polytechnic. So in 1854 the building of the Packer Collegiate Institute was opened to receive pupils and quickly became known as the most perfect establishment for the education of young women in the country. The original building has been added to and the curriculum has been changed and improved and strengthened to meet the needs of the time, and every change found in Mrs. Packer a liberal and zealous supporter until her death in 1892. It has a corps of 53 instructors and an average roll of 650 students. Under Dr. Truman T. Backus it has kept pace with the highest class of women's colleges and its equipment and curriculum are maintained with a zealous regard to preserve its traditions and its rich record of accomplishment.

The Adelphi Academy, founded in 1869, entered upon its new building in 1886 mainly through a gift of $160,000 by Charles Pratt, president of its Board of Trustees. It is a complete institution, preparatory, academic and collegiate, and takes a pupil into its kindergarten at the earliest age and fits him for the university or for a business or technical career. Its art department is possibly the most perfect and complete in the country. In 1889 the splendid buildings it occupies were seriously damaged by fire but the damage was soon repaired. It has generally between 1,100 and 1,200 pupils on its rolls.

Mr. Charles Pratt, who made a yet more princely provision for Brooklyn education in the establishment which bears his name — the Pratt Institute — was one of the partners in the Standard Oil Company. The land for this institution was bought in 1883 and work on the building was at once begun. It was designed by its projector to be "for the promotion of art, science, literature, industry and thrift," and he had been planning its features for twenty-five years or more, basing its curriculum on some of the English technical schools with the aim of so supplementing the usual educational training as to fit, by its evening classes, young men and women to apply themselves to the trade they had selected with the best technical and applied knowledge. Before it was fairly opened its donor passed away. May 4, 1891.

One of the early announcements of the institution gave-an idea of the comprehensiveness of the plan thought out by Mr. Pratt with the provisions for the day and evening classes in the following condensed "calendar;"

High School — A four-years course for both sexes, combining drawing and manual work with the usual studies of a high school or academy.

Department of Fine Arts — Classes in freehand and architectural drawing, clay modeling, wood-carving, design, art needle-work; regular art course; normal course for training of teachers; lecture course.

Department of Domestic Art — Normal domestic art course; courses in sewing, dressmaking, millinery, physical culture, combined course in domestic art and domestic science; lecture course.

Department of Domestic Science — Normal domestic science course, household science, hygiene and home nursing, public hygiene, cookery, laundry, food economics; lecture course.

Department of Science and Technology — Normal manual training, drawing, and machine designs; algebra, geometry, physics, chemistry, electrical construction, steam and the steam engine, strength of materials, machine design; mechanical drawing; carpentry, machine work, plumbing, house, sign and fresco painting; lecture course.

Department of Kindergartens — Training class for teachers, mothers' class, nurses' class, special classes; lecture course.

Department of Libraries — Free Library, Reading and Reference Room. Classes in library training, literature and cataloguing.

Department of Museums — Collections of inorganic substances, ceramics, glass, building and decorative stones, reproductive processes, organic compounds, textile fabrics.

The Thrift — Deposit, savings, and loan branches, the privileges of which are open to the public.

The Brooklyn Eagle Almanac for 1896, after the institution had been in operation for several sessions, gave the following account of its work, an account evidently supplied "on authority:"'

"The late Charles Pratt gave to the youth of Brooklyn an institution that is unique among the educational establishments of the country. While there are technological schools in other cities, there are none that were founded by a single individual that have anything like the range and influence that is exerted by the Pratt Institute. The buildings of this school are on Ryerson street, between Willoughby and DeKalb avenues, extending back for a block to Grand avenue. The main structure is 100 feet wide by 60 feet in depth, and six stories in height. The building devoted to science and technology behind this structure is 240 by 95 feet, while directly south of the main building is that of the High School, 50 by 80 feet, and three stories high. The latter was completed January 1, 1892. A new building has been erected on the west side of Ryerson street, that will contain the library. [This was completed and opened in May, 1896, and contains about 80,000 volumes and the collection is at the service of any resident of Brooklyn.]

"The object of the Institute is to promote manual and industrial education, as well as cultivation in literature, science and art; to inculcate habits of industry and thrift, and to foster all that makes for right living and good citizenship. Its aim is also to educate young men and women in handicrafts by which they will be made self-supporting; it encourages them, moreover, to practice those arts in a thorough and honest manner. The classes are open to everyone, but there is no room for shirkers and dawdlers. Nominal charges for tuition are made, but the Institute is in no way a money-making concern. The library of 52,000 in the new building is free to all citizens, children included. There is a reading room, with a reference department of nearly 2,000 volumes. On the second floor is an assembly hall, where lectures are given on the more general aspects of studies in the curriculum.

"The floor above is mostly devoted to domestic art — dressmaking, etc.; and on the second floor is a commercial department. The cooking schools are on the upper floor. The whole fourth floor is devoted to art — painting, drawing, designing, carving, modeling in clay — while the technical museum in the fifth floor and other parts of the main building contain works of art in textiles, etchings, photography, ceramics and metal. There is a fine collection of minerals. The large annex contains the engines, anvils, shops, foundries and other branches of the Department of Science and Technology.

"The High School is the Academic Department of the Institute. Its course of study covers three years and embraces manual training for both boys and girls. Pupils who have graduated successfully from a public grammar school are prepared to enter the High School, which fits its graduates for the highest scientific schools and colleges.

"In the basement of the main building is the library school for the training of library assistants, and the luncheon room.

"The Institute is under the control of a board of trustees. The average number of students is 3,000; instructors, 120."

Since then the work of the Institute has so increased that the last returns give the number of instructors at 134. The department called The Thrift is practically a building loan bureau and by it thousands of working people have been enabled to own their own homes.

But useful as the Pratt Institute is, the educational pride of Brooklyn is the "Institute of Arts and Sciences." It has done a great, work in the past, it is doing a great work in the present, but its future promises wonderful developments. It is the outgrowth of the old Apprentices' Library of 1824. In 1843 the name was changed to the Brooklyn Institute and for many years its annual lecture course was famous in the days when the lecture platform was a power in the land. Its main benefactor was Augustus Graham. He presented to its trustees the building on Washington street in which it was housed, and at his death in 1851 it was found that he had bequeathed to it $27,000 as an endowment. Of this the income from $10,000 was to be spent in scientific lectures and the purchase of scientific apparatus, the income from $12,000 was to provide Sunday evening lectures on religious topics, while the interest on the remaining $5,000 was to support a school of art. But somehow the interest in the institution began to fall off, the building was remodeled at a cost of $30,000 without improving its popularity, and as this amount was met by a mortgage the interest on Graham's endowment had to be devoted to its payment.

In 1887 a number of public-spirited citizens, foreseeing the evident end of the Institute, determined to revive it in accordance with modern ideas and on a scale that would be in keeping with the growth and importance of the city, with a grand museum as its central feature. A public meeting was held and much general interest was aroused and it was not long before the Institute building became a scene of daily activity. In two years the membership rose from 350 to 1,200, the library was reorganized and augmented at the rate of 50,000 books a year most of the scientific societies in Brooklyn joined the Institute and became departments of its work. In 1890 the building was partly destroyed by fire but the work went on, the various schools offering quarters for the use of the departments and in 1891 it had a total membership of 1,810. That year the Institute formally passed out of existence and its property was deeded to the Brooklyn Institute of Arts and Sciences, — the old society under a new name and with greatly enlarged powers. In 1892 the old building was acquired for bridge purposes and demolished and the departments continued to find refuge in the various schools and institutions until the new permanent home should be ready.

That home was the museum, so long talked about and anticipated. The city of Brooklyn was authorized to erect a section of the Museum building at a cost not to exceed $300,000. A tract of land facing the Eastern Parkway on the north, Washington avenue on the east, a line 100 feet south on the southern boundary oi old President street on the south, and land reserved for the Prospect Hill Reservoir on the west, containing eleven and nine-tenths acres and valued at $900,000, was leased by the city of Brooklyn to the Institute for a term of one hundred years.

On this site has been erected the first section of a Museum building, in classic style, and the entire structure, when completed, will cover an area of 560 feet square, with four interior courts, to provide light for the central portions of the building. The plan provides for collections illustrating the general history of Art and Architecture on the first floor, rooms for the illustration of the practical Arts and Sciences on the second floor, and galleries for the illustration of the history of Painting, Engraving, Etching and Decorative Art on the third floor. The central portion of the building is carried one story higher than the rest, and in this the Schools of Fine Arts and of Architecture will be located.

The first section of the building was completed in January, 1897, and was furnished and ready for occupancy as a Museum in May. It was opened to the public for the first time on June 2, 1897, and has remained open daily since. A second building in Bedford Park, on Brooklyn avenue, is used as an auxiliary to the main Museum.

The Board of Estimate and Apportionment in 1899 authorized the erection of a second section of the Museum Building and an appropriation to meet the cost of the same of $300,000. The second section is now in process of erection.

The departments now covered by the Institute's work include anthropology, archaeology, architecture, astronomy, botany, chemistry, domestic science, electricity, engineering, entomology, fine arts, geography, geology, law, mathematics, microscopy, mineralogy, music, painting, pedagogy, philately, philology, philosophy, photography, physics, political science, psychology, sculpture and zoology. It has a membership of 6,132 and its yearly work consists of courses of lectures on the arts and sciences, monthly meetings of each of the departments, concerts and dramatic readings. Its collections in anthropology, archaeology, architecture, chemistry, botany, entomology, ethnology, geography, geology, microscopy, mineralogy, photography and zoology, apparatus in physics, chemistry, electricity and engineering, and collections of paintings, sculpture and statuary are large and varied. The officers are A. Augustus Healy, Pres.: Chas. A. Schieren and Carl H. De Silver, Vice-Prests.; George C. Brackett, Sec.; Wm. B. Davenport, Treas.; Associate Members: Rev. Albert J. Lyman, Pres.;

James Cruikshank, Sec.; John A. Taylor, Treas.; Prof. Franklin W. Hooper, General Director of the Institute.

The early story of the drama in Brooklyn has already been told and its later history may here be rapidly sketched. The Brooklyn Theatre, destroyed by the awful calamity of December 5, 1876, was rebuilt in 1879 under a new name — Haverly's — but was not a success either financially or artistically and was torn down in 1890 to afford a site for "The Eagle" newspaper.

But somehow the drama has never acquired much of a foothold in Brooklyn and while stars and combination companies fill up a week's engagement very comfortably the taste of the people seems to run toward "variety" rather than to the "legitimate." Mr. Hamilton Ormsbee in 1898 summarized the closing days of the Brooklyn theatrical story as follows: An attraction was Hooley's Opera House, which occupied the upper floor of a building at Court and Remsen streets, where the Dime Savings Bank now stands, from 1862 to 1883. It was called an opera house, but was a place for minstrel show and is chiefly notable for the appearance of popular black-face performers and for the fact that that brilliant comedian, Nat C. Goodwin, used to do the imitations of eminent actors, for which he was once noted upon its stage at a very early time in his career. Another disused theatre is the Lee Avenue Academy in the Eastern District, which for many years after it was opened, in 1872, occupied the same position in the eastern end of the city as the Park did in the western. There was also once a theatre where is now Liebmann's Arcade, on Fulton street. R. M., Hooley and Thomas Donnelly opened it in 1869 as the Olympic. Hyde & Behman and John W. Holmes afterward conducted it and it disappeared about 1890. Music Hall, at the junction of Fulton street and Flatbush avenue, was used for a time about 1872 for negro minstrel exhibitions. The oldest theatre in the Eastern District is the American, on Driggs avenue, which was built as the Odeon in 1852, used in 1868 by R. M. Hooley as a variety house and has been both a variety theatre and a skating rink.

The conversion of an unused market on Adams street, near Myrtle avenue, into a variety theater in 1877 is notable, because it was the introduction to Brooklyn of the firm of Hyde & Behman, among the most extensive and prosperous managers in the theatrical business. Their Adams street house is one of the leading variety houses in the country, and they are the owners of six other theaters in Brooklyn, besides one in Newark. Their Brooklyn houses are the Grand Opera House, Amphion, Park and Gayety, used for drama, and Hyde & Behman's, the Star and Empire, for variety and burlesque. The Grand Opera House, in Elm Place, was built on the site of a church, and opened to the public in 1881. It was long managed by Knowles & Morris. The Amphion, on Bedford avenue, was built by the Amphion Musical Society, with the idea that it would occupy the same position in the Eastern District that the Academy of Music did in the Western. It was opened as a first-class theater, with C. M. Wiske as manager. This venture was unprofitable, and in January, 1888, Knowles & Morris took possession, conducting the house as a combination theatre. The control of Manager Edwin Knowles over this house lasted until the end of last season, and in that time he presented at that theatre the chief American and foreign actors of the day, with the exception of Henry Irving. Mr. Knowles was also the first manager of the Columbia, built for him, Daniel Frohman and Al Hayman, and opened March 7, 1892, with "Alabama." The Bijou Theatre was opened November 13, 1893, by H. C. Kennedy & Co., with Mr. Kennedy as the resident manager. The play was "Adonis," with Henry E. Dixey. In 1895 Colonel William E. Sinn, who had leased the Park Theatre since 1875, opened the Montauk Theatre, which was regarded as the most perfectly adapted house of its kind when completed. The Star Theatre was built about the time the Brooklyn Theatre was torn down, was used for a time as a combination house, and has since been occupied for variety and burlesque.

The leading event in the history of the Brooklyn little theatrical world in the closing days, however, was not its transformations or changes of management, but the final appearance of a world-renowned actor, who had, it would seem, lingered on the stage too long. This was Edwin Booth, possibly the greatest tragedian America has produced, who on April 4, 1891, made his last public effort on 'any stage at the Academy of Music. The play selected was "Hamlet." and as the Prince Booth had in the years of his prime won his highest need of praise. But his performance that night, as indeed on every night of his engagement, was a shock to all his admirers. It was mercilessly condemned by the newspaper critics, who did not see that the performance itself was a tragedy, — the ending in gloom of a career that had done more than aught else to lift the American stage above the level of "Uncle Tom's Cabin" and "The Dumb Man of Manchester." But it was the old story summarized in Johnson's famous line,

"Superfluous lags the veteran on the stage."

The National Guard after the war became a well-disciplined force. The Brooklyn contingent formed the second of the four brigades into which the State military forces were divided and was under the command of Brigadier-General James McLeer, one of the veterans of the Civil War and who for eight years had held the office of Postmaster of Brooklyn. The strength of the commands under him in 1897 was as follows:

| Organization. | No. of Members. |
|---|---|
| Brigade Headquarters | 11 |
| Thirteenth Regiment | 635 |
| Fourteenth Regiment | 616 |
| Twenty-third Regiment | 759 |
| Forty-seventh Regiment | 593 |
| Seventeenth Separate Company | 94 |

| | |
|---|---|
| Third Battery | 81 |
| Second Signal Company | 48 |
| Troop C | 100 |
| Total | 2,937 |

From the time of the close of hostilities between the States the Guard had been mainly engaged in holiday making, varied by shooting excursions to Creedmoor, but even amid the holiday making discipline and tactics were strenuously maintained, so that one of the officers used to remark that the Brooklyn National Guard was ready at any moment to go on any military duty. But the time came when the value of the militia was to be again tested. On January 14, 1895, 5.500 employees of the trolley companies went on strike. The merits of the dispute have no interest for us here and need not be discussed. Almost the entire system of street-car travel was brought to a standstill, and the apparent perfection of the strikers' plans seemed to give promise of a speedy termination of the trouble. But the employers were obstinate, and on the following day the strikers commenced to get ugly: Slowly the cars "began again to move," as new hands flocked in from all parts of the country, and on the 16th and 17th the police was able to handle whatever disturbances arose. On the 18th, however, the trouble got beyond their capability, a car was fired upon, a riot of considerable proportions raged for a time on Fifth avenue, and "fresh" conductors and motormen as well as passengers suffered, and on the following day the entire militia force, under General McLeer, was ordered out.

The military remained in possession of the streets until February 1st, when the struggle was given up by the strikers. During these eventful days the troops had hard work. Several of the rioters were shot, and it is hard to say how many were hurt in the daily charges of the cavalry. The streets were constantly patrolled by armed men, and here and there loaded cannons were placed on open streets ready to sweep an entire thoroughfare if necessary. Brooklyn breathed freely when it was all over and mourned the loss involved in human life as well as in money; but it was felt that the National Guard had saved the city from an era of mob violence and riot which would have brought about scenes at the very thought of which the boldest could not help shuddering.

In 1896 the Navy Yard was adorned with a rather ornate new main entrance at Sands and Navy streets, and its entire 112 ½ acres were by that time fully enclosed on the land side. The following description of the yard in 1897 is from "The Eagle:" "The Lyceum is a three-story structure. On the ground floor are the offices of the captain of the yard, and on the second floor offices of the commandant and his aides, and on the third floor the quarters of his clerks. Here the records are preserved, including such as pertain to ships, lists of officers and rosters of all clerks and the employees. In Trophy Park, a triangular green adjoining the Lyceum — not in the

Museum — is a marble column, commemorating twelve American seamen who fell at the capture of the Barrier forts, on Canton River, China, in 1856. It was erected by their shipmates on the "San Jacinto," "Portsmouth" and "Levant." About the monument are guns captured from the British frigate "Macedonian," and the iron prow of the Confederate ram "Mississippi." In 1890 the Naval Museum, containing priceless relics and trophies, was sent to the Naval Academy at Annapolis. A small octagonal building west of Trophy Park is the office of the naval surgeon, and beyond that there is a building for provisions and clothing. Here is cut out by machinery all the clothing used in the Navy, except that worn by officers, though the garments are sent away to be finished. Here, also, all the coffee used in the Navy is roasted, ground, put upon tins, and all canned goods, hard tack and condensed food for the Navy are stored.

"On the other side of Main street the cruiser "Cincinnati" was built.

"The workshops, machine shops and foundries are on Chauncey, Warrington and Morris avenues. On Chauncey avenue, which extends from Main street to Flushing avenue, are the cooper shop, mold shop, ordnance building, tank shed, now used for sand, coal and lumber; a building for anchor chains and rigging loft, coppersmith's, plumbing shop and boiler shops. Building No. 7, on Warrington avenue, contains various departments, the court-martial room, civil engineer's room and flag loft, where all flags and bunting used by our Navy as well as flags of other nations are made by women. Other buildings on this avenue are the blacksmith's shop, paint shop, yard and docks, construction department and steam engineering department. The avenue ends in a park. On Morris avenue are a joiner's shop, offices, boat house and iron plating shops. Most of the senior officers are pleasantly quartered on Flushing avenue, while some of them live in private houses, in the city. The spacious marine barracks and drill yard are entered from the gate on Flushing avenue, and the only department outside the enclosure is the Naval Hospital on Flushing avenue, separated from the yard by Wallabout market. In the hospital enclosure is the naval cemetery. The water front of the yard extends for 6,600 feet from Little street on the west to Division avenue on the east, and opposite the center is the Cob dock. This is an island nineteen acres in extent, and to resist the action of the tide a concrete and granite wall is built around it. It has a water front of 5,000 feet. Whitney Basin in this island has a frontage of 3,300 feet. The ordnance dock is also here. Communication is had by means of a steam rope ferry, and a causeway across Wallabout Channel, connecting the Cob dock with the main shore at the northeast boundary line, is now practically completed. This causeway is to be 522 feet long, with an extreme width of forty-one feet. Two forty-ton cranes, traveling on an eighteen-foot railway around the dry docks, are designed for lifting armor plates weighing from twenty to forty tons;

stepping steel masts, hoisting machinery and boilers and lowering them into place."

Among the most notable vessels constructed at the yard were the "Terror," launched in 1883, the "Puritan," launched in 1882, the 'Cincinnati," launched in 1892, and the "Maine," launched in 1890. The subsequent destruction of this last-named vessel in Havana Harbor was the first incident in the war with Spain of 1898, in which the United States acquired so much glory and territory.

About 1880 began the real transformation of the city in respect to its architectural attractions. Heretofore, as a rule, the architects were limited to churches mainly, with here and there an opportunity in an armory or mansion to show their skill and taste. But by 1880 the public sentiment, the public taste and the public wealth began to call for a higher order of things, and the response was most gratifying. With the City Hall and the Municipal Building, — of which latter one of the Brooklyn civic boasts used to be that it cost $20 less than the appropriation, — as a center, new structures of much beauty and commanding appearance began steadily to oust the old plain brick or marble front edifices so commonplace yet so comfortable. By 1890 a still further change was inaugurated. By that time the principle of skeleton construction had been introduced and the elevator system had been perfected, so that the height to which a building might be run up was a matter of money and calculation rather than of the thickness of the walls. So Brooklyn began to get sky-scrapers, and its office buildings vie with those across the river for their size and the perfection of their details. The Jefferson building rises to a height of 98 feet, the Mechanics' Bank to 140 feet, the Franklin Trust to 156 feet, and the Telephone building to 128 feet. It is not customary to mention the Havemeyer & Elders vast sugar mills, erected in 1883, as architectural beauties, but if beauty in architecture be, as some contend, the adaptation of building ideas to a means and an end, they must be accepted. Such structures as the Alhambra and the Fougera are equal in point of architectural perfection and elaboration of detail to any apartment houses in the world, and such structures as the City Railroad building, the new structures which have transformed parts of Montague, Court, Remsen, Fulton and many other streets within a radius of the center of Brooklyn's political life, afford much gratification to the visitor of taste as well as a theme for pardonable pride on the part of the citizens. The Hall of Records building, completed in 1886, is a handsome structure in the Renaissance style, three stories high, and cost $270,000. The Fire Department building, on Jay street near Willoughby, is a bold yet exceedingly graceful development of the Romanesque order. Its massive tower, rising some forty feet above the rest of the structure, gives it an individuality that at once attracts the eye. The Federal building, completed in 1892, at a cost of $1,886,115, is a wonderful change from the little store at the corner of Fulton and Front streets, where up to 1819 Brooklyn's first Postmaster, Joel Bunce, was wont to transact business. In what is known as the shopping district, — Fulton street from the bridge to Flatbush avenue, — the dry goods merchants have erected huge structures, eclipsing in their size and adaptability most of those in New York, and it is also said, far surpassing those across the river in the aggregate annual amount of business. Mention of the dry goods stores recalls the importance of these establishments in the daily history of Brooklyn, and might prompt a few lines further concerning them; but there are so many of them and of such varying degrees of importance that a selection might be invidious and would certainly be disappointing. But we may say a few words about the career of one of the greatest of these merchants, whose death early in 1900 is still mourned in many circles. This was Azel D. Matthews, who from a small beginning built up one of the largest trades in the city. His life story was, in fact, part and parcel of the modern history of Brooklyn. He settled in the place when it was a mere town of about 25,000 inhabitants. He began business in a small way, and as Brooklyn grew the Matthews establishment grew with it, until from a small shop in Main street the present large department store of A. D. Matthews & Sons in Fulton street evolved.

Mr. Matthews came of an old Cape Cod family. His father moved to Hinsdale, Massachusetts, where, on April 29, 1809, Azel D. Matthews was born. He began his mercantile career in Brooklyn in a small store at 93 Main street, which was then the business center of the town. He later established himself on Myrtle avenue, near Bridge street. Mr. Matthews was the pioneer among the dry goods merchants in the upper Fulton street movement. Recognizing the fact that Brooklyn was bound to grow, and that the march of trade would be up town, he rented a store at the corner of Fulton street and Gallatin place. That was thirty-five years ago. The Matthews store is now in the very center of the shopping district. From time to time additions have been made to the store, until it now covers the greater part of the block on Fulton street between Gallatin place and Smith street, extending back to Livingston street.

Mr. Matthews took a keen interest in the Church and Sunday-school life of Brooklyn. He early became identified with the Brooklyn Sunday-school Union, and continued his association with that organization almost up to the time of his death.

During this period the city itself was constantly effecting improvements. One of the most important of these, apart from roadways and the like, was the acquisition of the marsh lands of the Wallabout and their transformation into a public market. The ground in question had long been an eyesore, and besides was a constant source of danger to the public health. It was long thought that a public market or a public park might be erected there, as it was not deemed possible that the ground could ever be adapted for building purposes or that it would ever be needed for the Navy Yard, of whose territory it was a part. On September 12, 1883, the Grocers' Retail Protective Association urged the authorities, at a conference, to secure the land in question and turn it into a market, offering all the aid in their power. Acting on this, the city government entered into negotiations with the Navy Department and as a result obtained a lease of the property, with a view of practically testing the success or otherwise of the project. Part of it was at once drained and graded, divided up into streets and lots, a lot of two-story frame structures were quickly run up by market men, — cheap structures of the most flimsy description, for the whole affair was an experiment and the United States could cancel the lease at any moment by giving thirty days' notice, when the whole concern might be wiped out. The strength of the market lay in the open lots to which farmers' and other wagons brought produce direct from farm or garden, and there remained for half a day or a day until their load was disposed of. The scheme worked so well, in spite of the many adverse conditions, that the city in 1891 purchased about eighteen acres of the marsh land for $700,000 and the market became a fixed feature. In 1894 an additional twenty-seven acres was secured, for which Uncle Sam was paid $1,208,666. This tract, between Clinton and Washington avenues and from Flushing avenue to the East River, has been developed, says the "Eagle" Almanac, "largely into a shipping basin and pier system for vessels in the food supply traffic, and embracing facilities for loaded railroad cars to be transferred to the market without breaking freight bulk. The bulkhead wall along the south and west sides of the basin is 1,680 feet in length, and that along the easterly side of the basin, some 1, 080 feet. These walls, together with four of the five piers constructed, add a mooring frontage of over a mile in length to the city's wharfage room. The fifth pier. No. 2, has been leased to the Pennsylvania Railroad Company at the annual rental of $12,000. The preparation of this pier for service involved the outlay of $100,000 by the railroad company. The market is deriving great benefit from the operation of this terminal, and that of the Delaware, Lackawanna & Western Railroad, on the north side of Wallabout Canal, completed during last year. Cold storage, of which there was great need from the time the market was founded, has been provided in the opening to business last year of the establishment of the Kings County Refrigerating Company, with the preserving capacity of 700,000 square feet.

"In May, 1894, the city authorities and market people, acting conjointly, effected from the New York State Legislature the enactment of a law, chapter 569, which authorized the city authorities to issue upon lots rented five-year leases, with privilege of two renewals of similar duration at rates adjustable at the commencement of each term. The leases issued under this law required the erection of substantial buildings of brick, stc.ne and iron, uniform in external design, at the outlay of the lessees; the buildings at the termination of the leases to revert to the city upon payment of their appraised values. During the years 1895-6 the buildings were constructed."

By the close of 1897 it was estimated that the annual business of the market amounted to $25,000,000, and often in the summer of that year something like 550 wagons of produce would be disposed of every Saturday, while the financial return to the city for the year was $42,046 in the shape of rents, and $3,531 from the fees paid by farmers for wagon room.

This was a practical work. But the city was not forgetful of the adornments which came from the sculptor's studio, and which, besides adding to the beauty and interest of a street or park, serve to show that republics are neither oblivious to aesthetic requirements nor ungrateful to their great men. Several of these have already been mentioned. The statue of General Grant, unveiled in 1896, was a gift to the city from the Union League Club, and in the same year the statue of General Warren on the Park Plaza was unveiled. A statue of General Fowler, who commanded Brooklyn's "red-legged devils" in the Civil War, will shortly be placed beside it, and an equestrian statue of General Slocum, another war hero, is promised soon. A simple monument, but a most significant one, was placed on Battle Hill, Prospect Park, August 27, 1895, in memory of the four hundred Maryland soldiers who fell near the spot thus again consecrated in the fateful battle of Brooklyn, August 27, 1776. It is a plain but extremely elegant shaft of white marble, and its cost was borne by the Maryland Society of Sons of the American Revolution. It is at once a memorial to brave men who gave up their lives in the cause of patriotism, and it marks the center of a widespread battle-field on which it almost seemed as if that liberty for which they had died had been forever crushed out.

A peculiarity in the way of statues, — one erected by citizens to mark their sense of the labors of a citizen then still living. — was that which was unveiled at the main entrance to Prospect Park, on June 6, 1891. The man so honored was J. S. T. Stranahan. The idea of erecting a statue of this esteemed citizen in the people's playground which he had done so much to create was originated at a private gathering, and it was at once heartily endorsed, and in a short time the following committee was constituted to put the idea into shape: John Gibb, Chairman: John B. Woodward, Treasurer; Elijah R. Kennedy, Secretary; Richard S. Storrs, S. V. White, Darwin R. James, William B. Kendall, Charles Pratt, Henry B. Maxwell, George V. Brower, Samuel B. Duryea, C. N. Hoagland, E. F. Linton, William Carey Sanger, William Berri, Andrew D. Baird, Frederick A. Schroeder, Joseph F. Knapp, Bernard Peters, Thomas E. Stillman, Franklin Woodruff, David A. Boody, William A. Read, Abbott L. Dow, E. H. R. Lyman, A. C. Barnes, Charles E. Schieren, Alexander E. Orr, Benjamin D. Silliman and Gustave A. Jahn. In answer to a request for funds, money soon began to flow in, and the commission to execute the statue was placed with Frederick MacMonnies. His work was most satisfactorily completed, and the statue was unveiled amid much ceremony, at which Mr. Stranahan was privileged to be present and to listen to many kindly words about himself, notably those in the masterly address of Dr. Storrs.

Besides its progress in material wealth, in architectural beauty and commercial importance, the feature of Brooklyn's story during its last twenty years was annexation. The consolidation of Williamsburgh, Greenpoint and Bushwick in 1855 and the success of that experiment in the harmonious blending of the various elements had inspired a desire for "more." Besides, it was felt that Brooklyn was daily overflowing its old boundaries, and that the outlying districts were getting many of the benefits of the city government and privileges without being of any assistance in the matter of paying taxes, that what was spoken about as the "outside towns" were in reality prospering at the expense of Brooklyn. A beginning was made in 1886, when on May 13 a bill which had passed, the Legislature annexing New Lots became a law without the Governor's signature, thus taking from the town of Flatbush a vast proportion of its territory and adding a new ward, the Twenty-sixth, to Brooklyn.

The early story of New Lots has already been told, but the following interesting sketch by Mr. N. F. Palmer is interesting, as showing its modern development:

New Lots was originally settled by the well-to-do farmers of old Flatbush, and became an active farming district for market gardening, and all these New Lots farmers became prosperous and their influence was felt in the politics of Kings county. This influence prevented any innovation in the way of real estate development, and not until 1835, was there in the New Lots section a single parcel of land cut up into building lots. In that year Abraham H. Van Wyck and Peter Neefus purchased a parcel of land from the Johannus Eldert family, who owned a large farm extending from the Jamaica plank road to the old New Lots road next to the boundary line of the town of Jamaica. This locality had become famous by the horse race tracks at Union Course and Centerville, and a demand took place for building lots. Van Wyck mapped the lands into the first building lots, 25x100. in 1836, and lot No. 1 was near the corner of what is now Jamaica avenue and Eldert lane, in what is now known as the Cypress Hills section of the ward.

A few years after this, July. 1837, the farms of Major Daniel Rapelje and others were purchased by John R. Pitkin and a map made known as "Map No. 1. East New York lands, or the First Manufacturing District, lying on the Great Eastern Railroad, five and one-half miles from the city of New York."' This was the first use of the words East New York, and represented a neighborhood near the old Howard House. The Post office Department adopted the name, and it has stuck to it ever since. There never was any village corporation nor other form of government, except the town of

Flatbush, until 1852, when the town of New Lots was set off and created out of the eastern part of the town of Flatbush. Between Van Wyck and Pitken maps of 1836 and 1843 little was accomplished to create a boom in building on this tract. On the contrary, Pitkin was obliged to work hard to hold his own through the hard times of '36, and released from contract a vast area contemplated in this manufacturing district. On the 1st and 7th of July, 1841, and the 2nd and 15th of July, 1842, the titles (streets and avenues) were "made perfect through two great chancery sales," and a map was printed which gave notice: "East New York (center property), Union, monthly auction sale map. Notice: Several of the present proprietors of this valuable property have concluded to unite in establishing a system of monthly auction sales to persons wishing to make locations, or improvements. Persons can go out to see said property by the railroad cars from the South Ferry, Brooklyn side, at 9 ½ A. M., 4 and 6 ½ o'clock P. M. Tickets ½ each. Returning from East New York the cars leave at about 8 ¼ , 1 ¼  and 5 ½ o'clock. This is a good opportunity to secure very valuable property at low prices. It will soon be on the line of the great thoroughfare to Boston, the quick ten hour route per Long Island Railroad now nearly complete, and only about 22 minutes' time per railroad from the city, Brooklyn side. How can Newark and Lynn be so much better than E. N. Y.? They are not so well situated."

So wrote John R. Pitkin in 1843. more than half a century ago, and, strange to contemplate, he then could ride from the South Ferry to East New York in twenty-two minutes. He used the argument about time to get there with great foresight, for he realized that as an inducement to boom his venture nothing else could better be engraved on his map.

This map shows that there were only thirty-eight buildings in East New York at this time. The railroad was in the center of Atlantic avenue, and had a branch track down what was then, and is now, Pennsylvania avenue, into a building in "Block 14," south of South Carolina avenue, which we now call Liberty avenue, into the building of the New Jersey Mills, now owned by the Davis family, and still in operation. The Howards' Halfway House, on the Brooklyn and Jamaica turnpike at the end of Flatbush road at the head of Alabama avenue, is where the stage coaches made a stop. Opposite was the bourse of J. L. Williams, standing about opposite to the middle of the block, on the north side of Flatbush road. There were no streets represented on this map west of Alabama avenue, except the Flatbush road, nor any east of Wyckoff's lane, nor south of old Broadway. The following names appear as owners of lots: E. M. Strong, Isaac Bemis, Jacob H. Sackman, W. J. Furman, J. L. Williams, Vanderhof, W. van Voorliees, Frederick Lang and John Taphan along the south side of the turnpike. Along Virginia avenue (Fulton street) are the names: Johnson, Charles Gough, Wolcott March, Ransome Smith, and Turner. Along Alabama avenue, on the east side, were: Henry Grobe, Abrm. Van Siclen, Leonard Bond, Francis Keitz, Jacob H. Sackman,

Isaac Bemis, John W. Warth, Charles Heitkamp. On Georgia avenue: Ransome Smith, Potter J. Thomas, Charles Vinton, Charles Georig, William K. Teasdale, William Simonson, Rul Smith, Wentworth, Isaac M. Steevnorf (Stoothoofs). On Sheffield avenue were Wolcot Marsh, Jacob H. Sackman, J. L. Williams, Thomas I. Gerrald, Lewis Kendig, S. Frisbey, John Van Siclen. Pennsylvania avenue on the west side was all a courtyard, with no names on it. On the cast side were names: Vanderhoef, Ransome Smith, Samuel Judson, Sherman Institute Branch Depository Work and School, with Manson House corner of Atlantic avenue. H. F. Thrall on south side of Atlantic avenue, and south side of. North Carolina avenue (Liberty avenue) the factory building, now Davis' New Jersey Mills: on New Jersey avenue were Dutch Reformed Church, Turner, S. Shepherd, George Butcher, C. Goebel. Corner of South Carolina avenue (now Glenmore), M. F. Misenere, J. F. Bridges; on Vermont avenue were, corner Virginia avenue, Ransome Smith, Jacob H. Sackman; corner Atlantic avenue, Ransome Smith, John Lohmans, Morganthaler, Assalle Seldinger, Charles Beumaer, R. S. Winslow; on Wyckoff lane were, on west side, John Sopham, John Lohman, J. H. Sackman, C. Heitkamp, Charles Pieumer, F. Lang, John W. Worth, and at Broadway, Philip Obergirck. Not all of these occupied buildings, but they were the first investors in real estate in this locality.

In 1838 John R. Pitkin came out with a second map of the Second Manufacturing District in the easterly part of the town, laying out a large territory from the turnpike to the New Lots road. This was premature and the same territory was subsequently mapped by Rapalye, Walter Nichols, Lewis Curtis and others; only a few blocks of this old man remain. In 1849 Williams, Pellington & Furman laid out the land at the north side of the B. and J. plank road between old Howard place and old Pellington place. This was followed in 1851 by the Jacob H. Sackman map and in 1853 by Sackman, Barby & Delmonico. Horace A. Miller came out in 1853 with the map of eighteen blocks of land on the east side of Pitkin's East New York lands, between the plank road and old Broadway. Up to 1859 these were the principal lands of East New York. About this period C. W. Heitkamp was energetic and took a leading part in the affairs of the town. He published a map made "from different surveys and maps made and drawn by M. G. Johman, Esq." At this period the Broadway horse railroad had continued to circumnavigate around two blocks near the Howard House, but the Fulton street horse cars had got only to the Mattowak House, where the plank road company of the late Aaron A. De Graw stood on guard. At this period John R. Pitkin was general agent and signed a "map of East New York, Kings County, Long Island, N. Y., drawn by C. W. Heitkamp, lithographed and published by Gustav Kraetzer, May 1, 1859." The map said: "Great sale at auction of East New York (center) building lots, by James Cole & Son, at the Merchants' Exchange, New York, of 100 very valuable (reserved) center lots, belonging to George D. Pitkin, Israel W. Vanderveer and others. * * * This is all most desirable property within 4 ½ miles of New York City. By Broadway cars (fare 5 cents). About five miles by Fulton avenue cars from Fulton Ferry (fare 5 cents) and 5 ½ miles from South Ferry." No mention is made of the Long Island R. R. or how one could get from South Ferry.

The principal buildings at East New York in 1859 were: Howard House, by P. H. Reid; Mattowak House, by W. Simonson:, Railroad Hotel, by M. Bennett, on Atlantic avenue; Military Hall, by John Lohman, Liberty avenue: residence of C. R. Miller, of Bernhard McWilliams, Broadway and Hull street; Nicolson brick cottage, J.C. Middendorf, residence and grocery, corner of Sheffield avenue and Fulton street, with the old pump in front of it: William Alexander, residence on Flatbush road (East New York avenue); James L. Williams, residence, since moved, and is now standing on the north side of East New York avenue, opposite Williams avenue; C. Heitkamp, store and residence, on old plank road, where many a man has fallen up the three steps to get before the justice of the peace; C. A. Beckert, M. D., at Sheffield avenue, and G. Kraetzer, residence, Sheffield avenue.

East New York at this period had also the target companies shooting galleries of L. Altenbrand, of M. Bennett and of H. Luhrs, behind which now stands Breitkopt's Hotel, on the corner of Bushwick and Jamaica avenue, at the head of Pennsylvania avenue. At about this period, or in 1861, the city of Brooklyn had opened up the streets to the old patent line, along the ridge of hills, and the James L. Williams map had opened the intervening land from the Howard House to the old city line. 1 he old parade ground west of Alabama avenue and south of Atlantic avenue did not come out as lots until the Whitehead Howard map was filed in 1869, although the survey and map was made in 1857. The individuals whose names are mentioned, so far, were the pioneers of East New York, and the period to which they belonged was one peculiar to itself, and long to be remembered as East New York.

The return of the steam locomotive on Atlantic avenue and the opening of the elevated railroads just before annexation to Brooklyn in 1886 marks a middle period and one which was historical in its results, because at one bound this locality attracted capital, and a flood of it came, until hardly a farm was left to be purchased for the making of building lots, and East New York vanished and Brooklyn came to our doors and welcomed us as the Twenty-sixth Ward. Previous to that, and not since 1869, when Williamsburgh and old Bushwick were annexed to Brooklyn, had one square foot of territory been added to old Brooklyn. The sudden development of the Twenty-sixth Ward, after the opening of the elevated railroads, as the actual end of the Brooklyn Bridge, led up to conditions which eventually terminated in the annexation of all the county towns of Kings county and ended in consolidation with the city of New York. Surely East New York pioneers started a great project of suburban development. They came up to East New

York out of the crowded tenements of the old city for fresh air and prosperity, and they got both; peace to their ashes and respect for their courage.

Previous to the annexation of the town of New Lots to the city of Brooklyn an economical political government had made taxes small with very few public improvements. The first expensive improvement was the grading, curbing and paving in part of Atlantic avenue, which was done in 1870 by a special commission under an act passed April 16, 1869. This cost about $100,000. Thereafter a few principal streets in the old East New York section were improved by grading, curbing and flagging, which aggregated about $90,000 more expended under a New Lots improvement commission. When the agitation of the annexation question commenced, it was deemed wise to bond the town for $500,000 for public improvements, which was done.

There was a balance in this fund of accrued interest amounting to about $20,000, which was expended in part on certain other street improvements, or still remains to the credit of the ward.

Since annexation to Brooklyn the sewers have been laid and are being paid for by assessments on the property benefited.

The Park Department has improved Glenmore avenue, through the ward, and has also improved the eastern parkway extension and Pennsylvania avenue. These improvements were not assessed directly upon the property benefited, by an anomaly in political diplomacy.

The Twenty-sixth Ward, known up to 1886 as the town of New Lots, may deserve the credit of being the pioneer in annexation and consolidation to the city, because the annexation of that locality to Brooklyn caused a phenomenal boom to suburban property in the old town of New Lots that became a strong argument among real estate men and influenced the subsequent annexation to Brooklyn of all the other county towns of Kings county. The town of New Lots was ripe for annexation when it came, for it had secured perfect railroad transit via both steam and elevated railroads, as well as being the terminus of the trunk horse car lines to the Brooklyn ferries, which for five cents carried one to the ferry, day or night. Besides these railroad advantages water was secured at a small cost to the individual and without a dollar of town indebtedness. No wonder that the population of this ward increased from 10,000 in 1872 to nearly 80,000 in 1900.

Since annexation to Brooklyn the sewers have been laid and provided with the only perfect outlet in Kings county, and, as these sewers were prosecuted on long term bonds and as these bonds are about one-half paid off, it will be discovered ere long that the Twenty-sixth Ward has indeed secured great advantages in laying the foundation for a great and solid future to the real estate investor. This locality has passed through all the experimental schemes of suburban development, and whatever advantages it has had physically, they have all been a factor in its rapid growth. This ward may be said to be the gateway to Long Island, for all the bridges and railroads, elevated, surface or depressed, go through this gate to the island with their stream of travel. This ward will be the first to develop a water front on Jamaica Bay, and the wonder is that, with navigable water within two miles of a population of nearly 80,000 people, not a public dock for coal, lumber and all material necessary to cheapen the building and sustaining trade of such a community has been built.

There the annexation movement rested until, after much negotiation and delay. Flatbush became Brooklyn's Twenty-ninth Ward April 25, 1894, Gravesend became the Thirty-first Ward on May 8, and New Utrecht the Thirtieth Ward on July 1. This brought all of Kings county within the city of Brooklyn excepting the town of Flatlands, and that wheeled into line in 1896 and took rank with her old Dutch sister communities as the Thirty-second Ward. There was naturally great jubilation in Brooklyn over this consummation, and as by the time Flatlands had surrendered the trolley was opening -up new routes daily and the land boomers were organizing fresh tracts of land into home sites, it was felt that a splendid future had opened up for the enlarged city, — Greater Brooklyn, they called it, and the orators were wont to enlarge upon the extent and importance of a city that extended from the East River to the sea, that practically had space enough for a century's growth, that had a magnificent water front, a well-supplied treasury, a population of over a million and all varieties of landscape from the crowded streets around the City Hall to the festal scenes of Coney Island and the hopeful isolation of Flatlands and New Utrecht.

But even in the midst of this expansion and jubilation the evidences were not wanting that a much greater transformation was at hand; that once the comedy of annexation was over the drama of consolidation, — some regarded it as a tragedy, — would begin. The movement toward the consolidation of Brooklyn and New York had long been agitated. Mr. Stranahan had ventilated it for years, and with the completion of the bridge many thoughtful persons saw in that event but the first tangible evidence of the complete civic union that was bound to come. While the scheme was but a dream. Brooklyn regarded the matter somewhat jocularly, but in 1894, when the question became serious and agitation on the subject became acute, it was seen that the voting population was pretty evenly divided, for and against. In 1890 the advocates of union had so far matured their plans as to have a commission appointed by the Legislature to consider the expediency of consolidating the cities. The Long Island members were J. S. T. Stranahan, E. F. Linton and W. D. Veeder, of Brooklyn, and John H. Brinckerhoff, of Queens. Under the engineering of this commission a test vote as an expression was taken at the November election in 1894, with the following result:

| | FOR | AGAINST. |
|---|---|---|
| Kings county | 64,744 | 64,467 |
| Queens county | 7.712 | 4.741 |
| New York | 96.938 | 59.959 |

With the rest of the vote we are not here concerned. On the Long Island side the only district to give a majority against consolidation was Flushing (1,407 against, 1,144 for, union); but the most curious fact brought out was that Brooklyn's exploits in the way of annexation had really sounded the knell of its own separate history. The majority in Kings county for consolidation was only 277, and this was brought about by the vote of the annexed towns, for in Brooklyn city proper the vote showed a majority of 1,034 against. The vote had hardly been counted before definite action was taken by the opponents of the question which had now become a live and most important issue. The League of Loyal Citizens was formed and began a vigorous campaign, using the press, enlisting orators, issuing leaflets and even a newspaper which was called "The Greater Brooklyn." and introduced into the Legislature a bill supported by a petition signed by over 70,000 voters of Brooklyn, calling for a resubmission of the question to a vote of the people. On January 13, 1896, the league organized a mass meeting in the Academy of Music, where Dr. Storrs presided and declared that while resubmission was the topic to be considered, "there is now a strong sentiment against consolidation with or without resubmission." "Let Brooklyn's future remain in the hands of Brooklyn's people," was the watchword of the meeting. and its entire proceedings showed the keen antipathy which had been aroused to any attempt at union. In March, 1896, however, a bill favoring consolidation was passed in the Senate by a vote of 38 to 8 and in the Assembly by 91 to 56. When submitted as required by law to the executives of the municipalities affected. Mayor Strong, of New York, and Mayor Wurster, of Brooklyn, vetoed the bill, and Mayor Gleason, of Long Island City, approved it. When the bill was returned to Albany it was promptly repassed and became a law. A mass meeting in New York, in which A. A. Low and the Rev. Dr. Cuyler took a prominent part, asked Governor Morton to veto the bill, but it was signed on May 11, 1896, and so the first stage of the struggle was over.

By the terms of the act consolidation was to go into effect on January 1, 1898, and in the meantime a commission was to frame a charter for the proposed great municipality and setting out the basis of the union. This commission consisted of Seth Low, Benjamin F. Tracy, John F. Dillon, Comptroller Stewart L. Woodford, Thomas F. Gilroy, Silas B. Dutcher, William C. De Witt, George M. Pinney, Jr., and Harrison S. Moore. That body accomplished its task, and the charter it prepared, after being amended to please the whims of some of the legislators, was duly passed and became a law by the signature of the Governor on May 2, 1897. In November of that year the Mayor of the consolidated municipality and all the other elective officials provided by the charter were chosen after a heated campaign, and then the consolidation movement had only to wait a few weeks before coming to its full fruition.

It was truly a mournful gathering that assembled in the Council Chamber of Brooklyn's City Hall on the closing hours of December 31, 1897, to observe the passing into history of the City of Churches. There was no lack of expressions of hope for the future; it was even felt by many that Brooklyn was about to enter upon the highest phase of her history; that she was to preserve her individuality in the cluster of boroughs which the next day were to unite into the Greater New York; but even the most optimistic in the gathering could not but feel that they were face to face with "the end of an auld sang," as the Chancellor of Scotland remarked with the passing of the last vote which united that country to England. The meeting, — "the wake," someone irreverently called it, — was arranged mainly by the Society of Old Brooklynites and the city officials, and the following formed the committee in charge: Joseph C. Hendrix, William Berri, Herbert F. Gunnison, John S. McKeon, Richard Young, James L. Watson, D. T. Leverich, John Hess, E. D. White, Stephen M. Griswold, Mayor Wurster, Comptroller Palmer, Auditor Sutton, Aldermen J. R. Clark and David S. Stewart. The City Hall was bedecked with flowers and seemed gay even in the waning hours of its pre-eminence. Over the exercises Mayor Wurster presided, and in a graceful manner performed his last public official duty. The inevitable "oration" without which no American gathering would be complete was delivered by St. Clair McKelway, whose theme was "From Great to Greater." Will Carleton, the poet, read an original ode, "The Passing of Brooklyn," and Rev. J. M. Farrar, D. D., delivered an address on "Commerce and Church." An informal address was made at the close of the exercises by ex-Mayor Seth Low.

The proceedings were kept up until the tolling of the bell in the tower announced at once the dawn of 1898 and the end of the long and honorable story of the City of Brooklyn.

# QUEENS

## CHAPTER XLIII. QUEENS

With the advent of the Greater New York the old county of Queens became little more than an expression. Shorn of its ancient boundaries it retained its county organization, its County Clerk, District Attorney, Surrogate, Sheriff and other legal officials, but for administrative purposes it became one of the boroughs of the Greater New York with its representatives in the Council and on the Board of Aldermen of the great city, its own local Borough President, Board of Public Improvement, its school board and the like. It is as much a distinct borough as Manhattan or Brooklyn, with the same official staff as has any of the other component sections of the greater city.

But that fact does not make it any the less true that many of the old residents of the Queens County as it was, believe that in its present status as a borough much of its old glory has departed, that its birthright has been sold for a mess of pottage and that even that reward or price is still in the future. At the election of Nov. 6, 1894, at which the question of consolidation was decided by the people Queens county voted in favor of the change by 7,712 votes to 4,741, the large majority being rolled up mainly through the votes of Long Island City. Flushing township voted 1,407 against consolidation and 1,144 in favor of it.

The boundaries of the old County of Queens were as follows: On the east by Suffolk County, on the west by Kings County, on the north by Long Island Sound and on the south by the Atlantic, and included 410 square miles. In its territory was the North and South Brother, Riker (Hallet's) and several smaller islands. The whole was divided into the six townships of Newtown, Flushing, Jamaica, North. Hempstead, Hempstead and Oyster Bay. For a long time its population increased slowly — slowly, that is, considering its contiguity to Manhattan Island. In 1731 the figure was 7,895; in 1786, 13,084; in 1800, 16,983; in 1830, 22,460; in 1880, 90,574; and in 1890, the last official census in which the county figured.

Since the change which incorporated it into New York, what remains of the old county as the Borough of Queens still continues to show an increase, and that in a more marked degree than formerly. Long Island City has now an estimated population of over 50,000 and the other sections are increasing in great although not equal proportions. Of late years the land boomer has been energetically at work and devoting to Queens some at least of that energy which helped so materially to build up the old outlying sections of Brooklyn, and as a result many new settlements are opened up each year. But the increased facilities of travel with the various sections of the Greater City in the way of bridges over the East River and tunnels under it and the splendid programme of the Long Island Railroad as to its immediate extension and the adoption of improvements which will make it a trunk line are the surest reliances for the wonderful growth which will come to Queens within the next decade. Its population of 152,999 in 1900 will, it is confidently expected, be doubled.

For a long time in the last century the population of Queens increased very slowly so far as immigration was concerned. Little effort was made to entice settlement and it was so inconveniently situated that even intercourse between it and Brooklyn was difficult. Long after Brooklyn and its associate towns and even the villages of Westchester were more or less marked by the influx of settlers from abroad, Queens county went on the even tenor of its way, contented with its isolation, proud of its old families, and careful of the ancient customs which had been handed down, generation after generation. But such a state of things could not endure forever and the introduction of the railroad in Queens as well as elsewhere brought a change. Long Island City, for instance, may be regarded as a product of the railway, and it has had for years, as it has now, a larger proportion of foreign born citizens in its population than any other part of the borough. Jamaica, too, has felt the change, although it was not until the introduction of the trolley and its cheap and speedy method of transit that it began to really feel the full effect of the modern impulse.

But gratifying as this increase of population is in one sense — in every practical sense — it has not been witnessed without a sentiment of regret by some of the representatives of the old families. The late Gov. R. C. McCormick, who for fifty years had his home in Jamaica, remarked a few weeks before his death (1901) to the writer with considerable pathos: "I remember when I used to walk along these streets of Jamaica and everybody knew me and spoke to me. I knew all the children, and could send kindly messages of enquiry with them to their homes. I had something to say to every man or woman I met, I knew much of their history, their hopes, their disappointments, their anxieties and sorrows. They all knew me, knew of my interests, my politics, my purposes, my standing in the community. Now I can walk from my home here to the post office and back again and not exchange a word with any one. It is very sad; it is not as it used to be; we have lost the old friendliness and neighborliness, we are growing in strength, new streets are being opened up each year, we have no fault to find with the newcomers, they are here to found homes — the very best class of settlers who can come to any place, but somehow the old charm of personal acquaintance has been lost."

In one respect the statistics of Queens County are peculiar, as they show, until almost a recent date, a very small proportion of pauperism. In 1835, for instance, with a population of 25,130, there were only 71 persons receiving public relief. This slim proportion continued all through the history of the county until the introduction of the railway, and the figures before us tell the story so familiar to students of sociology that as the county advanced in wealth so did the number of its paupers increase. In a purely agricultural community, and especially in a community where the ground is tilled by its owners, pauperism does not flourish, and such a community was Queens County until it began to fall under the influence of the spirit of "modern improvements."

But the future of Queens borough is not to lie in agriculture; that much seems certain from a survey of existing conditions or conditions promised. It will be by the growth of its manufactures, the development of its seaside resorts and its advantages as a place for home building. Long Island City is already a manufacturing center, so is Jamaica, and scattered through the country are places like Steinway devoted solely to one branch of trade. All that is really needed to upbuild local manufacturing prosperity is cheap and adequate communication with the rest of the continent, and that is promised in the fullest measure in the near future. Land is cheap in every section of the borough and water privileges are plentiful. In the way of summer resorts contiguous to New York, it has splendid advantages. On the Atlantic coast the Rockaways, Arverne, Woodsburgh, Lawrence and Edgemere are already famous and popular; on the other side North Beach now attracts thousands each year, and Flushing Bay is ready to provide a dozen resorts, while College Point, Whitestone and' the shores of Little Neck Bay already boast populous summer colonies.

For home building with the trolley system daily becoming more ubiquitous, and the promised development of the Long Island Railroad, and the tunnels and bridges now in course of construction, all' insuring rapid and convenient travel, there is no section better for practical purposes on Long Island. Real estate in Brooklyn — throughout old Kings County, in fact — has long lost its old; time quality of cheapness — a quality that still presents itself abundantly in Queens. Then according to the schemes now being put through, Jamaica wilt really be nearer the center of business on Manhattan Island than are Flatbush or Gravesend.

A ridge of high hills runs east and west through the borough along its northern part, throwing out spurs to the Sound and breaking the shore into indentations of bays and headlands. On this ridge, facing the water, are some of the most finished home settlements in the city, while the broad interior plain stretching southward to the Atlantic is covered with agricultural villages, railroad towns and thriving suburbs. Throughout both the Sound and plains settlements city improvements, such as water, gas and electricity, are universal, and larger places, like Flushing and Jamaica, have sewerage systems.

Writing on the certain progress of Queens Borough, a recent writer, who evidently had the facts at his finger's end, wrote:

This tremendous prospective growth of population must of necessity follow the lines of least resistance, which, in the presence of adequate transportation, are determined by the cost of land. On this basis Queens should receive a disproportionate share of whatever investment takes place, for land in Queens is selling at hundreds of dollars as against thousands in the case of land in Manhattan and The Bronx at an equal distance from the Manhattan City Hall. The Long Island Railroad's passenger service will come into direct contact with the Manhattan Rapid Transit system at the Brooklyn terminal of the tunnel from the Battery and in Manhattan itself through the tunnel from Long Island City. Through these tunnels the principal settlements in Queens will be tapped without change of cars, except to board those of the Manhattan Rapid Transit road, and these new outlets to Manhattan will be supplemented by three others dispensing with water passage — the East Rivet Bridge, the Blackwell's Island Bridge and the bridge at Peck Slip, all of which are under way. The combined effect of two tunnels and three new bridges on the passenger service from Queens will be tremendous, revolutionizing travel not only over the Long Island Railroad, but over the elevated and trolley lines as well.

How susceptible the growth of the borough is to betterments of transportation appears from the progress made in the past three or four years. Consolidation with New York induced the construction of a network of trolley lines throughout the borough by the New York and Queens County Railway Company and the New York and North Shore Railway Company, which are identical as to management. The former system starts at the Long Island Railroad ferry in Long Island City and the latter at the terminus of the Kings County Elevated road at the Brooklyn borough limit. The two systems, which also connect with the Long Island Railroad and the Brooklyn Rapid Transit lines at numerous points in the interior, served the needs of local travel, besides bringing: formerly inaccessible places into contact with the highways of travel to Manhattan. The formation of the New York and Queens Electric Light and Power Company not only supplied the illuminant that is now essential in public lighting but made economical power for manufacturing available throughout the borough, except the Rockaway district.

These notable improvements, together with the admission to Brooklyn Bridge of the trolley and elevated lines of the Brooklyn Rapid Transit Company, which sends one branch of its system to Jamaica and another to Flushing, started a building movement which spread far beyond the customary limit of housing improvements. However, the bulk of the travel from the farther parts of the borough 'mist continue to be over the Long Island Railroad. Hence the supreme importance of the tunnels which will connect that road with the Manhattan Rapid Transit system, implying a saving of at least fifteen minutes in distance which now consume an hour in travel, besides dispensing with ferry transfers. But although the improvements in transportation that have been obtained since consolidation with New York appear slight by comparison with those now in sight, they were sufficient to initiate a far-reaching movement in real estate, until in 1900 the number of conveyances practically equaled those of The Bronx with its direct approach to downtown Manhattan and its years of start in municipal progress.

Outside of farming, only one of the old industries of Queens remains, that of horse racing, although it must be confessed that the sorry and sometimes silly exhibitions at Aqueduct are but a poor succession to the old glories of Hempstead or Union Course. Horse racing really was the first industry of Queens county and its meets were long the most famous in the country. In 1665 Gov. Nicolls ordered a race course to be set aside on Hempstead "for encouraging the bettering of the breed of horses which, through great neglect, has been impaired." His successor. Gov. Lovelace, also lent his aid to making the sport a success and it seems to have been a popular feature from the first. Daniel Denton in his "Brief Description" (London, 1701) says: "Toward the middle of Long Island lieth a plain 16 miles long and 4 broad, where you will find neither stick nor stone to hinder the horses' heels, or endanger them in their races, and once a year the best horses in the island are brought hither to try their swiftness, and the swiftest rewarded with a silver cup, two being annually procured for that purpose." The course itself was changed at least once, but the racing center continued to be on Hempstead plains until 1821, when it was moved to Union Course. The stakes at New Market, as the Hempstead Course was called, were as a general rule £50 for each event, although on two or three occasions £100 was the figure. It was on Union Course that horse racing reached its highest development in the eyes of the sporting fraternity, the gentlemen who make money on the turf. Gambling in fact was as much the feature of each meeting at Union Course as was horse racing itself; in reality, as in our modern days, the racing was but an excuse for the gambling. It was estimated that in the race in 1823 between "Eclipse" and "Sir Henry" for a stake of $20,000 a side $200,000 changed hands when Eclipse was declared the winner. The amount lost was even greater in 1842 when "Boston" defeated "Fashion" in two heats. It was estimated that 70,000 persons witnessed this race. It was probably the widely reported excesses of that race and its attendant circumstances that induced Dr. Prime to write:

"Here [Union Course] are regularly enacted twice a year, scenes which no imagination, however fertile, can depict without the aid of ocular demonstration. It has been stated, and the statement stands uncontradicted, that at a single course of races 50,000 persons attended and $700,000 were lost and won; and that during the five days that the "sports" continued the toll of the Fulton Ferry Company averaged $1,000 a day; and it is supposed that the other avenues of the city realized an equal sum. But the gambling, expense, and loss of time attending these scenes of dissipation form only a part of the evils with which they are connected. The drinking, the swearing, the licentiousness, the contentions and other nameless crimes, which are here periodically committed, with the countenance of law, are enough to sicken the soul of every man that fears God and is disposed to reverence His commands and must induce him to wish most devoutly for the time to come, and that speedily, when this crying abomination, with all its accompaniments, shall be banished from, this once sacred soil of Puritans and Huguenots."

Queens County had other tracks which while not so famous as that at Hempstead and Union Course still proved attractive enough to bring crowds to their "events" and to swell the notoriety which the county enjoyed — enjoyed even in England — as the headquarters of horse-racing in America. As early as 1757 there was a track in Jamaica, and one at Newtown in 1758. The "Fashion Association for Improving the Breed of Horses" had a course at Newtown in 1854, which continued with varying success until 1865, when it had to give way to the progress of the railroad. At Centerville, near Union Course, a trotting track was laid out in 1825 where, in 1847, the "Albany Girl" was tried to run 100 miles in 10 consecutive hours in harness. She actually accomplished 97 ½ miles in 9 ½ hours and then broke down. Surely such sport shows degeneracy somewhere.

With the decadence of the Union Course racing in Queens County ceased to be profitable, and it was abandoned altogether when Kings County took the sport up in earnest, until the establishment of the track at Aqueduct, where racing seems to be in reality another name for gambling. When horses are started to race in mud or by electric light the nature of the sport can easily be appreciated.

In the general chapters of this history reference has already been made to the position of Queens County in the War of the Revolution, so that it is needless to dwell upon that theme here. It had its Tories and its Patriots in probably equal numbers, it has been even asserted that the former were the most numerous, but however that may be, there can be no doubt that all sections were fully aroused to the evils of the system of government to which they had become subject and that the people of Jamaica have the right to claim their old suburb of Brushville as being the birthplace of the Revolution on Long Island.

It is not known what duties the County's militia performed at the battle of Brooklyn other than throwing up fortifications and standing guard at the outposts and ferries. Capt. Jacob Wright of Jamaica and Capt. Van Nuyse of Kings County formed two companies in Col. Lasher's 1st New York battalion in Scott's brigade. The Kings and Queens County Militia guarded alternate days at the Flatbush pass. On the day of battle Capt. Wright's men were in Cobble Hill fort. The Queens County Militia often spoke of lying behind the lines when the British shot whistled over their heads. Putnam rode along the line and every now and again, checking his horse, would say:

"Gentlemen, by your dress I conclude you are countrymen, and, if so. good marksmen. Now, don't fire till you see the whites of their eyes."

Next to the Revolutionary story the most interesting study in connection with the history of Queens County is thr.t of the incidents in connection with the transformation of the greater portion of it into a borough of the modern New York City. The story is well worthy of study and that it might be clearly and intelligently put before the reader by one who has made a thorough study we present the following written at the request of the publishers by Mr. Duncan Maclnnes, one of the expert accountants in the office of the Comptroller of New York, through whose hands all the papers in the case were passed and considered:

At midnight on the 31st day of December, 1897, there were forty-eight separate municipalities merged into the Greater New York, under the general name or title, Borough of Queens. These former municipalities consisted of Long Island City, the old towns of Newtown (from which Long Island City was originally created in 1871), Jamaica (in its earliest form the town of "Crawford"), Flushing' and that part of the town of Hempstead extending westward from the eastern limits of the incorporated village of Far Rockaway to the Rockaway Beach inlet. Eight incorporated villages were among the said municipalities, viz.: Flushing, College Point, Whitestone, Jamaica, Richmond Hill, Far Rockaway, Arverne, and Rockaway Beach; also fourteen school districts in the township of Newtown, eleven school districts in Jamaica, seven in Flushing, and three in Hempstead. These forty-eight separate municipalities were all within the corporate limits of that part (over two-thirds) of Queens County merged into the city of New York by the act of consolidation; and, together with the funded debt of the county, brought a legacy of bonded indebtedness alone to the greater city of $13,337,465. The total real-estate assessed valuation within said former municipalities was $83,263,593 on Dec. 31, 1897, and this was a great increase over what the same property was assessed at twelve months before, and an extraordinary increase over the assessment of 1895 and 1894.

On January 1, 1895, when the ten per cent constitutional limitation as to the debt of a city or county went into effect. Long Island City real estate, assessed valuation, was $16,667,332, and her bonded debt alone $3,033,500, or nearly twice the statutory limitation. Something had to be done, and the powers that then were proceeded to increase the assessed valuation of property, so as to scale down the ratio of the bonded debt, and the work was done effectually by increasing Long Island City real estate values in 1896 from $16,667,332 to $42,377,481, or more than the combined assessed valuation of 1895 of all real estate in Long Island City, the towns of Newtown, Flushing, Jamaica and that part of Hempstead which ultimately was merged into the Greater New York. These 1896 and 1897 values have since been reduced by the courts by upwards of six millions of dollars, which has the disadvantage of decreasing the proceeds to the City of New York from Long Island City tax arrears.

It will be noted from the table that the bonded debt of these Queens municipalities was more than doubled in the year 1897 as compared with a normal increase of several hundred thousand dollars in each of the years preceding; and the extraordinary increase during 1897 was practically all after the passage of the Greater New York charter in April of said year. As Comptroller Coler has said, "The worst mistake of the charter, it seems to me, was that it put a premium on the notion of the various communities (to be) consolidated going into debt."

The latter part of the year 1897 witnessed an orgie in Queens of lavish expenditure and debt-incurring obligations. Every town, village and school district was issuing bonds ad libitum, and generally on the most liberal terms to purchasers thereof. The county was also doing its share. The funded debt of the county park was increased in 1897 from $1,083,500 to $4,837,811, and everywhere was a feverish anxiety and haste to take in on the one hand and disburse from the other every cent that could be realized previous to Dec. 31, 1897, after which the authority to contract further liability or disburse a dollar was vested in the officials of the City of New York. It was a wild orgie while it lasted, and officials who in former years had never handled more than a few thousand dollars found themselves in possession and absolute disposal of hundreds of thousands of dollars, which was expended with the reckless lavishness of a Monte Cristo. Chapters might be written of the cow-paths that were paved by granite blocks, of the turnip and potato -patches that were lighted by electric lamps, of the by-lanes that were lit by gas and naptha lamps, etc., etc., and of the variety and questionable character of contract on contract made on the very eve of actual consolidation; and of the hundreds of thousands of dollars of floating debt that has since come to light and been foisted on the greater city, and the end is not yet! Consolidation has cost the Manhattan taxpayer, or rather Manhattan property, several millions of dollars for the honor of being the second largest city (numerically) in the world.

# CHAPTER XLIV. FLUSHING.

The earliest year of any settlement within the old township of Flushing, — Vlissingen, as it was called, — is 1643. Two years later Governor Kieft issued a town charter to the inhabitants, and this charter was afterward renewed by Governor Dongan in 1685. The town's early records and patents were destroyed by fire in 1789, but in 1792 a copy of Dongan's patent was furnished from the records in Albany under the seal of Governor Clinton, of the State of New York. There is a theory that the name given to the place was derived from that of a town in Holland, but the evidence as to this is a little hazy, and while the matter is practically of no moment, it seems fair to say that the honor of name giving to the Dutch town should not. be abandoned. The first settler was William Thorne (the name long survived in Thorne's Neck), who appears to have held views on religious matters which did not find sympathy among the Puritans, so he is said to have come to this neighborhood from New England in search of a place where he might enjoy liberty of conscience. What his views were is not exactly known, but they were of such a nature that he afterward found it congenial to throw in his lot with the Society of Friends. Soon he was joined by several others, and thus Flushing was another religious community, which, like Gravesend, was a standing reproach to the reputed religious toleration of Massachusetts.

The names in Kieft's patent of the settlers to whom it was issued were Thomas Farington, John Townsend, Thomas Stiles, Thomas Saull, John Marston, Robert Field, Thomas Applegate, Thomas Beddard, Laurence Dutch, John Lawrence, William Lawrence, William Thorne, Henry Sautell, William Pigeon, Michael Milliard, Robert Firman, John Hicks, Edward Hart. They were empowered to elect a Schout, to build fortifications, "to have and enjoy the liberty of conscience according to the custom and manner of Holland without molestation or disturbance from any Magistrate of Magistrates or any other Ecclesiastical Minister." In return for all this and other privileges they agreed to "reverently respect the High and Mighty Lords for their Superior Lords and Patrons," and pay a really moderate tax "in case it be demanded." All of those mentioned in the deed were not from New England, or exiles for religion. John Lawrence, who was one of the incorporators of Hempstead in 1644, was quite an enterprising gentleman, and was several times Mayor of New Amsterdam, and at the time of his death, 1699, was a Judge of the Supreme Court. William Lawrence was also prominent as an office-holder, and had the knack of "holding on" no matter what flag — Dutch or English — waved over the fort at New Amsterdam.

In Dongan's patent the names of the freeholders were Thomas Willett, John Lawrence Seinior, Elias Doughty, Richard Cornell, Moriss Smith, Charles Morgan, Mary Fleake, Wouter Gisbertson, John Masten, John Cornells, John Harrison, Denins Holdron, John Hinchman, William Yeates, Joseph Thorne, John Lawrence Junior, Matthias Harveye, Harmanus King,

John Farrington, Thomas Williams, Elisabeth Osborn, Joseph Havyland, John Washborne, Aaron Cornells, John Bowne, William Noble, Samuel Hoyt, Madeline Frances Barto, John Hoper, Thomas Ford, John Jenning, John Embree, Jonathan Wright, Nicholas Parcell, William Lawrence, Richard Townly, Edward Griffin Junior, John Lawrence at the Whitestone, Henry Taylor, Jasper Smith, Richard Wilday, Thomas Townsend, John Thorne, Anthony Field, John Adams, Richard Stockton, James Whittaker, Hugh Copperthwaite, Richard Chew, James Clement, Margaret Stiles, Samuel Thgrne, Thomas Hedges, William Haviland, Thomas Hicks, John Terry, David Patrick, James Feake, Thomas Kimacry, Phillip Udall, Thomas Davis, Edward Farrington, Thomas Farrington, Matthew Farrington, John Field, Joseph Hedger, John Talman, William Gael, William White, Elisabeth Smith, Thomas Partridge, William Hedger and Benjamin Field. Outside of the Lawrence, Farrington, and Thorne families few representatives of the original patentees appear in this list. But so far as can be learned they were of pretty much the same stamp as most of the pioneers — men and women whose law lay wholly in the sacred Scriptures.

Most of these people were farmers: most of them were from New England. Probably many had left the mainland to get rid of the religious notions prevailing there and enjoy freedom of worship in their own way. But they brought with them their Bibles and their own peculiar views, and were prepared to set up as much of a theocracy as circumstances would permit, — some even were determined to carry out their spiritual ideas no matter what circumstances presented themselves.

So it was as a religious colony that Flushing was to thrive. In 1647, by order of Governor Stuyvesant, the Rev. Francis Doughty settled in it as its minister. Stuyvesant was curious in his friendships, his likes and dislikes, and what there was in Mr. Doughty's composition that won him the personal interest of the Governor it is difficult to imagine. Doughty was an English clergyman, who had crossed the Atlantic that he might speak the truth, but his views on baptism did not suit the Puritans, and he was arrested, tried and ordered to leave Massachusetts. He promptly went to Rhode Island for a brief period, but in 1642 he went to Long Island, having with several associates secured a grant of 13,332 acres of land at Newtown. An Indian outbreak soon scattered this settlement, and Doughty took refuge in New Amsterdam for two years. In 1645 Doughty and most of the patentees returned to Newtown, but trouble and quarrels broke out, and as a result Doughty threatened to refer the matter to Holland, and thereupon he was arrested and fined twenty-five guilders. In this case Stuyvesant acted in haste and without warrant, and when he recognized this he was anxious to "do something"' for Doughty. A request from Flushing for a; minister reached Stuyvesant about this time, and he at once named Doughty. The good folks of Flushing, however, did not want the Newtown dominie, but Stuyvesant reasoned with them one by one. As a result Doughty was accepted and his salary fixed at 600 guilders. It was probably Flushing's complaisance in this matter that impelled Stuyvesant in 1648 to permit it to elect three Schepens and a clerk in addition to the primitive Schout. Doughty does not seem to have become popular in Flushing. His religious views were not pleasing to many, and that singular compound, Captain John Underbill, when elected Schout in 1648, at once ordered the meeting-house closed, as the preacher "spoke against his betters." Doughty wandered forth again, but returned. He had made his home in Flushing, and there his sons developed into splendid citizens, while his daughter Mary married Adrian Van Der Donck, a Hudson River patroon, who included what is now the city of Yonkers in his holding.

As a settled minister Doughty was a failure, and probably the citizens did not care to ask for another in his place. In 1656 one of the pioneers of the Society of Friends, William Wickendam, a shoemaker, settled in Flushing from Rhode Island, and the people seem to have accepted his views. They listened to his preaching and what he said appears to have united them under his spiritual leadership, and many were baptized by him. Even Doughty accepted the workingman's theological views and threw in his lot with the Quakers. Such a condition of things aroused attention in New Amsterdam and led to Stuyvesant's persecution of the Friends, which has been detailed at length in an earlier chapter of this work. But this persecution failed, like most persecutions of similar nature, to stamp out the object of its enmity, and Flushing became more and more deeply a religious, — a Quaker community. In 1660 quite a number of Huguenots settled in the township, and their presence and pronounced views on matters of faith made Flushing more than ever before a center of religious thought.

In June, 1672, George Fox, the founder of the Society of Friends, made his memorable visit to Long Island, and, as might be expected. Flushing was one of his stopping places. He stayed in the home of John Bowne, Stuyvesant's victim and victor, and the couch on which he was wont to rest and other articles of furniture used by him or in use during his sojourn are still preserved. Fox in his diary mentions holding one large meeting in Flushing, "many hundreds of people being there."

Although, however, Flushing was thus in a sense a center of Quakerism, it was not until 1690 that a meeting-house was erected. After Stuyvesant's experience in the case of John Bowne the Friends seem to have been permitted the utmost freedom of worship, so far as the civil government was concerned. Lender the English rule, indeed, they were more or less in trouble, because in accordance with their principles they refused to train in the militia service, a service which by law was made compulsory on all able-bodied men. This refusal was punished by the imposition of a fine, and as it was not in keeping with their ideas of religion and right to pay this fine, their goods were seized and sold in satisfaction. This procedure the Quakers regarded as an infringement of liberty and conscience, as a religious persecution; but it was not so in reality, as the law made no provision for creeds, the militia was for the defense of the people and the Quakers enjoyed the security of that defense and should contribute their share in it. A much more dangerous disturber Of the peace of the Quakers, and indeed of the community, was the attempt made in the reign of James 11 to establish the Church of England throughout the province. We say attempt, because, although it is the fashion for some writers to argue as though that church was established in New York, just as it was in England, it never really succeeded. Royal instructions and Gubernatorial edicts notwithstanding. The King's orders to Governor Dongan, in fact, avoided the question of "establishment," although that result was implied. "You shall take especial care that God Almighty be devoutly and duly served throughout your government; the Book of Common Prayer as it is now established read each Sunday and holiday, and the Blessed Sacrament administered according to the rites of the Church of England." He was also ordered not to present a clergyman to any benefice within his gift "without a certificate from the Most Reverend the Lord Archbishop of Canterbury of his being conformable to the doctrine and discipline of the Church of England." Still he was to "permit all persons, of what religion soever, quietly to inhabit within your government without giving them any disquiet or disturbance whatever for or by reason of their differing opinions in matters of religion." So far as Flushing was concerned, these instructions had little interest, and it was not until 1702, under Governor Cornbury, — one of the most disreputable of men and blindest of churchmen, — that any effort was made to foist an Episcopalian minister on the town. Then the turbulent George Keith came upon the scene, but as the story of his experiences and of his persecutions of Quakers inspired by him have already been told in an earlier chapter, the story need not be repeated here. Ecclesiastically in the Episcopalian fold, Jamaica, Newtown and Flushing were united for a time under one rector. The first, Patrick Gordon, died: a few days after his arrival, and then Cornbury sent the Rev. James Honeyman among the people to preach to them until he could determine upon a rector. This rector, the Rev. William Urquhart, was put in possession of the charge in June, 1704, and continued to minister to such of the people as adhered to him until his death, in 1709. Flushing did not take kindly to him, nor did he to Flushing. "Most of the inhabitants thereof are Quakers," he wrote, "who rove through the county from one village to another, talk blasphemy, corrupt the youth, and do much mischief." He held services once a month in the Guard House, which was amply sufficient for his auditory. Mr. Urquhart's headquarters were in Jamaica, and there, too, as we shall see, his path was not one strewn with roses. His successor was the Rev. Thomas Poyer, a Welshman. Flushing still continued obdurate, and matters were not much brighter in Jamaica, which still continued to be the rectorial headquarters, but Mr. Poyer "wras 'led" on amid a host of discouragements, as we will read in the story of Jamaica, until his death, in 1731. Two years later the Rev. Thomas Colgan was given the charge, and under him, in 1746, the first Episcopalian Church in Flushing was erected. Mr. Colgan seems to have got on better with the Quakers than any of his predecessors, and one of them, it is said, actually aided the new congregation by a gift of money. As was customary, the Society for the Propagation of the Gospel (in London) sent to the new church a Bible and Prayer Book, and that gift is now among the treasures of St. George's Church. On the death of Mr. Colgan, in 1755, the Presbyterians and others endeavored to seize control of the ecclesiastical affairs in the three towns and elected a Presbyterian minister. Sir Charles Hardy, then Governor, would have none of this, and presented the Rev. Samuel Seabury to the charge. Mr. Seabury had not a very high opinion of Flushing, which he said was "in the last generation the ground seat of Quakerism, is in this the seat of infidelity," but under him the church was finished and in 1761 it received a charter from King George HI under the title of St. George's, which it still retains. His leading lay helper in Flushing was Mr. John Aspinwall, whom he described in one of his letters as "a man of low birth and strong passions, and violent in his resentments, who, having acquired a great fortune in privateering, removed thither from New York, and has really done very considerably toward finishing the church and giving it a good bell." Not much of an angelic character, certainly, but this reformed pirate was a benefactor to the Flushing church in many ways, even to the extent of "bringing over many Quakers and Calvinists, so that I myself," wrote Mr. Seabury, "have been a joyful witness of a numerous congregation in a church wherein, within three or four years, seldom assembled above ten or twelve persons." It is sad to think that the friendship of Mr. Aspinwall and Rector Seabury should have ended in a violent rupture caused by an effort on Aspinwall's part to make Flushing a separate charge under a new rector, but so it was. The effort did not succeed, and Seabury remained until 1765, when he removed to Westchester. Afterward he was the first Episcopalian bishop in America. His successor in the three towns was the Rev. Joshua Bloomer. The tripartite rectorial arrangement continued until 1802, when Flushing and Newtown united in calling a rector, leaving Jamaica to its own course, and in 1809 Flushing and Newtown separated, and the Rev. Brazella Buckley became first sole rector of Flushing.

From then until now St. George's has held a long list of earnest, devoted rectors, but the name that stands out in boldest relief is that of the Rev. William A. Muhlenberg, who presided over it from 1826 to 1829. This famous preacher and practical philanthropist founded the once famous Flushing Institute for the education of boys, and out of its success grew St. Paul's College, of which he continued to act as principal until 1844, when he accepted a call to New York.

Until 1811 St. George's Church and the meeting-house of the Society of Friends contained the only two organized religious bodies in Flushing. In 1811 a congregation of colored Methodists was organized, although it did not possess a church edifice until 1837. The white Methodist brethren built a church in 1822, the Roman Catholic Church had its beginning with twelve adherents in 1826, when the Rev. Father Farnham celebrated mass for the first time in Flushing, and in 1835 the first place of worship was fitted up. In 1854 a second Episcopalian Church, St. Michael's, was erected, and St. George's Church was rebuilt for the third time, the second building having been erected in 1812. The Baptists also erected their first Flushing church in 1854.

The most prominent of the early industries of Flushing, next to agriculture — farming — was that of fruit and tree growing. The Huguenot settlers introduced many of the fruits of their native land, and their product won quite a measure of fame and brought them considerable profit. In the early years of the eighteenth century a number of English gardeners settled in Flushing, attracted by stories of the varied nature of its soil and its adaptability to fruit raising, and established market gardens. Its fame, however, in horticultural circles was really won by a native, William Prince, who was born in Flushing in 1766, and died there in 1842. His father, William Prince, in 1750 laid out a tract of land in Flushing for the propagation of trees, such as apple, plum, peach, cherry, nectarine and pear. This venture proved quite a success, and the area of ground was steadily enlarged and the varieties grown extended to almost every variety possible in the climate, almond and fig trees, flowering trees and shrubs, berry bushes. So famous did the place become that General Howe, when maneuvering in Flushing on August 29, 1776, ordered it to be guarded so as to prevent any depredations on the part of his soldiery. The nursery, however, did suffer considerably during the British occupation, and for the time its business was paralyzed. In 1789 the place was visited by General Washington, who had long heard of its beauties, but what he saw did not answer his "expectations," for at that time the business was just beginning to recover. By 1792 Mr. Prince had twenty-four acres under his operations. His son brought the nursery up to the fullest measure of its usefulness. In 1793 he entered into business relations with his father and extended the area under cultivation until it exceeded sixty acres. He sent far and near for trees, fruits and plants for experimental purposes, successfully acclimatized several hundred, systematized the nomenclature of the best-known fruits, such as the Bartlett pear and the Isabella grape, and wrote a "Treatise on Horticulture," the first work of the kind issued in the United States. The London Horticultural Society named the William Prince apple in his honor, and he enjoyed the personal friendship of all the celebrated botanists and naturalists of his time. The Morus multicaulis, long so well known in the manufacture of silk, was first grown here in 1826 by

Mr. Prince from trees imported from France a year after they had been received there from the Philippine Islands. Perhaps this should entitle him. to be regarded as the pioneer in the great American Philippine trade which is so certain to come as the result of more recent events!

Flushing had many other famous nurseries, such as that of Samuel Parsons, a man noted for his benevolence, his enterprise, his public spirit and his steadfast adherence to the Society of Friends, before which body he frequently preached. His love of trees led him to plant many along the streets of Flushing at his own cost, and he went into the business of tree raising simply for the good he might accomplish rather than as a commercial speculation.

With the upward progress which attended so many of the Long Island towns after the Revolutionary War Flushing had but little share. Its business had been sadly shattered by that armed conflict, and its geographical position was such that it was by no means easy of access. In the closing years of the eighteenth century communication with New York was had twice a week — -Tuesdays and Fridays — by passenger boats, and that service sufficed until the advent of the nineteenth century. In 1801 a daily coach service was established, running from Flushing through Newtown to Brooklyn, and such coach service, with slight changes as to route, continued until 1854, when the opening of the Flushing & North Shore Railroad forced its cessation. But long after the railroad was an assured fact the carrying trade in merchandise continued to be done by packets. The first steamboat from Flushing to New York was run in 1822. It was a small concern, but proved so successful that in the following year "The Linnaeus," a much more substantial and roomy vessel, was put on the route.

In 1837 Flushing began to feel that she really was becoming prosperous, and in that year it applied for and received its charter as a village. The population was then about 2,000, the number of real estate owners was 103, and the assessed valuation $465,360. Robert B. Van Zandt was elected the first President under the charter.

The Rev. H. D. Waller, to whose interesting "History of Flushing" this sketch has been much indebted, says: "The village boundary line began at the creek just beyond the bridge on the College Point causeway and ran east, crossing Whitestone avenue about 300 feet beyond Bayside avenue, just including the Osgood property. At a point near the junction of Bayside avenue and Parsons avenue the line turned south and ran to the corner of Sanford avenue and Long lane (now South Parsons avenue). From this corner, which marked the furthest limits of the village in that direction, the line ran west to the creek, forming an acute angle with Sanford avenue and crossing Jamaica avenue just south of the Jagger homestead (now Captain Hinman's). Sanford avenue was not open below Jamaica avenue. Bowne avenue was the street furthest east. Long lane began at the village limits and ran south. Jagger avenue was a private lane leading from Main street to the Jagger house; Lincoln street was then called Liberty street; Amity street was not then opened; neither was Locust street east of Main. A tide mill, kept by William Hamilton, stood at the bridge on the College Point causeway. There were no houses northeast of the park except a few which stood in large country places. * * * The lower part of Main street was more thickly settled, but even there the houses stood apart from each other with gardens between. The Pavilion, once a famous hotel, stood at the corner of Bridge street and Lawrence avenue, where the old electric power house now stands. The Town Hall stood where the fountain now stands, facing on Main street, the school-house being on the lot now occupied by the Empire Hose Company's building in Lincoln street."

From the time of her incorporation as a village until the closing scene in her history, when she became part and parcel of the Greater New York, the story of Flushing was one of great progress. It was regarded as a residential quarter, sufficiently retired to be the scene of several county fairs, where abundant educational facilities were provided, and church, social and professional circles were all of the most desirable qualities. The Board of Education commenced work in 1848 in accordance with an act of the Legislature passed that year, and under its direction the educational system of the village was steadily extended: in 1874 the Douglass Pond water supply was introduced and made the occasion of a grand demonstration and parade, with the usual oratorical accompaniments. In 1883 the old area of the village was considerably extended by a new act of the Legislature, and in the following year the Flushing Hospital and Dispensary was incorporated, a building being rented for its purpose until 1887, when the hospital was ejected on ground presented for the purpose by the late John Henderson. "The village of Flushing," writes Mr. Waller, "has always been a place of residence. Those institutions have been fostered that would render the village attractive to persons seeking homes; manufacture has not been encouraged. The village streets are macadamized, well shaded with fine trees of many varieties, lighted by gas and electricity and swept and sprinkled at public expense. The sidewalks are -paved with stone flagging. A complete system of sewers extends throughout the village. The steam and electric cars make frequent trips between Flushing and the city. These conveniences and improvements have made Flushing an attractive home for business and professional men of New York. Here they find pleasant homes and rural surroundings within easy reach of their places of business."

Such are the salient points in the history of Flushing township in general, and especially of Flushing village, the center of its life. There are several settlements or villages throughout the township which are deserving of some mention, however brief.

College Point (formerly Lawrence's Neck) on Flushing Bay was first settled by immigrants from Germany. It was the scene of the operations of Dr. Muhlenberg's St. Paul College and from that got its modern name. It has some manufactories and a population of some 6,000. Within recent years it has become quite a suburban residential village, boasting all modern improvements in the way of gas, electricity, etc., and many remarkably fine residences have been added to its attractions during the past year or two. It is confidently expected that it will continue to grow in favor.

Whitestone is regarded as being, next to Flushing village, the oldest settlement in the township. It derived its name from a large white piece of rock in front of it in the East River, and although several efforts have been made to change the name the efforts have failed. Even De Witt Clinton's popularity, which inspired a meeting of citizens. to give it the name of Clintonville, failed to make the change any more than a passing whim. Another name once given to it "Cookie Hill," did not find many admirers at any time, so Whitestone has clung to it throughout its modern history. That history really amounts to very little. In 1800 it had less than twelve houses. It was not until 1853, when J. D. Locke & Company established a tin and copper ware factory, that it began to attract settlers, and a year later it had advanced sufficiently to induce Uncle Sam to establish a post office within the village. Some of its clay soil has been found eminently suited for making tobacco pipes, flower pots, flower vases and the like, and in connection therewith several establishments have arisen, and the village now boasts a population of about 3,400. Whitestone is the terminus of the North Shore branch of the Long Island Railroad. It is one of the stations of the New York Yacht Club. and already before consolidation contained a considerable colony of New York business and professional men. The village has a new athletic club, and a school-house costing $200,000 has recently been completed. A tract of land fronting nearly a mile on the water is held jointly by the Realty Trust and the Cedar Cliff Park Association, part of which is tinder development by Edwin P. Roe.

Francis Lewis, one of the signers of the Declaration of Independence, whose seat in Whitestone was one of the centers of Revolutionary activity, was born at Llandaff, Wales, in March, 1713, and was educated at Westminster School, London. In that city he also obtained his mercantile training. He sold all his property in England in 1735, and came to this country, where he at once engaged in business as a merchant, establishing houses in New York and Philadelphia. He met with remarkable success, and probably was the leading shipper in New York at that time. His enterprise was unbounded, and he paid frequent visits to Europe on business ventures, going as far as Russia, and was twice shipwrecked. As a supply agent for the British army he was taken prisoner at Fort Oswego when it was surprised by Montcalm, was carried to Montreal, and from there to France. After his liberation he returned to New York to find the conflict between the Colonies and the mother country already practically commenced; and, joining heartily in Revolutionary movements, he was in 1775 unanimously elected a delegate to the Continental Congress, where his business experience, executive talent and knowledge of commerce made him a valuable member. At the next session he with his fellow patriots signed the paper to the maintenance of which they pledged "their lives, their fortunes and their sacred honor." Having some time previous purchased a country seat at Whitestone, he removed his family to it in 1776, and then entered actively upon the performance of duties of importance with which he had been entrusted by Congress, one detail of which was the importation of military stores, in which he expended the bulk of his large fortune, and for which he was never repaid. Hardly had his family been settled at their home in Whitestone before they were visited, in the fall of 1776, by a body of British light horse, who plundered his house, wantonly destroyed his extensive and valuable library, and, taking Mrs. Lewis a prisoner, retained her several months, without a change of clothing or a bed to rest on! Through the influence of Washington she was released, but with her health so broken by the abuses she had suffered that she drooped and died — another victim to English chivalry in the eighteenth century. Mr. Lewis resided here until 1796, when he disposed of his property and retired to New York, where he died December 30, 1803, in his ninetieth year.

The second son of this patriot, Morgan Lewis, afterward Governor of New York, also lived at Whitestone for many years. He served in the War of the Revolution as a captain, and afterward as major, retiring with the rank of colonel, to resume his legal studies and qualify for the bar. He soon acquired distinction in that profession, and in 1792 became Chief Justice of New York's Supreme Court. In 1804 he was elected Governor. In the War of 1812 he became a major general and served on the Niagara frontier. But the details of his career are too interesting to be condensed and we must refer the reader to the sketch of India Delafield, containing a sketch of his life and that of his father. Governor Lewis died in 1844.

Bayside, on Little Neck Bay, although in many respects a modern settlement, has really a history of almost equal antiquity with Flushing village, but its story is uninteresting, although it contained a building which, like so many hundreds of others, bore the designation of Washington's Headquarters. It was really simply a scattered group of rural residences until within a comparatively few years, and its progress has been slow. It has a population of 700, but is steadily rising into favor as a residential village, as it presents many advantages in the refined society already to be found there and the many beautiful villas which adorn its streets.

As much might be said of Little Neck, a similar community on the other side of Little Neck Bay and close to the Nassau county boundary line. The property was in the hands of the Hicks family from the time Thomas Hicks drove the Indian owners off the lands by force until a recent date; indeed, some of that redoubtable land grabber's descendants are still to be found in and near the village. Douglass Point, however, as it is now called, one of the most beautiful "bits" of landscape on the sound, passed from their hands early in the last century. Little Neck is slowly but surely rising in popular favor, and its population of 600 are doing all that is possible to add to its attractiveness. Willets Point, Douglaston and several small settlements are also gradually finding their way into public favor and are certain to increase as the years roll on.

In fact, there seems little doubt that the whole of the old township of Flushing is destined to be the "home land," as it were, of a great population of home owners, — the best possible class of citizens. A recent article in one of our daily papers, speaking on this point evidently with the knowledge of an expert, says: "Flushing, with a population of 9,700, on the ridge overlooking Flushing Bay, is a village of Dutch Colonial antiquity, of historic associations and substantial growth. Originally an agricultural community, its chief characteristics have come to be those of a suburban home settlement. It has good Toads, schools and churches, libraries, banks, stores, shops and a complete system of public works. Fine old mansions, set in spacious grounds, break the uniformity of development present in more distinctly modern places, and the water affords variety to the enjoyment of nature and outdoor life. In the outskirts of the village are important suburban additions, developed by private enterprise, as Ingleside and Bowne Park. Both are located on high ground, abutting on fine residential streets, which are continued through them.

At Ingleside the Realty Trust has sold some hundred detached frame dwellings at $3,500 to $6,750, besides a number running as high as $10,000. Building sites are sold to investors at $260 to $1,000 a lot. At Bowne Park, where John Dayton & Company have built extensively, similar conditions as to prices of houses and lots prevail, this place, like the former, having maintained a high grade of suburban construction. Among smaller groups of houses in the market are eight dwellings at the Broadway station that are quoted at $3,000 and upward. These are offered by John N. Falkinburg, who is also improving a tract at Bay side, a station just east of Flushing, with houses selling at $3,500 to $6,000. Land in the various additions under development at Flushing has been carefully restricted against uses objectionable in a residential community, the aim having been to keep in harmony with the social and natural features which have made the village attractive to quite a colony of artistic and professional men.

"Corona, with a population of 2,700, is another center of suburban development in the section overlooking the Sound. Until recently houses were for the most part built by intending occupants with assistance from co-operative building and loan associations. Construction work is now largely carried forward on extensive tracts, as Luona Park and Hamilton's Homes. At Luona Park, laid out by the Realty Trust, several hundred houses have been built. The prices prevailing have been between $2,400 and $3,500. At Hamilton's Homes, developed by William J. Hamilton, quotations range from $2,000 to $3,000.

"Elmhurst, nearby, with a population of 3,000, is composed of two principal elements, an old village of Dutch origin and a modern suburban settlement. The newer Elmhurst comprises a tract of 1,800 lots controlled by Cord Meyer & Company. Houses are sold to intending occupants at $3,500 to $10,000.

About two hundred and fifty families have been drawn to the neighborhood since the tract was opened in 1896. Provisions are contained in all the deeds reserving the land for private residences, and property is thus guarded against construction which might tend to depreciate values. The management refuses to sell lots unless assurance is given that no house is to be erected without the plans having been approved by the company. This makes speculative building impossible. On the other hand, the village elsewhere offers attractive opportunities for building operations, and a group of new houses by Warren & Combes were for the most part readily disposed of last season at $3,800 to $4,300."

# CHAPTER XLV. NEWTOWN.

In the old Gazetteers the township of Newtown was described as bounded on the north by the East River (including in its limits Riker's, the two Brother and Berrian Islands), on the south by Jamaica, Flatbush and Bushwick, and west by Bushwick and the East River. It was held to contain 10,683 acres. These rather vague boundaries are now of little use, except in an antiquarian sense, for the town is described very differently nowadays, when it is apportioned between the First and Second Wards of the borough of Queens and has its boundaries indicated by named streets or avenues.

For a long time Newtown was the stepchild of the metropolitan area, its backyard, so to speak. Whatever was too offensive for the rest of the area found lodgment there, and the odors from some of its works often aroused indignant protests even from dwellers on Manhattan, while Newtown Creek, once one of the sweetest bits of water stretching into Long Island from the river, became a synonym for all that is vile. Much of its territory was used as a dumping ground, its manufactories were those which could not be carried on close to any large city, the making of glue, the rendering of fat, the distillation of oil and the like, and the establishment of each of these made the surrounding territory only the more barren and bleak. Back from the coast line the land was flat and the landscape uninteresting, and as agriculture decayed the old farms, many of them, began to be cut up into market gardens, while discolored and deserted barns became mute evidences of the glories of the past. In the entire district pools lay stagnant, helping by their exhalations to make the territory uninviting even to the land boomers, who found "Newtown lots" invariably the hardest sort of proposition to tackle when the lots were away from within sight of the river. The place had gradually lost caste and settlers were few. Astoria had flourished, the beauties of Ravenswood had invited a colony of home builders of the better class, Hunter's Point was boomed for many years as a suitable site for the homes of Manhattan workingmen, but the lots failed to command anything like attractive prices outside of Astoria, and Ravenswood was somewhat exclusive. Within the last ten or twelve years a change for the better has taken place and many thriving communities have sprung up, thanks to the increase in the metropolitan population, the facilities of transportation and the more responsible efforts of the land speculators, and such places as Winfield, Elmhurst, Woodside, Louona Park, Corona, are not only beautiful and attractive settlements, but are an illustration of the effect of business principles, capital and thoughtful, well-planned enterprise being applied to the once wild and irresponsible business of land booming. But even in spite of the number of these settlements, and their surrounding evidences of prosperity, there are not more dreary and uninteresting trolley rides in the area of the Greater New York than those across old Newtown township, say from Greenpoint Ferry to North Beach.

Tt used to be a standing joke, — a somewhat grim one, — to say that Newtown's greatest industry was that of funerals, that it was the great burying ground of New York and Brooklyn. Certainly it is plentifully dotted over with cemeteries, the cheapness of the land and its apparent unpopularity with the living having induced churches and corporations to buy up large lots or "parcels" and developing them for burial purposes. Except such as the extensive holdings of the Roman Catholic Church and some smaller places owned by other religious bodies, these cemeteries are all ruled by corporations, pay dividends or are expected to pay dividends on the money invested in them, and are managed on business principles and with a view to the profits just the same as any other piece of property would be. The largest of these cemeteries is Calvary, now inclosing some 300 acres, and the smallest the little Quaker resting place in Middle Village, which is hardly one acre in extent, while the Methodist cemetery, near the latter, only encloses two acres, but it has a history of its own which antedates the Revolution, for it was laid aside for its present purpose in 1770. The Lutheran cemetery and St. John's, also at Middle Village, Machpelah, St.Michael's. Mount Olivet, Mount Nebo, Union Field and parts of Evergreens and Cypress Hills are among the best known of the other silent cities which so long were Newtown's most potent attractions for throngs of visitors from the neighboring centers of population.

In another way the township of Newtown is peculiar among the old Long Island communities. In Jamaica, Flushing, Hempstead, Oyster Bay and other places the first settlement, the first place which gave the name to the township, has retained its original importance and maintained its place as the center of its population, — the local capital, as it might be called. Not so Newtown. In 1870 its most densely populated comer, including Astoria, Ravenswood, Hunter's Point, was concentrated into one municipality and elevated into the dignity of a city, with the result that Long Island City now has a population of 52,240, while Newtown still struggles on as a village with a population of about 2,500. Still the old village is growing, has added about 1,000 to its population in a decade, and in spite of the prominence of the city it is to the village we must turn when we write of the history of the township until at least within the last three or four decades.

Antiquarians have decided that the first settlement in the township was made at what was afterward known as Fisher's Point and which is known at the present day as North Beach. The pioneer Hendrick Harmansen received a grant of land there from Governor Kieft in 1638, and appears to have at once settled. Not long after Richard Brutnell received a grant of land near the modern Dutch Kills, while amidst a slowly gathering procession we find a blacksmith named Jorissen, who was the first white man to become possessor of the beautiful tract later known as Ravenswood. That he was killed by a party of Indians is simply to say that he was the victim of a contingency which he and all other pioneers, and even dwellers in towns, in those picturesque but happily remote days had to face.

The first general name applied to the territory was Mespat, so named after a small tribe of Indians who hunted around Newtown Creek. The Rev. Mr. Doughty 's settlers twisted it to Maspeth, a name which still lingers in one of the villages of the township. After the Doughty forces were shattered by the terrible Indian rising of 1643, the whole of Newtown's territory was, in fact, pretty well cleared of settlers by the avenging hosts of the red man. When peace was restored and a truce had been made with the aborigines, the pioneers, who slowly returned, found they had a new grievance, — the pretensions of Mr. Doughty. That gentleman seemed to have caught the land fever pretty severely and tried to set up as a patroon, but the other original patentees stood up for their rights and won their case when they appealed to the Governor and his Council. So in his wrath Mr. Doughty gathered up his skirts and forsook Maspeth forever.

Immigration helped the territory but slowly, a spot here and there only being cleared, for although lying temptingly near to New York, the swift and treacherous currents in the river were not 'much to the liking of the longing eyes on Manhattan. In 1652, however, a little colony came from Connecticut, mainly English people, and after prospecting around settled on a spot which answered all their requirements in the way of meadowland, abundant and pure water and the like. As was necessary, application was made to -Governor Stuyvesant for a town warrant or charter, which he at once granted, giving the name of Middleburg to the place and conferring on the colonists all the privileges which had been awarded to the other towns on Long Island which had asked that favor from him. This was the beginning of Newtown.

The first Magistrates were Robert Coe, Richard Gildersleeve and Thomas Hazard. The usual system of town meetings seems to have governed as far as possible all the local arrangements, but it is unfortunate that nearly all the early records have been lost. But enough has been left to show that Middleburg was a peaceable and law-abiding community, that it admitted newcomers to the privileges of settlement only after being satisfied as to character and after a vote had been taken, and when a citizen did not walk according to the local ideas of right and wrong he was unceremoniouslv ordered to betake himself elsewhere. Serious crimes were apparently unknown among them; they had no lock-up for offenders, and imposed liberal fines upon all who violated any of the local ordinances. Some offenses were too heinous to be condoned by a fine, no matter how severe, and in 1660 we read of the just and merited penalty inflicted on a "ne'er-do-weel" who stole some corn from Magistrate Coe's bairn. This reprobate had to walk through the village with two rods under each arm and drums beating in front of him, and having suffered this humiliation he was to make "amends" to the party he had robbed. Besides all this he was ordered to keep to his house at nights and so give no cause for suspicion as to his movements. Why he was not summarily ordered out of the community is not disclosed. Very likely there were sufficient reasons for not imposing this last dread penalty. The citizens united in paying premiums for the slaughter of wild beasts, especially wolves, and in mutual protection against the Indians, but the latter continued troublesome, and in 1653, so great was the apprehension of a general rising of the Ted men, that the whole colony passed over to Connecticut for safety. They soon returned, however, and resumed the usual tenor of their ways, but in 1655 the Indians did make a raid which caused much bloodshed and destruction.

The people from the first seem to have been dissatisfied with the Dutch government in New Amsterdam, although they fulfilled all their obligations to it honestly and paid their tithes with commendable regularity. In 1662 Connecticut, under its charter, laid claim to jurisdiction over Long Island and the English towns excepting Gravesend seem to have accepted this claim joyfully. Those which were near New Amsterdam, however, had to be cautious in their preference, because the redoubtable Peter, the doughty Silver Leg, had his eye upon them. So Middleburg had to await events while cherishing her hope of getting away from Dutch rule. In 1663, however, her citizens openly professed allegiance to Connecticut, threw away their Dutch name and adopted that of Hastings. Then they were landed in a slough of despond by news that Connecticut had deserted them as the result of a treaty with Stuyvesant, and hailed the arrival of Captain John Scott as the direct representative of English authority, elected him their President, but he did not rule very long. Peter Stuyvesant had too much on hand to think of the contumacy of Middleburg or Hastings, and in 1664 Captain Nicolls wrested the entire province from his rule, and Middleburg or Hastings had an English government at last, an English government de facto, which of course had never been realized under the Connecticut claims. With that change, too, the old names were abandoned and "the New Towne" took their place.

In the convention of 1665, which accepted "the Duke's laws," the limits of the different townships were discussed and to a certain extent determined, for the original charters were, as has been noticed frequently. So, too, was the determination of the convention. However, in the following year the freeholders secured by purchase all the remaining lands in the possession of the Indians, or lands claimed by them, and on March 6, 1667, Governor Nicolls issued a brand new charter in which he gave the people all the privileges of a town government, ordered that the town should continue to be known as New Town and vaguely set out its boundaries as "east by Flushing Creek, north by the Sound, south by the Jamaica line which runs on the south side of the hill and west by Mespat Creek or Kills." The boundaries as thus set forth continued practically to be those of the township although the courts had afterward to be appealed to very frequently. A bract of meadow land which was in dispute between Bushwick and New Town was awarded to the former after quite cantankerous legal proceedings in 1669. In 1684 Newtown, Brooklyn and Bushwick had a three-cornered fight over their boundaries, and a year later Flatbush secured a patent for some land which Newtown claimed. A long and wearisome contest ensued, all the other towns apparently joining issue, most of them against Newtown, asserting that she claimed tracts of territory which had been patented to the others. Sometimes the trouble was before the law courts, sometimes before the Governor, sometimes before the Legislature. There is no practical purpose to be gained by following its details and it may be dismissed by saying that after dragging along for some 80 years it was finally adjusted by an act of the Legislature in 1768. The sudden overthrow of the English government and the appearance of Anthony Colve in 1673 as the representative of the Dutch authorities, appear to have been received by the Newtown people with equanimity. The Duke's laws and the Duke's methods had been tried and found decidedly wanting by a people who valued the privileges of freedom. However, when Colve's representative visited Newtown to administer the oath of allegiance he found only 23 out of the 99 male adults which his papers showed the place contained. New Town was united with "Rustdorp, Heemstede, Vlissingen and Oyster Bay in the election in the usual roundabout way of a sheriff and clerk who were to execute the laws in those five towns. Toward the close of 1674 the Dutch rule gave way to the English, the Duke's laws were again operative, and the Dutch officials were removed. But the people were far from satisfied, and when the news came that King James had fled from his ancestral kingdom and been succeeded by the Dutch prince, William of Orange, there was great rejoicing among the freeholders' generally, Dutch as well as English. They were represented in every convention and in their excess of zeal actually voted to provide two soldiers for the defense of the fort at New Amsterdam and to fully provide for the maintenance of that brace of heroes!

Newtown, throughout its early history, by which may generally be understood its prerevolutionary history, was essentially an agricultural community, and it is said that it became so 'famous for its crops of wheat, rye, hemp, tobacco and potatoes, that in 1732 all of the land within its boundaries had been taken up mainly for fanning, grazing or fruit growing purposes. Horses, cattle and sheep were reared in great numbers and much attention was given to breeding, importations being made from New England and Holland. The fruit raised was particularly good and the Newtown pippins became famous at an early date. In such a community few trades were in demand, for the people were content with their own product and the wealthier had slaves who were generally handy men on the farm or did the rough work in the domestic establishments. Then, too, money was scarce and business transactions were conducted on the basis of barter. Thus in 1661 a house was sold for "six hundredweight of tobacco, a thousand clapboards, and half a fat [vat] of strong beer." Still the community supported several such tradesmen as butchers, weavers, tailors, carpenters, coopers and blacksmiths. In some instances the trades were represented by a single representative, but there were half a dozen weavers although every household had its spinning wheel, and sometimes its own loom. Milling in such a community was a remunerative as well as a most necessary business and as early as 1657 John Coe had set up a flouring mill. The first trace of manufacturing pursuits occurred in 1691 when Thomas and Edward Stevenson were given permission and the necessary ground to set up a fulling mill. In 1721 a bark mill and tannery were put in operation by William Vallance. Then followed a starch factory, a brewery and a grist mill. Most of these were in operation when the Revolutionary War broke out and managed to struggle through it, although while the struggle lasted all business was depressed except agriculture and where that was permitted without molestation it was no longer profitable. When the war broke out Newtown was found like every other town on the Island, especially on the island west of Oyster Bay, to be hopelessly divided. The Newtown farmers saw their stock carried off by order of Congress to prevent it being used by the British and the news of the result of the battle of Brooklyn made it only too apparent that their property would never be returned. Some of their citizens, too, who formed part of General Woodhull's little force were captured along with that hero and sent to the prison ships. The British troops were visible in Newtown village on August 28 and the Whigs knew then that their doom was sealed. Those who could fled before the arrival of the redcoats, most of those who remained were seized and imprisoned or taken out of the town and their property confiscated. Feeling in the crisis rose high and a Tory thought it no disgrace to turn informer against his Whig neighbor, a proceeding which the latter repaid with full interest when his turn came in course of time. Newtown on the surface, at least, became intensely loyal and joined heartily in a petition which prayed that the whole of Queens County might be restored to royal favor. It was restored and Newtown raised a couple of troops of horse to guard its borders against the depredations of the despised Whigs. But the wages of loyalty was soon found terribly exacting, exasperating, and beggaring. Martial law prevailed during the seven years of the "occupation" which followed the battle of Brooklyn, and the civil courts were suspended. Many, troops were quartered at Newtown from time to time — the 17th dragoons, the Maryland Loyalists, the 42nd Highlanders, the 33rd regiment and a battery of artillery. The soldiers were mainly billeted in the houses of the Whigs, but the farmers. Whig or Tory, had to supply the army with their produce at a price named by the army officials, or see their oats, wheat, straw and provisions confiscated and themselves harshly maltreated by the soldiery or imprisoned, perhaps both. Robbery was a matter of daily occurrence and toward the end of the seven years life, liberty and property were held by the slenderest of tenures. Little wonder that Newtown, Whig or Tory, hailed the return of peace with many manifestations of delight.

While we do not think of Newtown as a religious settlement such as was Gravesend, or even as a theocracy like Hempstead or Jamaica, there is little doubt that the pioneer settlers were earnest God-fearing people, fully imbued with the devout spirit of New England. Still their purpose in leaving the land of the Puritan was to secure a stretch of fertile soil and earn a livelihood rather than to obtain any further religious freedom than the law or public sentiment there tolerated. Mr. Doughty, of course, might be cited to prove an exception to this, but while he had to leave New England mainly on account of his views on baptism, there is no evidence to show -that he intended setting up a religious community when he settled in "Mespot." Indeed he appears more anxious to attain the dignity of patroonship rather than the barren honor of spiritual leadership. But his connection with Newtown was too brief to give full scope to his ambition, temporal or spiritual, while certainly the course of events showed that whatever his views may have been as to the founding of a little theocracy, they were not shared by those who were his fellow-patentees in 1652. It has been asserted, however, that the first settlers were organized in a congregation prior to setting up their homes in Mespot and that accompanying them was their pastor, the Rev. John Moore. That this minister was among the pioneers seems undoubted, and it is very likely, nay it is certain, that he would preach to his neighbors and perform his holy offices among them; but there is nothing to show that he was accepted as their leader, that his voice and influence were all-important in their councils as was so often the case in other settlements. We are told that be preached in the "town house," which served him also as a dwelling, and which had been erected soon after the settlement was effected, but all that relates to him is so disjointed and meagre that his personality adds little to our history. He died in 1657, so that at best he was not permitted to enjoy for many years the associations of the community he had helped to found. It was not until 1671 that the first church building was erected in Newtown. The Rev. William Leverich was at that time the pastor and he is generally regarded as the first settled minister in the town. Mr. Leverich had quite a history before settling in Newtown, where his life work was destined to end, about 1694. It seems, however, that several years before that he had retired from the active duties of the ministry. He was a native of England, and after being educated for the ministry at Cambridge crossed the Atlantic in 1633 to become pastor of the church at Dover, N. H. He remained there two years or so and then, after holding several brief charges, became, in 1640, minister at Sandwich, Cape Cod, where, it seems, he took a particular interest in the work of spreading a knowledge of the Gospel among the Indians. He removed to Oyster Bay in 1653, where he had acquired some land, and was chosen as minister lay the people at an annual salary of £15. He remained there for some two years as pastor and then became minister at Huntington, where he remained until 1670, when he settled in Newtown. He seems to have been a man of singular ability, about as learned in the law as in the Gospel, and seems to have engaged in many enterprises outside of his sacred calling, and his lawsuit or lawsuits with his predecessor as religious teacher in Huntington still form an interesting story in the early annals of that town. Mr. Leverich certainly prospered in his worldly affairs and seems to have been much beloved in Newtown. His descendants are still among the most prominent citizens of Long Island.

The successors of Mr. Leverich at Newtown were amiable men, and the church prospered so that about 1697 or thereabout a house and lot were set apart for the use of the ministry. In 1703 the church was taken possession of by the Rev. Mr. Urquhart of the combined charge of Jamaica, Newtown and Flushing, under the orders of Lord Cornbury, just as in the case of the Jamaica church, and an effort was made to suppress Presbyterianism. The Rev. John Hampton was openly arrested in Newtown and imprisoned for attempting to preach without first obtaining a permit from the precious scamp who then represented the majesty of Britain — Lord Cornbury. In spite of this the Presbyterian flock was able to keep together and in 1708 the Rev. Samuel Pumroy accepted a call to the pastorate and entered upon his duties on September 18th, that year, although he was not ordained for some fourteen months later. Under him the church waxed strong and in 1715 it was received into the Presbytery of Philadelphia and built a new and much larger tabernacle, which seems to have been used for religious services from that date, although it was not fully completed until 1741. By that time, however, the labors of Mr. Pumroy were nearing an end, for he died in 1741. The most noted of his successors was the Rev. Simeon Horton, who held the charge for some 26 years. Then he retired and waited for the end, which came to him May 8, 1786. He had the mortification of seeing the church in which he had labored so long without a pastor (for his successor, Andrew Bay, was not a success in any way and only lasted a couple of years), used by the British troops as a hospital, a guard house, and finally demolished. It says wonders for the steadfastness of the people that in 1787, four years after the last British troops sailed through the Narrows homeward bound, they commenced the erection of a new house of worship.

For many years after the zealous Mr. Urquhart captured the Presbyterian meeting house at Newtown, the story of the Episcopal Church in Newtown is bound up with the story of its progress in Jamaica and Flushing and has already been told in the sections devoted to these towns. It does not seem that at first the old meeting house was much used or that Newtown was regarded as much more than a preaching station. But in 1735 a building was erected for the use of the church and services were commenced in it although it was not completed until 1740. Newtown continued part of the tripartite charge until 1797, when the Episcopalians attained the long-sought privilege of having a minister of their own and tire Rev. Henry Van Dyke entered upon the sole charge. Five years later he retired. Newtown then united with Flushing and the Rev. Abraham Clarke became joint rector. This arrangement lasted until 1809, when it was dissolved and Mr. Clarke was rector of Newtown until his death in 1810. The Rev. Evan Malbone Johnson became rector in 1814 and continued until his removal to Brooklyn in 1827, when he was succeeded by the Rev. George A. Shelton, who was rector for the long period of 33 years, from 1830 to 1863.

The first Dutch Reformed Church was erected in Newtown in 1732, but the congregation for several years thereafter was dependent upon the service of such ministers as might be sent them from New York or Kings County. In 1739 the people united with the other Reformed churches in Queens County and this arrangement continued until 1802, when the Rev. Jacob Schoonmaker became minister of Jamaica and Newtown jointly. He labored in Newtown until 1849 and the church throve under him greatly and built in 1833 a new house of worship. But years began to limit even his great capacity for work, so he confined himself for the remainder of his days to Jamaica, and Newtown went forth alone and prospered under the care of the Rev. Thomas C. Strong, who was installed December 12, 1849.

As early as 1661 a school was held in the town or meeting house under the direction of Richard Mills and thereafter under a success of high attainments. The children in the county sion of teachers, some of than apparently men were never without means of learning as much at least as the three R's, which was all that the American common school system aimed at until within comparatively recent years. As the population increased schools were established at different points and by 1740 there were no fewer than five in the town, and in 1762 an advanced school, where writing, arithmetic, the "Italian method of book-keeping by double entry," Latin and Greek were taught, was opened at Hallet's Cove.

After the Revolutionary struggle had been fought and won Newtown relapsed into its old quiet ways as an agricultural community and slumbered on. It had a population when the rule of Uncle Sam commenced of about 2.000: forty years later (in 1830) it had only increased by some 500. Communication with the outside world was difficult and dangerous on the one side and. expensive and tedious on the other. The currents on the East River were treacherous and a knowledge of their peculiarities had never been thoroughly mastered even by those living on its banks, so that a voyage from Newtown Creek to the opposite shore might last an hour or take up the best part of a day, and the landing place depended not on the will of the passenger but on circumstances. All was well provided fair weather was vouchsafed; if not the simple trip might furnish terrors enough to enthrall a farm fireside for a generation to come. If the journey was made by land up to 1798 the means of accomplishment were few and far between, unless one had the command of horses and wagons. In that year, however, a "light, airy coachee, hung on springs," was put on the route between Newtown and Brooklyn, running through Maspeth, across Penny Bridge to Bushwick, Cripplebush and Bedford, and the cost for the trip was 3 shillings. The "coachee" carried seven passengers and' left Newtown three days in each week. In 1805 the extension of the Cripplebush road brought Newtown more easily in touch with Brooklyn and in 1816 it was placed in direct communication with the Williamsburg ferry and so in easy reach, comparatively, of Manhattan Island. It was not, however, until 1854, with the opening of the North Side Railroad, that Newtown was brought into touch not only with Brooklyn and New York but with the outlying sections of its own territory and began to make ready for the threat advance which was in time to come with the trolley, railroad, rapid transit and annexation.

So far as the township was concerned the modern advance in population commenced in 1830, but little of that advance was felt in Newtown village. In fact it steadily began, almost with the opening of the last century, to lose its primal place in the story of the township and to become a quite subordinate village.

Even Maspeth in time surpassed it. That early English settlement, almost as early as Newtown village itself, has had a most curious history. For years it was a stronghold of the Quakers, but that body abandoned it long ago. Writing-in 1845 Dr. Prime said: "The only public edifice is an ancient Friends' meeting he use which is now very much in decay, and is seldom used as very few of that denomination are to be found in this vicinity. It is supposed to be about 100 years old, but there is some reason to believe that it is even more ancient." But whatever its age it has long since disappeared altogether and so have most of the country homes of the merchants and others of New York which in the early part of the nineteenth century made it the best-known village in the township. Here De Witt Clinton had his country seat to which he was glad to retire at frequent intervals to think out his many schemes for the upbuilding of New York and to escape from the worry and wiles of the politicians, and one is almost inclined to think that the local statesmen were more numerous, more irrepressible, more zealous in their plans for emptying the public treasury either by way of salaries or appropriations than now. The old house is still standing, seemingly in as good condition as when it was inhabited by Walter Franklin, Clinton's father-in-law, whose New York house was Washington's residence when he became President of the United States and whose name is still kept alive in Franklin Square, on which the Presidential dwelling stood. Many modern villas and cottages, even little settlements, have arisen in Maspeth since De Witt

Clinton's day, but it still retains much of its rural aspect except in the spots where manufacturing has sprung up.

To-day it would really be termed a manufacturing village, and has been such since 1842 when John Murch began the manufacture of cord and twine, and that business is now carried on in several establishments, the industry giving employment to several hundred hands. In 1852 Cord Meyer started a factory for producing animal carbon. Oil cloth making was another industry, established in 1863, and since then a number of other establishments of various kinds have given employment to a population estimated to-day at 2,500. During the past few years the building up process going on so unceasingly in New York and Brooklyn has added what may be called a new industry to Maspeth in the opening up of picnic grounds and athletic grounds which attract at intervals large crowds of visitors each summer. It is well supplied with churches and can now be so easily reached that there is no doubt its popularity as a site for homes and factories will steadily increase.

Middle Village is another old settlement, but it is mainly given over in these later days to cemetery purposes, although it supports a living population of some 1,300. It received its name from its geographical situation, being midway on the old turnpike betwen Williamsburg and Jamaica. In it was built in 1713 the first Methodist church on Long Island, but that structure has long since disappeared. The late Joseph Wesley Harper, of the famous New York publishing house, had his home in Middle Village from the time he reached manhood until his death in 1871, and did much to improve the amenity of the village as a place of residence. The Harper family originally hailed from Newtown, where the father of the founders "J. & J. Harper" was long a farmer. Corona has lately come into prominence as a manufacturing village and home site, having been much favored by the land boomers, and as much may be said of Laurel Hill, full of memories of the old Alsop and Rapalye families and which began to be laid out for "improvement" in 1853. About the same time Woodside became known as a desirable place for residential purposes and several elegant villas were erected. It dates from 1850, when the late J. A. F. Kelly came north from South Carolina and sought retirement from active life amid its beautiful surroundings. It still continues to be a village of homes and its business interests are mainly confined to floriculture and market gardening. East Williamsburgh, Charlotteville, Glendale, New Suffolk and several other settlements arc among those likely to become soon prominent through the impetus which rapid transit and consolidation have even already brought about. What may be called the old part of Newtown township has an interesting history in the past, but its future promises to surpass it in incident, in importance and in real achievement.

# CHAPTER XLVI. JAMAICA.

To Governor Stuyvesant must be awarded the credit of bringing this town into existence, the old village of which is destined to become in the near future one of the great railroad centers with the usual accompaniments of trade, business and industries of all sorts, of this part of the continent. Stuyvesant issued his first warrant for settlement March 21, 1656, and a more ample and more imposing document in 1660. When Gov. Nicolls sent Stuyvesant to enjoy the comforts of his Bouwerie, he confirmed all the rights and privileges which had been granted Jamaica by a deed dated Feb. 15, 1666, and Governor Dongan twenty years later gave it another charter mainly for the sake of the fee involved. On March 7, 1788, it was reorganized as a town by the state government and so it remained until it was swallowed up in the Greater New York.

Such in brief is what might be called the municipal history of Jamaica from beginning to end. There is much doubt about the origin of its name, but it is generally accepted as being a modernized rendering of the old Indian name Jameco — the name of a small tribe located on Jamaica Bay. How or when this name was first applied is not clear. The Dutch authorities called it Rusdorp — town in the country; and this was long its official designation. Some of the settlers called it Canorasset, others -Crawford, but Jamaica, by whoever introduced, kept to the front and remained. Very likely it was called Jameco before the white man came along. But there have been all sorts of surmises and speculations over the name and the etymologists as usual have given their fancy-free reins over it with wonderful results: even so staid a personage as the late Dr. O'Callaghan, the famous local historian, formulated a theory that the word was derived from the Indian name for beaver as translated by the French "Amique."

Where the first settlers came from is a point that has not been exactly determined, but there is little doubt that they came over from Connecticut with the view of establishing a religious colony, or rather a colony where religious tolerance might be enjoyed. Those who signed the request to Stuyvesant, therein described themselves as "inhabitants of the town of Hempstead and subjects of this province," so it is very likely that some of them had been for a time residing in Hempstead and spying the land. They told the Governor that the wanted "a place to improve our labors upon; for some of us are destitute of either habitation or possession, others, though inhabited, find that in the place they are they cannot comfortably subsist by their labors and exertions." So they asked for the Governor's consent to settle on a tract of land "called Conorasset and lyes from a river which divideth it from Conarie see to the bounds of heemstead, and may contain about twenty families." This tract they had already "bought" from the Indians for "two guns, a coat and a certain quantity of powder and lead." Stuyvesant had to be petitioned three times before he consented, but when he did confirm the request he did it in a most handsome manner, giving them permission to elect magistrates and conduct their affairs on the same lines as Brooklyn, Midwout and other Dutch towns. The names of the petitioners were Robert Jackson, Nicholas Tanner, Nathaniel Denton, Richard Everit, Rodger Linas, Daniel Denton, John Eazar, Abraham Smith, Thomas Ireland, Thomas Carle, Edward Spray, John Rhoades, Andrew Messenger and Samuel Matthews. These fourteen may therefore be regarded as the first citizens of Jamaica. By 1660, when Stuyvesant gave the town a regular charter and the name of Rusdorp, there were some forty additional freeholders in the town. It was a little republic in itself; its town meeting regularly settled all its affairs and even regulated who should and who should not be admitted to citizenship. One Benjamin Hubbard, for instance, in 1649 had bought a house lot without having first obtained the sanction of the town meeting, so it required him to give assurance of his good behavior. Of course with such additions to the population more land had to be secured from the local Indians from time to time, and we find several records of purchases made in exchange for such articles as soldiers' coats, kettles, "bottles of licker," powder, lead, guns, blankets and the like. The value of the Dongan patent of 1686 was that it clearly defined the limits of the township and showed that several of the original patentees were still prominent in the town. The names given in this patent were, Nicolas Everit, Nathaniel Denton, Nehemiah Smith, Daniel Denton, John Oldfields, William Creed, Bryant Newton, Benjamin Coe, Jonas Wood, William Foster, John Everit, Edward Higbie, Daniel Whitehead, John Carpenter, John Furman, Samuel Smith, Richard: Rhodes, Thomas Lamberson, Joseph Smith, George Woolsey, John Baylis, Thomas Smith, Wait Smith and Samuel Mills. The town government seems to have gone at once into operation on receiving Stuyvesant's first permit (it should hardly be called a charter, although in effect it was one). The town meeting, as has been said, determined everything, subject, of course, to the Governor's veto, but Stuyvesant seems to have given the English settlements much more liberty than he did the Dutch, and so practically the town meeting of Jamaica was supreme within its bounds. Attendance at these meetings was compulsory and absence without cause was the subject of a fine. A keeper was hired in 1661 to look after the cows and calves of the lieges, thus saving a lot of individual time and worriment, and they gathered in their crops in squadrons under appointed officers for mutual protection against any overt effort on the part of Indians. It must be said, however, that the settlers did all they could, according to their light, to deal justly with the red man, and held frequent conferences with his representatives while the conclusions seem to have been mutually satisfactory. In 1662 they hired Abraham Smith, one of the original patentees, to beat the drum on Sundays and on the days of public meetings. They laid aside a lot ten rods square as a burying place and this, in 1668, they had reverently enclosed with a wooden fence.

The glimpses we get of the community show it to have been prosperous from the first and steadily advancing in material wealth, reminding us in many respects of the English settlements on the eastern half of the island. The population steadily increased, although as early as 1664 the adventurous, roving spirit of some of the early settlers asserted itself and Daniel Denton, John Baylis and Luke Watson headed a new migration which passed over into New Jersey and there commenced the settlement of Elizabethtown. Denton, however, seems to have returned within a few years to Jamaica and resumed his original holding there. It is worthy of notice that in the petition to Gov. Nicolls for a tract of land on which to settle in New Jersey, Denton and his associates dated the document "from Jamaica, commonly so called." From this paper, in which they speak of the "decease of the Dutch interest" in the Province, we see how thoroughly English at heart were the pioneer settlers at Jamaica. They had fled from New England intolerance and from nothing else and built up right under the official dictatorial regime of Stuyvesant as complete a little republic as was any of the communities in Massachusetts which sent representatives to the General Court. In all essential matters they were masters of their own municipal destinies — and so continued for many years.

While not a professedly religious community like Gravesend, or enrolled under clerical leadership like Southold, there is no doubt that from its inception Jamaica was a theocratic society — one in which the affairs of the little commonwealth were regulated by the teachings of the Scriptures rather than the statutes of their High Mightinesses. The life of the community revolved around its church and the recognized fathers of the church were the natural leaders of the people, so that for a long time after the settlement was begun the story of its religious development is really the entire story there is to tell. Stuyvesant's permission for settlement was dated March 21, 1656, and it was not until 1662 that a town meeting decided to erect a house of worship, a meeting house, and united in a call to the Rev. Zachariah Walker to join with them and become the first minister of Jamaica, which he accepted. It is not to be imagined, however, that during the four or five years which elapsed before this preacher that the community was without any regular religious services. Undoubtedly one or more of their number was quite capable of conducting public worship and fulfilling all the duties which could be performed by a lay preacher. Services would be held in any convenient barn or in the winter time in any hospitable kitchen. With the erection of the meeting house, however, the people had a place where they could worship God or discuss affairs of state or assemble for any purpose, religious or secular, as they saw fit. The little frame edifice (20 feet square) was at once the church and the Town Hall. About the same time a house was built for the prospective minister and a lot laid aside for his use. It would seem that an effort was made to try the experiment of listening to one of Stuyvesant's ministers before finally calling one from New England and accordingly in answer to a petition Stuyvesant sent there the Rev. Samuel Drisius, who was able to preach in English and who, on Jan. 8, 1661, delivered two sermons and baptized eight children and two women. Probably all this was done to please the irascible Governor and to pave the way to the peaceable settlement of the minister of their choice. Mr. Walker seems to have won the affections of his people, although one would think from the records that he was as much a farmer as a clergyman. He received, however, much "encouragement" in the way of having his stipend increased and the like, but he decided on trying another sphere of operations and in 1668 removed to Connecticut. The Rev. John Prudden, a Harvard graduate, then became Jamaica's minister at a salary of £40 and the use of the minister's house and land. He was a Congregationalist and the majority of the citizens were Presbyterians and they seem to have been unable to agree, although what the real difference was between the two, considering the time and circumstances, it is difficult to realize. It is not so stated, but probably the people did not want any connection with the Congregational churches in Connecticut, while Mr. Prudden at that time regarded New England as the hub of the entire religious system. The Jamaica citizens seemed to have appreciated his services and were desirous of retaining him, but he retired in 1674. His successor, the Rev. William Woodruff, whose salary was fixed at £60, did not seem to please the people. Mr. Prudden, on full reflection, thought he might go further and fare worse, so in 1676 Mr. Woodruf seems to have been released and Mr. Prudden once more presided over the table in the meeting house. It was an amicable arrangement on both sides. Mr. Prudden became a Presbyterian and his salary was to be £40 a year. Besides, he had the use of forty acres of meadow land and 19 of the brethren agreed each to bring him a load of firewood each year. Then he was housed in the minister's home and to encourage him it was agreed that if he remained as minister for ten years the house and lot which had been set apart for the use of the minister should become his own property. Under him the congregation prospered. In 1690 a new and more commodious meeting house was erected — 60 feet long and 30 feet wide, and a year later the minister's salary was raised to £60 with all firewood and other privileges. In the following year, however, he accepted a call to Newark, N. J. His ministry had extended six years beyond the ten which made the minister's house and lot his personal property, but before leaving he transferred the holding to the congregation, receiving in return land elsewhere. Jamaica seems to have been invariably liberal in its treatment of its ministers and to Mr. Prudden's immediate successor, the Rev. George Phillips, the promise was made that if he should remain in charge until the close of his life his annual salary of £60 would be continued to his widow. The minister's salary being paid mainly in produce, or as a result of sales of produce, sometimes a little difficulty arose in connection with the collection, owing to the dilatoriness of human nature, but such details were to be expected.

In 1699 a stone meeting-house was built partly by subscription among the people, and when that source failed by a rate passed by the trustees. By that time, it should be noted, several of the ratepayers were opposed to the Presbyterian form of worship and refused to pay the rate, but payment was finally made compulsory. It was a small square structure, forty feet square, surmounted with a belfry. Its interior was plainly fitted up with high-backed, uncomfortable pews, and a high pulpit, high enough to bring the preacher on a level with the gallery, on the south side, had the usual huge sounding board, an arrangement which good Dr. Prime used to think was an arrangement of the devil. Much of the history of Jamaica centered around the church until it was demolished in 1813.

Its historic interest began immediately on its completion. The Rev. John Hubbard, who had been ministering to the people for some time, was formally called to the charge in January, 1702, and was duly installed and given possession of the minister's house and lot. He had hardly more than got accustomed to his new dignity when he was dispossessed of both church and manse in the summary procedures already recorded in a previous chapter of this work.

By that time, it should be remembered, the Presbyterians were no longer tine sole dictators of Jamaica. The growth of population had long overstepped the old necessity of submitting a certificate of character on the part of prospective settlers to the town meeting, and people had become citizens to whom Calvinism was a thing abhorred.

As early as 1657 we find Robert Hodgson, a preacher of the Quaker persuasion, visited Jamaica and was lodged in the house of Henry Townsend (one of the first petitioners to. Stuyvesant for settlement privileges), who for his hospitality was promptly fined eight Flemish pounds. A few months later Townsend, who seems to have adopted the views of the Society of Friends, repeated his offense by housing another preacher, and was again fined, this time at a higher figure. But Townsend never failed in his hospitality, and welcomed each wanderer and gathered a congregation to listen to the preaching of the new doctrine until Stuyvesant, tired of hearing such contumacy, sent down to Jamaica a squad of soldiers to see that his edicts were respected, and then Townsend and several others removed to Oyster Bay and so placed themselves beyond Stuyvesant's jurisdiction. But in spite of soldiers and local opposition the number of friends grew. They stubbornly held their views in spite of opposition, declined to pay the rate imposed for the support of the "priest of Jamaica," and had their goods distrained as a result, but held their ground. As a result their services were more numerously attended year after year, and Jamaica was declared in 1686 a place for holding quarterly meetings, although it was not until 1706 that they erected a meeting-house.

About 1702 a Dutch Reformed congregation seems to have been organized, meeting in the stone church, which, as has already been pointed out, was never intended, even by the Presbyterians themselves, for their sole use. It was not until 1716, that the Reformed Dutch people erected a little tabernacle of their own.

The year 1702 also marks the formal introduction of the Episcopalian body, when, according to the authorities of that denomination, Jamaica, Newtown and Flushing were spiritually united under one rector. After the forcible ejection of Mr. Hubbard the Rev. William Urquhart continued, in spite of strong opposition on the part of those he styled "nonconformists" and sometimes amid much and sometimes bitter controversy, to hold the church and the minister's house until his death, in 1709. Air. Hubbard died in 1705, and was succeeded by the Rev. Francis Goodhue. We do not find whether he was elected to the pastorate by the people or was simply set down among them by the rascal who then represented Queen Anne. But he must have been a rather weak-kneed brother or he would never have accepted such a document as the following prior to entering on his duties:

By his Excellency Edward Viscount Cornbury Captn Genl & Govr in Chiefe of ye Provinces of N York, New Jersey & of all The Territories & Tracts of Land Depending thereon in America & Vice Admiral of the same &c. To Mr Francis Goodhue, Greeting.

I do hereby Licence & Tollerate You to be Ministr of the Presbvterian Congregation at Jamaica in Queens county on the island Nassaw in the sd Province of New Yorke & to have & Exercise the ffree Liberty & use of yor Religion pursuant to Her Matys pleasure therein signified to me In her Royal Instructions & during so Long Time as to me shall seem meet & all Ministrs & others are hereby Required to Take notice hereof Given undr my hand & scale at ffort Anne in New York this day of this Instant January in the ffourth year of Her Matjs Reign Annoq: Dni 1705.6.

CORNBURY.

By His Excys Command

William Anderson D secy

Goodhue only lasted about a year and then went home to New England to die. With his departure the Presbyterian flock had no shepherd until in 1710 the Rev. George McNish entered upon the work of the ministry among them. In July of the same year the Rev. Thomas Poyer was appointed Rector of Jamaica, Newtown and Flushing under the Episcopalian banner. Then the battle royal between the two forces was on. Both of these men were of marked ability and of earnest devotion to their work. Perhaps McNish was the brainiest of the two, the most brilliant of the two. but Poyer was one of those diligent, plodding individuals whose dogged perseverance makes up, in the way of actual accomplishment, for genius. It is not certain whether Mr. McNish was born in Scotland or in the north of Ireland, but his name demonstrates clearly that he was of the Scottish race. Mr. Poyer was a Welshman and came direct from the Mother Country to at once enter upon his duties here. Mr. McNish came to America in 1705, in company with the tainted Mackemsie, and with him assisted in the formation of the Presbytery of Philadelphia — the first in North America, and to him is generally awarded the credit of bringing about the first Presbytery on Long Island, in 1717. However, he remained a member of the Presbytery of Philadelphia until his death, in 1722.

McNish seems to have been a natural leader, and if Poyer lacked that essential quality to success in public or professional life, he had at least the backing and support of the representatives of the Royal Government, the authorities of the church and the powerful society in London which was then engaged in sending out men like him as missionaries to "propagate" the Gospel in foreign parts. Such were the two men who were destined to oppose each other in support of their respective standards in Jamaica for several years. The echoes of the battle rolled over Newtown and Flushing, over all of Queens County, in fact, but Jamaica was the battle ground; there the leaders resided and there was the center of attack, the prize for the victor, the little stone church.

Certainly Mr. Foyer had officially the most exacting position of the two. Mr. McNish had his energies concentrated in Jamaica, and although he made his influence felt throughout Long Island, and seems to have travelled all over it doing missionary work, his parochial labors must have been light. But in Mr. Foyer's case there was steady parochial work all the time and a host of other troubles — pecuniary mainly — while the opposition confronted him at every step. From some of his letters we get a capital idea not only of his own little troubles, but of the condition of the places over which he was set to hold spiritual supervision.

The first position in the struggle was won by McNish. Settling in Jamaica before the arrival of Foyer, he took possession of the church and for some reason or another, Mrs. Urquhart, the widow of Foyer's predecessor, vacated the minister's house and turned it over to McNish. Gov. Hunter saw to it that the church was turned over to Foyer, but McNish, "an independent North Britain preacher who has had the assurance in the face of the contrary to aver that the Bishop of London as no power here," held on to the dwelling and the people, the ratepayers, not only refused to pay Mr. Foyer his stipend, but actually handed over part of it to Mr. McNish. To oust McNish from the dwelling a suit at law was necessary and Gov. Hunter seemed unwilling at first to spend his money in that manner: besides the Judge before whom the matter would likely come was a Dissenter. Afterward he seemed willing to aid in bringing the case into a court of law, but by that time Foyer hesitated about following such a procedure and aroused the ire of the Chief Executive. It seemed a paltry case throughout, one in which Foyer had the worst of it — his salary unpaid or only partly paid, his dwelling withheld, his appeals disregarded at headquarters, his congregation growing slowly, and personal indignities being heaped upon him on frequent occasions. But for gifts of money from the home society it is difficult to see how he could have maintained the struggle. His brother clergy, however, stuck to him all through and really forced the authorities to take some action — getting some special instructions in his case from the Queen in Council; but even all that had paltry practical results. Even a suit at law which he instituted for the recovery of his salary dragged along so slowly as almost to banish all hope of legal relief. Here are two of his letters to the Secretary of the Society for the Propagation of the Gospel, whose missionary he was, which are pathetic in their presentation of his case:

Jamaica L. I. Novr. 2d 1714.

Honored Sir — It will be five years the last day of next month since my most honored patrons the Venerable Society were pleased to order me to embark to proceed on my Mission which I obeyed and embarked that same Jay but there were more hindrance than one that detained the Fleet till the loth of April and in the interim I was tossed about from one expensive harbor to another with my family having my Wife visited on board with two fits of sickness and obliged each fit to bring her ashore for the help of a Doctor which was not a little trouble & charge to me and besides all this the £20 it was forced to pay for our passage & the twice laying in of sea Stores put me to very great straits the loth of April we left the Lands end of England and had a very tedious and uneasy passage of 13 weeks lacking two or three days. In this passage I had great experience of the goodness of God and often had occasion to reflect on the Royal Psalmist's expressions in Psalm 107. 23 &c where he has these words — They that go down to the Sea in ships and occupy their business in great waters these men see the works of the Lord and his wonders in the deep &c. I saw indeed & wondered and often expected in the great tempests we had to have been swallowed up of the merciless waves, but when we were in our trouble and almost brought to our wit's end We cried unto the Lord and he was graciously pleased to hear us and bring us tho' not into the haven where we would have been yet unto a Christian shore yea unto the Island where my, Mission was to terminate about 100 miles from my Parish Here the ship and part of her Lading was lost on the 7th July but not the life of one person.

The week following I did set out for this place where to this time I have not ceased (according to the ability that God hath given me) to instruct the Flock committed to my charge I have labored faithfully in my Lord's Vineyard and in my private advice from House to House as well as public discourses I have exhorted them to faith in Christ and amendment of life and to live in Love I have likewise endeavored to possess them with as due a sense of the fundamentals of our religion as I could and the Great God has vouchsafed to give such a blessing to my poor yet well meaning endeavors the number of the communicants of the Church of England here before my time never exceeded 30 I have had above 60 — of the Independents who are the most numerous in my parish T have gained some and of the Quakers more some that were very rigid Independents since I came and that have reflected very much on our Church and constitution are now very frequently my hearers; and among the Quakers where my predecessor Mr. Urquhart thought it not worth his while to go I seldom have so few as fifty and often more than one hundred hearers.

And notwithstanding I have all along discharged the duties of a Parish Minister yet have I never received one penny of the Salary due to me by the laws of the Colony how to come by it I can't tell; and without it or an augmentation of my Salary from my Right Honble & Right Revd Patrons I cannot live in this dear place. I live very near much below the character of a Missionary and yet am running myself in debt. I am spending my strength & yet cannot get a competency wherefore I humbly beg the Venerable Society will be pleased to consider my condition, it is very necessitous indeed.

But I will trouble you with no more at this time but refer you to the Revd Mr. Vesey who I understand is safely arrived in London how I have led my life here and in how mean circumstances I am he can if you'll be pleased to enquire of him very well inform you.

I have no more to add but my most sincere & hearty prayers to the Lord to bless prosper & keep my most honored Patrons and when the time of their departure hence shall come may God who is the rewarder of those who make it their study and delight to enlarge Christ's Kingdom here take 'em to the eternally happy enjoyment of himself in Heaven is the prayer of

Honored Sir &c &c

Thos. Poyer.

Jamaica 15th Jany 1716-17

Honored Sir — By suit at Law for the recovery of my Salary here is as backward as my last gave you an account, so that I have nothing new to add on this head but that one of my lawyers is dead which put a stop to it last Term & what progress will be made in it the next I cannot tell, you shall be acquainted of the proceeding by every opportunity.

The continuance of my troubles (which alas have no prospect of an end) and the tediousness of this lawsuit have almost wearied me out, I find a daily decay in myself thro" the continual fatigue I undergo in this large parish which consists (as I have formerly observed) of Three towns which I serve alternately & how I have discharged my duty to the Souls I am entrusted with is well known to my good God and Great Judge & will I hope be testified by some of my people. I humbly beg the favor of you to give my most humble duty to my most Honble Patrons & acquaint them that their poor Missionary is laboring under many difficulties & reduced to the want of a great many necessaries: two Gowns and Cassocks I have already worn in their service a 3rd is worn very bare and my family wants are so many and pressing that I know not how I shall procure another.

But pray give me leave to assure you that I am not reduced to this necessitous Condition thro' any extravagance in my way of living, 'tis well known to many here Dissenters from us as well as friends to the Church that I am contented to want many necessaries the better to be enabled to be hospitable, which is expected from the established Ministers here and which with my being conversant with them hath (I praise God for it) removed the prejudices of some and effectually brought others to us.

But under all my troubles this bears me up and is great comfort that God is so good lo me as to continue his Blessing on my endeavors I have lost none but have gained many the number of my hearers consisting of about 400 & Communicants above 3 Score, 1 have this last week gained two families from the Anabaptists & Quakers and baptized them. Many are often coming over to us and I am assured more would, were there according to their desire a Minister of the Church of England to preach to them in this Town every Lord's day.

But this I leave to the consideration of the Honble. Society and hope they will be pleased to consider my necessities and administer a little comfort to me in my troubles.

I pray God to bless guide preserve and keep my most honored Patrons may they be enabled to send out many faithful Laborers into Christ's Vineyard & amply rewarded for all their pious and good deeds. This is what offers at present from

Your most humble Servt

Thos. Poyer.

Mr. Poyer's appeals to the home authorities for help were backed up by his own people in the following statement which was forwarded to London:

February 6th 1716

We humbly pray leave to lay before our Honble Patrons a true state of the case of the Church here and that as briefly as the nature of the thing will bear.

The Independents here being the most numerous do annually choose the Church Wardens & Vestry out of those of their own persuasion who are the most inveterate against the Church, every freeholder having a vote by virtue of an Act of Assembly for settling the Ministry made in the year 1693 in which act there is a clause empowering them to call a Minister, the act also provides that such a Minister shall be inducted & established to entitle him to the Salary of £60 per annum given by the same Act.

Now this Dissenting Vestry & Church Wardens have (as no other could be expected of them) after the death of the Revd Mr Urquhart (who enjoyed the Glebe & Salary undisturbed for about six years) called one Mr Geo: McNish who because of that call has seized upon the Parsonage House & Glebe pretends to all and has actually received some part of said Salary. This call is the only argument on which they insist & on pretense whereof they defraud the rightful minister both of the Glebe and Salary contrary to the known laws and continued practice of all the other places in this Province that stand upon the same foundation. To confute therefore their absurd notion the case may be stated thus. In Feb 1702 the Vestry & Church Wardens (being as always Dissenters) called one Mr Hubbard a Dissenting Minister (one whom some of us have heard declare it a sin to sav the Lord's Prayer). In the year 1704 Mr Urquhart was sent here by the Venerable Society & Bishop of London and was immediately inducted and established by the then Governor of this Province the said call given to Mr Hubbard (who never did officiate as Minister of the Parish ) being deemed to be invalid because the person called was not qualified to accept & this proceeding of that Governor was declared to be right by another Act of Assembly in 1705 for the better explaining the former Act — Thus in like manner after Mr Urquharts death as is said before they called the said Mr McNish who being a Dissenter like the other not qualified to accept thereof, our present Governor for the reasons aforesaid on the arrival of Mr Poyer immediately caused him to be inducted and established by the Chaplain Mr Sharpe on the 18th day of July 1710 which we think (with submission) makes the matter very clear that the Salary & Glebe can belong to none but him; for the Cure must not lie vacant for want of a call or presentation & not to call at all or to call a person in himself incapable of accepting is all one. And it can never be supposed that the Law intended any other than an Orthodox Minister for if otherwise nothing but confusion must ensue about the disposal even amongst the Dissenters themselves all having an equal right.

To this false argument of the Church Wardens & Vestry (as well as their principles) may be attributed the many affronts by them at sundry times given to our Minister even to the excluding him from sitting in the Vestry contrary to the Governors express Injunctions from the Crown signified to them.

Yet notwithstanding the imperious behavior of these our Enemies who stick not to call themselves the Established Church & us Dissenters we can with Joy say the Church hath increased very considerably both in its number of hearers & Communicants by the singular care pain and industry of our present Laborious Minister Mr Poyer who notwithstanding the many difficulties he has struggled with has never been in the least wanting in the due execution of his Ministerial Function but rather on the contrary has strained himself in travelling thro' the Parish even beyond his strength & not seldom to the prejudice of his health which is notorious to all the Inhabitants for almost 7 years last past in all which time he has not received one farthing of his Salary allowed him by the laws of this Province nor any private contributions that by the nicest search we can find out except about £18 (this Country money) which was presented to him by some of his people at his first arrival here purely on the account of the tediousness of his voyage from England & his having with his family been shipwrecked on this island about 100 miles from his parish and at divers times since Gifts on the whole not amounting to Fifty pounds.

A year later Mr. Poyer reported a little progress in spiritual matters, but the situation unchanged in other respects, writing to London, under date of October 24, 1717. he said:

Jamaica. October 24th, 1717.

The State of the Church in this Parish is much the same as. my last gave you an account of saving that I had two new members added to it since, & baptized besides several Infants & some adult persons.

And Here I must desire you to pardon me while I acquaint you that I have undergone more trouble in the discharge of my Ministry here than I am able to tell you — for besides the frequent abuses and affronts I receive from some of the Enemies of our Constitution besides that they make it their constant endeavor to tire me with their ill usage and to starve me as some of the most inveterate among them do sometimes express themselves; the service of the three towns which this Parish consists of bears hard upon me, and affords me as much business as I am able to go through with. I serve them by turns every other Sunday besides frequent Lectures on week days. Now to do this and to visit my people which I am often obliged to who live distant from me many of them about 12 miles, I am necessitated to keep two horses which is very expensive & troublesome to me & consumes me more Clothes in one year than would serve another that is not obliged to ride for 3 or 4. In Newtown & Flushing for want of the convenience of private houses I am forced to make use of Public ones which is a very great charge to me for I bring some of my family generally with me. If I did not they would be the half of the year without opportunities of public Worship.

Mr. McNish held the fort — the house and glebe — until his death, in 1723, but the passing of that doughty antagonist made no difference in Mr. Foyer's worldly prospects. In fact they were worse, for the Presbyterians were actually at law with him for the recovery of the church building, and in this they were finally successful. Tired of it all, Mr. Poyer became anxious to give up the struggle, and wrote i touching letter to London asking to. be relieved. The letter was dated June 16, 1731:

By this opportunity I beg leave humbly to represent to my Honble Patrons the Venerable Society for Propagating the Gospel in Foreign Parts that I have been their Missionary here 21 years & may without incurring the imputation of boasting say that my diligence in the discharge of my functions has been little inferior to any I pray God to give a blessing to the seed sown but so it is that besides the great and almost continual contentions that I have struggled withal amongst the Independents in this parish having had several law suits with them before I could have the Salary which the Country has settled upon the Minister of the Church of England several other law suits for some Glebe lands which we have lost and at last even the Church itself of which we had the possession 25 years is taken from us by a trial at law (with what justice I can't pretend to say) tho' I say I have endeavored as patiently as I could to bear up under all these trials besides the loss of two Wives & Several children yet the infirmities of old age bear very hard upon me insomuch that I find myself almost unable to officiate at the three towns of Jamaica, Newtown and Flushing as I have hitherto done and which is absolutely necessary for the Minister of the Parish to do.

The intent of these are therefore to beg that my distressed state and condition may be laid before the Venerble Society and that they will be pleased to permit me to quit my Mission and to return to Great Britain as being for the reasons aforegiven not capable of bearing such fatigues and discharging my duty as I have done for so many years in this place. I humbly beg of my most honored patrons to consider my case & circumstances & I remain &c

Thos. Poyer

His resignation was accepted, but before the arrangements were completed he was called higher and passed away January 15, 1732.

We must now return to the Presbyterian camp. Mr. McNish, broken in health, seems to have either retired from the active work of the ministry a short time before his death or to have obtained leave of absence, for he passed away at Newtown, New Jersey, March 10, 1722. It was under his successor, the Rev. Robert Cross, "an Irish gentleman," Thompson called him, that the crowning victory of the restoration of the old church was won. The dissenters — Presbyterians and Quakers — could not, however, avoid the payment of the salary for the maintenance of the Episcopalian minister, and this salary was paid out of the rates with grumbling and sometimes only after a legal process had been indulged in. The Quakers invariably paid under protest, when they paid at all. The result of the Revolutionary War put a end to all this.

In 1738 the Rev. Walter Wilmot, one of the best beloved of Jamaica's ministers, entered upon his work in the little stone church.

His ministry was spiritually a success, and the historic tabernacle had all it could do to hold the worshippers. Under him the local Presbyterians lost much of the harshness which had come to them as a result of more than a generation of fighting with Friends on the one hand and Episcopalians on the other. They had won the victory and Mr. Wilmot was essentially a man of peace, a man who had taken no part in the warfare and so was better able to heal up the wounds among the laymen, the result of years of friction. He was a native of Southampton and had married a daughter of the Townsend family, a family which had been locally famous for its devotion to the doctrines of the Society of Friends, even before that society was fully organized. She was a devoted Christian and on her marriage openly embraced the Presbyterian views held by her husband. His ministry was destined to be a brief one. Mrs. Wilmot died February 24, 1744, in the twenty-third year of her age, and her husband joined her on the 6th of August following, when in his thirty-fifth year.

Under a succession of ministers and itinerant preachers or students designated as "stated supply," the cause of Presbyterianism barely held its own in Jamaica for a long term of years after Mr. Wilmot passed away. At times the membership fell off greatly, and in 1761 we read that it had but twelve communicants. There were several causes for this. The preachers were, as a rule, able men, but there was continual difficulty in the payment of the stipend, and there were the usual divisions in the congregation itself, so common in the history of Presbyterian societies, which led to schisms of more or less importance. During the Revolution the minister was Matthias Burnet, who was installed' in 1775, when in the twenty-sixth year of his age. He seems to have been an amiable but rather a weak brother, had married a lady belonging to an Episcopalian family and was opposed to the Revolutionary movement. It was to his pro-British sentiments, however, that the little stone church was saved, during the occupation after the Battle of Brooklyn, from the desecration which befel most of the other places of worship on Long Island. When the struggle was ended the feeling against him on the part of the people generally was so intense that he was compelled to resign. He removed after a time to Norwalk, Connecticut, where he accepted fully the views of the Episcopalian body and became rector of one of its churches. We are told, however, that he paid an annual visit to Jamaica, and in 1790 preached to a large congregation in the stone church. That fact is significant as showing how early the first bitterness engendered by the great struggle had passed over — so far as Jamaica was concerned.

The stone church served until 1813. when it was pulled down and a more commodious structure was erected in its place and opened for worship in January, 1814. At that time the Rev. Henry Wood was the pastor.

The English Church, even after it had lost the stone building and turned forever from all thoughts of possessing it again together with the glebe, seemed to wax in strength, slowly, but none the less surely. Its official position was of itself a tower of strength, and the payment of the stipend was about as well assured as anything worldly could be. The Rev. Thomas Colgan. who was the successor to the unfortunate and long-suffering Poyer, and who entered on his duties January 31, 1733, was a much more diplomatic and congenial gentleman. He aimed to make friends all around and to antagonize no one and appears to have succeeded. He seems to have accepted the situation as he found it and began holding services in the building which then served as a court house. The old animosity seemed to die out rapidly, the lawsuits ceased, his stipend was paid as the law directed and he slowly built up a congregation. Six weeks after he began his work he was able to report that 200 persons attended his services in Jamaica. The court house soon proved too small for the work, and with quite an effort, aided by help from New York and elsewhere, the people secured a lot and erected a building for their own use. Under the name of Grace Church it was opened for service April 5, 1734. Governor Cosby and his family attended in state, the military lined the front of the building and the throng was so great that many persons had to be turned away. It was a memorable occasion — one which would have cheered the heart of poor Mr. Poyer beyond measure and set Mr. McNish to measuring out unstintedly the vials of destruction. Many gifts were made to the church, notably a Bible, Prayer Book, surplice and pulpit and communion table cloths by the wife of the Governor. After such an auspicious opening Grace Church flourished. Here are some extracts from Mr. Colgan's letters to the London society which used to get such dolorous reports from Jamaica:

Jamaica Novr 22d 1740

We have yearly for these seven years last past increased in Church Members, so these buildings are generally well filled in time of Divine Service, & the worship of God is duly performed with decency and good order, the several sects which are around us do look upon the Church with a more respectful eye than formerly, there being not wanting either in myself or people any Christian like or prudential means necessary to form a reconciliation & union amongst us, some itinerant enthusiastical teachers, have of late been preaching upon this Island the notorious Mr Whitfield being at the head of them & among other pernicious tenets, nave broched such false & erroneous opinions concerning the doctrine of Regeneration as tend to the destruction of true religion & of a holy and virtuous life and therefore I take this opportunity to beg that the Society would be pleased to bestow upon the people of this parish a few of Dr Waterland's pieces on that subject, & of his Lordship the Bishop of London's Pastoral letters upon lukewarmness and enthusiasm.

Jamaica Decemr 15th 1741

However in the mean time be pleased to accept this general account of the State of my Mission there being three Churches belonging to my Cure, that of Jamaica Newtown and Flushing, I must with a great deal of truth sav that not only they are in a growing condition & the members thereof generally of an exemplary life and conversation but that the Church of England here was never in so much credit and reputation among the Dissenters of all sorts as at this day, their opinion concerning her doctrine as well as discipline being vastly more favorable than ever. Enthusiasm has of late been very predominant amongst us but is now in a declining state several of the teachers in that way as well as their hearers being found guilty of the foulest immoral practices and other of them have wrought themselves into the highest degree of madness — these occurrences together with those good books lately sent over by the Society have taught people what the true spirit of Christianity is and what it is not & that it is to be found in a more sober rational Scheme than that delivered to mankind by Mr Whitfield that Arch Enthusiast and his adherents, having nothing more to add but the promise of all due diligence & fidelity in the discharge of all the Offices belonging to my Mission.

Jamaica March 23d, 1743

Our Church here is in a flourishing condition her being depressed of late by those clouds of error & enthusiasm which hung so heavily about her. has in effect tended to her greater illustration & glory.

If the Society would be pleased to order me some small tracts, such as The trial of Mr Whitfield's spirit: An Englishman directed in the choice of his Religion, Bishop Stillingfleet's Unreasonableness of separation &c. I'm your most obt &c.

Thos Colgan.

Jamaica Sept 29th 1743.

Our Church here was never in so thriving a way as at this time — for it has increased both in number & esteem with those who are without her pale, these eight or ten years last past more than it did for 30 years before being one of the oldest Missions from the Society — This must be an argument with them, that under the benign influence of Heaven and their pious Care & bounty, my faithful endeavors have not been wanting to promote and answer the end & design of my mission to this place I would further acquaint the Venerable Society that since my last accounts I have baptized 17 persons belonging to 3 families in this parish, consisting of Men Women & children who before were tainted with the corruptions of Anabaptism S: Quakerism & have now before me a fair prospect of doing the like good office for others in a little time.

Jamaica Sept 29th 1744.

The several Churches belonging to my Cure (as those of Jamaica, Newtown & Flushing) are in a very peaceable & growing state, whilst other separate Assemblies in this Parish are in the utmost confusion & this I can write with a great deal of truth that Independency which has been triumphant in this town for the 40 years last past is now by the providence of God in a very faint & declining condition which gives us hopes that better Principles than such as issue out thence will generally prevail amongst us & that we shall be belter united than heretofore.

Jamaica Sept 29th 1746

These are to acquaint the venerable Society that my endeavors in the work of my Mission are by the blessing of God attended with success a late & remarkable instance whereof we have in the conformity of a Family of good repute in ye Town from Independency to the Doctrine Discipline and Government of our Church which considering all circumstances may be thought worthy of notice.

In, my letter of the 26 March last I gave information to the Society of our being in a very likely way of having a Church erected in the town of Flushing a place generally inhabited by Quakers & by some who are of no religion at all which indeed has all along from the first settlement of the town been a great obstruction and discouragement to an undertaking of this kind but now by the kind providence of God (who has raised up Friends & money for the purpose ) the work is actually begun so that I have hopes of performing divine Service in this new Church in about 3 months time and also that the Society will bestow upon it a Bible & Common Prayer book according to their usual bounty for certainly there can be no set of People within this Province who are greater objects of the Society's pity & charity than those belonging to the town of Flushing of which I have been so truly sensible that it has brought me (if I may be permitted thus to express it ) to double my diligence in that place where error & impiety greatly abound nor have I been wanting (thro' the Divine assistance) in the other parts & duties of my Mission for the space of almost one and twenty years to approve myself a faithful Laborer & my trust in God is that I shall continue to approve myself such whilst

Jamaica March 28th, 1749.

I have great hopes that our Church at Flushing will in a little time gain ground among the Quakers who are very numerous there, and it is somewhat remarkable and may be thought worthy of notice, that a man who had for many years strictly adhered to the principles of Quakerism, when that new Church was opened & a collection made he gave money for the use of that Church, but , thinking he had not put enough in the Plate, went immediately after service and gave more to the Collector.

Mr. Colgan died in 1755 and then the "dissenters" tried their coup — long famous locally — of at once installing one of their own ministers, .Simon Horton, into the vacancy, but Governor Hardy made short work-of that and Samuel Seabury, Jr., was inducted to the charge of the three towns. He was not a success by any means, and by 1760 he complained that the communicants in Grace Church were less than 20. Under these circumstances the full amount of his stipend was not forthcoming and the constant attention necessary to keep the church in repair was relaxed with the usual result. With the view of improving matters, Seabury got up the idea of having Grace Church incorporated, and the following document, which explains itself, was drawn up, signed and presented to Cadwallader Colden:

To the Honourable Cadwallder Colden Esq President of his Majestys Council and Commander in Chief of the Province of New York and the Territories depending thereon in America &c

The Petition of the Minister of the Parish of Jamaica & Sundry of the Inhabitants of The Town of Jamaica on Nassau Island Communicants & professors of the Church of England as by Law Established Most Humbly Sheweth

That the Inhabitants of the town of Jamaica: Members & professors of the Church of England as by Law Established: did some years ago by Voluntary contributions Erect & finish a decent & Convenient Church in the Town of Jamaica: for the Celebration of Divine Service according to the use of the Church Of England, but that through the Want of some proper Persons to Superintend the Affairs of the Same: With Legal Authority, the Building is now Considerably out of Repair, and There is Danger Least moneys contributed for the Repair of the Same may be Improperly Applyd to the Detriment of your Petitioners: & Thro' the want of Such Persons it also comes to pass yt Pious & Well Disposed People are Discouraged, in their Designs of Establishing & Erecting proper Funds for the Support Of the Church & its Ministry Your Petitioners Therefore Humbly beg that yr Honor Takeing these things into Consideration Would be Pleasd to Grant us a Charter (Incorperateing such Persons as upon Mature Deliberation shall be found Worthy) with such Privileges & Immunities as in Your Wisdom you shall think Proper And Your Petitioners as in Duty bound Will Ever Pray Aprill the 8th 1761'.

Samuel Seabury Jur Minister
Robert Howell
Benjamin Carpenter
John huchiens
John Smith
Jacob Ogden
Joseph Olfield
Joseph Olfield Junr
Jhno Troup
John Comes
Gilbert Comes
Thomas Truxton
Thos Braine
Benj. Whitehead
Samll Smith
William Sherlock
John Innes
Richard Betts.
Isaac Vanhook

Thos Hinchman

Adm Lawrence

The charter was granted, the church was repaired as the result of a subscription which netted £93 18d, but the people did not flock to Air. Seabury's ministrations in any greater numbers than before. So he gladly went his way when an opening occurred for him at Westchester, and the Rev. Joshua Bloomer was installed in his stead. Mr. Bloomer commenced his ministry May 23, 1769, and soon was able to announce that his services were well attended — "crowded assemblies who believe with decorum." But the times were sadly out of joint and it was not long before he had some trouble in getting payment of his salary as it fell due. When the crisis came Mr. Bloomer found it necessary to close his church for a few weeks; some of his members were sadly persecuted by order of Congress, several even sent to prison or to Connecticut, but with the victory of August 21, 1776, all went well and the good, loyal minister was again permitted to pray for King George and the royal family without hindrance. In 1778, as a result of a lottery, $780 was realized for the purchase of a glebe, and with the money a farm of seventy acres was bought about a mile west of Jamaica village. It was not the first time a lottery had come to the aid of Grace Church. By one, in 1747, the bell in its steeple had been bought. The glebe does not seem to have proven a profitable adjunct to the church, and it was offered for sale in 1786. With the cessation of hostilities, Mr. Bloomer seems to have passed over the crisis of the sentiment against everything British undisturbed, and ministered in his three charges until 1790, when he passed to his reward, and his remains were laid in the chancel of Grace Church.

After Mr. Bloomer's death, however, the congregation began to dwindle, although most of the rectors were men of more than ordinary ability. In 1808 the money received at a communion season was only $234. There is no doubt that the influence and generosity of the King family was the most potent agency in carrying the church through its darkest days, which may be said to have lasted from 1796 until 1815, and the first substantial token of that interest was a gift from Rufus King of real estate in New York sufficient to yield the rector $500 a year. The same generous hand in 1820 started the movement for the erection of a new church, and as a result the second Grace Church was built and opened for service July 15, 1822. This building served the congregation until January 1, 1861, when it was burned to the ground and to the building which took its place, a beautiful gothic structure of stone, and which was consecrated by Bishop Horatio Potter January 8, 1863, the King family were princely subscribers, while their subsequent gifts were numerous and munificent.

The Dutch Church seemed to have had its beginning in Jamaica in 1702, and for a time its services were held in the little stone building erected by the Presbyterians. For some years the congregation was ecclesiastically attached to the Kings County Consistory, but in 1715 they managed to build one of the little octagon edifices such as the early Dutch congregations delighted in, and tried to get a minister of their own, but they failed to offer enough in the way of inducement and that project slept. Afterward when there were small congregations formed at Newtown, Success and Wolver Hollow further attempts were made to get a clergyman to devote himself to the four, but it was not until 1741 that they succeeded, and the Rev. Johannes Henricus Goetschius settled among them. He and his successors were able men, but they did not attract large congregations somehow and the people did not seem to act as a harmonious unit with regard to them. During the Revolution the church was unceremoniously used by the British as a storehouse, the people were without any stated pastor, but Dominies Rubell and Schoonmaker, of Kings county, visited them at intervals and held services in Grace Church. After the war was over the Rev. Rynier Van Nest became the pastor of the four churches. It was decided, in 1794, to have half of the services in English, as it was thought that the younger people might wander away, seeing that the tongue of the motherland was thoroughly understood by only a few. But the old Dutch service continued to be a feature and old Dr. Schoonmaker, who was minister of the church when the old building was abandoned, June 23, 1833, delivered the farewell sermon in Dutch, although not over half a dozen could follow his words clearly. The new church, a frame structure, was consecrated July 4, 1833, by which time the octagonal edifice had been demolished. With this change the congregation (it had parted company with the other Reformed Churches in the county) seems steadily to have waxed in strength. The building was burned to the ground on November 19, 1857, but on October 6, 1859, the present tabernacle was opened for worship. It cost over $20,000.

The Methodist Episcopal body had a congregation in Jamaica in 1784, but it was not until 1810 that they erected a church. The first Roman Catholic Church, St. Monica's, was erected in 1839 and the first Baptist Church in 1869. In 1873 the German Reformed Church was erected.

From the consecration of churches we pass easily as a corollary to the God's acre, where the fathers of the village sleep. There are several of these in Jamaica township, notably that at Springfield and the quaint Hebrew cemetery at Woodhaven, but the oldest of them all is that in Jamaica village. It was first set aside — to the extent at least of ten rods square — in 1668 and with considerable additions has been used since then, although the oldest existing stones bear such comparatively recent dates as 1732 and 1737. It has been much beautified in recent years and the chapel at its gateway, the Chapel of the Sisters, built by Nicholas Ludlam, of New York, in 1857, in memory of his daughters, is an attractive piece of architecture. In Jamaica village also the Roman Catholic, Methodist and Protestant Episcopal Churches each have their grounds "sacred for the resting place of their dead." In the ground of the last named is the grave of Rufus King and of many of the other members of that famous family.

At first, as might be expected, agriculture and hunting were the two industries of Jamaica most generally followed, the two industries in which the early settlers found their employment and their amusement. It was not long, however, before the area of industry was widened. In 1663 John Ouldfield, at a town meeting, was voted a home lot and twenty acres of meadow land on which to settle and pursue his occupation — that of a tanner. He was admonished to stick strictly and constantly to his trade and to take care only to produce good leather. How he behaved himself after "getting in" we are not told, but as the eyes of the leaders of the community were upon him it is very likely that he fully met their views. In 1669 the settlers offered James Hubbard, of Gravesend, ground on which to erect a mill, but he preferred to remain in Lady Moody's bailiwick. Benjamin Coe, however, fell in with the offer in the following year and the people agreed to build a dam for the mill which he agreed to erect and work. It was part of the agreement that in return for the lot and the other bounties conferred upon him, he should grind the corn of the townspeople in preference to that of strangers on days to be mutually agreed. Mr. Coe carried out his part of the agreement so well that they added ground for a grist mill. The milling business after a time fell into the hands of Joseph Carpenter and Caleb Carman on the same terms as Coe had received and which did not pan out very well with him, but whether owing to his incompetency or neglect history sayeth not. The new firm, however, were also allowed to erect a saw mill and were to be permitted to feed it from the common lands of the township under a few restrictions pertaining to growing trees. Their work according to the peculiar ideas of the time was to be done cheaper for the townspeople than for others, but even toward outsiders they were not permitted to make extravagant charges. This arrangement seems to have proved eminently satisfactory all around. Milling privileges were awarded in 1685 to Benjamin Coe and John Hansen, but there is no record as to how Coe profited in this venture by his first experience. There is also a record of half an acre of land being voted to a cooper on condition that he work at his trade, build a home "and supply the town with such cooper's work as they shall stand in need of." In 1704 permission was given to Jonathan Whitehead and Benjamin Thurston to establish a fulling mill to "full [shrink] all kinds of cloth, press the same for three pence the yard, and to full for the townspeople before other townspeople." For a long time the milling industry in Jamaica was a most important one, but little has been heard of it in recent years.

In 1676 the first record of a local school appears in the record, for in that year Richard Jones was given the use of the little stone church "for to teach scoule in for ye yere ensuing, provided he keep ye windowes from breaking and keep it deasent and cleane on Saturday nights against ye Lord's Day and seats to be placed in order." How Brother Jones fared and how long he kept "scoule" is not stated. Nine years later mention is made of a girls' school kept by "Goody" Davis. In 1705 Henry Lindley was licensed by Governor Cornbury to teach school in Jamaica and a similar authority was conferred in the same year on Thomas Huddleston. The ministers of the Church of England generally were in receipt of small grants from the London Society for the Propagation of the Gospel to provide teaching facilities, but the amount was never, in the case of Queens county, sufficient to secure more than temporary service. Thus the Rev. Mr. Foyer complains, in 1724, that while there were schools in Jamaica, Newtown and Flushing, they were taught by Quakers or Presbyterians. A public meeting was called in 1726 to consider the possibility of establishing a free school, but nothing came of it, probably owing to theological differences. Still the educational facilities of Jamaica seem to have been ample at all times, and several of the teachers, such as James Lockhart, Thomas Temple and John Moore, all preRevolutionary schoolmasters, were men of more than ordinary education. In 1777 Andrew Wilson opened a grammar school, and in 1784 the Rev. Matthias Burnet, the Presbyterian minister, opened a private school, in which he proposed to teach Latin and Greek, and for which he had engaged "a person" to teach the common branches, writing, bookkeeping, vulgar arithmetic and the like. The opening, in 1791, of Union Hall Academy led the way to other schemes of higher education. The history of that institution has already been referred to. In 1812 the common-school system of the state superseded all private enterprises to a great extent and put all the primary schools in the commonwealth within a short time on a standard basis. Still even under that system, as it progressed, much was due to the work and intelligence of local teachers and superintendents, and in this regard we must recall the work of Henry Onderdonk, Jr., who was the first superintendent of common schools under the law passed in 1844.

Jamaica has never figured much in the outside world. The General Assembly of the Province of New York met in the village in 1702 and again in 1753, and in 1790 it received a visit from George Washington, who seemed to have been fully satisfied with his reception and his entertainment. The village received a charter in 1814 and an additional patent of the same class in 1855. The town meetings were held at first in the meeting house, which has been generally spoken of as the stone church, but afterward when that place became the Episcopalian sanctuary they were held in the court house. That building was torn down by the British troops in 1777 for military reasons, and from that time until 1858 they were convened at various inns and public houses.

In 1858 a town hall was erected on Herriman street, near Fulton street — a wooden two-story structure, inconvenient and dangerous. It served its purpose, however, until 1870, when the present town hall was completed and was then converted into dwellings.

In 1827, so far as the records show, the first made road in Jamaica was laid out, and it was followed by several others, but it is not likely that any of these early highways are still used and their original boundaries are not now exactly determinable. In 1786 the people in town meeting decreed that no hogs should be permitted to roam about the streets, and we see plenty of other evidences of a desire to improve the amenity of the town much earlier than was the case in many other Long Island villages. It was not until 1830, however, that the township was divided into ten road districts, and a systematic effort made at their improvement and maintenance.

While Jamaica was in all moral respects quite a clean community, yet the people seemed to be at all times in a condition to punish such evil doers as might turn up among them. The early town meetings were liberal in their scale of fines for contraventions of local laws and a significant appointment was that of whipper, to which office Joseph Prue was appointed in 1772. His work, it is true, lay principally among negroes, but still he stood ready to suitably admonish any one the law thought deserving of such treatment. In those early days theft was a capital offense, and as late as 1782 we read of two unfortunates — William Guthrie and Joseph Alexander — Being hanged at Jamaica for stealing from a farmer at Cow Neck. But hanging was too expensive a luxury to be indulged in by a country town like Jamaica. Such corrective agencies as the lock-up or cage, or even the stocks, were much more in vogue. In fact as late as 1808 new stocks were ordered to be erected.

When the Revolution was over, the redcoats gone and peace had been proclaimed, Jamaica celebrated the result with huzzas and ovations and feasting, and then quietly settled down to the even tenor of its days. Of course, it felt remotely the trend of the outside world, it had a reverent funeral procession when the news reached it that George Washington was no more, and it felt a revival of the old patriotic thrill when the news came in 1812 that war with Britain was again on; it was stirred to its depths around each election time, but such flurries soon passed over and left little trace. Its splendid fishing in Jamaica Bay seems to have attracted few adventurous spirits and the islands which dot that inland sea, and which were included in the boundaries of the township, were untenanted and unknown. It had its newspapers — the Long Island Farmer was started by Henry C. Sleight in 1819, and the Long Island Democrat first saw light at Jamaica in 1835, — and these in a measure supplied the news of their day and more or less sage comment and communication was kept up with the outside world by means of lumbering stages, which run -uu the schedule time which was formulated each trip by the caprice and in accordance with the temper of the driver.

A revival, the great modern revival, set in in 1837, when the Brooklyn & Jamaica Railroad was opened. With that came, slowly at first but surely, wonderous changes. The once famous plank road of 1854 has already been spoken of, and other road improvements were soon in vogue. By and by the horse car supplemented the service of the railroad, but the advent of the trolley and the introduction of something like rapid transit by the railroad brought the old village nearer and nearer, as it were, to Brooklyn.

As the means of transit increased the land boomers began to turn their attention in the direction of Jamaica, especially after it began to be understood that the elevated railroad system of Brooklyn was certain, sooner or later, to be extended there. Lender their manipulation such places as Dunlin, Richmond Hill, Woodlawn, Clarenceville, Morris Park, Woodhull Park and half a dozen settlements were opened up and the lots disposed of with remarkable celerity. Even the old pre-Revolutionary village of Springfield — a place in fact not many years the junior of Jamaica village itself — felt the impulse of the change, and Woodhaven, founded in 1836 by John R. Pitkin, talked confidently of extending its manufactories. In 1863 Messrs. Lalance & Grosjean entered upon the manufacture of agate ware in an old factory building and extended the business so rapidly that in 1870 it was necessary to organize a joint stock company to operate and control it. The capital stock was fixed at $500,000 and the operations grew steadily year by year. In 1876 its buildings were destroyed by fire, but the calamity in the long run really helped the corporation, for the old structures were at once replaced with modem buildings, in which the most advanced appliances were introduced. The goods made by this establishment are now to be found all over the country.

Queens, another of Jamaica's suburbs, has also felt the impulse of the modern movement, and has gradually been opened up to settlement. It still, however, retains much of its primitive agricultural aspects, although in the recent railroad changes which have been discussed it seems likely that Queens will, more than all the outlying portions of the old township, receive its share of the material prosperity so confidently anticipated.

Just as these lines were being penned a telegram brought the news of the death of one of the most devoted citizens of Jamaica — ex-Governor Richard C. McCormick — at his home, 88 Herriman avenue, in that village. In this work he took a deep interest, made many valuable suggestions and promised to aid it from his rich stores of Long Island historical data. He was a most enthusiastic student of county history and had gathered together a valuable library containing published volumes of local history from all over the country, for, as he said, in such works the real story of the nation and its people is to be found. In conversation with the writer a few weeks before his death he told the story of the now forgotten movement to erect at Jamaica a statue of General Nathaniel Woodhull and regretted that that grand hero was apparently forgotten in the region where he was best known and where he gave up his life for his country.

Both the political and the business career of Governor McCormick were anything but commonplace. In recent years he had been engaged in mining operations, with offices at 1 Broadway, New York, but in earlier life he was active as a Republican, and had the confidence of such men as General Grant, Zachariah Chandler, and William H. Seward. This was considered somewhat remarkable, as he married a daughter of one of the most distinguished Democratic statesmen of the day, Allen G. Thurman, of Ohio.

Mr. McCormick was born in New York City on May 23, 1832, and was descended from several old Long Island families. He was elected Trustee of Public Schools for the Eleventh Ward in 1858, and two years later was a member of the Republican State Committee, taking an active part in the campaign of that year in support of Lincoln, as he had in the canvass four years previously, when General Fremont was his party's candidate. He was made Chief Clerk of the United States Department of Agriculture in 1862, and a year later became Secretary of the Territory of Arizona. So well did he attend to the duties of this office that in 1866 he was appointed Governor of the Territory by President Johnson, and at once set about placing the people in a better condition for defending themselves against the hostile Apaches. It was on his advice that General Crook was sent to this section.

Governor McCormick served three terms as a delegate in Congress from Arizona, and declined a fourth nomination in order to accept the appointment of Commissioner to the Centennial Exposition. He was appointed Assistant Secretary of the United States Treasury in 1877, and Commissioner General to the Paris Exposition in 1878. Returning to New York and settling in Jamaica, he devoted himself to promoting the large mining enterprises with which he had become identified. He was President and Director of the Boreel Mining Company and the Small Hopes Consolidated Mining Company, a Director of the Leadville Consolidated Mining Company, and a Trustee of the Citizens' Savings Bank. He served a term in Congress from the First New York District, taking his seat on March 4, 1895.

During Governor McCormick's stay in Arizona he kept Secretary Seward informed as to Maximilian's movements in Mexico. He was one of the founders of the Long Island Historical Society and the author of "Arizona: Its Resources," and of several other works, and was a member of the Union League Club, the American Geographical Society and of the Military Order of the Loyal Legion. He was also a Commander of the Legion of Honor of France.

# CHAPTER XLVII. LONG ISLAND CITY

On May 27, 1870, Governor Hoffman signed the bill which took away part of Newtown from that ancient township, including some of its most thriving villages, and incorporated it into a distinct municipality under the title of Long Island City. Such a union had been agitated for several years, mainly since the terminus of the Long Island Railroad had been established for good at Hunter's Point, and the concentration, there of a large population seemed inevitable in the not very distant future. But it is difficult now to see what was to be gained by taking a section of territory with several villages widely separated from each other and having little in common and dubbing it a city. It was hardly a political measure; it seemed rather a move on the part of the people, headed by Father Crimmin, of St. Mary's, Hunter's Point; the wealthy residents were opposed to it and with reason, for there was not even a city treasury in sight and the imposition of city taxes on a sparsely settled community meant a startling increase. That increase it was urged would keep manufactures from coming to the section and would result in an increase of assessments on real estate without any increase in the actual market value of the property. From a financial standpoint there was nothing to be said in favor of the change, and the events which followed from the signing of the bill of incorporation until the later bill was signed which wiped the city out of existence amply justified all the arguments against it. It became in its consolidated state a prey to the machinations of the local politicians, its treasury was ever empty, its police force was never adequate, its educational system was deficient; the taxation was increased without adequate return, the several sections incorporated by law did not incorporate in reality, except in the Hunter's Point section, the expected tremendous increase in population did not materialize, transit throughout the section was slow and uncertain until 1890, when the trolley began its work; and when consolidation took effect Long Island City was the weakest point in the aggregation which made up the Greater New York. Its most noteworthy feature was a bonded indebtedness of $3,849,000, on some of which interest was paid at the rate of seven per cent. The Long Island Railroad had done its work well in spite of local political opposition. It had built up a vast terminal depot, brought the place into close and frequent communication with Manhattan Island and made it a place of entry in reality for the business of Long Island; but the city itself failed to take advantage of its opportunity and became more noted for the antics of its politicians, its local "statesmen," than for aught else.

The localities incorporated into Long Island City were Astoria, Hunter's Point, Ravenswood, Dutch Kills, Blissville and Middletown and several small settlements, while the two Brother and Berrian Islands were thrown in for variety. The city had a splendid stretch of water front from Newtown Creek to Bowery Bay, but although settlement was early effected within its borders it never had any history worth writing about except that which comes from the stories and traditions of the old families who built it up and the more or less straggling communities of which it was composed. These communities may now be considered in detail.

Governor Kieft seems to have given patents to many settlers for lands along the water front from a farm at Hell Gate to an Englishman named William Hallet to another at a point overlapping Newtown Creek at the other end of the territory now under consideration which was given to Everardus Bogardus, the first minister or dominie of New Amsterdam, and from that fact the point was named Dominie's Hook. The property stood in the name of the dominie when he went down into the waters off the Welsh coast in 1647, along with Governor Kieft himself, in the wreck of the "Princess." His widow, the still famous Aneke Jans, secured a fresh patent for the point from Governor Stuyvesant, and it was purchased from her heirs in 1697 by Captain Peter Praa, whose descendants, along with those of Aneke, have enjoyed many a most exciting hunt after mythical real estate, to the enjoyment of the public and the enrichment of the lawyers. Peter Praa (or Pratt) was a Huguenot, and came here from Dieppe, France, in 1659. He appears to have been a man of means, for soon after his arrival he bought a bouwery at Gowanus. He died in 1663. His son. Captain Peter Praa, the purchaser of the Dominie's Hook, was born at Leyden in 1655, and therefore was but a child when he came here. He developed into one of the largest land owners in the vicinity, owning vast tracts in Bushwick and elsewhere as well as extending his original purchase of the Dominie's Hook by much additional territory on the water front as well as inland. He died in 1740. One of his daughters, Annetie, had married William Bennet, and died some years before him, leaving a young family, and to these children Captain Praa bequeathed the Dominie's Hook property. Thus in course of time its popular name became Bennet's Hook. One of the family, Jacob Bennet, bought up the entire interest in the estate of the other heirs and at his death bequeathed it to his daughter Anne, wife of Captain George Hunter. She died in 1833, leaving the property, which by that time had again changed its name to Hunter's Point, to her children. The last of these to reside on the family homestead was Jacob Hunter, who died in New York City in 1875.

It is noticeable that some of the deeds in the early part of the last century conveying lots at Hunter's Point call it Long Island City. It continued to be a straggly, dreary, poverty-stricken place, with few settlers and these of the poorest class, until the Long Island Road, because it could not make the necessary arrangements in Brooklyn, selected it as the main terminus of the road. Since then it has steadily increased in population, and as the First Ward of Long Island City it rapidly assumed the lead in the destinies of that now happily departed shade. Railway and manufacturing interests have steadily built up its population and added to its material (resources, most of which, however, were mercilessly squandered by political intriguers.

The Second Ward of Long Island City, Blissville, was founded by Neziah Bliss, the patriarch of Greenpoint, but it really calls for little mention, not having yet fulfilled the ambitious hopes once held as to its future. At all events, it has not yet felt the upward movement which the advent of the Greater City has brought to so many other outlying places. Its history has yet to be written. It formed part of the old Dutch Kills section, and was a corner of the old dominie's farm.

With Ravenswood, which became the Third Ward of the city, we find better material for historical study. This is certainly one of the prettiest "bits" in the whole of Greater New York, and as a residential neighborhood it has been a favorite from the beginning of the nineteenth century. In the first edition of his "History of Long Island," issued in 1838, Thompson says: "The site is sufficiently elevated to afford the most charming view of the adjacent country and possesses charms which almost equal some descriptions in eastern romance. The situation will hardly suffer by comparison with the beautiful scenery of the Thames at Windsor. Already several houses have been completed and others are in course of erection. In the vicinity are the valuable farms of the corporation of New York, upon which' buildings have been constructed for the accommodation of more than 500 orphan children who are maintained at its expense." Grant Thorburn, the noted Scotch florist of Astoria, whose seed store in New York was long one of the landmarks of the city, describes his sensations when, once passing this institution, he saw 600 children enjoying themselves. But the enterprise, or benevolence, or whatever it may be called, did not continue for many years. Its ultimate fate created quite a riot. In French's Gazetteer of New York we read: "About 1834-5 the corporation of New York City erected extensive buildings about one and one-half miles south from Astoria for a pauper establishment, which were sold at public auction April 15, 1847, upon the removal of these institutions to the islands in the river. Three large buildings, called the 'Boys' Nursery,' 'Schoolhouse' and 'Infants' Nursery,' the property of William W. Miles, were leased May 25, 1847, to the Commissioners of Emigration for a ship fever hospital and other purposes. A public meeting was held immediately thereafter at Astoria to express indignation at the appropriation of the property to these uses and to remonstrate against it. The people failing to obtain their object, the premises were assailed and destroyed on the night of May 26-27 by a mob in disguise. An attempt was made to fasten the expense of these losses upon the town, and after repeated efforts the owner recovered $3,000 from the State by act of March 15, 1855." With this threatened discord out of the way, Ravenswood resumed its quiet and dignified serenity, and many fine villas were erected within its neighborhood from time to time. It still retains its old description as a residential quarter, although business and manufacturing requirements are beginning to make inroads upon its domain. It was long, however, the aristocratic section of

Long Island City. In 1849 St. Thomas's Episcopal Church was organized, and since then most of the social life of Ravenswood has revolved around that little tabernacle.

Steinway, the principal settlement in the Fifth Ward, was laid out in 1872 by the famous firm of New York piano-makers. There they erected a splendid suite of buildings for their own uses and around these buildings the little village of Steinway was soon built up. It has now an estimated population of 1,500, and several other enterprises are carried on in it, while its beautiful situation on Long Island Sound has made it attractive to hundreds of home-seekers. It is a thriving place in every way and will likely undergo many important developments before many years pass by.

Astoria, which became the Fourth Ward of the city, was long the most populous and most popular village within it. It was incorporated as a village in 1836, and at that time its name was changed from Hallett's Cove. The name originally proposed: was the old Indian one of Sunswick, still kept alive in the name of a creek, but one of the men prominent in the matter of the incorporation, Mr. Stephen A. Halsey, suggested that if it were named in honor of John Jacob Astor he might pay for the foundation of a female seminary which was to be one of the features of the new village. Mr. Halsey spoke as one having authority. He had been engaged in the fur trade for many years, was intimately acquainted with Mr. Astor, and it was supposed possessed much influence with him. But Mr. Astor was not exactly the man to be caught with such chaff, and when approached on the subject rather threw cold water on the matter by saying there was already a city named Astoria and one was enough. However, Mr. Halsey persevered, Astoria became the name, and Mr. Astor contributed $100 to the institution which it was expected he would erect and maintain. Mr. Astor was a liberal enough giver according to his lights, but the race of modern benefactors had not then arisen.

Hallet's Cove received its name from William Hallet, an Englishman, who got a patent for a tract of land of 160 acres at Hell Gate from Governor Kieft. In 1655 his home was destroyed by Indians, and he was glad to escape to Flushing, of which place Stuyvesant appointed him sheriff. However, he did not hold that office long when the Governor deposed him for entertaining a traveling preacher from Rhode Island. When the trouble had blown over be returned to his property at Hell Gate, and afterward added more acres by purchase from the Indians until he owned pretty much all of the coastline from Sunswick Creek round to about where Steinway now is. Anneke Jans also managed to get a slice of real estate nearby. She seemed to know how to manage to secure choice parcels of land better than any of her contemporaries, and she certainly managed to hold on to what she got. Bit by bit several farmers settled in the district, and in 1753 Captain Jacob Blackwell and Joseph Hallock built and operated a mill at the mouth of

Sunswick Creek, on its right bank. Around the mill a small colony gradually sprung up. Possibly there was not when the Revolution broke out over half a dozen houses altogether, but behind lay a thriving colony of prosperous farmers. One evidence of this is found in the fact that in 1762 an English and classical school was established at Hallet'sCove, while thirteen of the near-by farmers were willing to board one or more of the scholars at a yearly rate of $45. But the institution did not last long, and Hallet's Cove resumed its sleep.

With the War of 1812 the sleep was broken. Large parties of experts visited the cove with the view of surveying its importance as a defensive position, covering as it could the approach from the Sound through Hell Gate to New York. One of the results of this survey was the erection of Fort Stevens. But the flurry was soon over, although its effects were of incalculable benefit to Hallet's Cove. The many fine, even romantic, sites suitable for residential purposes which surrounded it had become known, and many New York merchants secured choice plots in the neighborhood. But the most noted of the new arrivals was General Ebenezer Stevens, for whom Fort Stevens had been named. A member of the famous Boston Tea Party, a hero of two wars and a popular man in social life, his advent would have caused a stir in any community and would have been the occasion of a warm welcome. Such he found in Hallet's Cove. He built a splendid home on an eminence just opposite the northern extremity of Blackwell's Island, and gave the name of Mount Bonaparte to his property.

Mr. Henry Whittemore, the well-known Long Island historian and genealogist, gives the following interesting record of the family of this hero and his achievements in "The Heroes of the Revolution," a work of great value and research:

John Austin Stevens, the founder and first President of the Society, comes of a line of distinguished New England ancestors, who have been prominent in Church and State affairs for two hundred years.

Erasmus Stevens, the first of the family mentioned in this line, appears in 1714 as one of the founders of the New North Church in Boston, He had a son, Ebenezer (1).

Ebenezer Stevens (1), son of Erasmus Stevens, was probably born in Boston. He lived in Roxbury, where he married Elizabeth Wild. They had a son, Ebenezer (2).

Major-General Ebenezer Stevens, of the War of the Revolution, son of Ebenezer and Elizabeth (Wild) Stevens, was born in Boston, Massachusetts, August 22, 1751. He was an ardent patriot, and led the famous "Tea Pairty," 1773, in disposing of the obnoxious cargo by "committing it to the deep." He made little effort at disguise, being recognized by the officers of one of the ships. He soon afterward removed to Rhode Island, where he raised two companies of artillery and one of artificers, and was commissioned Lieutenant, May 8, 1775, and took part in the expedition against Quebec. He joined Henry Knox's regiment of artillery, was made a Captain on January 11, 1776, and on November 9, following, was brevetted Major. He commanded the artillery at Ticonderoga and Stillwater. As senior officer of this arm of defense in the northern department, he directed the artillery operations in the encounters which led to the defeat and surrender of Burgoyne, and soon after received a brevet commission as Lieutenant-Colonel, with a special resolution of thanks from the Continental Congress, for merit as Commandant of the Artillery of the Northern Department in the campaigns of 1776-7. He was at this time in the Massachusetts line. On April 30, 1778, he was commissioned Lieutenant-Colonel and transferred to Colonel John Lamb's regiment of the New York line, in which he served to the end of the war. He was entrusted with the defenses of the Hudson River, and had chains and other obstructions placed across the river to prevent the ships of the enemy from ascending. In 1781 he prepared a train of artillery for the southern service and was selected by General Lafayette to accompany him on his expedition to Virginia.

Owing to impaired health he returned home for a time, but after a brief respite he was commissioned by General Knox to prepare the artillery force which was to operate against Cornwallis. This was collected and transported from West Point. Philadelphia and Baltimore, and played an important part in the final siege which led to the surrender of Cornwallis. This completed his active service, though he continued his command till the army was finally disbanded. It is believed that no officer of his grade in the army rendered more arduous, various and important services than Colonel Stevens, and his characteristic energy, courage and perseverance gave assurance that, had the opportunity occurred, be would have signalized himself in a manner worthy of his patriotism and his ambition.

After the Revolution he started in business in New York, and without any previous experience, but relying on his own prudence and foresight, he met with extraordinary success and became one of the leading merchants of New York City. As agent of the War Department he constructed the fortifications upon Governor's Island in 1800. In 1812 he was commissioned Major-General of the State Militia, and with Morgan Lewis mustered for active service against the British, in September, 1814, at the time of an anticipated attack upon the city. He resigned his command in 1815 and withdrew from all public employment. He married, first, in 1775, Rebecca Hodgson, of Boston. In 1784 he married Lucretia, widow of Richardson Sands, a daughter of John Ledyard and sister of Colonel William Ledyard, the hero of Fort Groton. By his first wife, Rebecca Hodgson, he had issue three children, viz.: Horatio Gates, George, Rebecca (married John P. Schermerhorn). By his second wife he had Byam, William, Henry K., Samuel, Dr. Alexander H., John Austin, and Mary, wife of Frederick W. Rhinelander, Esq.

John Austin Stevens, Sr., was born in New York City January 22, 1795, died October 19, 1874. He was graduated at Yale in 1843; entered mercantile life and became a partner in his father's business in 1818. He was for many years Secretary of the New York Chamber of Commerce, and was one of the organizers and the first President of the Merchants' Exchange. From its first establishment, in 1839, till 1860, he was President of the Bank of Commerce. He was chairman of the Committee of Bankers of New York, Boston and Philadelphia, which first met in August, 1861, and decided to take $50,000,000 of the Government 7-30 loan. They subsequently advanced $100,000,000 more, and the terms of the transaction were arranged chiefly by Mr. Stevens, as the head of the treasury note committee. His advice was frequently sought by the officers of the Treasury Department during the Civil War.

John Austin Stevens, Jr., the first President and one of the incorporators of the Society Sons of the American Revolution, son of John Austin Stevens, Sr., was born in New York City January 23, 1827; was graduated at Harvard in 1846, engaged in mercantile business in New York, and in 1862 was elected Secretary of the New York Chamber of Commerce, continuing in office six years. He was librarian of the New York Historical Society, and devoted himself to the investigation of topics of American History. He founded and for many years edited the Magazine of American History. He was the author of numerous works, among which were "The Valley of the Rio Grande; its Topography and Resources" (New York, 1864); "Memorial of the New York Chamber of Commerce on Steam Navigation" (1864); "Colonial Records of the New York Chamber of Commerce" (1867), containing illustrations and biographical and historical sketches; "The Progress of New York in a Century" (1876); "The Expedition of Lafayette Against Arnold," published by the Maryland Historical Society (Baltimore, 1878), and other works.

General Stevens' eldest son married the daughter of Albert Gallatin, Secretary of the Treasury under Jefferson and Madison, and that venerable statesman died in the home on Mount Bonaparte in 1849. By the middle of the century quite a number of manufactories had located around Hallet's Cove, which had become quite a village. In 1828 St. George's Episcopalian Church was founded, and in 1834 a meeting-house was erected for the use of the Presbyterian and Dutch Reformed congregations. In 1837 the once famous female institute was founded. The Rev. Alexander H. Bishop was installed in 1840 as minister of the Dutch Church, and the Presbyterians, having given up their interest in the building, erected jointly, it was given over to the sole use of the new pastor. The Presbyterians worshipped in the district "school-house until 1846, when they entered a new church they had built, and chose the Rev. F. G. Clark as their pastor.

About the middle of the last century Astoria became noted for its nurseries and gardens, the leader in that business being Grant Thorburn, whose grounds were once the most extensive of any devoted to the raising of garden seeds to be found in the country. Thorburn's gardens were near the river, — the Sohmer piano factory now stands on part of the property, and he himself was postmaster of Hallet's Cove for some time, and assisted in the organization of the Reformed Dutch Church in 1839. A useful man, the founder of a local industry and one who made a considerable mark in the world of letters, it is worthwhile to recall the salient features of Thorburn's career before he became connected with Astoria.

In the "Statistical Account of Scotland," vol. I, page 495, is the following brief notice:

"Mr. Grant Thorrburn, seedsman. New York, the original 'Lawrie Tod,' though a native of Newbattle parish, where he was born on the 18th of February, 1773, lived in Dalkeith from his childhood until he sailed for New York on the 13th of April, 1794. He is a man of great piety and worth, though of a remarkably lively and eccentric character. He visited Dalkeith in 1834, when he published his "Autobiography," which he dedicated with characteristic singularity and elegance to Her Grace the Duchess of Buccleuch."

It did not suit the purpose for Mr. Peter Steele, the gifted schoolmaster who in 1844 wrote these words, to give any indication of Thorburn's career in Scotland. Political feeling then ran very high and political resentment was very bitter, and the teacher could not, had he so inclined, say a word commendatory of Thorburn's early life without bringing upon his own head the ill will of the Buccleuch family and its adherents. So like a canny Scot he acted the part of the Highlandman's parrot, which "thocht a guid deal and said naething ava." Thorburn learned from his father the trade of a nail-maker, and became quite an expert at it long before his apprenticeship was past. Like most of the Scottish workmen of the time, — a time when the old order of things was fast changing and the governing powers tried to quell the popular advance and the popular aspirations with trials for treason, sedition and the like, — Thorburn became deeply interested in politics, and in Dalkeith was prominent among those who advocated Parliamentary reform and a generous concession to the claims of the people to a voice in the conduct of affairs. The result was that when opportunity offered he was arrested for treason, and after a short time in prison was released on bail. This arrest made him a marked man and blocked any prospect of his making his way in the world, so, believing that the star of freedom blinked bonnily across the sea in the new republic which had thrown off the yoke of the same Parliament he had protested against, Thorburn left Scotland, and, settling in New York, tried to earn his living at his trade of nail-making. It, however, did not promise much for the future, and in 1801 he started in business as a grocer at 20 Nassau street. "He was there," writes Walter Barrett, "some ten or twelve years, and then he moved to No. 22, and about the time of his removal, in 1810, he changed his business and kept garden seeds and was a florist. He established a seed-raising garden at Newark, but it proved unsuccessful, and thereafter he confined his attention to his business in New York and acquired considerable means." In 1825 he secured land and opened his garden in Astoria, where he built a home for himself.

From the beginning of his American career almost Thorburn became known for his kindly heart, and he did much practical good in a quiet way, not only among his countrymen, but among all deserving people whose needs touched his sympathy or aroused his compassion. For many years his store in Liberty street was not only a lounging place for the merchants who bought flowers, but for the practical gardeners who grew them, and his place became a sort of clearing house for the horticulturists in the city, and every Scotch gardener who arrived in New York from the old country made Thorburn's place his headquarters until he found employment, and hundreds used to say that the advice and information they received from him at that critical stage in their careers were of the most incalculable value to them through life. In 1854 Mr. Thorburn in a sense retired from business and returned to Astoria. From there he moved to Winsted. Connecticut, and finally to New Haven, Connecticut, where he died in 1863.

Air. Thorburn possessed considerable literary tastes, and under the *nom de plume* of "Lawrie Tod" wrote in his later years at frequent intervals for the "Knickerbocker Magazine" and other periodicals. He gave to John Gait much of the information which that genius incorporated in his story of "Lawrie Tod; or. Settlers in the New World," and his published books of reminiscences, notably his "Forty Years' Residence in America" and "Fifty Years' Reminiscences of New York," still form interesting reading. So, too, does a now scarce volume published in 1848, under the title of "Lawrie Tod's Notes on Virginia, with a Chapter on Puritans, Witches and Friends." This book is one of those contributions to American social history which will become of more value as time speeds on, although its importance will be more appreciated by the student than by the general reader.

Until the incorporation of Astoria as a village it progressed on somewhat slow yet eminently satisfactory lines. In fact, it was regarded as prosperous. After incorporation it progressed more rapidly. The "horse" ferry gave way to a steamer in 1839, and in 1853 a gas company was organized and many other improvements were introduced. Its advantages as a residential village were kept well before the people and every inducement was offered to people likely to become good citizens to settle. It was a quiet, orderly community, a home community, a law-abiding, peaceful community: and even after the formation of Long Island City, of which it became a ward, when other parts of the township were offering protection to blacklegs and swindlers, when the liquor dealers united openly to defy the law, when it was loudly boasted that in Long Island City a man might even defy the law and escape justice,

Astoria held aloof from the maelstrom of license and crime and pursued the even tenor of her way, conscious that if other members of the family had thrown open their doors to crime she at least had preserved her name unsullied. But it cannot be said that her incorporation with Long Island City proved for Astoria's benefit; now she will fare in the Greater New York still remains to be seen.

An event which for a time attracted the attention of the entire country, and indeed of the scientific world, to Long Island City was the blowing up of. Hell Gate so as to provide a clear channel for navigation. This event belongs to the annals of Astoria because the main obstructions destined to be removed lay off her shore line and' the operations were directed from headquarters established in her territory. The wonderful story of that great engineering enterprise has been so often fully told that there is little need of plunging into the details in these pages. Suffice it to say that the work was begun in 1870 by the United States Government and placed under the direction of General Newton. For six years the work progressed, and after some minor obstructions had been removed every effort was directed to the destruction of Hallet's Reef, the most dangerous in the whole passage. A shaft had been sunk and passageways cut out in the interior of the rock until its whole extent was opened up. Into holes drilled into these passageways 52,206 pounds of dynamite and other explosives were inserted, a network of electric wires connected the whole with a series of batteries on shore, and these again were controlled by a single wire operated by a button. The work was pronounced complete, and on Saturday, September 23, 1876, water was let into all the passageways and on the following day the little daughter of General Newton touched the button and in two seconds Hallet's Reef was a mass of broken rock. The whole scheme had worked to perfection, almost exactly according to the schedule of the engineers. Flood Rock was afterward destroyed in the same way and several smaller obstructions were successfully removed. Hell Gate with its dangers is now a thing of the past, and this was amply demonstrated in the early summer of 1901, when a United States war vessel of the first class successfully passed through a channel which formerly was deemed too dangerous to be attempted in time of peace except by river craft manned by river pilots, and was always dangerous. Readers of Fenimore Cooper's interesting novel, "The Water Witch," will recall a most thrilling description of the passage through Hell Gate as it was in the days before Uncle Sam undertook to remove its dangers.

To the student of American municipal matters the history of Long Island City as a distinct community during its existence of some twenty-eight years, is an interesting study, if a somewhat nauseous one. It is not intended to follow its details here, for, excepting for the purposes of such study, the story is really purposeless; so a few details will suffice. As the new city became the legal center of Queens county it became the seat of the law courts and so attracted quite a new order of business to the whilom Hunter's Point, a class of business which it still holds. To accommodate this legal business it was deemed necessary to build a court house. One was authorized in 1872 and in 1875 it was completed and opened. The original cost was fixed at $150,000, but the actual cost was $278,000, and the local politicians thought it escaped them too easily at that! The first election under the charter was held on July 5, 1870, when Abram D. Dittmars was elected Mayor, but the charter proved unworkable and full of faults, so that within a year a second charter had to be given the city. Each of the five wards were represented by three Aldermen, but in 1879 the number was reduced by limiting the wards to one city father each, while two were chosen by the city at large. Henry S. Bebevoise was elected the second Mayor in 1873, and in 1876 Mr. Dittmars was re-elected, but soon resigned. The most famous of all the Mayors, — famous for his vulgarity, his defiance of law and his aptitude for holding votes, — was Patrick Jerome Gleason, the last of the city's own rulers, and who, after a curious career, be came a political nonentity, a bankrupt, and died poor and heartbroken early in 1901. One of the newspaper accounts of his career said: "Patrick Jerome Gleason, who in late years was never mentioned without his emblem, the battle-axe, being spoken of in the same breath, was a unique figure in American politics. For years he practically carried Long Island City in his vest pocket and was the autocrat of the place. He was its Mayor for three terms, running over eight years, and from the time of his appearance there until his death his name was constantly before the public in one form or another.

"Gleason was fond of notoriety and liked to talk about himself and his deeds. He declared that the laborer and school children had in him a champion, and in the fight for more school-houses he continually led the van. One of his latest feats was to write an autobiography, which it was his intention to publish in book form. He could not keep it long enough, however; he said it was too good for that, — so he gave it to the newspapers a chapter at a time.

"It was in the parish of Drum and Inch, County Tipperary, the birthplace of Senator John Morrissey, that Patrick J. Gleason was born. He said in his book that he had a twin brother and six other brothers and one sister. Patrick was the pigmy of the family, and he stood six feet one inch when he had attained his growth.

"In May, 1862, when the Civil War was raging, Gleason came to this country. He used to tell that he had not been here two days when he was assaulted by two volunteer firemen, and he added, 'we had to be separated by a policeman.'

"Mr. Gleason's twin brother became a member of Mosby's guerrillas, but Patrick elected to stand by the Stars and Stripes, although the Ninety-ninth Regiment, in which he was a lieutenant, never got to the front. The next step in his career was as a distiller in Flushing, but the plant was confiscated by the Government and Gleason found himself bankrupt. He became a bidder for a street railroad through Williamsburgh into Long Island City, and got a franchise. Then came his first plunge into politics at the time of the Greeley campaign, when he was defeated for the Assembly.

"With a capital of fifty cents, Gleason thought of California as a haven, and he said he went to a friend to borrow $150, telling him be need never expect to see it again. The friend gave him $300 and he went to the Golden Gate. He had brothers in San Francisco, and finally sold his distillery secret for $5,000, dabbling in stocks and increasing his capital to $32,000. He heard that someone was trying to get his franchise in Williamsburgh, so he came East, built his road, acted as conductor, driver, president and general superintendent, and began to increase his rolling stock.

"It was as Mayor of Long Island City that Gleason came into the greatest prominence. He was a strong supporter of consolidation, and when the Greater New York was finally an accomplished fact Mr. Gleason announced himself as a candidate for Mayor of the greater city. The battle-axe was his emblem on the ballot, but his candidacy was looked upon as a joke."

With the story of this interesting personage, whose name for fifteen years or so was the most familiar one in Long Island City, we might fittingly close this chapter, for in one sense he was its most representative citizen, in that he could for many years rally a majority of its votes to his assistance to support his schemes. But before closing it may be proper to recall one locality which practically has passed out of existence. Dutch Kills still has a quasi-existence in local talk, although it has legally been wiped out, but Middletown, on the eastern boundary line of the city, seems to have been entirely passed into the forgotten. In the Revolutionary era it came into prominence from the movement of the British troops, Sir Henry Clinton and General Robertson having their headquarters there for brief periods, just as Lord Cornwallis seems to have had a brief station at Dutch Kills. But historic tradition alone is not enough to give vitality to a place, and so Middletown gradually fell from its one-time prominence and is now practically a memory.

# CHAPTER XLVIII. SUMMER RESORTS.

Long Island, throughout its whole extent, might most fittingly be styled the garden of New York, or Greater New York, the amusement and recreation ground of America's greatest city. It gratifies every taste. The lover of quiet can find it in abundance, can settle down in places apparently so far removed from the din of commerce, the roar and bustle and struggle of humanity, that he might easily imagine himself a thousand miles away from any habitation excepting his own and hear no sound save the hum of the bee, the twitter of the bird, or the musical duet of the katydid when night falls and darkness closes in on the little world to which he has resigned himself. If he wants society and fun and frolic and excitement, he can find it in abundance at many a popular caravansary, where he can be associated with people from all parts of the world, get the newest hints as to social life and study the most recent fad in the fashionable world. If a sportsman, he can find full use for rod and gun; and if he desires to fish in the deep blue sea, the waters of the Atlantic or of Long Island Sound are ready at his command. The fishermen can find no place where a day of more genuine fun can be had than in Jamaica Bay, or he can have a day worthy of being remembered by engaging in snipe shooting at Westhampton; if he wants excitement with his sport, let him spend a day or two in an open boat off the Great South Bay; if he be of the quiet, contemplative, philosophical kind, Izaak Walton description of a sport, a gentle "angler," why, such places as Sayville are ready to receive and welcome him. If a golfer, the finest courses in the world are at Babylon, Ouogaie, Flushing, Port Washington, the Shinnecock Hills and a dozen other places. If a polo expert, he will find many noted players in the Meadow Brook Club, one of the most famous sporting organizations in the land, whose kennels are a sight to see and whose annual hunting record is the best and most exciting in the country. If a bicyclist, he has only to secure a little tag and go meandering over some of the finest cycle paths to be met anywhere in this vale of tears and of spent tires and smashed wheels. He may even enjoy scorching now and again, and. most wonderful of all, will never once in his journey on the island be denounced as a nuisance. Sea-bathing, rolling and tumbling in the breakers or floating lazily in still waters is everywhere at command or within easy reach; and some of the most magnificent stretches of sandy beach to be found anywhere are of frequent occurrence along the whole extent of the South Shore. The harbor facilities for yachting purposes are unexcelled, and the sport, one of the grandest ever invented by human agency, is enjoyed to the full by the dwellers on the island. No prettier sight can anywhere be found than the snug harbors of Port Jefferson or Shelter Island during the height of the season. If one is of a poetic mind, loves to realize how small an atom he is in the cosmopolis, he can sit on the rocks at Montauk Point and mourn the glories of a vanished race, a royal race, and realize the mutability of earthly greatness and comprehend his own insignificance as he watches the wide expanse of horizon and sees the wide limitless expanse of water kissing the rocky coast when in placid mood, or hurling against it with resistless fury when the angry fit is on.

A rare place indeed is Long Island for all sorts and conditions of men, and the beauty of it all is that every section of it is within easy reach of America's metropolitan city, Greater New York, part of which, indeed, is now on the island itself. Even to the sojourner, with only an hour or two to spare, the attractions of the island are open. Coney Island is less than an hour's distance by water, or even by the trolley, and a ride on some of these vehicles really carry the visitor through a stretch of ground more crammed with historical interest than can be found in an hour's ride even in history-burdened Continental Europe. We traverse the scene of the Battle of Brooklyn and through old villages, now, however, so sadly modernized and annexed that only glimpses here and there of the relics of other days present themselves. But we. in spite of changes, do pass through Flatbush and Flatlands and Gravesend, and each of these names recalls to the student of modern history a flood of treasured memories. Coney Island itself is a picture, a unique "city of the sea," with its bands, its noise, its touts, its shows, its merry-go-rounds and its cafes and saloons. A little bit vulgar, some people call it: possibly they are right; but there are many tastes in this world to be gratified and every taste that is right and proper and in keeping with morals and ethics has to be catered to. Coney Island has but one mission, and that is to please the public; and as it is visited every year by about a million persons it can hardly be said not to fulfill that mission. But people who think it vulgar, who find it not to their taste, can pass it by and go on to Manhattan Beach and the Oriental, where they can listen to classical music, hear now and again an opera or burlesque, associate with the salt of the earth, be waited upon by Austrian dukes and Italian counts rigged up in swallow-tailed coats, eat the culinary masterpieces of French chefs, and see a grand display of fireworks before ascending to their bedrooms to be lulled to sleep with the gentle moan of the deep blue sea. In the season "the sport of kings." as horse racing is called, can be enjoyed at Sheepshead Bay or at Gravesend. Another resort near at hand is Rockaway, a long stretch of sand lying between Jamaica Bay and the ocean; while east of it, on the same stretch of sand, is Arverne, with its huge hotel and cottages, a center of social pleasure for three months every year.

The trolley system of Brooklyn is one of the most comprehensive to be found anywhere, and by it one may journey over very considerable distances of interesting country for a cost that is almost nominal. From Brooklyn Bridge to Jamaica is perhaps the acme of cheap and pleasant traveling, and so in the trip from the Broadway Ferry to Flushing or North Beach. Jamaica is the railroad center of the island. Flushing one of its old historic towns, and North Beach a summer show place; and to get to each of these places the cars pass through a wide extent of varied country, sometimes more or less thickly populated, sometimes so thinly peopled that the car bowls along with increased speed, irresponsive to the beauty of the surroundings or the story of the wayside, so as to make up the time lost in threading its way through the city's streets. Traveling by trolley is a delightful pleasure on a warm day, for the car itself "makes a breeze," as the conductor tells us, and there is a certain degree of excitement or exhilaration always obtainable when one is bowling along through an open country, now passing a village, now a church, now a green field, and ever and anon dashing through some little collection of pretty villas, the beginning of some future popular summer resort.

But the trolley has its drawbacks; and as we look at the motorman we realize what a wide difference there is between that mechanical development and the old-fashioned stagedriver of our younger days. The motorman is a part of the machinery, and nothing more. The stage-driver was a gentleman, and, in his way and so far as his observation went, a scholar and a philosopher. He could tell you the story, the romance, of every field as he passed it by, name the owners of each house, tell you how much the head of each family was worth, relate all sorts of village scandal and gossip, and point out the scene of every remarkable occurrence within his view for a hundred years back! Your motorman is a different personage. He attends strictly to business, and his business is to get his car to the end of his route and nothing more. We question if there is a motorman in Brooklyn who could point out to you a bit of the ground fought over in the Battle of Brooklyn in 1776, or who ever heard that such a battle had ever been fought. His mind is fixed on other things.

The resorts on Long Island are very numerous, and all of them seem to grow in popularity year after year. We cannot recall one that has gone back to its primitive condition of solitary wildness: although most of them have their ups and downs, their good years and their bad ones, the story is one of steady progress all along the line. Some seasons the "gilded youth" of both sexes prefer one place to another, and forsake, say Shelter Island for Glen Cove; but new arrivals take the place of the departed ones, and the story of success goes steadily on. There is more reason for this than appears on the surface. The people who really make these resorts are the dwellers in the large cities, and as these increase in population year after year so does the cry for summer homes, and summer breathing places increase. Then Long Island fills the bill. It is so easily reached and yet affords such a welcome change! But, more than all that, its schedule of prices are moderate, and a man can spend a season at on€ of its best hotels as cheaply as he can in such establishments anywhere. Land is cheap, and a site for a dwelling is not costly, nor is labor extravagant in its demands. A man can choose a site overlooking the seashore or in some picturesque nook in the center of the island, all for a moderate cost, while he can have his provisions from New York or from some of the towns on the Connecticut shore as cheaply and promptly as though he were still a dweller in the busy haunts of men. He can enjoy city privileges and rural felicity without drawing more heavily on his purse than though he never stirred away from the noise and clamor of a city. Long Island is every year becoming an island of homes in the sense that Brooklyn used to be called a "city of homes." It is drawing to itself all classes of the community, — the millionaire and the clerk, and the mansion and the cottage, both find congenial surroundings.

In recent years a new development has taken place on Long Island, in the holding by individuals of vast extent of its territory, such as the property at Oakdale of William K. Vanderbilt and the estates of F. G. Bourne, of W. H. Whitney and others. These demesnes are veritable baronial holdings and rival in beauty and elegance many an English show place. But they are much more home-like, and the residences erected on them are a thousand times more comfortable than most of the storied old-world castles we read so much about. The old owners of manors on Long Island would have gazed with wonder at these estates, the modern successors of their vast holdings. The modern manors are not so large as the old ones, and their title deeds do not convey any questionable "rights," — rights which sometimes sadly interfered with "life, liberty and the pursuit of happiness;" but they are better worth living on and give to their owners more genuine pleasure and comfort than any of the old patriarchs could derive from their broad but bleak and sterile acres.

Of late years a feature of summer-home life on Long Island has been the organizations which club together, buy a piece of property, erect a club house and cottages and restrict the rights of property-owning on their domain to their own members. By this means many a pleasant colony has been formed of people who are acquainted with each other and whose company is congenial. Some of these places are most attractive, their co-operation permitting many expenses which the members could not indulge in single-handed, and they afford as a result of the benefits of co-operation all the pleasure of rural outdoor life at a very moderate cost.

But the multitude of people who go to Long Island flock to the resorts and the number of them is legion. Take Patchogue, for instance. It is in itself an old and settled community, lying in the shelter of the Great South Bay, in a little bay which bears its own name, with a railroad station in its midst, and one of the best roads in the island reaching from its center right across to Long Island Sound, to Port Jefferson. It has an industry pre-eminently its own, its oyster trade, as well as several manufacturing establishments. Little need for it one would think, to spread bait to catch summer visitors; yet season after season they flock to it by the thousand. Its wide streets charm every one; and its churches, villas as well as its general air of comfort and cleanliness are satisfying somehow to the dweller in cities. Of course it caters to this annual trade and has all the attractions which an up-to-date seaside resort should have, and, unlike many of the smaller towns in Suffolk county, it spends money on improvements with no niggard hand. As a sea-bathing resort it has all the adjuncts which fashion demands, and a fleet of oar-boats or sailing vessels or naptha launches are daily riding in its harbor, waiting the beck and call of any who want to enjoy a sail on the Great South Bay. If one is tired of the seacoast he can easily turn his steps inland; he can enjoy a glimpse of the country, or, by hiring a gig. can drive for many hours through rich and varied scenes and never once catch a glimpse of the coast until he returns to his hotel or boarding-house, and boardinghouses are as plentiful in Patchogue as dollar bills in a bank.

For those who desire seaside with very little, comparatively, of country, a tract of Long Island has been coming slowly into vogue in recent years, and that is at its eastern end along the shores of Great and Little Peconic Bay. A recent writer speaks of this section in the following enthusiastic fashion, — a fashion which, however, is truthful, in spite of its enthusiasm:

"Along Peconic Bay are a number of towns and villages whose fine climate, good roads and general attractions are making them prime favorites with summer visitors. The bay itself is a beautiful body of salt water, on whose placid bosom all manner of pleasure craft can be seen during the warm months, bearing happy groups of care-free folk. They sail or row over the blue waters in land-locked security from the rollers of the open sea. If they wish to take a dip in the surf, good beaches offer the alluring opportunity.

"On the north side of the bay, after leaving Riverhead, one soon comes to the town of Aquebogue, a name admirably descriptive, for water and bog make up the bay-front side. The Saxon half of the name and the sedgy flats about the town suggest the marshes of Runnymede, where the barons wrested the Magna Charta from King John.

"The land rises as one reaches Jamesport, and here are hills crowned with old churches and pleasant homes. This town has become so popular for a summer holiday that the difficulty frequently met with is getting accommodations, a fact that has served as a stimulus in the erection of many cottages.

"Franklinville is a pretty village, 'at peace with all the world.' Contentment exhales from it as a fragrance, and it always has a colony of summer residents.

"A little way on down the narrow Italy-shaped peninsula into which the north side of Long Island is here tapering is the modest village of Mattituck. Both to the north end and to the south it has fine water views. Having comfortable inns and hospitable farmhouses for the entertainment of visitors, it has won deserved repute as a place of summer outing. One of the diversions of those sojourning here is found in a little creek flowing toward the Sound and abounding in crabs. In both sea and bay fish are plentiful.

" 'Just sneeze and you pronounce it:" that is a remark the writer overheard as descriptive of the name Cutchogue. But this description is suggestive in other ways than phonetically. A sneeze is apt to result from too much oxygen, and in the air that blows fresh from the water over sightly Cutchogue oxygen is abundant. This pretty town has other advantages than good air and a fine view. It is on one of the best roads in America, the long, straight highway leading from Riverhead to Orient. But good roads on Long Island, it should be said, are the rule rather than the exception. Every natural advantage in surface and soil helps their construction and maintenance. The drainage is good, the grades seldom steep, save near the ocean, and there is plenty of land to give the roads needed width. As a result these highways between verdant stretches of farm land, in the shade of noble trees, by the shores of shining lakes, and in sight often of the mighty sea, offer a perpetual invitation to walking, cycling and driving.

"One's first impression of Peconic, formed from a glance down its broad, shaded street, is favorable, and closer acquaintance with the old town confirms this impression. Jutting out from the shore is a headland called Nassau Point. Southold, a few miles east, lays claim to antiquity in its name, and points to the fact proudly that its first settlers secured a concession from the Indians and from a church as early as 1640. There is a contention between Southold and Southampton, across the bay, as to which is the older. In August, 1890, Southold celebrated, with much ceremony, the two hundred and fiftieth anniversary of its founding. The town has a center where the stores, schools, and churches are grouped, and about it the houses are scattered widely. Whichever way the wind may blow the old place is fanned by a sea breeze. In this fact some antiquarians profess to have found a reason for the great age of some of the inhabitants, a few of whom, it is gravely claimed, antedate the founding of the place. "Journeying to the very end of the main line of the Long Island Railroad one reaches the progressive and interesting town of Greenport. It has over 3,000 inhabitants, and is both a resort and an important business center. Besides the trade that comes to it from being the terminus of the railroad, it has a considerable commerce through its boat connections with Shelter Island, New London, and Sag Harbor. Within the safe haven of its harbor a mighty fleet could find anchorage. The town's large summer population is drawn from a wide territory — New England and the West being represented as well as New York and Brooklyn. These sojourners have pleasant stopping places in well-appointed hotels and comfort-giving cottages. They find every means of outdoor diversion. Boating, sailing, fishing, and shooting are excellent, and many pleasant trips can be made awheel, afloat, or afoot. The view one gets from a bluff north of the town is expansive and exhilarating. Dancing in the sunlight are the waters of the Sound stretching away to the green shores of Connecticut; to the south lies Peconic Bay, a glittering sapphire set between the green heights of Shelter Island and the trees of Greenport, with spire and roof peering through them; to east and west the eye travels over water to the far horizons. This north prong of Long Island pushes on from Greenport, beyond the pretty town of Orient, with its one thousand people, to its end at Orient Point. Here the land, which has been gradually becoming narrower, dips into the sea, and what, in some of the geological epochs of the past, was a greater Long Island here becomes the bed of the Atlantic."

To many, the central portion of Long Island will always be its most attractive feature. Jamaica itself might be a resort, deserves to be a resort in fact, for its antiquity, its natural beauty; and the important part it has played in the history not only of Long Island but of the country at large ought to commend it to many classes. To a certain extent and up to a certain time it was a "resort," but since it became a railroad center it is so no longer; yet for one who wants to explore Long Island no place is better adapted as headquarters unless one is prowling around Montauk Point, or meandering solemnly in the outskirts of Wading River. It is surrounded by a cluster of pretty home-like towns, — Hollis, in the one direction and Woodhaven in the other, each worth a visit to get a good understanding of the comforts and discomforts, the joys and drawbacks of the individual the comic papers like to run foul of as the suburbanite.

It is not very far by rail from Jamaica to Garden City, a place which has acquired so much prominence from the beautiful cathedral and schools founded by the late A. T. Stewart and his widow. Stewart was a strange individual. The most successful merchant of his time, every speculation he entered into in connection with his legitimate dry-goods business turned to gold: everything else he touched turned to dross. One of his pet schemes was to found a city on Long Island, and with that end in view he purchased a large tract of land in the township of Hempstead. He knew that a town must have some reason for its existence, and he furnished the reason — the cathedral. He also built houses for the people to live in; but none was to be sold, all to be rented, and the rentals in turn was to help support the cathedral and its work. It was a failure. Americans do not like to live in an atmosphere of restriction, and that was what life at Garden City meant. The cathedral is a thing of beauty, the architectural beauty of Long Island, and the schools associated with it are the best of their kind; but it was not until Stewart was dead and the silly restrictions were removed that Garden City began to attract people. Its growth has been slow: the word "city" as its title has proved a misnomer. It will in course of time be peopled: that is inevitable; but it will never be in itself a city, for the next time that the Greater New York stretches itself it will be swallowed up as have so many more popular places.

For sylvan beauty no section of Long Island can more commend itself than that around Lake Ronkonkoma. Says the writer we have already quoted:

"The sheen of its limpid surface sparkles like the eyes of an Indian maiden. Fed by springs at the bottom, its waters are as pure as they are clear. The lake is about three miles around, and its shores form the shape of a pear. In places it is over sixty feet deep. As a shady fringe around it are many trees, and clustered about are a number of cottages. Along the beach of white sand a road runs, and the view from it over the crystal face of the lake is beautiful. This is the largest body of fresh water on Long Island. It is fifty-five feet above sea level. Through some mystery of nature it has periods of ebb and flood, but these are not coincident with the tides or by any possibility connected with them. On the sloping banks daisies nod to their relatives the lily-pads in the water. In the darkling depths, bass, catfish, and perch disport »themselves. Floating now and again over its bosom, as if calling its Indian name, are the sounds of bells from St. Mary's-by-the-Lake, and from other steeples. A legend has it that a phantom canoe now and again goes noiselessly over the waters bearing an Indian girl, love-lorn, and in search of the young brave to whom she has given her heart. With the dawn her birchbark boat skims away into the ether and the sun looks down into the mirror face of Ronkonkoma."'

But we must cease mentioning places, for wherever our eye falls on the map some great hotel like that at Long Branch or some quiet, old-fashioned inn like that at Roslyn comes before us demanding a word; and the summer delights of Southampton, or Cold Spring or Moriches or Shelter Island troop up calling for more detailed description than can well be given them individually in a chapter devoted to all as a class. Then too many historic spots are recalled, such as the early home of him who when a wanderer far from it wrote the plaintive words of "Home, Sweet Home," — one of the world's songs; the old Indian Canal at Shinnecock; the memorial to Nathan Hale; the haunts of Captain Kidd, and even the late tumult and excitement at Camp Wyckoff, where our soldiers rested afeer their return from their short but glorious campaign in Cuba, — all these bid us linger, all inspire a desire to tell their story; but such things cannot be crowded into a chapter and had better, here at all events, be left untold.

For fifty years or thereabout Long Island has been a paradise for the land boomers. Money has been made in its real-estate field, and much has been lost. The land boomer is an evil: of that there is no doubt; and the story of his doings in Williamsburgh and other places have won for him a memorable reputation. He has done harm in many quarters, — harm which exists to this day, because he has floated a half-considered and ill-advised scheme, and then when the "bottom fell out of it" left it hopelessly a wreck. Such results are painfully evident all over Long Island. But still the boomer has been of service. He quickened the extension of the old city of Brooklyn by his efforts more than did any other agency; he it was who opened up its farms and turned them into streets and squares and won for 'it its title of "city of homes;" he, too, has been the means of bringing to the front most of Long Island's most popular resorts. They have been started in the first instance by his glowing descriptions and his confidently expressed hopes, and once he induced the people to believe as he professed to believe the rest was easy. He made money. He turned strips of sand into foundations of wealth, won a price for old farms which would have astonished the old holder of a manor patent; but the people got something for their money, something they could use for health and pleasure. It was said of a once famous real-estate auctioneer and boomer in Brooklyn that he sold more sand and mud than any other man living. So he did. But people built hotels on the sand and homes on the mud, and so all were benefited. The boomer should be gratefully remembered when we think of the marvelous prosperity which Long Island has for so many years enjoyed for its pleasant country homes, its suburban pleasures and the wealth which the vast throngs of summer visitors yearly bring to its resorts.

But if the boomer has passed a greater power has arisen to perform his work, to perform it more honestly, more thoroughly, and with more beneficial and permanent results. That power is the railroad system of the island. There is no doubt that the plans now in progress for the extension and development of the Long Island Railroad will open up the entire island to business and pleasure to an extent even now little dreamed of and make it become a veritable fairyland of homes and resorts, and that, too, at a not very far distant day.

# CHAPTER L. FREEMASONRY ON LONG ISLAND.

As might readily be supposed, Brooklyn is a city of societies of all sorts — secret, fraternal, political, sporting, dramatic and fashionable. Most of its organizations are popular, that is to say, their membership is practically open to all who apply and who have the requisite qualifications as to taste, acquaintance, reputation and the wherewithal to pay the entrance fee and the annual dues. Some on the other hand are as exclusive as can be imagined, and it would seem the more exclusive a certain club or society may be the larger is its waiting list. In the long list of Brooklyn clubs and societies nearly every taste seems to be catered to, every nationality has its circle, every trade and profession has its social home, and every recreation its temple. Even the ladies have their chosen societies and the number of those open equally to both sexes — notably the dramatic and singing societies — run into the hundreds.

The time indeed was when the people on almost each block in Brooklyn formed practically a little social organization among themselves. That was in the days prior to the advent of the tenement or apartment house and the appearance of the trolley. In the pleasant summer afternoons people would gather on the stoops and verandahs in front of their homes and receive the visits of their neighbors, while the ladies would ramble from one home to another and indulge in their dearly loved and kindly gossip. Each block had its own passing affairs to discuss and business to regulate, and it was done in a pleasant, neighborly fashion as the evening hours slipped away. The children played in the streets right under the eyes of their elders, and without any of the modern dread which the bicycle, the trolley and the automobile have inspired, and the adult male population discussed the latest turn in politics or canvassed the most recent news. Each household seemed to unite for the time being into but one family, having the same interests, the same anxieties, the same ideas of hospitality and amusement. So it went on, night after night, during the spring and summer, and when winter came each house in turn held sweet converse with its neighbors, unless, indeed, when a sleighing excursion carried practically the whole adult and active population on a wild and health-giving rush along one of the old plank roads. All this is now a thing of the past. We are not so friendly with our neighbors as we were wont to be, for the influx of population is steady and changes are continual. But Brooklyn is still a city of social instincts, and instead of holding forth on a stoop, we now spend our evenings in our clubs and there seek that solace, that kindred association, that inspiration from congenial souls which tends so effectually to lighten the burdens and dissipate the cares of the moiling and toiling of our daily existence and which make life after all seem really worth living.

Ill point of antiquity the credit of being the premier among the existing organizations on Long Island must be given to the Masonic fraternity. The records of the Grand Lodge inform us under date of February 4, 1784, that it was then

"Voted unanimously that the petition of James Gardiner, John Leverel Hudson and Joseph Corwin requesting an Ancient Warrant to form a lodge on Long Island be granted."

There is, however, no further record of this lodge, and, indeed, it is doubtful if it was ever constituted. The three surnames mentioned frequently appear in the annals of the island, but diligent investigation has failed to locate them exactly. It is generally supposed that they were residents of Brooklyn, but even for this there is no warrant. The record shows, however, that in some part of Long Island there were, in 1784, members of the Ancient and Honorable Fraternity in numbers sufficient to think of uniting into a lodge. It is worth noting, too, that the then Grand Master, Bro. William Cock, although a lawyer in New York, was a native of Long Island, and a representative of one of its oldest families.

In 1787, however, another Long Island application for a charter reached the grand body, over which Chancellor R. R. Livingston then presided, this time from brethren at Jamaica. This was granted and Jamaica Lodge was duly constituted on September 5, that year. It does not, however, appear to have gained much headway, and in 1792 surrendered its charter and passed out of existence. In the following year some brethren at Oyster Bay, headed by Moses Blackly, applied for the necessary authority to organize a lodge in that town, and the application was referred to a committee. So far as the records show that ended the matter. Probably the field in that stronghold of Quakerism did not seem to the committee very promising. At all events there is nothing in the minutes to show that they even dignified the application with a report. On March 22, 1793, a lodge was constituted at Huntington, but it seems to have been a weak organization from its very beginning. It struggled on, however, until 1806, when so far as can be ascertained it ceased holding any meetings and was abandoned. Its last master was Ruluf Duryea, but local history concerning him is silent.

On December 7, 1796, application for a warrant for "a lodge in Suffolk county, Long Island, by the name of Suffolk Lodge" was made to the Grand Lodge of New York, and it was at once granted. Grand Lodge was not so particular then as now and little time was wasted either in making Masons or warranting lodges. It was not, however, until March 10 following that the first regular meeting of the new body was held and the lodge "duly opened and in order for business." The officers were installed, the first master being William Wright, a past master of Independent Royal Arch Lodge, No. 2, New York City. The visitors present at the opening meeting were seven brethren from Huntington Lodge, No. 26, and "Brother Fagan from Ireland." The first applicant for initiation was Woodhull Smith, who was afterward passed Fellowcraft March 16 and raised April 11. The lodge increased rapidly at first.

In the course of its opening year it initiated nineteen candidates, the highest number reached in any given twelve months in its entire career. The people around were mostly farmers or seamen, and while the seamen were enthusiastic at first their vocation did not permit them to attend lodge meetings regularly and after a time most of them lost all interest and dropped out. Those who did retain their connection were of little practical use. The lodge was seldom represented in Grand Lodge meetings even by proxies, but it managed to pay its dues with more or less regularity until 1820. In 1822 it was reported in arrears for two years. Long before that it began to decline, and in the seven years from 1806 to 1812 partly inclusive it initiated only seven candidates — in 1806, 1807 and 1811 two in each year, in 1810 one, and in 1808, 1809 and 1812 none. From 1812 onward things seemed to improve. In 1813 it had three initiations, in 1816 the number reached seven, and in 1820 the records show five additions. From then the story of the lodge is simply that of slow progress to dissolution. Even in 1816, which looked as if the early success had in a measure returned, of the seven initiates five went no further than the first degree, and in 1820, when there were five initiations, two remained Entered Apprentices to the end of time, so far as Suffolk Lodge was concerned. This, of course, is a bad sign, but the cause for this particular weakness we cannot trace. In spite of many discouragements the lodge met regularly and elected officers each year until December 11, 1822, when J. M. Williamson was elected Master. He does not seem to have been installed, and after that date the meetings were held infrequently and irregularly, the last entry in the old minute book bearing the date of September 14, 1825. That may be accepted as the date of dissolution.

The writer of a manuscript history of the old lodge, from which the facts here set forth have been gleaned, comments on the downfall of this lodge in words which are as applicable to the craft at this date as they were when written nearly forty years ago. He wrote: "Two causes may be found for this decline. First, too little care was taken in the examination of the characters of persons proposed for membership. So far as the minutes show there was not always a committee of inquiry appointed, but the candidate was proposed, received and initiated at the same meeting. It was this want of due discrimination in the admission of members which explains a fact that appears on the records, viz., that in 1805 there were more suspensions and more of lodge discipline than through all the existence of the lodge. The other cause which may account for the decline of the lodge was the neglect of the brethren to pay their dues regularly. It is not certain that they always paid the fees for degrees. At a meeting of the lodge in February, 1800, when it had been organized three years and had about thirty members, a note in the treasurer's accounts states that there was 'Cash on hand, $64.19; due from members, $103.75.' Four years afterward the state of the finances was in a still worse condition, the report being $221.80 due from members and no cash at all in the treasury. It was this un-Masonic conduct in the members not paying dues, and the neglect of the lodge in not using its power of discipline that led to its extinction in the end. A very brief examination into this will teach a lesson which the wise among Masons will be ready to learn." So far as we can learn the body fulfilled all its duties perfectly with the exception detailed in the above quotation. We have, of course, no idea of how the "work" was rendered, but we may conclude it was at least equal to that of the other Long Island lodges. It observed the two saints' days, sometimes by a dinner, sometimes by a sermon, sometimes by book, and it readily responded to all claims upon its charity. One lamentable feature of the records is the amount of ill feeling that seemed to prevail among the brethren or some of them. As early as 1799 we find a committee at work straightening out a quarrel between two brethren. The committee reported and the report was accepted, but what they did report the minutes do not state. The compiler of the manuscript says: "In 1802 two brethren were called to account by the lodge itself and a committee appointed. This committee duly reported that although the said I. B. and S. C. may be considered as respectable members of society, they, as Masons, have acted without the square and compass and ought to be considered as refractory members until something favorable on their side may be produced.' In 1805 the lodge became more severe. Brother S. S. was called upon to answer the following charges presented against him by a committee appointed for the purpose: 1. Refusing to discharge his dues; 2. non-attendance at lodge meetings; 3. slandering and injustice to his brethren. S. S. pleaded guilty to the first two, but defended himself against the third. The lodge after considering the defense proceeded to ballot for his expulsion and the ballot was unanimous."

Another brother was charged with "defrauding the fatherless and the widow," but the minutes do not show what was done with him. In 1802 the lodge was summoned to examine into a "matter of difference" between two of its Past Masters. It did examine on the promise of both to abide by the .decision of the brethren, but the one who was held to be in the wrong refused to accept the conclusion arrived at, and the matter was carried into a law court. Such things do not add to the prosperity of a lodge, and the wonder is that old Suffolk carried the banner of Masonry in Setauket for the number of years it was so privileged.

The present Suffolk Lodge, No. 60, which meets at Port Jefferson, claims to be the successor and heir of the old organization with whose history we have just been dealing. The modern No. 60 is a most prosperous body with over one hundred members, and is proud of the earlier lodge whose name it bears. As the old lodge went out of existence in 1824 and the new one was warranted in 1856, it can hardly be said that the theory of continuity is much in evidence. Thirty-two years is a long time in American Masonic history, and that fact makes us feel that the connection between the old lodge and the new is one of sentiment rather than continuity. But then sentiment is a powerful factor in all that concerns the fraternity.

The year 1797, when Suffolk Lodge was chartered, was a busy one, apparently, among the Freemasons on Long Island. Morton Lodge at Hempstead was then organized and still continues, having celebrated its centennial with great éclat June 23, 1897, when Grand Master Sutherland and a host of dignitaries took part in the proceedings. It was probably an offshoot from Huntington Lodge, at least the brethren applying for a warrant seemed to be members of that organization. The centennial exercises created quite a degree of interest in local circles, and many stories of the older brethren found their way into print. From these we select two. The first incident is that of two brothers who lived on the north side of the island, perhaps twenty miles from Hempstead. They reached the lodge by what is called the "ride and tie" method. That is, they both started together early in the morning, one riding the single horse on the farm, and the other walking. The rider proceeded to a place agreed upon, where he tied the horse and took up his journey afoot. When the first walker reached the horse he mounted and after passing his walking journey tied the horse again at another place of agreement. So the journey was made to the lodge, and the return on the following morning was a repetition of the scheme.

The second story is told of a man named Piatt Stratton, living near what is now College Point. Stratton was a candidate for Masonry and rode into Hempstead on horseback at about noon. Having looked after his horse in the barn, he went to the hotel through the kitchen, which was as fashionable a way as the front door at the time. In the kitchen he found an old colored cook standing over a great fire in the large chimney place, across which was a gridiron of very ample proportions.

"What's the gridiron for, Aunty?" asked Stratton, to which the old cook replied: "I'se don' know, marsa, zackly, 'cept that the Masons meet ter day an' dey genly uses it when dey meets." This was enough for Stratton. He returned to the barn, mounted his horse and rode off. Nothing was ever heard of him again by the lodge, and he doubtless died in the faith that the gridiron was intended for him.

The various committees who arranged for the celebration of the centennial were as follows, and included the master, Robert A. Davidson, and all the living past masters of the lodge:

Invitations — Wor. Bro. B. Valentine Clowes, Bros. George W. Terry, Carman Lush.

Grand Marshal— R. Wor. Charles L. Phipps. Aids — Lewis H. Clowes, Israel W. Williams, William B. Osterhont, Jotham Post, Henry Floyd Johnson, Royal Harvey.

Railroad and Transportation — R. Wor. Robert A. Davison, Wor. Augustus Denton.

Music — Wor. Bros. Augustus Denton and Oliver E. Stanton.

Press and Printing — Wor. Bros. Oliver E. Stanton, Lot Van de Water, Jr., and B. Valentine Clowes.

Tent and Hall — Bros. Lewis H. Clowes, Eugene V. Willis and John Findlay.

Refreshments — Bros. William M. Akley, Lewis H. Clowes, William McCarthy, Eugene V. Willis, Jotham Post, Foster L. Oakley, Benjamin Griffin, Edward Willis, Morris Sherwood, John Findlay, Richard C. Campbell, Thomas" W. Albertson, Walter N. De Nyse, Israel W. Williams, George W. Terry, John Miller, C. Gardner Miller, William B. Osterhont, William S. Hall, Wor. Oliver E. Stanton.

Decorations — Bro. Richard C. Campbell.

Reception — R. Wors. Robert A. Davison and Charles L. Phipps, Wors, Augustus R. Griffin, Benjamin A. Haff, B. Valentine Clowes, John W. De Mott, Joseph E. Firth, Robert Seabury, Augustus Denton, Lott Van de Water, Oliver E. Stanton and John R. Sprague, Bros. George W. Terry, Israel W. Williams, Richard C. Campbell, Thomas W. Albertson, William McCarthy, M. J. Gildersleeve, Lewis H. Clowes, Walter N. De Nyse, C. Gardner Miller, Joseph H. Bogart, M. D.; C. G. J. Finn, M. D.; Charles F. Lewis, Timothy J. Bird, Thomas B. Seaman, Thomas J. Sammond, Charles Davison, Samuel S. Rhame, William H. Patterson, William S. Hall, John Miller, William P. Miller, Foster L. Oakley, George Emery, Eugene V. Willis, William B. Osterhout.

In 1797, too, the first known Brooklyn lodge of which we have any record — St. Alban's — was constituted. There are vague indications that, apart from the lodge warranted in 1784 and which, as has been pointed out, may or may not have been a Brooklyn body, there was one lodge existing there prior to 1797 — Mechanics, No. 1. But all we know about that is its name. About St. Alban's Lodge we certainly know little more. It only existed for about two years, and then it was permitted to disappear. At all events, it was mentioned as "lately held" in the petition presented December 4, 1799, to the Grand Lodge by a number of its members and others for a new warrant under the name of Fortitude Lodge. The warrant was at once issued, and bore the signature of Chancellor Livingston.

That lodge is now undoubtedly the oldest in Brooklyn, and it celebrated its centenary in December, 1899, with a banquet and reception which will long be remembered with pleasure by all who were permitted to take part in the proceedings. The first meeting place of the lodge was in the upper room of a tavern near "the Ferry," as Fulton Ferry was then called, and the keeper of the tavern, Martin Boerum, was one of the charter members. Soon after its institution the lodge was called upon to make its first public appearance, when it took part in the local procession on the death of George Washington, and it marched in one of the processions which, in 1824, welcomed Lafayette on his memorable journey through the country which he had helped to mold into a nation. There was always a good deal of patriotic sentiment in Fortitude Lodge when occasion arose, and it was one of the lodges which, in 1814, under the immediate direction of the Grand Lodge, helped to build the fortifications around Brooklyn and so protect it from the British invasion then expected.

Fortitude has had its ups and downs like all our older lodges, but it managed to pull through, although it was hard pressed in 1832, when an epidemic of cholera made things unpleasant in Brooklyn. The history tells us that "the first record of the conferring of degrees was on January 13, 1806. The fee for each degree was two dollars, but at a meeting oi the lodge held January 20, 1806, the fee for each degree was raised to five dollars." The history also tells us that "refreshments appear to have been an important part of the proceedings of the lodge. The amounts of money spent for this purpose ranged all the way from five dollars to sixty dollars per night. Upon the night of November 16, 1812, there is the record in the minutes of a charge of £41 12s 10d. which is something over two hundred dollars. The regular refreshments for meeting nights during the earlier history of the lodge were cheese, crackers and wines." "Besides this the records show that the expenditures for charity were continuous and liberal. How they managed it all, with their small income, I cannot understand, unless it be that the brethren "chipped in" very frequently and that fines were liberally imposed and willingly paid. The great curse of all our early lodges was the drinking habit. When they went to refreshment the brethren went in reality instead of symbolically, as we do at present, and the junior warden's duties as superintendent of the feast meant more than mere words. But the costliness of the custom led to its abolition, although some of the lodges had to adopt heroic measures before the abolition was complete. Had the habit not been stopped we would have had a very different history of Freemasonry in New York than that to which, in the language of the political platform makers, we now 'point with pride.' Our early brethren, both here and in Britain, were jolly fellows and the lodges were often places of pleasant retreat, where the flowing bowl and the merry song made life seem rosier and happier than in the currents of life appeared possible. They performed their Masonic work with dignity and with care, they were scrupulous, possibly more scrupulous than we are in these days of rush and commercialism, as to who they admitted to their charmed circle, they zealously fulfilled all the Masonic duties they professed, and when they turned from their labors to 'rest and refresh themselves' they did it with a thoroughness and abandon that sometimes stagger us, as we read the story. In many instances the records of the old lodges tell us more of the refreshment episode than of the incidents of the time devoted to work, the old 'monitors' and 'companions' and 'vade-mecums' present us with page after page of the songs and glees and 'catches' they used to sing, and as most of the poetry is miserable doggerel, and refers to drinking, love making and law defiance, we are apt to get rather a poor opinion of the morals and manners of the early brethren unless we probe a little beneath the surface. But give these fathers "all the credit to which they are entitled, it is impossible to study the Freemasonry of 1800 and that of 1900 without coming to the conclusion that the craft is one of the most progressive of organizations; that if it holds as steadfastly as possible to the old landmarks, it is earnestly seeking forth after new ones. "To me, the most interesting part of Masonic study has been, not its rules, not even its ritual, but the character and standing of the men who have been prominent in its ranks. If Masonry has been worth anything, if it has really proved a moral factor, if its philosophy is sound, it cannot have failed' to impress itself upon the lives and thoughts and aspirations of those who have been prominently identified with it. Fortitude Lodge has had quite a number of brethren on its roll who have won a measure of fame, sometimes local, it is true, hut still sufficient to show that they were distinguished above their fellows, and who can say that the teachings and mellowing and broadening influence of the lodge did not aid these men in winning such distinctions and honors as they received? The first master of Fortitude Lodge, Dr. George A. Clussman, who held the office until the close of 1801, was the most prominent physician of the time in Brooklyn, and although physicians, like actors, are soon forgotten when they cross old Charon's ferry, this man's memory is still held in sweet remembrance in the story of the community in which he lived and labored. Fortitude's first Senior Warden (afterward Master), Daniel Rhoades, was a grocer and a soldier, and in the war of 1812 was a member of the military company locally known as 'the Katy-dids,' which failed to win national renown only because the British forces did not come to this neighborhood during that struggle with the old country. Still though the opportunity did not come, Rhoades and his comrades proved that they were ready to meet it. The more notable of the early officers, however, was the junior warden, Henry Eckford, the greatest shipbuilder of his time. A native of Scotland, but a typical American citizen, he constructed most of the vessels which on the Great Lakes won so much fame in the war of 1812 for the American navy. The once famous battleship Ohio and many other noted war vessels were built from his designs, and in fact he was the reconstructor of our navy at the time when America successfully wrested from Great Britain— for a while, at least — the undisputed sovereignty of the seas. He afterward went to Turkey and became chief naval constructor for that country. He died in 1832. All his biographers bear witness to the loyalty and sweetness of his disposition, to his true Christian spirit and to his possession of every true Masonic virtue."

The first chaplain of the United States Navy, the Rev. John Ireland, was also a member of Fortitude Lodge. He was one of the chaplains of the Grand Lodge. Another brother of Fortitude who held this honor was the Rev. Evan M. Johnson, one of the most notable of the long list of clergymen who have made the name of Brooklyn famous as "the City of Churches." He was a zealous worker in the Master's service, freely gave of his own means to the cause in which he labored, and for years preached without fee or reward, building one or two churches where they were needed — among the poorer classes of the city — among the lapsed masses. He was a roan of rare courage, and in the pulpit and out of it never hesitated to proclaim his loyalty to Masonry even in days when persecution was abroad and zealous Masons were content to hide their light under a bushel. It is singular that men like Ireland and Johnson did not hold the appointment of Chaplain in the lodge, but from the list in the volume now published it would seem that such officials were not formally recognized and appointed until 1864.

Masonically, probably the best known name on the long list of members of Fortitude Lodge is that of Nathaniel F. Waring, who was its master in 1834 and again in 1848. For many years he was one of the most active Masons in New York, and came into special prominence in connection with what is known as the Phillips Grand Lodge. He was elected grand master of that body in 1857, and when it was received into the legitimate Masonic fold in 1858 he, according to the agreement, carried with him into "the" Grand Lodge his honors as a past grand master. We can hardly regard him, even when in opposition to the regular Grand Lodge, as being clandestine, for his opposition was based upon honest principle, and he was an honest man, one of those who would rather be right than be president, as the saying goes.

Fortitude Lodge at present is a flourishing body of craftsmen. It has some two hundred members on its roll, and ranks high among the lodges of Brooklyn. It is fully conscious of its position as a representative lodge, is proud of its antiquity, and is a splendid example of that Masonic spirit which with one hand holds steadfastly to the past and with the other reaches out for all that is beautiful and worthy and commendable in the days which are passing over us.

On July 26, 1804, a lodge was constituted at Sag Harbor, but it passed out of existence in 1818, and appears to have had a struggle for existence until 1818, when it disappeared. An interesting history of this lodge and its successor, the Wamponamon Lodge of the present day, has been written by one of the Past Masters of the latter. Brother Brinley D. Sleight, which we here reproduce:

During the first decade of the present century the Masonic fraternity established its organization in Sag Harbor. The first officers of Hampton Lodge, No. ill, were: Elias Jones, Master; Ithuel Hill, Senior Warden; Joel Fordham, Junior Warden; Moses Clark, Treasurer; Benjamin K. Hobart, Secretary; John Godbee, Senior Deacon; Aaron Clark, Junior Deacon; John Morrison, Tyler.

Five years afterward we find the same officers in the East and West, with Nathaniel Havens, Junior Warden, and Luther Hildreth, Secretary. The list of members comprised about fifty well-known citizens, — names famous in the historic annals of the east end of Long Island, such as Howell, Hildreth, Worth, Crowell, Jennings, Gardiner, Glover, Bishop, Briggs, Baker, Conkling, Hedges, Harris, Topping, Seabury and others. The communications of the brethren were held in the attic of the house of Moses Clark, on the corner of Division and Union streets. The house is still standing, having been moved further up the street, next south of the residence of Miss Julia King.

Hampton Lodge, No. iii, was at that time the only civic society in Sag Harbor. Neither were there military, firemen's or other organizations. The mystery attached to the name and ceremonies of the order lent an attractive interest to every occasion when the brethren appeared in public, and well-accredited tradition says that the schools were dismissed, and the people turned out en masse "to see the Masons parade."

After a while fraternal activity languished, and eventually in 1819 the lodge surrendered Its charter, having for fifteen years been "steadfastly held in the Port of Sag Harbor." About this time politics infested Masonry. In 1827-30 exciting partisan contests followed, in which anti-Masonic sentiment was a powerful agency.

On the east end of Long Island all Masonic affiliation was abandoned. For thirty-eight years thereafter the Masons had no habitation in Sag Harbor, but in 1857 some brethren from other jurisdictions abiding among us, together with the few remaining members of Hampton Lodge, mindful of the precept, "once a Mason always a Mason," concerted to institute a new lodge. Others desirous of joining the order were initiated, passed, and raised in Peconic Lodge, No. 349, of Greenport, with the understanding that they were to become charter members of the new organization when the requisite number was obtained. The charter members of the new lodge were: Henry S. Roscoe, Eastern Star, No. 227, New York City; Joseph Stanton, Widow's Son Lodge, North Stonington, Connecticut; Charles H. Reeves, Star of the East, New Bedford, Massachusetts; J. W. Nickerson, Lebanon, New York City; Noah Washburne, Jacob Leek, Thaddeus Coles, Nathan T. Fordham, Zebulon Elliott, of defunct Hampton Lodge, No. Ill, and James E. Smith, Roswell Warner, Thomas Lister, Nathaniel Dominy, John Stein, John R. Sayre, P. H. Douglas, raised in Peconic Lodge, Greenport. These sixteen men having taken the obligation and agreed, to dwell together in unity, established Wamponamon Lodge, No. 437, F. & A. M. The name was settled upon after thoughtful consideration. There were those who desired the old name and number to be retained. "Hampton" had local signification, and the three units were unique and easily fixed in the memory. Besides, they indicated seniority in the list of Masonic lodges. But the newly-initiated brethren wished to imprint their own individuality upon their offspring, and so they literally "left the west and traveled east" in search of a new name. Wamponamon is the

Indian appellation for the easternmost point of the promontory of Montauk, and signifies "to the eastward." It is found in the records of the town of Easthampton, and a correlative term in the Indian deeds. It is quaint, original and not likely to be appropriated by other societies.

The first men made Masons in Sag Harbor under the new order of things were: Joshua B. Nickerson, Abner D. Smith, William White, William L. Parsons, Sylvester F. Brown. They were raised under a dispensation in January, 1858, the charter of the lodge not being issued until the June following. The lodge was dedicated on June 16, A. L. 5858, and on the same occasion the following officers were duly installed: Henry S. Roscoe, W. M.; James E. Smith, S. W.; Roswell Warner, J. W.; Joseph Stanton, Treasurer; Sylvester F. Brown, Secretary; Nathaniel Dominy, Senior Deacon; Pulaski A. Douglas, Junior Deacon; Thomas Lister and William White, Masters of Ceremonies; Noah Washburn, Tyler.

The first meetings were held in the rooms of Suffolk Lodge, I. O. O. F. Afterward the third story of the south side of the present Nassau House building was obtained. It was furnished not without elegance and comfort, in part due to the good taste and generosity of Dr. Frederick Crocker, for many years treasurer of the lodge.

In 1883 it became necessary to look about for a new home. After the consideration of various schemes it was duly determined to purchase the old Presbyterian Church, then owned by the Episcopal society. A contract of sale was signed with the vestry of Christ Church on December 17, 1883. A fund was raised by bonding the property, which, together with the moneys already accumulated, provided for a thorough reconstruction of the building. The present Masonic Hall is the result. The new hall was opened with a festival and promenade concert on July 8th next ensuing. On the evening of November 20th following, the ceremonies of dedicating the new lodge room were impressively conducted by Right Worshipful Frank R. Lawrence, Deputy Grand Master of Masons, and his associate officers of the Grand Lodge. Public addresses were also given in the large hall, and a collation served in Crowell's Hall. The occasion was a memorable one. Thus, the structure originally erected in 1817 for the worship of God was again consecrated to the Supreme Architect of the Universe and dedicated to the memories of the Holy Saints John.

It may not be inappropriate to refer, in passing, to the early Masters of the lodge, those who have gone before us, who have seen the Great Light, and who are now no more among the living.

Henry S. Roscoe, the first Master, was a swarthy, dark-eyed man, with black hair and flowing beard. He was of dignified demeanor, well up in his work, and a conscientious believer in the tenets of Freemasonry. Restless and nervous, and something of a nomad, he went from this place to East Hampton, and thence to Connecticut, where he died.

The second Worshipful in the East was James E. Smith, an active business man, identified with our early prosperity as a commercial mart. He came here from Connecticut when a young man, and lived here until his death. His final mercantile venture was the building of a vessel at the foot of Main street. It was the last one built in Sag Harbor, and was sent to the Pacific coast, where it still bears on its stern the square and compasses which signalized its bridal with the sea, in the waters of our bay.

Joshua B. Nickerson succeeded Captain Smith. He had been one of the argonauts in the search for gold in California. He returned home, having been more successful than many others. Entering into the business activities of our village, a prosperous career was before him, but the insidious disease, consumption, cut him off in the strength of his manhood.

Following came Captain A. Smith French, a typical whaleman, in our characteristic whaling times. More than once had he circumnavigated the globe carrying the emblems of Masonry and Masonic charity to the confines of the earth. He was raised in Hawaiian Lodge, No. 21, Sandwich Islands, but was a native of this county. He sleeps beneath the quiet shades of Oakland cemetery. Next came Abner D. Smith, merchant and citizen of good repute, methodical, correct, attentive, who served the lodge with fidelity and zeal, both as Master and Secretary, for several years. William H. Gleason, a graduate of Yale, wielded the gavel after Smith. A scholar, a politician, a lawyer and a divine, his life work was well done and his career active and; honorable.

Of those who have more recently occupied the East, but who have passed beyond the veil, are Benjamin F. Huntting, whose name is especially associated with the purchase and reconstruction of the present hall. He was the chairman of the Building Committee and threw all the enthusiasm of his nature into the work, making it a labor of love, and Thomas F. Bisgood, whom we have so lately borne to the silent tomb, a wise counselor, a steadfast and genial friend. These are "the dead but sceptered sovereigns who rule our spirits from their urns."

The lodge was constituted but three years before the beginning of the war of the Rebellion. Our numbers were few, but Wamponamon supplied its honorable quota to the list of self-sacrificing heroes who voluntarily imperiled their lives in defense of the Union. Dr. L. D. Hall, one of the early initiates, and Drayson Fordred, another, a promising young man, were killed upon the field of battle. Several returned after having won the laurels of honorable conflict.

Among the living members who have achieved Masonic distinction may be mentioned David A. Emory, who has found light in .the East, having become a Deputy Grand Master of the Northern District of the Empire of China. He is still a resident of the Flowery Kingdom. The brother of longest official record is Right Worshipful Elbridge G. Howard, who, in a period of twenty years, extending from 1869 to 1889, occupied the Master's station twelve times. In 1884 he was made Deputy Grand Master for this district.

There have been memorable occasions in our history which can only be alluded to here, as matters of record. Conspicuous among these are the public installation, given in December, 1884, and previous to this, in the same eventful year, the entertainment of July 8th, and the dedication of the lodge, November 24th. The commemoration of the emancipation from debt of the order in the State was duly observed April 24, 1889, and the celebration of the one thousandth communication of the lodge en May 2, 1895, was a jubilee of fraternal interest transcendent in our annals. In this festivity Peconic Lodge, of Greenport, joined with us in a body. The whole membership of Wamponamon Lodge since the beginning numbers two hundred and ninety-four. There are now living, and in good standing, one hundred and twenty Master Masons, who have traveled the same road and are bound by the same ties of brotherhood.

May the mystic bond never be loosened. Fresh as the green sward upon the promontory whose name it bears, may the memoryof our lodge forever be; bright as the beacon light from its headlands, which bids God-speed to the parting traveler; glad as its beckoning rays that cheer the homeward bound, may its future ever shine. Long live Wamponamon! Esto perpetua!

In 1808 a lodge was warranted at Newtown, which seems to have flourished about a decade and then passed away. It was one of the lodges which, in the panic of 1814, worked a couple of days on the Brooklyn fortifications, but that is about the only glimpse of it which we get. Then, so far as can be learned, Hohenlinden Lodge, No. 338, organized in 1821, and still extant, and Naval Lodge, No. 391, warranted in 1826, but which almost on receipt of its charter abandoned it, were the other lodges instituted on Long Island prior to the outbreak of the Morgan controversy, which played such havoc with Freemasonry all over the North American continent, compelled hundreds of lodges and chapters to pass out of existence, raised up a powerful if short-lived, political party, attempted to seat a President in the White House and almost brought about the complete annihilation of the Masonic fraternity.

From that persecution the craft slowly recovered and in time was restored to its old strength. Long Island felt the change, although it was not until about 1852 that the upward movement still going on may be said to have fairly begun. In that year the whole of Long Island was united with Staten Island and several Hudson River counties into the First Masonic District. In 1859 Long Island was divided. Kings county being placed in the Third Masonic District and Suffolk and Queens in the Fourth. In 1868 Kings county itself was made the Fourth District and in 1873 it was divided. Frequent changes, as a natural result of the wonderful progress made by the fraternity, finally resulted in Long Island being divided into three districts — the first three on the roll of the Grand Lodge — and that arrangement seems destined to endure. According to the latest official returns there are now on Long Island about fourteen thousand members of the fraternity and seventy-six lodges. In addition there are a great many members of the fraternity residing in Kings county and in Queens borough who are members of lodges meeting on Manhattan Island. Taking that into account it is safe to estimate the entire membership of the craft on Long Island at nearly twenty thousand.

About the date of this writing there is a movement on foot looking to the erection of a Masonic Hall in Brooklyn. That there is need of such a structure is apparent to every one; and that the brethren in the borough are numerous enough, wealthy enough and influential enough to make such a movement successful if it is proceeded with, there is no doubt. Yet there are so many things to be considered that a natural conservatism is apparent about actually beginning the work. At the same time an option on a site has been secured, quite a large sum has been pledged and an outline architectural scheme has been prepared and so the matter rests, awaiting developments. In the meanwhile, as may be seen from the statistical tables already given, the Brooklyn lodges, as well as the chapters and commanderies, meet in apartments and halls scattered all over the borough. What might be called the headquarters of the fraternity is the structure known as the Aurora Grata Cathedral, the local home of the Scottish Rite bodies, the Mystic Shrine of many lodges and of the Aurora Grata Club, the leading Masonic social organization of the borough. The Aurora Grata Club was organized in 1887, and has some four hundred members, all connected with the Masonic fraternity. The building fit occupies was formerly the parsonage of the Bedford Dutch Reformed Church, and is a comfortable, roomy structure, but the good old dominies of that closely Calvinistic body would hold up their hands in pious horror could they see the improvements and changes which the Masonic brethren have introduced. Even what used to be the holy man's study — his sanctum sanctorum — is almost nightly — in season, of course — given over to merry parties; and there are bowling alleys, billiard tables, a reading room and all other accessories of an up-to-date social club. Adjoining the house occupied by the Aurora Grata Club is the cathedral of the same name — the old Reformed Dutch Church — now adapted for Scottish Rite and other Masonic purposes. The Brooklyn Veterans' Association meets in the basement, and in one corner is their library, a small but wonderfully useful and well selected collection of books. The building itself has seen its best days and the wind on a stormy night seems to have free access to the several apartments. A modern Masonic temple is certainly needed in Brooklyn. The Brooklyn Masonic Veterans' Association is one of the best and grandest developments of the social side of Freemasonry of which we have knowledge. All members must have belonged to the .fraternity for at least twenty-five years and all are therefore men who have passed at least into mid-life, but the organization's motto, "The best of life is yet to come," shows how they face the setting sun slowly sinking in the west. The Veterans' annual dinners are possibly the jolliest "functions" of their kind which we know. They combine a splendid bill of fare, splendid singing and some of the best after-dinner oratory heard in Brooklyn. They are generally attended by the most active Masons in Brooklyn, as witness the following partial list of those at the gathering of 1901:

Josephus L. Wood, president of the Brooklyn Masonic Veterans; Henry A. Powell, A. H. Nichols, E. W. Mascord, John W. Richardson, James T. Burdick, John H. Visscher, Richard E. Shaw, C. K. G. Visscher, Sidney L. Rowland, Charles F. Bloom, Claudius F. Beatty. Andrew B. Martin, Joseph H. Cummin, Dr. James T. Terhune, Frederick L. Jenkins, C. W. Hubbell, Rufus L. Scott, John S. Mowry, Edward A. Dubey, R. Van Valkenburgh, Joseph C. Abell, W. T. Ramsbotham. Commodore Edward Hooker. William Van Sise, Charles A. Shaw, J. K. Van Sise, Frank Mapes, J. Carlisle Loudon, John W. Palmer, John T. Palmer, J. Fred Marble, Lee C. Moore, Augustus C. Tate, John W. Mott, L. E. Nicholson, Charles W. Held, George W. Foote, Frank E. Wilson, Dr. J. J. Terhune, W. O. Cloges, Stephen W. T. Tennant, J. Harris Balston, Wilmon Whilldin, Howard W. Ennis, George W. Arnold, Abram H. Dailey, Robert Rogers, James A. Babcock, Theophilus: Pratt, Herman Canter, Thomas Heilson. William E. Stein, Lawrence MacNaughton, Charles S. Buell, D. G. Griffiths, Daniel J. Morrison, W. H. Armstrong, Theodore Thieler, John Cuthbert, W. J. Smith, Charles W. Hayes, W. Westlake, C. O. Cowtan, Joseph W. Ray, David S. Bruen, Obediah Harned, Thomas W. Corrigan, William P. Christmas, William H. Johnson, Gustavus C. Weber, John C. Waldron, James D. Wright, Wi .A. Mathies, F. Frederick Lenhart, Alfred Sims, W. J. Allen, Augustus W. Boerner, Joseph H. Loomis, W. A. Campbell, Eli R. Denniston; J. W. Smith, A. E. Leach, Louis Nathan, Rudolph R. Bennett, Isaac Hicks, James E. Martin, G. B. Martin, J. R. Bennett, J. M. Kerrigan, L. A. Lewis, J. T. Ross, Harry T. Cook, J. W. Hawkes, W. H. Jamton, John K. Torfts, James Divisch, Charles Christmas, James L. Waldon, J. G. Ramee, Dr. W. T. Millington, E. L. Spike, T. M. Goddard, Charles Goddard, D. M. Meninger, I. Dunn, Colo Venoni, Isaac S. Waters, Edwin Selvage, Judah Moses, James Parsons, James Macbeth, W. H. Steers, S. Wasserman, Samuel Steinbrink, Washington Irving Comes, William M. Clark, G. Turner, J. W. Stopford, H. McKeon, B. A. Levett, H. A. Aechtemacht, Almet R. Latson, H. G. Buswell, A. E. Biederman, George W. Wilson, John W. Carme, George W. Brown, James A. Byxbee, William L. Burke, William Burns, Henry Scheele, Herman Pietsch, M. L. Mann, George W. Cook, G. Greve, C. F. Graves, William Cheviton. Charles Schabaker, William H. Phillips, George S. Patton, Joseph M. Cord, Robert E. A. L. Estrange, H. T. Giberson, John Fleming Duncan, Walter MacBain, Charles G. Smith, Elmer E. Cain, William Clowninzer, James Sinn, Dr.W. H.

Clowninzer, Henry A. Phillips, Henry E. Tuthill, Burton AI. Balsh and Thomas G. Singleton.

At the dinner of 1893 addresses were delivered by three prominent citizens of Brooklyn— William Sherer, chairman of the New York Clearing House; "Deacon" William Richardson and Mr. St. Clair McKelway, of the Brooklyn Eagle. These addresses are so elevated in tone and so full of interest to the general reader that we are tempted to reprint them here:

Brother William Sherer responded to the toast of the Grand Lodge, saying: "I am here to-night for the purpose of partaking of this banquet and do what I can to extend the brotherly feeling in Brooklyn. It was my assignment, I believe, to speak for another Grand Body, the 'Grand Chapter.' I loaded myself with sufficient ammunition, I thought, to do execution in that direction; I come here and find that owing to the absence of our Grand Master I am called upon to fill in space to be occupied by either of those gentlemen, so that much abused institution, the Grand Lodge of the State of New York, that has suffered so often at my hands, is again to be a victim to-night. Brethren, you know the story of the Grand Lodge, now one hundred and twelve years old, representing the constituencies of seven hundred and fifty lodges formed with us. You know the purpose for which this annual assemblage of Masons is held. You know every lodge in this State, no matter how small or how large, is afforded equal representation in your own Grand Lodge, and you know the voice of the representative of the most humble New York body receives as much attention as though he came from the most desirable one in the State, and for harmony, dignity and justice of ruling the Grand Lodge of the State of New York sets an example that the several Houses of Congress and State Legislature may well follow. And it is this fact that will, in years to come, as it has in years that have passed, be of great importance to the fraternity in this State, and when you come to think that this Grand Body, without danger and without confusion, represents a grand feeling of brotherhood extending amongst more than one hundred thousand men, then you see the force that there is in that body. Representatives of more than one hundred thousand men are there to legislate, for what? In the interest of "brotherly love and respect for all that is good. No matter what may be a man's political opinion, no matter what may be his religious, creed, if he believes in our recognized Supreme Being and in the brotherhood of man, he finds his representative and his place. Socialists, anarchists, reformers and national men have tried for ages to find the panacea for human wounds, but I will tell you that the solution rests alone in this fact and in this condition, when men will treat' their brother men as brethren, when they will do to them as they expect to be done by, then we will have no need of reformation in anything. Now, Brethren, we do not pretend, we do not claim, to stand in the place of any man's creed or religion, but we do believe that we have the foundation of all that is good and substantial, the foundation of every creed, and that is love to God and love to all. Our Grand Lodge during its one hundred and twelve years of existence has exalted all that I have just mentioned in these few brief words. That your several Grand Bodies have other uses I will not deny. You cannot compel every man to follow in the same rut and in the same line, and if a man finds that his usefulness to his fellow man and his usefulness in Masonic circles is growing by taking an interest in the other lodges, they give him freedom to go there, but never lose sight of this fact, that the Grand Lodge Of the State of New York, through whom indirectly the authority came to bring this association to light, is the mother of all that stands for Freemasonry in the grand State of New York.

"It has been my great good" fortune to be a" member of that body for twenty-four years. I have sat under the gavel of many Grand Masters that have passed away; I have sat under the gavel of so many of them that to-night I cannot recall their names, but I have yet to see a-man in that position and in the chair who has ever given way to personal spite or personal feelings in carrying out the official position in which his brethren placed him. Now, Brethren, recollect, he who serves you so serves without the hope of reward. There is no salary attached to the office of Grand Master of the New York Body, nor for many years past has one ever thought that his position was any reason why he should go before his fellow citizens as candidate for any office. "We are enabled by our great system of brotherhood to eliminate partisanship and every selfish motive and every other motive which might bring us down from the pinnacle upon which we stand."

Brother William Richardson, responding to the toast of the Brooklyn Masonic Veterans, said: "It is with a feeling of pride that we recognize ourselves this evening to be Masonic Veterans. The City of Brooklyn, by reason of recent events, is well and favorably known amongst all the cities of the world. It has been the fashion amongst a certain class of Brooklyn men, when traveling, to register themselves as from 'New York.' That time has passed by. Hereafter, in registering, no man will be loath to put himself down as from Brooklyn. It was claimed by St. Paul, of old, that he was 'a citizen of no mean city,' and we can certainly claim, in view of recent events, that we are 'citizens of no mean city,' and one which contains very few mean people.

"The motto of our Association is 'The best of life is yet to come;' and that is a worthy motto for those whom' we may look upon as being amongst the 'sifted wheat' of the Masonic lodges of this city. "After the length of experience which we must attain before being eligible to membership in the Masonic Veterans, we may reasonably — and without too much egotism — look upon ourselves as illustrations of the truth of the doctrine of 'the survival of the fittest.' But while we can more thoroughly and sensibly enjoy the present, one of the most important things for us to feel and enjoy is the hope of the future, that 'the best of life' is yet to come, — not merely during the few more years which we may spend here, but in the life eternal in that great beyond. In this connection you will pardon me if I recite a few verses written by Thomas Campbell, a Scotch poet, who lived the latter part of the last century and the earlier part of this. For the theology of the poem in a critical sense I will not vouch; for the poetry of it I am willing to be held responsible:

" 'All worldly shapes shall melt,
The Sun himself must die in gloom,
Before this mortal shall assume
Its immortality.
I saw a vision in my sleep
That gave my spirit strength to sweep
Adown the gulf of Time.
I saw the last of human mould
That shall creation's death Behold,
As Adam saw her prime.
" 'The Sun's eye had a sickly glare.
The Earth with age was wan,
The skeletons of nature were
Around that lonely man.
Some had expired in fight: the brands
Still rusted in their bony hands;
In plague and famine some.
Earth's cities had no sound nor tread,
And ships were drifting with the dead
To shores where all was dumb.
" 'Yet, prophet-like, that lone one stood,
With dauntless words and high.
That shook the sere leaves from the wood
As if a storm passed by.
Saying, we are twins in death, proud Sun.
Thy face is cold, thy race is run;
'Tis mercy bids thee go;
For thou ten thousand thousand years
Hast seen the tide of human tears,
That shall no longer flow.
" 'Go, let oblivion's curtain fall
Upon the stage of men,
Nor with thy rising beams recall
Life's tragedy again.
My lips that speak the dirge of death.
Their rounded gasp and gurgling breath
To see thou shalt not boast.
The eclipse of nature spreads my pall.

The majesty of darkness shall
Receive my parting ghost.
" 'Go, Sun, while mercy holds me up
On nature's awful waste,
To drink this last and bitter cup
Of grief that man shall taste:
Go tell the night that hides thy face,
Thou saw'st the last of Adam's race,
On earth's sepulchral clod.
The darkening universe defy
To quench his immortality
Or shake his trust in God.'

"It was well said by the old patriarch of Uz, Job: "For I know that my Redeemer liveth; and that He shall stand at the latter day upon the earth: and though after my skin worms destroy this body, yet in my flesh shall I see God, Whom shall I see for myself and mine eyes shall behold, and not another, though my reins be consumed within me.' Again, another patriarch who lived long after him, the Psalmist, King of Israel, cried out in ecstasy: 'As for me, I shall behold Thy face in righteousness, I shall be satisfied when I awake with Thy likeness;' and in this connection I may again quote the lines of a poet:

" 'There is a land where every pulse is thrilling
With rapture, earth's sojourners may not know;
Where heaven's repose the weary heart is stilling:
And peacefully life's time-tossed currents flow.
'Thither our weak and weary steps are tending;
Savior and Lord! with Thy frail children bide.
Guide us towards home, where, all our wanderings ending,
We shall see Thee and 'shall be satisfied.' "

"But, while we have the duties of life here, we must not be entirely engrossed with the thoughts of the best of life being yet to come, even in the great hereafter."

President Haskell in response to the toast, "The Mason as a citizen," said: "Even those who are skeptical as to the extent to which Masonry controls men's actions, will admit that if tenets of Masonry are made the rules of men's lives there will be better sons, better fathers and better citizens."

St. Clair McElway, responding to the same sentiment, "The Mason as a Citizen," said: "Every American Mason should be a good American citizen. I do not so far lay out the duties of other men as to say that every American citizen should be a Mason, but I do say that of every American citizen were a Mason some questions which are now before the public would be settled at once and forever. There would be no question in such a case about the eternal divorce between Church and State. There would be no question in such a case about an end at once and forever of legislative appropriations to sectarian schools. There would be in citizenship, as there are in Masonry by legitimate evolution, natural and qualified leadership. For a thousand years Masonry has been the epitome of an honest registration and an honest vote. The last twenty years our country has witnessed the deterioration of the legislative arm of government, but in Masonry the legislative arm represented by our Grand Lodge of this and other States, and of other nations, was never stronger, was never purer, never more simple, never more worthily trusted, and never more universally respected than now. In the one hundred and twelve years of its existence it has commanded the approbation of man, the allegiance of the Brethren, and it has deserved, not only the considerate judgment of mankind, but it has received, whether in adversity or prosperity, the gracious favor of Almighty God. Masonry was invisible in the duties of citizenship and ever should be. It was, however, much invisible, not unfelt, not unfelt in its professional, its fraternal capacity, but strongly felt in the underlying principle of the golden rule and the brotherhood of man and the equal rights of all before the law, which are the foundation stones of this supreme, magnificent order. As Masons we know what our charter is, we know where we got it, we know to whom we owe allegiance and obligations under it, and we know its invaluable advantage to our order. Now let us as Masons believe what we please concerning protection, believe what we please concerning revenue reform or free trade, believe what we please concerning sound money, but let us bear in mind that home affairs are not political affairs, that neighborhood affairs are not State affairs. Under the Declaration of Independence the right of man to liberty is regulated by law. I congratulate you upon your numbers and your enthusiasm, and I thank you for your courteous attention. I regret that I have not been able in previous years to be with you. To-night, I am, if you will allow me to indulge in a personal remark, so fatigued with labor finished, and yet awaiting me, that I hardly hoped to be with you. I have been brought into good company, and this will become a pleasure of memory; associated with other occasions of our brotherhood down at the St. George, where I have met them at the festive board, and is suggestive of a few verses, which I think I can remember, although I would not dare match my poor memory alongside of the magnificent mental faculty of the Deacon, whom I found but did not make, and in labelling him I had only acknowledged the fitness of things.

" 'There is an isle.
And the name of that isle is the Long Ago;
And we bury our treasures there;
There are brows of beauty and bosoms of snow.
There are heaps of dust; but we loved them so;
There are trinkets and tresses of hair.
" 'There are fragments of songs that nobody sings,

And a part of an infant's prayer,
There's a harp unswept, and a lute without strings,
There are broken vows and pieces of rings,
And the garments she used to wear.
" 'Oh. remembered for aye be that blessed isle,
All the days of our life fill night,
And when the evening comes with its beautiful smile.
And our eyes are closing in slumber awhile,
' May that 'Greenwood' of soul be in sight.""

"What manner of men may these Freemasons be," is a question that was once asked in London when the fraternity began to attract notice outside of their lodge-rooms, and it is a question that is often asked even yet wherever Freemasons by their numbers stand out in bold relief in any community. So far as Brooklyn is concerned the roll of membership of the various lodges might be said to include the foremost representatives of every walk and condition in life, ministers and mechanics, bankers, lawyers, political war-horses, teachers, merchants and professional men of all sorts. The writer of this has an abiding conviction that the best interests of the Masonic fraternity can always he most readily subserved by naming for public discussion the men who are, or have been, prominent in its ranks, rather than by enlarging upon the moral and other lessons which are inculcated in its lodge. Contrary to the general belief. Freemasonry has no secrets. It has. of course, grips, words and signs peculiar to itself, but these are not what are considered "secrets" in the popular sense. Outside of these all that the fraternity dwells upon is contained in the pages of the Holy Book, which ever lies open on its altars. "Study the Bible," Grandmaster Thornme once said in addressing a mixed audience, "and you will be not only iii possession of every Masonic secret, but be as good a Mason as anyone in the ranks." Of that there is no doubt. Most men are the result of their associations, and are just what their associations make them, whether these associations be found in the home circle, the political forum, the church parlor or around the Masonic altar. So it is safe to say, when a man becomes prominent in public life or in any walk of life and we find that he is also active in Masonry, has been, in fact, active in Masonry long before he became prominent in other good work, that it is the teachings of the craft which have directed his path and strengthened his effort in air good works. A good Mason must be "also a good citizen and exhibit in his walk and conversation all that which makes for peace, order, law, progress and advancement in any community. One or two examples of Masonic biography may enable us to understand this more clearly.

The first we select is that of a man whose memory is yet cherished among the members of the fraternity of Brooklyn and who was, and is, justly regarded as the most typically representative Freemason which Long Island has given to the great brotherhood. This was Joseph D. Evans, who, in 1854, succeeded the famous Chancellor Walworth as-Grand Master of the State of New York, and who, while by no means the most brilliant chief executive the Grand Lodge had chosen up to that time, proved by no means the least useful.

The following sketch of the career of this distinguished brother is reprinted from the Standard History of Freemasonry in the State of New York, issued a few years ago by the publishers of the present work:

CAREER OF JOSEPH D. EVANS.

Brother Evans was born in the city of New York in 1807. His parents removed to "Richmond, Virginia, and there the future Grand blaster received his education and business training. In 1842 he was made a Mason in Marshall Lodge, No. 39, Lynchburg, and afterward affiliated with St. John's Lodge, No. 36, of Richmond, and in 1846 became its Master. Two years later, when he left Richmond to take up his residence in New York the brethren presented him with a Past Master's jewel.

Taking up his abode in Brooklyn, he affiliated with Anglo-Saxon Lodge. His business interests, however, lay in New York, and here it may be said that his commercial career was as brilliant as his Masonic one. As president of the New York Tobacco Board of Trade he exerted himself greatly in the struggle of 1871-3 to retain the bonded warehouse system in New York City, and he was the first president of the New York Naval Stores and Tobacco Exchange. His business career was marked by industry and, probity, his word was as good as' a bond, and, while he paid close attention to details,: he acted with a breadth of view and, a wholesome liberality that showed him to be animated by as much ambition to promote the general good as to conserve his own personal ends. He was a man of humble piety and of deep religious sentiments and his memory is yet held in loving remembrance in the Church of the Messiah, Brooklyn, of which he was vestryman and clerk for many years.

In Anglo-Saxon Lodge Brother Evans became Master in 1850, was elected again in the following year and declined re-election in 1852. In the Grand Lodge he was noted for his loyalty and his conciliatory spirit. When the Phillips division took place in 1849 Anglo-Saxon Lodge went out with the dissidents, but Evans exerted all his influence upon the brethren and submitted a resolution; which, on being adopted, brought the Lodge back to its allegiance; As Grand Master he tried hard to restore harmony in the jurisdiction and, though he did not fully succeed, there is no doubt that his influence hastened the final union of the various bodies among whom union was desired. In fact, it was to his direct initiative that the measures were taken in 1858 which in 1859 finally closed the disunited ranks. He was a; strong advocate, of the representative system between the different Grand Lodges and wrought hard to make it universal, and to him is due the inauguration, of the District Deputy system as we have it today — a system that has done much to preserve the unity of the craft and to lessen the labors of the Grandmaster and other executive officers of the Grand Lodge. '

On retiring from the Grand Master's chair, after being twice elected, Brother Evans stepped down to the ranks again only to resume his active. work. In 1859 he dimitted, from Anglo-Saxon Lodge affiliated with Prince of Orange Lodge, No. 16, and became its Master in 1860. In 1864 he aided in the organization of Hillgrove Lodge, No. 540, and later, in 18-67, when Hillgrove had become prosperous, he helped to organize Mistletoe Lodge, No. 647, Brooklyn, and served its Master until 1870. All this time he was more or less active in all the Masonic branches. Chapter and Crypt had no mysteries for -him and chivalric Masonry claimed him as a faithful knight. In the Ancient and Accepted Scottish Rite he received. the highest degree. Sovereign Grand Inspector General, and for two years presided over the Grand Consistory, Northern Jurisdiction, while as Grand Minister of State he accomplished much good work.

As a Mason he was a stanch advocate of maintaining the simplicity and purity of the order; and in showing the brethren that the ritual, while beautiful, was simply an introduction to a wonderful system of philosophy, religious and moral, he never tired. The landmarks of Masonry formed a theme which engaged his attention for many years and his concise arrangement of these much disputed essentials found great favor in New York. This arrangement is to be found printed in the current edition of the constitution, a position of honor which it should always occupy. There never lived a more devoted Mason or one who interwove Masonry more completely into his daily life. All of his sons in this respect emulated his example. The entire family of Brother Evans was noted for its interest in Masonry, and his eldest brother, James, was at one time Grand Master of Virginia. Joseph D. Evans died at Brooklyn September ii, 1888, when in the eighty-second year of his age.

As an evidence of how thoroughly he himself could apply the teachings, the philosophy of Masonry, we quote the following from his address in 1855, when referring to the death in that year of John Van Buren, who was an enthusiastic Mason and had been Junior Grand Warden and Senior Grand Warden during four years under the Grand Mastership of Morgan Lewis:

"The soul of our beloved brother, John Van Buren, has taken its everlasting flight; his well-known seat is vacant; it was, as you well recollect, always near the East. His manly form, benignant demeanor and unobtrusive deportment are vividly impressed upon our memory. He was ever watchful of the true interests of the institution, a friend to the needy and oppressed, and a firm and unflinching adherent to our ancient laws and regulations; in his death we have sustained a great loss, but we have the consolations afforded by the happy reflections that he has gone to meet a rich reward, and that his memory will ever flourish as the green bay tree. Brother Van Buren died in January last; at his request his remains were consigned to the tomb by his brethren, who assembled in large numbers to unite in the sorrows of the family and participate in our last solemn rites, and as the sympathetic tear which silently expressed their grief at their unexpected loss fell upon his grave, the evergreen deposited by hundreds of kindred hearts within the tomb proclaimed with trumpet power the everlasting truth that his body will rise and become as incorruptible as his soul."

As might be supposed, the ritual came in for a large share of his official attention while Brother Evans exerted a direct influence on the craft as Deputy Grand Master or as Grand Master. In 1852, at his suggestion, one important piece of uniformity was attained when the Grand Secretary was instructed to notify all Lodges that it was a violation of the constitution to transact any business other than conferring degrees, except when in a Lodge of Master Masons; another regulation that did good service in keeping the craft free of undesirable material, or assisted to that end, was that passed the same year requiring a candidate to be an actual resident in the vicinity of a Lodge before being in a position to apply for membership. A Masonic funeral service drawn up by H. G. Beardsley, of Hamilton, New York, was also adopted by the Grand Lodge and recommended to the fraternity of the State. Such a compilation was much needed and it served a useful purpose at the time, although it has since been superseded. It would have been thought that Freemasons would have respected the Sabbath, but unfortunately in the multiplicity of interests which then prevailed some organizations, both 'cheap and nasty," found it profitable to work the degrees on the Lord's day, even without the justification that they were Hebrews and held sacred the seventh day of the week; so it is gratifying to find the Grand Lodge putting squarely on record for the second time a declaration that Masonic meetings on Sunday, except for burial purposes, are improper and prohibited, and also that the use of profane language should render a brother liable to discipline. Being himself a man of strong religious sentiments, there is no doubt that Brother Evans' influence was at work in bringing about such legislation. Doubtless all such matters were thoroughly understood by the brethren long before his time, but they were not given legislative force until he took the initiative.

The necessity of having the esoteric work uniform throughout all the Lodges of the State had been a theme of anxious interest throughout the jurisdiction since the days of Livingston, but, although many means had been tried, Grand Visitors and District Visitors appointed, the desired uniformity could not be brought about, and now that Lodges were springing up in all directions it was seen that something had to be done or the wildest confusion would ensue. To overcome this, if possible, Oscar Coles, in 1852, introduced a motion, which was adopted, that the Grand officers should constitute a Lodge of Instruction, to meet once a week, and appoint a sufficient number of Grand Lecturers so that each Lodge could be visited at least once a year and exemplify the standard work. The Grand Lecturer was to receive compensation from the Lodge so visited. This was virtually the beginning of the present Committee on Exemplification of the Work, and under it the lectures were thoroughly revised and submitted to the craft. The system thus compiled was favorably received, but in 1855 the experience of the committee led to the permanent employment of a Grand Lecturer. This subject is thus summarized by the late C. T. McClenachan, who as a ritualist had in his time no superior in the jurisdiction: "The revised work of the craft," he wrote, "was pronounced by the Grand Master, Joseph D. Evans, as very gratifying, meeting with general approbation; that if was 'the same taught by Preston, Webb, Cushman, Cross and men of their day, and was in general practice throughout the United States; that Past Grand Master Walworth, our Grand Chaplain, the Rev. Brother Town, together with four other old Masons, recognized and stamped it the same, substantially, as that taught to them forty to fifty years ago. As to the above-named ritualists, Preston and others, there seems ample room for surprise, for the above and similar remarks occur in the Grand Master's address of June 5, 1855. The inconveniences in the Revision are thus set forth: 'It is now three years since the Grand Lodge commenced a revision of the work. * * * The chaotic rubbish had to be removed, predilections and prejudices overcome, before truth could rear her towering arch, self-supporting and self-capped, to the admiring gaze of the devotees of Masonry's ancient landmarks, but, thanks to patience and perseverance, success equal to all expectation has crowned the effort. Its merits have borne it on approving wings to distant quarters of the State, and it is now practiced and adhered to in the main by scores of our Lodges.' The subject of the new revision went to a committee, who reported on the following day, recommending the election of a Grand Lecturer, under the constitution, at a salary of one thousand dollars, who shall reside in the city of New York, and other Lecturers, who shall receive for their services their actual expenses and two dollars per day during the time they are attending a call. * * * On June 8 Brother A. Colo Veloni was declared elected Grand Lecturer and on the succeeding day the Grand Lodge resolved 'that the work of the Grand Lecturer be submitted to the Grand officers, with power to receive or reject his standard, as they may see fit.' Accordingly, at the close of the session * * * the Grand Lecturer exhibited his version of the ritual to the Grand Master and the Grand Secretary and it was rejected." The reasons for this very drastic conclusion were many, but the main one was the brother's imperfect pronunciation of the English language and a certain amount of extraneous matter, which was not suited to the taste of American Masons. Further on, McClenachan says:

"On June 7, 1856, the Grand Lodge abolished the Lodge of Instruction; voted Brother A. Colo Veloni, for his services as Grand Lecturer, five hundred dollars; elected Brother William H. Drew the Grand Lecturer without a fixed compensation. * * * An appropriation of five hundred dollars to -Brother Drew was made on the following June, and the sum of two hundred and fifty dollars to Brother Veloni as his assistant. The services of the Grand Lecturer were then settled at three dollars per day and necessary expenses, to be paid by the lodges employing him. The lengthy reports presented by the Grand Lecturer, William H. Drew, to the Grand Lodge and printed in full in the proceedings of 1857 and 1858 are remarkable documents and worthy of frequent reference. It was in this latter year the compensation to the Lecturer was made one thousand dollars. It was ordered that the State be divided into Grand Lecture Districts, designated by Senatorial districts, and that conventions be held in each."

It was this legislation that placed the "standard work" right before every Lodge in the State and gave the New York brethren a reputation as ritualists which has never been surpassed by those of other jurisdictions.

It was under Grand Master Evans, too, that the present Grand Lodge library really had its beginning, although for such purpose donations of books had already been received on various occasions. He brought the heed of such an annex so clearly before the brethren in his address in 1855 that the first five officers were appointed a Library Committee, with power to commence the formation of a library and to draw on the Grand Treasurer for five hundred dollars during the year to purchase books. Subordinate Lodges were asked to aid in the work, and a really good beginning was made, although the work afterward, for various reasons, was permitted to languish. It was Evans' idea that the Grand Lodge library should be a sort of central lending organization, giving the brethren all over the country the advantages of studying whatever treasures it possessed, but this was soon 'afterward abandoned as unfeasible. It was not, in fact, until the Grand Lodge got settled in his own home that much practical headway was made in the' collection of a library worthy of the institution'.

Grand Master Evans governed the craft wisely and well, and, while discussion prevailed in the craft, the Grand Lodge steadily advanced in popularity and power. When he retired at the close of his second term there were three hundred and nineteen lodges under its jurisdiction and, besides, thirty-two lodges were working under dispensations, while the New York fraternity was recognized all over the world for its power and well-directed energies.

A more modern Mason, yet one who in his earlier days was often associated with Evans and who died in November, 1901, was John G. Barker, Masonic bookseller, who was probably known, by name at least, to every reading member of the fraternity in the United States an-d Canada. His home was for years in Brooklyn and some of the Masonic organizations of which he was a member had their headquarters there, but his place of business was in New York City. For 'some thirty years he published Masonic books, but the great feature of his business was its half-yearly auction sales of Masonic books, gatherings from all sorts of places of volumes of interest to members of the order and' to no one else. Sometimes not over half a dozen buyers would attend .these sales, but as a rule nothing was exactly sacrificed — Barker attended to that. He was very proud of these auction sales and claimed, with justice, that they were not only helpful to the members of the craft, but that he was of real benefit to the widow or heirs of a book-loving Mason by securing for his literary treasures better prices than could be obtained were they sold in open market. But, as he sadly used to admit with a grim smile, "book-buying brethren" seemed to get smaller in number year after year; as to the brethren in New York and Brooklyn who read books — Masonic books — he was wont to aver that they "might be counted on the fingers of both hands and still leave us two or three fingers for additions." For the "bright Masons" of the present day he had nothing but the most contemptuous words and was ready on all occasions to demonstrate that such burning and shining lights are not Masons at all.

But still, it must be admitted that Barker himself was behind the age. His place of business was in a street that was once a Masonic center, but had long ago lost its preeminence in that and in every other respect, except for manufacturing industries. He had a large stock, but it was never displayed properly. When you wanted anything you had to ask for it, and Barker generally had it, no matter how rare a bibliographical treasure it might be. Yet it may be questioned if even he had a complete knowledge of all that his stock contained, for human memory has its limitations.

The establishment in Bleecker street, New York, was not an inviting one. It was not at all tidy.; the furnishings were "the remains of former grandeur," and the presence of half a dozen cats did not add to the neatness of things. Three or four chairs were disposed around an old stove, chairs so well-seasoned that they could not be destroyed by rough usage, and therein lay their supreme comfort, for you could sit in them as you liked, elevate them to your notion of the fitness of things, and if you so desired tilt your feet on the stove at any angle. It was not a handsome spot, the surroundings were venerable and decrepit, yet around that stove more Masonry has been talked, and discussed during the past quarter of a century than probably in any other spot in the State of New York. Mr. Barker himself was a living encyclopedia of local Masonic history, and if his educational training had only been commensurate with the opportunities that came to him and with the facilities his business opened up, he would have been a power in the fraternity. But his early education appears to have been limited. For several years he edited and published a Masonic magazine, which had more errors on the page — errors in grammar and in spelling, involved and dense sentences, misquotations and the like, than any publication the writer of this ever knew, yet he was never aware of them. His sale catalogues were useless for bibliographical purposes because of their mistakes in names and dates, yet such errors he never seemed to think amounted to much. But if someone had pointed out to him a misspelled name in one of Albert Pike's publications he would have gloated over it for a month and denounced the ignorance of Pike in the bitterest terms to all and sundry.

In fact, denunciation was his great forte. At times he was wont to denounce everything. The name of Albert Pike used to arouse his ire much as a red flag is said to arouse the dander of a bull, and the name of the late Enoch Terry Carson uncorked all the vials of his wrath. Even some of the Grand Masters of his own jurisdiction did not escape his ire and of some of them the language he used was such as if here repeated might lay the publisher open to legal proceedings. Of the Grand Masters of recent years he knew nothing, except John Stewart and Wright D. Pownall, for both of whom he entertained the highest regard, but all the others since the days of Frank R. Lawrence were to him little more than names. He admired Grand Master Lawrence's work, or rather the magnificent outcome of it. although he did not admire Lawrence's methods; but then Barker was one of those whom Lawrence himself used to denounce as the Past Masters who led the New York fraternity into the mire of debt from which only heroic measures and masterly leadership enabled them to get out of.

But. in spite of his gift of denunciation, which, as usual, grew more virulent as years crept on, John G. Barker had a kind heart. Many a time have we seen a beggar enter his store, and experience a share of his wrath, winding up with the stern admonition that "this is a place of business and not a bureau of charity;" and we always noticed that when the speech was near the close his hand was in his pocket and the supplicant went away satisfied. Once a fellow walked in and solicited a dime, saying he was a brother of a lodge in Boston and had tramped the streets in search of work until he was played out. Barker, after the customary discourse, gave him the ten cents. "That fellow wants a drink," the writer said after the scene was over. "Well, ' said Barker, "what if he does? He asked me for a dime for food and I had the dime to spare. If he has lied about it, I have at least done my part." But his kindliness of heart showed itself in many other ways. No young brother ever applied to him for a bit of information as to work, or law, or procedure, or history without having the point at issue fully explained, no matter how much of his time it took up, and he would not only give his own views but would back them up with authorities, ransacking his whole store, searching in safes, desks, pigeon-holes and all sorts of corners for the necessary books or data. "Proceedings" of Grand Lodges were his favorite study, and probably he knew as much of the contents of these as any man living. Now and again he used to talk of editing a volume or two of selections from the valuable contributions to Masonic history which lie buried in these "books which are not books," but he seemed unwilling to undertake the task owing tc his advanced years.

Barker was a genuine example of the old school of Masons, of the type that prevailed in New York forty years ago. At that time Simons, Holmes, Phillips, Macoy, Sickels, Henry C. Banks, Somers, and Evans were in the height of their usefulness. Grand men, they were, all of them. Although one or two gave way to the cup which inebriates, they were not drunkards; they were "convivialists," as they used to call themselves, but there is no doubt that their fondness for looking on "the wine when it is red" lowered their standing in the social scale and more or less wrecked their lives. But whether *bon vivants* like Holmes, or prim, devout, hard-working merchants like Evans, they were all men of brains. When Barker was raised in Silentia Lodge in November, 1862, he had known Simons, Holmes, Sickels and most of the rest of these leaders for some years, and he had quite an intimate acquaintance with that apostle of unrest — that most wonderful of ritualists — Henry C. Atwood, who passed away from the storms and distresses and conflicts of this life to, let us hope, a haven of rest above, two months before Barker signed the by-laws and was acknowledged a Master Mason. Still, although he thus dated legitimately in a Masonic sense from 1862, it is difficult to tell when Barker's acquaintance with the craft began. They were not so particular then as now about many matters and Barker laughingly once told a group of listeners that his initiating, passing and raising showed him nothing new as he had "many times seen the whole business before." In fact he had often tyled a lodge when he was in that state of darkness which the elder brethren stigmatized so eloquently as being that of a "cowan," although not one of them could tell the exact meaning of the word. Neither can any of the brethren of the present twentieth century, for that matter. Of course it was wrong to let a boy act as tyler, but if the fact of a non-Mason being tyler had been called in question Simons would have found ample precedent for it in the Scotch system which did not demand in those days — and possibly does not make it obligatory even yet — that the tyler of a lodge must be a member of the fraternity.

For many years Barker was a prominent figure in Grand Lodge circles although the only official appointment he ever held was that of grand librarian for some four years. But the library was a small affair in his day, containing little beyond loose numbers of proceedings, and during his tenure of the office he attempted little beyond arranging and completing these.

The fact is that he became active in Grand Lodge circles at a time when a library was hardly likely to be a theme of immediate interest. The first year he attended the Grand Lodge as a representative the purchase of the present site of Masonic Hall was announced and then followed the excitement of corner-stone laying, of seeing the building in process of erection, of its dedication, and the long years of doubt, money-raising, and even despondency, until

Lawrence lifted the load. It was in these years of financial darkness that Barker was prominent. For the past decade he seemed to take more of a direct interest in Scottish Rite matters than in anything else. He was the secretary and real leader of what the brethren in Brooklyn and New York generally speak of as the Gorman Cerneau council, and he supported its claims to being the genuine article with all the force and vehemence of the old controversial school in which Hyneman and Folger almost to our day carried on the argumentative methods of Lawrence Dermott himself. Into this feature of his career, however, this is not the place or time to enter.

Since the days of the leadership of Joseph D. Evans, Brooklyn has given two Grand Masters to the craft in New York, Joseph J. Couch and William Sherer, and in all probability will in 1902 furnish yet another in the advancement to the highest honor in the gift of the fraternity of Elbert Crandall, now Deputy Grand Master. A lawyer engaged in active practice on Manhattan Island, Mr. Crandall's home was long in Brooklyn and his entire Masonic affiliations are centered here. He is a member of Ridgewood Lodge, No. 710; of Ridgewood Chapter, No. 263; of De Witt Clinton Commandery, No. 27; Aurora Grata Consistory, Scottish Rite, and of Kismet Temple, Mystic Shrine. In the Grand Lodge, before being elected to his present office, he was chief commissioner of appeals, and his eloquent voice has often been heard in that capacity as well as in urging measures and matters of importance to the general welfare of the fraternity. He has proven a wise and conservative counselor, has rendered loyal service to a succession of Grand Masters, and is thoroughly equipped by long years of practical training and by the dictates of his own heart to assume the leadership of the big army of New York Masons — an army now numbering over one hundred thousand.

Possibly the course of time will place yet another Long Island Mason in the highest office. At present Townsend Scudder is chief commissioner of appeals in Grand Lodge, and somehow that office has come to be regarded as a stepping-stone to greater honors. Townsend Scudder was born at Northport July 26, 1865, and has represented Suffolk county in Congress. As a lawyer he ranks high, having been counsel for Queens county at the time when its affairs were being adjusted prior to annexation. In Masonic circles he is popular everywhere, and the same high regard follows him into every walk in life, for there is no doubt that but for his own determination to quit active political life he would have been returned to Congress from his district as often as he cared. He proved a most useful and' reliable representative of his constituents, and while he was in Congress he never permitted his associates to forget that there was a place called Long Island, a place that had many and just claims upon their consideration, and he managed somehow to get quite a large proportion of these claims satisfactorily and liberally adjudicated.

Made in the USA
Middletown, DE
18 July 2017